THE IDEA
OF A
SOUTHERN
NATION

THE IDEA OF A SOUTHERN NATION

Southern Nationalists and
Southern Nationalism, 1830–1860

JOHN McCARDELL

W · W · NORTON & COMPANY
NEW YORK   LONDON

Copyright © 1979 by W. W. Norton & Company, Inc.
Published simultaneously in Canada by George J. McLeod Limited, Toront
Printed in the United States of America.

Library of Congress Cataloging in Publication Data

McCardell, John.
    The idea of a Southern Nation.

    Includes bibliographical references and index.
        1. Nationalism—Southern States—History.
    2. Southern States—History—1775–1865.   3. Southern
    States—Intellectual life.   I. Title.
    F213.M13   1979   320.9′75′03   79–12896
    ISBN 0–393–01241–7

                    1 2 3 4 5 6 7 8 9 0

For my Father and Mother

Contents

Acknowledgments ix

Introduction 3

1. Duty Bound to Interpose 11
2. The Great Distinguishing Characteristic 49
3. The Degrading Shackles of Commercial
   Dependence 91
4. A Southern Republic of Letters 141
5. Northern Domination in our Schools and Pulpits 177
6. The Mission and Destiny Allotted to the Anglo-
   Saxon Race 227
7. The Man and the Hour Have Met 277
   Conclusion 336

Appendices 339
Essay on Sources 355
Index 376

Photographs following page 150

Acknowledgments

The publication of this volume, I now realize, marks not an end but a beginning. Only a naive graduate student lacking both experience and therefore modesty would dare to have proposed a dissertation topic studying the development of Southern nationalistic thinking from 1830 to 1860. Such a study requires research in an inexhaustible supply of materials and runs a dual risk of either oversimplification or diffusion. Every subject discussed in the following chapters deserves further investigation, which I hope to continue. Whatever merits the present study may possess is a tribute to numerous organizations and individuals who offered me support and encouragement in my pilgrim's progress toward humility and appreciation of the historian's craft. It is a great pleasure to acknowledge those contributions here.

This study actually began with an interest in Southern history aroused during my undergraduate years at Washington and Lee University by the late, inimitable Professor Ollinger Crenshaw, and his skilled and friendly colleagues, Professors Allen Moger and Robert McAhren. I continue to profit by their examples as teachers and scholars.

One of the more pleasant aspects of this project was becoming acquainted with the staffs and holdings of many of the excellent research facilities in the South, where most of my primary research was conducted. Students of Southern history are well served by the efforts of the fine people at the Louisiana State University Library, the Mississippi Department of Archives and History, the Alabama Department of Archives and History, the University of Georgia Library, the South Carolina Historical Society, the South Caroliniana Library of the University of South Carolina, the Southern Historical Collection in the library of the University of North Carolina, Chapel Hill, and the Perkins Library, Duke University. The Houghton Library, Harvard University, has granted permission to cite various materials from its extensive holdings.

A number of organizations considered this study worthy of their support, and for their confidence I am deeply grateful. At various stages the Colonial Dames of America and the Charles Warren Center for Study in American History provided needed assistance. The Faculty Research Fund at Middlebury College helped defray the costs of revising the manuscript. The Society of American Historians, in awarding the dissertation on which this volume is based the Allan Nevins Prize, provided a helpful financial and psychological boost, which sped the book into print.

Most of the manuscript was drafted in Eliot House at Harvard University, which proved an ideal setting. For comfortable surroundings and good fellowship I thank Alan Heimert, house master, and my fellow tutors, especially Alan Brinkley, Alan Kantrow, and William Kuntz. They and several other tolerant fellow graduate students, Michael Chesson and Nan Stone, read portions of the manuscript and discussed problems of methodology and interpretation to my great benefit.

Other scholars, too, have read portions of the manuscript and offered valuable insights. William Cooper, whose forthcoming work on the politics of slavery will enrich our understanding of that subject, read the entire manuscript as did Frank Freidel, whose pungent critique was timely and encouraging. Portions of the manuscript profited from the criticisms of D. D. Bruce, John G. Clark, and Stanley Engerman. Jim

Mairs and Drake McFeely at W. W. Norton have been patient and exceedingly helpful editors. At Middlebury College Travis Jacobs, William Catton, and Thomas Cox have been supportive as professional colleagues and friends.

My greatest debt, on which this book is but a token payment, is to David Herbert Donald. His meticulous reading of numerous drafts of the manuscript, for which he sacrificed considerable time and energy, his insightful criticisms, his patience, and his warm friendship far exceeded what I had any right to expect. His scholarly example and deep personal concern for his students ennoble the historical profession.

And, finally, there are those who, for various reasons, found themselves closer to this book than they may have wished to be. Patricia Denault, my typist, endured a bizarre summer of special delivery mailings from faraway places and, under great pressure, performed her task with skill and good cheer. My wife Bonnie, having spent a long and patient courtship with the idea of a Southern nation, has contributed to this study in countless intangible ways. The dedication acknowledges inadequately the love and support of the people who have paid for this volume many times over.

THE IDEA
OF A
SOUTHERN
NATION

Introduction

I

The idea that there exists an 'irrepressible conflict' between the two systems of labor prevailing in the States, is fanciful and superficial. On the contrary, the two systems mutually aid each other." So spoke Senator James Chesnut of South Carolina on the eve of secession and civil war. To him the source of sectional tension was deeper and more complex. "There is," he declared, "a conflict—a conflict of ideas irreconcilable. The opinions of those who give life and energy to the antislavery party touching government, society, the relations of man to both and to each other, are radical and revolutionary. If these prevail, there can be no peace, North or South."[1]

Despite Chesnut's rhetoric, it is incorrect to think of Northerners and Southerners in 1860 as two distinct peoples. Their intellectual, political, social, and economic beliefs were generally shared and were not determined solely on sectional grounds. But on one issue the sections disagreed, and that issue—slavery—gave such an ideological charge to all other questions that by 1860 America was on the verge of civil strife. The peculiar institution came to represent for Southerners a

---

1. *Speech of the Hon. James Chesnut, Jr., of South Carolina, April 9, 1860* (Baltimore: John Murphy and Co., 1860), p. 21.

whole ideological configuration—a plantation economy, a style
of life, and a pattern of race relations—which made Southerners believe that they constituted a separate nation.

Thus, Chesnut's remarks were significant because they
recognized that by 1860 sectional tensions had reached the
point where many Southerners *perceived* an ideological difference between themselves and other Americans. According
to the anthropologist Clifford Geertz, ideology is a response to
social, cultural, or psychological strain. "And," he continues,
"it is, in turn, the attempt of ideologies to render incomprehensible social situations meaningful . . . that accounts both for
the ideologies' highly figurative nature and for the intensity
with which, once accepted, they are held."[2]

The ideology of Southern nationalism first appeared during the crisis over the tariff in South Carolina, which was a
response to accelerating social, political, and economic changes
of the 1820's. The South was becoming increasingly aware of
its minority status within the Union. Compounding the difficulties of this position were the declining economic fortunes
of the seaboard states coupled with a growing concern over the
future of slavery. Each of these problems—beginning with the
Missouri crisis in 1819–20, continuing with the social and economic dislocation of the 1820's, and intensifying with the
launching of William Lloyd Garrison's abolition newspaper
The Liberator in 1831—converged and crystallized during the
tariff imbroglio of the early 1830's. The resulting strain
aroused and sharpened sectional awareness. Many Southerners were finding, in Geertz's words, their social situation
incomprehensible. And, as a result, they turned to Southern
nationalism to render their situation meaningful.

As Geertz suggests, then, the tariff struggle awakened a
sense of sectional consciousness that had up to that time been
wholly subordinated to an intense love of the American
Union. With South Carolina leading the way, Southerners

2. Clifford Geertz, "Ideology as a Cultural System," in *Ideology and Discontent*,
ed. David Apter (New York: Free Press of Glencoe, 1964), p. 48.

began for the first time openly and seriously to question the value of the Union. A few went even further in advocating secession. The idea of a Southern nation was born.

II

This book is a study of the origins, development, and impact of the idea of a separate Southern nation prior to the Civil War. In order to follow the argument, it is important for a reader to know exactly what is meant by the terms *sectionalism, nationalism,* and *Southern nationalism.*

Sectionalism results when the inhabitants of a geographical entity possess or perceive a common interest in a specific issue or set of issues. Sectionalism has existed throughout the history of the United States. A commonality of interest has been variously exhibited, as in New England's dissatisfaction with the War of 1812, the plains states' advocacy of free silver in the 1890's, or the "solid South's" Democratic voting pattern up until recent times.

Nationalism need not exclude sectionalism. So long as a national government is able to embrace and preserve diverse interests—whether those interests be sectional, class, ethnic, political, social, or economic—it will retain the loyalties of the various elements in its population. Provided that local and national goals can remain coordinated, local allegiances can reinforce nationalism. Josiah Quincy showed the process in 1811 when he stated that "the first love of my heart is the Commonwealth of Massachusetts. . . . The love of the Union grows out of this attachment to my native soil." So, too, could a North Carolinian in 1832 rank his loyalties: "I belong first to No. Carolina, and then to the Southern Country, and then to the U. States, and then to the Human Family."[3]

3. Hans Kohn, *American Nationalism: An Interpretative Essay* (New York: Collier Books, 1961), pp. 122–23; David M. Potter, "The Historian's Use of Nationalism and Vice Versa," in *The South and the Sectional Conflict* (Baton Rouge: Louisiana State University Press, 1968), pp. 36, 48, 62–63; Joseph Seawell Jones to Daniel M. Barringer, December 11, 1832, Daniel M. Bar-

In the United States, then, allegiance to the nation grew out of loyalties and commitments to immediate, local, and familiar scenes, people, and institutions. American nationalism, such as it was in the early nineteenth century, comprised not so much a universally shared culture or way of life as it did a widely if not universally shared set of experiences and goals. The common heritage of the American Revolution and a general commitment to its meaning as expressed in the Constitution formed the core of American nationalism as well as a base for disputes over how best to fulfill the commitment. Originating in a very general ideological consensus, American nationalism included sectionalism as well as countless other "isms" of the early national period.

Southern nationalism emerged when sizable numbers of Southerners began to perceive that their own set of shared interests were becoming increasingly incompatible with those of the rest of the Union and were, in fact, being threatened. This perception, which began to evolve at the height of the Nullification crisis in the early 1830's, was a response to economic, social, and political strains from the 1830's on that repeatedly seemed to reveal the South's permanent minority position. It fostered a belief that Southerners were a "conscious minority" whose outlook and needs differed from those of other Americans.[4]

---

ringer Papers, Southern Historical Collection, University of North Carolina, Chapel Hill. Other writings on the concept of nationalism that have been of inestimable value in preparing this study include Carlton J. H. Hayes, *Essays on Nationalism* (New York: Macmillan Co., 1926); Boyd C. Shafer, *Nationalism: Myth and Reality* (New York: Harcourt, Brace, and Co., 1955); and Louis L. Snyder, *The Meaning of Nationalism* (New Brunswick, N.J.: Rutgers University Press, 1954).

4. Paul C. Nagel, *One Nation Indivisible: The Union in American Thought, 1776–1861* (New York: Oxford University Press, 1964) is a thoughtful study of the cohesive and enduring power of the idea of union. Nagel's *This Sacred Trust: American Nationality, 1798–1898* (New York: Oxford University Press, 1971) argues suggestively that many Americans have harbored doubts about the American experiment in nationhood. Fred Somkin, *Unquiet Eagle: Memory and Desire in the Idea of American Freedom, 1815–1860* (Ithaca, N.Y.: Cornell

Nullification made Southerners view every aspect of American life in a new light, transmuting values and goals previously associated with the American nation into virtues and distinctions peculiarly Southern. Out of the tariff crisis grew a systematic defense of the South's peculiar institution of slavery. Proslavery quickly became the position around which all Southerners, no matter how much they might disagree with one another on other questions, could unite. And a concern for the future of slavery lay at the base of Southerners' views on every other issue of the day.

But if slavery was the *sine qua non* of sectional ideology, it was not the only component. During the 1830's Southerners also began trying to reconcile their desires for maintaining a distinctive way of life with their dreams of effecting economic self-sufficiency through industrialization. Calls arose and spread for a distinctive Southern literature. Religious nationalism became more intense. Educational movements made overt sectional appeals. Eventually the South convinced itself that it must expand southward and westward, and "Manifest Destiny" came to mean the acquisition of territory in Latin America. The political tensions of this expansive thrust eventually ruptured the national parties. Finally, as a result of activities in all these areas, enough Southerners became convinced that the Union so threatened their interests and their security that the idea of a Southern nation at last achieved fulfillment.[5]

University Press, 1967) is an important study of underlying tensions in America's quest for national identity. An important contemporary study of the ongoing debate over the meaning of the Constitution is Francis Lieber, *Two Lectures on the Constitution of the United States* (New York: Baker and Godwin, Printers, 1861).

5. Yehoshua Arieli, *Individualism and Nationalism in American Ideology* (Cambridge: Harvard University Press, 1964) is an excellent analysis of the relationship between individual needs and national goals and policies. One of the best contemporary scholarly studies on the nature and limitations of government is Francis Lieber, *On Civil Liberty and Self-Government*, 2 vols. (Philadelphia: J. B. Lippincott and Co., 1859). Vernon L. Parrington, *Main Currents in American Thought: An Interpretation of American Literature from the Beginnings to*

III

Research on all these aspects of Southern nationalism is abundant. Scholarly studies of such important subjects as the proslavery argument, the Southern economy, education, religion, literature, territorial expansion, and party politics have broadened and deepened knowledge about life in the antebellum South. So valuable has been the work of these students of Southern history, so thorough their research, that a comprehensive examination of the growth of an ideology of Southern nationalism is now possible. Taking a broad perspective on the work of these scholars produces fresh conclusions about the nature of the secession movement.[6]

This book is an attempt at such a synthesis. Its organization is topical, its approach within each chapter both biographical and chronological. Southern nationalism manifested itself in a variety of forms. Individuals who influenced the course of Southern nationalism will be examined in detail to produce a composite portait of the Southern nationalist. Ideology is added to this portrait by examining the coming together of the various nationalist movements. While the movements started out independently, interaction developed. Men who were literary nationalists were frequently educational nationalists, and men who were proslavery polemicists were also expansionists as well. Slowly the movements merged so that by 1860 the "Southern nationalist" was characterized by a distinct set of motives and beliefs.

Chronologically, this study will trace the course of each

1920, 3 vols. (New York: Harcourt, Brace and Co., 1927), 2: 3–182 brilliantly analyzes the changing orientation of the Southern mind from 1800 to 1860.
6. The only full-length study of Southern nationalism is Avery O. Craven, *The Growth of Southern Nationalism, 1848–1861*, vol. 6 of *A History of the South*, ed. Wendell H. Stephenson and E. Merton Coulter (Baton Rouge: Louisiana State University Press, 1953), which, though well researched and written, neglects some important topics—expansionism, commercial conventions, and the various cultural movements, for example—and thus does not consider Southern nationalism as a comprehensive ideology. In fact, the major conclusion of the book is that Southern nationalism was nonexistent.

Southern nationalistic movement from about 1830 to 1860. At the same time it will present certain related patterns of development. For instance, it will consider and explain the movement of Southern leadership from Virginia to South Carolina and then westward to the cotton states. It will also trace and evaluate the hardening and closing of the Southern mind as fundamentalism, environmentalism, and organic, pre-evolutionary thinking replaced rationalism and a faith in progress and man's perfectibility. In every case the aim will be to show how and suggest why certain Southerners first perceived their differences from other Americans and the ways in which they proceeded to draw from those differences an ideology of separate nationhood.

A majority of Southerners, probably even in 1861, still hoped that their sectional rights could be maintained within the existing Union. They viewed secession and a separate Southern nation as a dreadful last resort. They were sectionalists, but they were not Southern nationalists.

Thirty years of growth, expansion, and change in America, however, during which the Union seemed to have become less of a boon and more of a burden, had wrought in many Southern minds the perceptions so forcefully expressed by James Chesnut in 1860. A growing, conscious, and vocal minority of Southerners believed that the only way for the South to retain its rights was to sever the bonds of Union on the grounds that the constitutional compact had been violated. They wished to form a more perfect Union of Southern states to restore the rights that seemed imperiled. These men considered secession and a Southern nation the happy issue out of all the Union's afflictions. They were the Southern nationalists.

CHAPTER ONE

Duty Bound
to Interpose

THE LAST OF THE SIGNERS IS DEAD," mourned the black-bordered *Baltimore American*. On November 14, 1832, Charles Carroll of Carrollton, the last surviving signer of the Declaration of Independence, died. "The only remaining link which connected this generation with the past, with that illustrious race of statesmen, philanthropists, and patriots, the founders of American Independence, and the benefactors of the world, now, and for all time hereafter—is broken."[1] An era had ended.

Carroll's death symbolized the end of one period of American history and the beginning of another. On the gray November day that the venerable signer's remains were committed to the Maryland soil he loved, the government he had helped establish was on the brink of a serious constitutional crisis. In the White House, triumphant, sat Andrew Jackson, savoring his recent massive reelection victory and planning how to employ his new mandate in the service of the Union. In Columbia, South Carolina, a convention called to plan resistance to a high tariff was about to issue an "Address to the People of South Carolina," which proclaimed, "It is in vain to tell South Carolina that she can look to any administration of the

1. *Baltimore American*, November 14, 1832.

federal government for the protection of her sovereign rights, or the redress of her southern wrongs." It added at once ominously and hopefully, "If South Carolina should be driven out of the Union, all the other planting States, and some of the Western States, would follow by an almost absolute necessity."[2]

The Union seemed on the verge of dissolution. Governor Robert Y. Hayne of South Carolina ordered the immediate formation of a volunteer force of 10,000 men. "Let them come prepared with Guns or Rifles," he urged, "and come in the shortest time possible." Meanwhile, in Boston, Massachusetts, a large crowd converged on Faneuil Hall, the "cradle of liberty," to express their loyalty to the Union and their hostility to South Carolina. A Southerner present at the meeting viewed the proceedings with great alarm:"The gentleman who first addressed the meeting closed his speech with an angry sketch of the burning plantations—the shrieking families—and the brutal and merciless slave[s]—amidst thunderous applause. . . . Say what they will of the prejudice of the Southern people against the North," he concluded, "I saw and overheard more prejudice today against the South than ever was generated in Charleston. . . ."[3] Section was poised against section. The spirit of compromise and conciliation that, however briefly, had prevailed when Charles Carroll and his associates were founding a nation seemed to have gone to the grave with the last of the signers.

2. *Journal of the Convention of the People of South Carolina: Assembled at Columbia on the 19th November, 1832, and again, on the 11th of March, 1833* (Columbia: A. S. Johnston, 1833), pp. 6, 77.

3. "Governor Robert Y. Hayne's Military Preparations," in William W. Freehling, ed., *The Nullification Era: A Documentary Record* (New York: Harper and Row, 1967), pp. 155–56, 160; Joseph Seawell Jones to Daniel M. Barringer, December 17, 1832, Barringer Papers, Southern Historical Collection.

I

In the North they are	In the South they are
cool	fiery
sober	voluptuary
laborious	indolent
independent	unsteady
jealous of their	zealous for their
own liberties and	own liberties, but
just to those of	trampling on those
others,	of others,
interested	generous
chicaning	candid
superstitious and	without attachment
hypocritical in	or pretentions to
their religion.	any religion but
	that of the heart.[4]

So wrote Thomas Jefferson in 1785. Though white Americans had a great deal in common, he thought, they also had certain differences. One of the most important differences was sectional, North and South.

Since there was no confederation of states prior to the Revolution it is impossible to determine if Southerners perceived themselves as constituting a distinct region by 1776. There is scant evidence that Southerners recognized that their region possessed peculiar and unifying characteristics. On the whole, the years leading up to the Revolution witnessed an ever increasing sense of colonial community irrespective of sectional boundaries.[5]

4. Thomas Jefferson to the Marquis de Chastellux, quoted in John Richard Alden, *The First South* (Baton Rouge: Louisiana State University Press, 1961), p. 17. The most comprehensive study of the South in the early national period is Thomas P. Abernethy, *The South in the New Nation, 1789–1819*, vol. 4 of *A History of the South*.

5. An original and suggestive study of the developing sense of colonial community is Richard L. Merritt, *Symbols of American Community 1735–1775* (New Haven: Yale University Press, 1966).

But sectionalism—Northern as well as Southern—was apparent in the earliest sessions of the Continental Congress. Whether the dispute concerned selecting a commander of the Continental Army, permitting Negroes to fight, empowering and financing some sort of central government, or deciding upon peace terms, representatives from North and South frequently acted on the basis of what would most benefit their section. Yet though debate was often heated, a common danger and a common purpose made cooperation not only desirable but also necessary. Although such nationalists as John Adams of Massachusetts, Richard Henry Lee of Virginia, and Henry Laurens of South Carolina received some criticism, they succeeded in maintaining a common front against a common British foe.[6]

By war's end the united colonies agreed sufficiently on political principles to produce a framework for a common government. The Constitution embraced the beliefs for which the colonists had fought; it represented a definition of the new American nation. Yet no sooner had Americans expressed their commitment to the principles set forth in their new charter than they began to detect differences among themselves. As the anthropologist Geertz has noted, "commonality of ideological perception may link men together, but it may also provide them . . . with a vocabulary by which to explore more exquisitely the differences among them."[7] Agreement on the principles of the American Revolution—freedom, independence, representative and popular government—almost immediately led to disputes over just what those principles meant.

Some of the more serious disputes were sectional in nature. By the time of the constitutional convention there was a distinct geographical entity known as "The South." Though

6. Alden, *First South*, pp. 33–73; Andrew C. McLaughlin, *The Confederation and the Constitution, 1783–1789* (New York: Harper and Brothers, paperback ed., 1962), pp. 174–77; Gordon S. Wood, *The Creation of the American Republic, 1776–1787* (Chapel Hill: University of North Carolina Press, 1969), pp. 420–21.
7. Geertz, "Ideology as a Cultural System," p. 48.

diverse in population and topography, and though similar to other sections in reliance upon agriculture, the states south of Pennsylvania, as Jefferson well knew, composed a peculiar section. In the constitutional convention Charles Pinckney of South Carolina considered the difference to be the methods of agriculture, while James Madison of Virginia was more explicit in defining the difference between North and South on the basis of slavery.[8]

The new nation soon felt the effects of sectionalism. When Secretary of the Treasury Alexander Hamilton introduced his comprehensive financial program, which included funding the national debt with new securities, assuming the outstanding state debts incurred during the Revolution, passing a protective tariff on certain imported goods in order to stimulate domestic manufacturing, and creating a national bank, opposition immediately formed. Jefferson, then Secretary of State, became the leader of an anti-Hamilton faction that included the Virginians in Congress. They particularly objected to the assumption of the state debts, since their state had already liquidated a large portion of its debt, while states like Massachusetts had done little. The Southern congressmen provided an almost unanimous bloc against the bank, which had equally strong support in the North. Though a compromise (in which the Jeffersonians supported Hamilton in return for the relocation of the nation's capital on the banks of the Potomac River) avoided irreparable damage to the new government, partisan strife—which was often sectional as well—had clearly emerged.[9] A recurrent argument of the Jeffersonians was that Hamilton's program discriminated against the South. So concerned was Jefferson for the future of the Union that he beseeched George Washington to stand for re-election to the presidency in 1792, claiming that

8. Jesse T. Carpenter, *The South as a Conscious Minority, 1789–1861: A Study in Political Thought* (New York: New York University Press, 1930), pp. 8–9.
9. Joseph Charles, *The Origins of the American Party System* (New York: Harper and Row, 1956), pp. 11–25; Merrill D. Peterson, *Thomas Jefferson and the New Nation: A Biography* (New York: Oxford University Press, 1970), pp. 409–13.

. . . the confidence of the whole union is centered in you. Your being at the helm will be more than an answer to every argument which can be used to alarm and lead the people in any quarter, into violence and secession. North and South will hang together if they have you to hang on.[10]

So long as Washington remained as president, sectional strife was contained, but during the administration of Washington's successor, John Adams, from 1797 to 1801, sectionalism became more pronounced. During these years there emerged the doctrine of states' rights, which was the premise from which later notions of resistance were derived. In 1798, after the Federalist majority in Congress passed the Alien and Sedition Acts, which intended to curb dissent at a time of grave international crisis by fining and imprisoning opponents of administration policy, the legislatures of Virginia and Kentucky passed a series of resolutions protesting. Written by Jefferson and Madison, the resolutions were a statement of states' rights philosophy.

The resolutions were a clear expression of the Jeffersonian position. Declaring loyalty to the Union, the Virginia Resolutions announced that in case the national government undertook "a deliberate, palpable, and dangerous exercise of powers" not granted by the federal compact, "the States, who are the parties thereto, have the right, and are in duty bound to interpose for arresting the progress of the evil and for maintaining . . . the authorities, rights, and liberties appertaining to them." When Federalists charged that the Kentucky Resolutions, which reiterated the same views, were intended to foment disunion, the Kentucky legislature adopted a second set of resolutions in 1799, which vowed "attachment to the Union" but stated that "the rightful remedy" against "all unauthorized acts done under color of [the Constitution]" against the states was "a nullification by those sovereignties. . . ." The purpose of all these resolutions was not to dissolve the Union

10. Douglas Southall Freeman, *George Washington: A Biography*, 7 vols. (New York: Charles Scribner's Sons, 1948–1957), 6: 359.

but to preserve the essential features of federalism. When a hopeful Virginian suggested at the time of the passage of the resolutions the possibility of forming a Southern Confederacy, Jefferson repudiated the notion.[11]

In 1801, after a vicious campaign and a stalemated election, the House of Representatives selected Jefferson for the presidency. In his inaugural the Virginian set forth his belief that Americans of all political persuasions and all sections shared a commitment to strict constitutional principles. He declared that "every difference of opinion is not a difference of principle. We have called by different names brethren of the same principle. We are all republicans; we are all federalists."[12]

But events during the first dozen years of the new century soon dispelled even the illusion of unity and demonstrated that neither sectionalism nor disunion was an exclusively Southern notion. Through a series of mishaps, Jefferson's successor, Madison, took the path to war with England in 1812. Support of the war was noticeably lacking in New England. In 1814 a group of New England Federalists met in Hartford, Connecticut, and assailed Madison's conduct of the war, which had brought the invader to New England's unprotected shores. Moreover, a trade embargo had caused great hardship to New England's mercantile economy. Noah Webster of Massachusetts circulated a message announcing that "the southern states have an influence in our national councils altogether disproportionate. . . ." He urged a "convention of all the northern and commercial states . . . to consult upon measures in concert. . . ." Though the resulting assembly at Hartford

11. Adrienne Koch and Harry Ammon, "The Virginia and Kentucky Resolutions: An Episode in Jefferson's and Madison's Defense of Civil Liberties," *William and Mary Quarterly*, 3d series, 5 (1948): 145–76; Ethelbert Dudley Warfield, *The Kentucky Resolutions of 1798: An Historical Study* (New York: G. P. Putnam's Sons, 1887), pp. 123–26; Philip G. Davidson, "Virginia and the Alien and Sedition Laws," *American Historical Review* 36 (1931): 336–42.

12. Dumas Malone, *Jefferson the President: First Term, 1801–1805*, vol. 4 of *Jefferson and His Time* (Boston: Little, Brown, and Co., 1970), p. 20.

limited itself to a call for peace, amendments to the Constitution, and stronger military defense, it stated in strikingly familiar language that "in cases of deliberate, dangerous, and palpable infractions of the constitution, affecting the sovereignty of a state, and liberties of the people, it is not only the right but the duty of such a state to interpose its authority for their protection." If conditions did not improve, the convention planned to reassemble, and there was little doubt that a second convention would disrupt the Union. The coming of peace, however, forestalled further action.[13]

Just as the end of the Revolutionary War sparked in the new nation a desire to incorporate its political beliefs into the Constitution, so did the coming of peace in 1815 inspire a new burst of exuberant American nationalism. Buried, at least for the moment, were old antagonisms. Political parties had disappeared; prosperity was on the rise; peace prevailed. "A nation united can never be conquered," wrote Jefferson to his old enemy Adams in 1815. "My temperament is sanguine. I steer my bark with Hope in the head, leaving Fear astern."[14] If the passing generation of leaders was optimistic, the rising generation was ecstatic. A young nationalist from South Carolina, John C. Calhoun, declared:

> . . . we are charged by Providence, not only with the happiness of this great people, but . . . with that of the human race. We have a government of a new order . . . founded on the rights of man. . . . If it shall succeed . . . it will be the commencement of a new era in human affairs.[15]

In North and South the cry arose for things peculiarly American. Young Henry Clay of Kentucky favored an "Amer-

13. James M. Banner, Jr., *To the Hartford Convention: The Federalists and the Origins of Party Politics in Massachusetts, 1789–1815* (New York: Alfred A. Knopf, 1970), *passim*, but esp. pp. 315–16, 339, 342–43.

14. Lester L. Cappon, ed., *The Adams–Jefferson Letters*, 2 vols. (Chapel Hill: University of North Carolina Press, 1959), 2: 456.

15. Robert L. Meriwether and W. Edwin Hemphill, eds., *The Papers of John C. Calhoun*, 8 vols. to date (Columbia: University of South Carolina Press, 1959–), 1: 329–30.

ican System" of economy. "What is our present situation?" he
asked. "Respectability and character abroad—security and
confidence at home. . . . We should have our wants supplied
when foreign resources are cut off. . . . Let us now do something to ameliorate the internal condition of our country."
Clay, supported in 1816 by Calhoun, began to develop a program of internal improvements, a national bank, and a protective tariff, which looked to the achievement of American self-
sufficiency.[16]

As early as 1783 Noah Webster had led the advocates of a
distinctively American language. In ensuing years he published his *American Reader*, *American Grammar*, *American Spelling Book*, and, in 1828, his monumental *American Dictionary of
the English Language*. Echoing such expressions of educational
nationalism was the *Southern Literary Messenger*, published in
Richmond, which urged that "universal mental cultivation.
. . . of the heart and intellect" was "required of Americans,
from the nature and structure of our government." The North
Carolina legislature declared in 1819 that "education . . . [is]
the only durable basis of every thing valuable in a government
of the people. . . ."[17]

At the same time came a call for an American literature.
In 1815 a group of young Boston writers founded the *North
American Review* to encourage an indigenous literature. In a
speech at Harvard College in 1818, Edward T. Channing, one
of the *Review*'s editors, delivered an address entitled "Literary
Independence." America must establish, he said, "a domestic
literature upon what is peculiarly our own—our scenery, our
institutions, our modes of life, our history, and the antiquities
of our country." Joining the cry were leading periodicals. *Niles'*

16. James F. Hopkins, ed., *The Papers of Henry Clay*, 5 vols. to date (Lexington:
University of Kentucky Press, 1961–), 2: 140–58.
17. Alice Felt Tyler, *Freedom's Ferment: Phases of American Social History from the
Colonial Period to the Outbreak of the Civil War* (New York: Harper and Row,
paperback ed., 1962), pp. 231–32; *Southern Literary Messenger*, 3 (1836): 386;
Charles S. Sydnor, *The Development of Southern Sectionalism 1819–1848*, vol. 5 of
A History of the South, p. 60.

Weekly Register and the *Portico* in Baltimore called for literary achievement commensurate with American military power. The *Southern Review*, founded in Charleston in 1828, announced its intention of arresting "the current [from abroad] which has been directed against our country generally and the South in particular." The *Southern Literary Messenger* stated in its first issue its readiness to aid in "building up a character of our own, and imbodying and concentrating the neglected genius of our country."[18]

Each of these campaigns underscored the fact that during the first half of the nineteenth century America was an incomplete nation, lacking those cultural components by which nations had been traditionally defined. There was no distinctive American language or literature, no American educational system, no American economy. The coming of peace in 1815 activated those forces that were to begin defining the contours of American nationality. Inevitably those forces—which included economic development, social and political reform, the encouragement of literature, education, and religion, the expansion of territorial boundaries—would force choices upon Americans about the ways in which their lives might be changed. Inevitably, too, the resulting changes would elicit various responses and produce unforeseen tensions. But these problems lay in the distance. For the moment, at least, the impulse toward definition was urgent, exhilarating, and universal. A unifying spirit of American nationalism overshadowed sectional feelings.

II

Nowhere was the incompleteness of the new nation more apparent than in the still imprecise nature of the relationship be-

18. Benjamin T. Spencer, *The Quest for Nationality: An American Literary Campaign* (Syracuse: Syracuse University Press, 1957), p. 55; Edward T. Channing, "Literary Independence," *The Key Reporter* 26 (1961): 4; *Southern Review* 1 (1828): 1; *Southern Literary Messenger* 1 (1834): 2.

tween the state and national governments. The United States in 1815 was a confederation of states, each of which pursued its future with little direction or interference from Washington. Indeed, many politicians spent as little time as possible in the nation's capital, which, like the government, was still unfinished. They preferred living back home near the center of political activity; this, usually, was the state house.[19]

It was on the state level that most important decisions were made. Businessmen wishing to begin a railroad had to deal with the state legislature. State universities, which began to spring up in the early nineteenth century, relied upon the state government for financial support. Military defense was provided not by a national army but by a state militia. Taxes were levied not by Congress but by the state legislatures. The inevitable result was a lack of uniformity, whether in railroad track gauges, military preparedness, or tax rates, that caused Americans to refer to their country as "the Union" of states and to use the plural verb form when speaking of the "United States."[20]

Whenever crisis struck it was generally on the state level that a response was worked out. Not long after the peace of 1815 a series of crises struck the seaboard South. The first was economic. Between 1815 and 1818 the American economy, released from the inhibitions of wartime, soared to new heights of prosperity. In the South the boom was reflected in the rapid increase of the price of agricultural products. In Virginia, severely depressed when war closed European markets, tobacco prices recovered from a wartime low of 2 cents per pound and by 1818 sold for as much as 25 cents. The 1816 prices of both

19. James Sterling Young, *The Washington Community, 1800–1828* (New York: Harcourt, Brace, and World, 1966), pp. 13–37.
20. George Rogers Taylor, *The Transportation Revolution, 1815–1860*, vol. 4 of *Economic History of the United States*, ed. Henry David *et al.* (New York: Harper and Row, paperback ed., 1968), pp. 71, 189; Edgar E. Knight, *Public Education in the South* (Boston: Ginn and Co., 1922), *passim;* Marcus Cunliffe, *Soldiers and Civilians: Martial Spirit in America, 1775–1865* (Boston: Little, Brown, and Co., 1968), pp. 44–45, 201–12; Sydnor, *Southern Sectionalism*, pp. 77–86.

wheat and corn, of which Virginia was the leading producer in the South, were double those of 1813. In South Carolina, where rice and sea-island cotton were the leading products, rice prices increased from 3.6 cents per pound in 1814 to 6.1 cents in 1817, and sea-island cotton skyrocketed from an 1812 low price of 17.5 cents per pound to an astounding 1818 high of 63.2 cents. Short-staple cotton, which was being produced in ever increasing quantities in the South Carolina upcountry, leaped from an 1811 price of 8.9 cents per pound to an 1817 price of 29.8 cents. Planters responded predictably. Many took out mortgages on their existing lands to purchase additional acreage and agricultural production soared. Banks recklessly overextended their resources to finance speculation in land. Credit was easy, prosperity assured.[21]

In 1819 disaster struck. The supply of agricultural products began to exceed demand. At the same time, the new management of the Bank of the United States began to call in its loans, and the state banks followed suit. The results were catastrophic, especially in the slaveholding states. The price of sea-island cotton tumbled to 24.5 cents by 1823, short-staple cotton to 11.5 cents; corn fell to an 1823 low of 34 cents, wheat to an 1825 low of 79 cents, rice in 1823 below 3 cents for the first time in thirty years. Many a planter fell deeply into debt.[22]

At the very same time these economic woes set in a political crisis of great magnitude erupted. Since 1815 four new states had been admitted to the Union. Two, Mississippi and Alabama, permitted slavery, and two, Illinois and Indiana, did not. When Missouri applied to the Union as a slaveholding state in 1819, a dispute immediately arose in Congress. At issue was the balance in the Senate between slave and free

21. Lewis C. Gray, *History of Agriculture in the Southern United States to 1860*, 2 vols. (Washington: Carnegie Institute, 1933), 2:766–67, 1030–31, 1039; William W. Freehling, *Prelude to Civil War: The Nullification Controversy in South Carolina, 1816–1836* (New York: Harper and Row, 1965), pp. 25–26.
22. Gray, *History of Agriculture* 2:1030–31, 1039; Sydnor, *Southern Sectionalism*, pp. 104–33.

states. After protracted debate the Congress voted to admit Missouri as a slave state but to exclude slavery in the remainder of the Louisiana Purchase north of 36° 30′. To keep the balance in the Senate, Congress admitted nonslaveholding Maine at the same time. The precedent for simultaneously admitting a free state and a slave state lasted thirty years.

Some Southerners viewed the Missouri controversy with alarm. Though only Virginia vocally opposed any sort of compromise, there was considerable dissatisfaction throughout the South with the pledge in the so-called Missouri Compromise to exclude slavery from all states created north of 36° 30′ in the Louisiana Purchase. On the other hand, some Southerners enthusiastically endorsed the Compromise. Calhoun averred that the admission of Missouri would "settle forever" a "question, which has so deeply agitated this country. . . ." The press in Natchez, Mississippi, quarreled over whether the Compromise or outright prohibition of slavery in Missouri was the correct course.[23]

An underlying concern of Southern opponents of the Missouri bill was an awareness of the South's declining political influence in the national government. As the population in the North grew rapidly, Southern population could not keep pace. In 1790, almost exactly half of the population of the United States resided south of Mason and Dixon's line. By 1820 that percentage had declined to 46.7 percent, and that figure included slaves. If whites only were counted, the Southern percentage of the total population was only 35.8 percent. The political consequences were highly significant. The South in 1789 held 46 percent of the membership of the House of Representatives but held only 42 percent in 1820. A similar decline occurred in the number of presidential electors from the Southern states. The Missouri crisis awakened portions of the

23. Glover Moore, *The Missouri Controversy, 1819–1821* (Lexington: University of Kentucky Press, 1953), pp. 170–217, 248; John C. Calhoun to John Ewing Calhoun, January 8, 1821, in J. Franklin Jameson, ed., *Correspondence of John C. Calhoun,* Annual Report of the American Historical Association for the Year 1899, 2 (Washington: Government Printing Office, 1900): 181.

South, then, both to its shared interest in slavery and its declining sectional power in the Union. Congressman Spencer Roane best expressed this feeling when he advised President James Monroe that Missouri and other "western people . . . have an identity of interests with us. . . . The influence of a Southern sun has given to them a justice and generosity of character, which we look for in vain, among the Northern Yankees."[24]

Sectional tension did not abate after 1820. An outgrowth of the Missouri controversy was a renewed discussion over the future of slavery. In 1821 *The Genius of Universal Emancipation*, an antislavery newspaper published first in Ohio, then in Tennessee, and later in Baltimore, first appeared. In 1829 a free North Carolina Negro, David Walker, published a tract in Boston calling on slaves to revolt. In 1831 William Lloyd Garrison's famous abolitionist *Liberator* was first published. Moreover, during the 1820s the American Colonization Society, founded to relocate freed blacks in Africa, was at its busiest, receiving support from both North and South.[25]

Southern planters were extremely sensitive to any discussion of Negro emancipation. Their degree of hostility to abolitionism generally corresponded to the size of the black population in their midst. The earliest systematic defenses of slavery were written by men in Virginia and South Carolina who resided in areas where the black population outnumbered the white. In Virginia, which had led the opposition to the Missouri Compromise, planter attitudes against any suggestion of emancipation were firm. Depression had positively devastated the Old Dominion, and a number of the tidewater planters,

24. Carpenter, *South as a Conscious Minority*, pp. 21–23, 178–79. See Tables 1 and 2, Appendix I.

25. Two good general studies of the antislavery movement are Dwight L. Dumond, *Antislavery: The Crusade for Freedom in America* (Ann Arbor: University of Michigan Press, 1961), and Louis Filler, *The Crusade against Slavery, 1830–1860* (New York: Harper and Row, 1960). On the Colonization Society see Early Lee Fox, *The American Colonization Society, 1817–1840*, Johns Hopkins Studies in Historical and Political Science, 37 (1919): 9–231; and P. J. Staudenraus, *The African Colonization Movement, 1816–1865* (New York: Columbia University Press, 1961).

blaming the seemingly infertile soil, packed up and moved west to the rich grain and tobacco lands of Kentucky or to the equally fecund cotton lands of the southwest. Between 1810 and 1820, Virginia's rate of population increase was the lowest of all the Southern states, and most of that growth occurred in the counties west of the Allegheny Mountains, where non-slaveholding farmers, many from the North, were settling. After Monroe the birthplace of Presidents would produce no more elected chief executives for almost a century. By 1820 the state that had had the most congressmen under the 1790 census fell behind both New York and Pennsylvania. The Golden Age of Virginia was passing.[26]

It was the embattled planter of the tidewater region who reacted most vigorously to any suggestion that slavery ought to be ended. In 1825 the *Richmond Enquirer* published a series of letters by a pseudonymous correspondent, Caius Gracchus. Charging that the aims of the Colonization Society, which the Virginia legislature had voted to support financially, looked toward emancipation, Gracchus sketched the outlines of an argument that would soon become familiar. Emancipation meant the "surrender of $300,000,000" in property, but, even worse, it threatened

> to revolutionize the whole character and habits of the people of the South. . . . Even our bodies, as well as our minds have been moulded under the influence of the principle of labor among us. . . . Proud, high spirited and independent, the love of freedom and jealousy of invasion of their rights, either individually or politically, have ever, I think, been characteristic of the Virginian and the South.

26. *Statistical Views of the Population of the United States from 1790 to 1830 Inclusive* (Washington: Duff Green, 1835), pp. 60–63; Avery O. Craven, *Soil Exhaustion as a Factor in the Agricultural History of Virginia and Maryland, 1606–1860,* University of Illinois Studies in the Social Sciences, 13 (1925): 91–121. Craven correctly blames careless agricultural methods for Virginia's decline, but he overstates the unprofitability of Virginia agriculture. Recent studies suggest that Virginia agriculture was unprofitable only by comparison with production elsewhere. Also, as the experience of Edmund Ruffin demonstrated, Virginiians themselves, not their soil, were primarily to blame. For a full treatment of this problem see Chapters Two and Three following.

Though the letters received wide exposure through the large circulation of the *Enquirer*, they were also published as a pamphlet a year later to reach an even wider audience. Virginia was getting a strong taste of Southern sectionalism.[27]

As the shadows of economic depression lengthened in Virginia, as the character of its population changed and the vigor of its leadership declined, a tug of war took place over control of the state government at Richmond. For some time the population of western Virginia had objected to the disproportionate influence held in the state legislature by the tidewater gentry, who thwarted internal improvement measures because to do otherwise would require a higher tax on their slave property. Agitating for state constitutional reform to apportion representation more fairly, the nonslaveholders of the transmontane region got their wish in 1829.[28]

At issue when the convention assembled was the basis of legislative representation. The eastern planters supported the status quo, which followed the federal lead in counting each slave as three-fifths of a man, but the westerners, realizing that the federal basis greatly augmented planter influence, desired a change to a "white only" basis. A leading western reformer hoped to remove the "odius yoke of slave representation" while an eastern planter, Abel P. Upshur, responded by arguing that such a revision assumed an identity of interest between slaveholders and nonslaveholders that was actually nonexistent. "Be assured," warned Benjamin W. Leigh, a planter spokesman, "that fanatics are at work, and that the political power to which the possession of Negro slaves entitles the South hangs in the balance." Thus, when Virginians debated representation, they were really debating slavery.[29]

27. Quoted in William S. Jenkins, *Pro-Slavery Thought in the Old South* (Chapel Hill: University of North Carolina Press, 1935), p. 75.
28. Charles Henry Ambler, *Sectionalism in Virginia from 1776 to 1861* (Chicago: University of Chicago Press, 1910), pp. 142–44; Robert McColley, *Slavery and Jeffersonian Virginia* (Urbana: University of Illinois Press, 1964), pp. 10–12, 117, 183.
29. Alison H. G. Freehling, "Drift Toward Dissolution: The Virginia Slavery Debate of 1831–1832" (Ph.D. diss., University of Michigan, 1974), pp. 54,

The outcome was a modified constitution that apportioned seats in the lower house about equally among four sections of the state and allocated seats in the upper house among two larger sections, with the combined tidewater and eastern section in a slight majority over the section west of the Blue Ridge. Though the easterners could have lost more, they were only grudgingly satisfied with the compromise. The planters, now politically as well as economically in retreat, cast about for a villain and pitched on democracy. "Universal suffrage" was a "plague" comparable to "the influenza—the smallpox—the varioloid—the Hessian fly." Worse, the diseases seemed always to originate in the North, "and they always cross above the falls of the great rivers: below, it seems, the broad expanse of waters interposing, arrests their progress." Lamenting, they asked, "What has become of our political rank and eminence in the Union? Whither . . . has the Genius of Virginia fled?"[30]

A number of South Carolinians were asking a similar question, though they expressed it in terms of their section rather than their individual state. Economic conditions were not improving in the Palmetto State, and more and more Carolinians during the 1820's were departing their native soil for the west. Of the Southern states, South Carolina's population was increasing at a rate slower than any state but Virginia. Moreover, its black population, which had surpassed the white between 1810 and 1820, continued to grow at a much more rapid pace, making South Carolina the only state with a black majority.[31]

244; *Proceedings and Debates of the Virginia State Convention of 1829–30* (Richmond: Samuel Shepherd and Co., 1830), pp. 319–20; Ambler, *Sectionalism in Virginia*, p. 158. Upshur and Leigh represented Northampton and Chesterfield counties respectively. In both counties the black population outnumbered the white. See U.S. Census Office, *Fourth Census* (Washington: Gales and Seaton, 1821).

30. *Proceedings and Debates*, pp. 407, 404.

31. Donald B. Dodd and Wynelle S. Dodd, eds., *Historical Statistics of the South, 1790–1970* (University, Ala.: University of Alabama Press, 1973), p. 46; Freehling, *Prelude to Civil War*, pp. 46–48. See also Tables 3 and 4, Appendix I.

Geography and climate had conspired to fit South Carolina peculiarly to become the spokesman of the slaveholding states. With the invention of the cotton gin, production of short-staple cotton, for which the soil of upcountry South Carolina was ideally suited, rapidly increased. The state became uniquely homogeneous as cotton planting (and, with it, slavery) expanded far into the interior. There were numerous intermarriages between the leading families of the upcountry and the lowcountry. As a result there was little of the intrastate sectionalism that plagued such states as Virginia, and the state's government reflected the monolithic character of its society. The South Carolina legislature was omnipotent. Its membership, the only popularly elected state officials, chose governor, United States senators, and presidential electors. This extraordinary power, combined with a property qualification for voting and the disproportionate representation of the lowcountry barons in the legislature, stifled dissent, made organized political parties an impossibility, and rendered the state a virtual unit on any national issue.[32]

Though Carolinians were distraught during the 1820's they expressed their concern in different ways. The lowcountry planters were particularly sensitive to any suggestion of federal interference in state affairs, especially because of their large slave holdings. For example, in 1825 Whitemarsh Seabrook, a young lowcountry rice planter, wrote a detailed defense of slavery in response to an emancipation proposal by the Ohio legislature. Perhaps equally important in motivating Seabrook was a rumored slave rebellion in 1822 led by Denmark Vesey, which proved abortive. Seabrook delivered his message before the Agricultural Society of St. John's Colleton District in the lowcountry, where whites constituted only 20 percent of the total population. "By what authority can we be divested of *our whole property?*" he cried to his fellow

32. James M. Banner, Jr., "The Problem of South Carolina," in *The Hofstadter Aegis*, ed. Stanley M. Elkins and Eric McKitrick (New York: Alfred A. Knopf, 1974), pp. 60–93. See also Map, Appendix II.

planters. Emancipation would bring not only economic destruction but also "desolating convulsions" to the social fabric, "wide spreading conflagration" in which would be raised up "a Spartacus or an African Tecumseh, to demand by what authority we hold them in subjection." The sober citizens of St. John's had Seabrook's speech published and circulated widely throughout the lowcountry. His concerns were evidently theirs as well.[33]

Seabrook and his neighbors were much more concerned about the slave population in their midst than they were about immediate economic conditions. Despite the sharp decline in the prices of rice and sea-island cotton, these planters were relatively better off than the residents of the Carolina upcountry. Though the price of rice had dropped, it leveled off not much below its pre-1815 average of 3 cents, where it remained through the 1820's. Even then it had fallen no further than the cost of living. Like the rice planter, the sea-island cotton planter's cost of living had dropped about as far as the price of his crop. But, also like the rice planter, the lowcountry cotton planter was far from economically prostrate. If he should ever have a grievance against the general government, it was unlikely that economics would be the cause.[34]

While the lowcountry had escaped the prolonged depression in relatively good condition, upcountry South Carolina

33. Freehling, *Prelude to Civil War*, p. 366; Gray, *History of Agriculture* 2:1030; Whitemarsh B. Seabrook, *A Concise View of the Critical Situation, and Future Prospects of the Slave-Holding States, in Relation to Their Coloured Population*, 2d ed. (Charleston: A. E. Miller, 1825), pp. 6, 13, 20. Freehling argues (p. 81) that Seabrook in this speech declared that Carolinians "detested" slavery. In fact, Seabrook was directly quoting a speech by Patrick Henry in 1788, which warned that because many Americans "detested" slavery, at some future date they might try to effect emancipation. Seabrook, reaffirming this fear, prophesied that Henry's "appalling prediction is about to be verified." Neither Seabrook nor his audience "detested" slavery; they "detested" abolition.

34. Freehling, *Prelude to Civil War*, pp. 25–48. I am very much indebted to Freehling's analysis of pre-Nullification economic conditions in South Carolina, which is thoroughly researched, clearly presented, and persuasively argued.

was in poor financial shape. The upcountry planter differed from his lowcountry counterpart both in the crop he raised and in the life he lived. The great names of old Carolina were mostly lowcountry names. St. Philip's and St. Michael's churchyards in Charleston held the remains of most of the distinguished old families. Wealth, position, and a distinctive style of life were transmitted from one generation of lowcountry gentry to the next and served as a buffer against the onslaughts of life. The upcountry planter, however, had achieved his wealth and prominence only recently, as the spread of short-staple cotton displaced the yeoman farmer with a rugged, aggressive, and frequently uncouth breed of frontiersman, who reaped rapid and great wealth from the soil. A planter aristocracy of sorts had arisen, modeled after the lowcountry aristocracy and centered in Columbia. The upcountry parvenus, imitating their Charleston betters, affected the culture and breeding their ancestry belied. They overextended themselves financially, and, when depression came, it struck with a vengeance.

Though the upcountry planter viewed federal activities with the same negative attitude as the lowcountry gentleman, his concerns were somewhat different. Between 1818 and 1829 the price of upcountry short-staple cotton plummeted 72 percent, while the cost of living fell only about 50 percent. Faced with such a crushing discrepancy, selling their cotton in a contracting free market while buying clothing and other supplies in an uncertain market regulated by import duties, the upcountry planter—searching for a cause of his distress—naturally seized upon the tariff. The tariff seemed to be a barrier designed to impede his economic freedom. An upcountryman called it "the tax of agriculture for the benefit of manufactures." The plaintive warnings about abolition from the monied lowcountry had little impact, for neither the threat nor the consequences of abolition seemed particularly real. If the planter in the upcountry had a grievance, it was purely and genuinely economic.[35]

35. Avery O. Craven, *The Coming of the Civil War*, rev. ed. (Chicago: University of Chicago Press, 1966), p. 59.

Though the concerns of upcountry and lowcountry differed, the peculiarities of South Carolina politics and geography helped bind them together. Unlike Virginia, there were
no intrastate political battles to fight, for South Carolina was
wholly committed to cotton and slavery and wholly determined to improve its prospects. The response of the state to
federal policy employed rhetoric that suited both the bankrupt
upcountryman and the fearful lowcountryman. It was rooted
in the same concerns that moved the embattled Virginia
planters to stand up for their distinctive minority rights. It was
perhaps best expressed in 1824 by the lowcountry-dominated
South Carolina Senate, which cited "the supreme and permanent law . . . of self-preservation" in answering a challenge by
Secretary of State John Quincy Adams. Adams had declared
that a South Carolina law requiring free Negro seamen to be
imprisoned while their ships were in Charleston harbor violated both the Constitution and a treaty with England. In response, the Carolinians asserted that a state's duty "to guard
against insubordination or insurrection . . . is paramount to all
laws, all *treaties*, all constitutions . . . and will never, by this
state, be renounced, compromised, controlled, or participated
with any power whatsoever." [36]

The relationship of state and nation remained unsettled,
since South Carolina continued to arrest Negro seamen. But
that "supreme and permanent law . . . of self-preservation"
had not had its last test.

III

The young vice president of the United States, John C. Calhoun, was greatly worried. The Washington heat of early May
1828 had penetrated the Senate chamber over which he pre-
sided, where a momentous debate was about to begin. The
House of Representatives had just passed and sent on to the
Senate a new tariff bill, which raised import duties from 33

36. Freehling, *Prelude to Civil War*, p. 115; Herman V. Ames, *State Documents
on Federal Relations: The States and the United States* (Philadelphia: University of
Pennsylvania Press, 1900–1906), p. 207.

percent to 50 percent. To an agricultural, exporting state like South Carolina, the tariff had become a symbolic target of blame for hard times. Calhoun recognized the explosive possibilities if the tariff should pass. As an upcountryman he, too, believed "that [the tariff] is one of the great instruments of our impoverishment; and if persisted in must reduce us to poverty," or, worse, "compel us to an entire change of industry." Calhoun, like a number of Carolinians in 1828, looked "on the present unequal action of the system with deepest anxiety."[37]

Calhoun stood at the crossroads of a promising political career that had thus far been enthusiastically nationalistic. Born in 1782 of moderately wealthy, slaveholding, Scotch–Irish parents in upcountry South Carolina, Calhoun was a graduate of Yale College and Litchfield (Connecticut) Law School. He was admitted to the bar in 1807. In 1811 the tall, handsome Carolinian, who possessed sharp features and an equally sharp intellect, married the daughter of a wealthy low-country planter and, financially independent, the couple removed to an upcountry plantation. Calhoun was elected to Congress in 1812, where he was a strong supporter of the war with England. When the war ended he proclaimed the exuberant nationalism of the new political generation. Appointed in 1817 as Monroe's Secretary of War, Calhoun was a staunch supporter of internal improvements that looked toward strengthening national defense. "Let us, then, bind the Republic together," he cried. "Let us conquer space." In addition, he and most of the Carolinians in Congress supported the 1816 protective tariff, which taxed imports at a mild rate of 25 percent. In those years, to a man with a brilliant future and great capacities for hard work, all things seemed possible.[38]

37. Freehling, *Prelude to Civil War, p.* 138; Calhoun to James Edward Calhoun, May 4, 1828, *Calhoun Correspondence*, p. 265. Freehling's book is by far the most recent and most authoritative treatment. Two other old but still useful studies are Chauncey S. Boucher, *The Nullification Controversy in South Carolina* (Chicago: University of Chicago Press, 1916) and David F. Houston, *A Critical Study of Nullification in South Carolina* (New York: Longmans, Green, and Co., 1896).

38. *Calhoun Papers* 1: 401. All biographical information in this and succeeding paragraphs is taken from the following sources: Margaret Coit, *John C. Cal-*

The postwar optimism of South Carolinians quickly soured. Increasingly they began to question the benefits of certain federal policies. Thomas Cooper, president of South Carolina College, even went so far as to urge his fellow citizens to "calculate the value of the Union." The state legislature in 1825 and again in 1827 declared that protective tariffs were discriminatory and therefore unconstitutional. The tariff policy, which Calhoun as war secretary and later as John Quincy Adams's vice president continued to support during the 1820's, was coming under fire at home, and the young Carolinian, possessing ambitions for the presidency, could not afford to alienate his constituency. Yet to oppose the tariff was to risk losing support in the North that would be crucial for a presidential bid. In 1827, protesting that the rate was becoming oppressively high, Calhoun cast the tie-breaking vote against the Woolens Bill, which would have raised the duty on imported woolens from 33 to 50 percent.[39]

Now a similar bill again faced the Senate in 1828, and Calhoun feared that this time its passage was assured. The Carolinians, seeking tariff relief, were in fact responsible for what they called the "Tariff of Abominations." Presidential politics was to blame. Desiring the election of Andrew Jackson in 1828 over Adams and knowing that northeastern support was crucial for victory, the South Carolina congressmen planned to support absurdly high tariff provisions on raw materials and then join with New England to vote the entire tariff bill down. The strategy backfired, however, as Northern Jacksonians managed to reduce the rates just enough to secure passage of the reckless act, which put duties at an unnecessarily high level. The Carolinians had done themselves in.[40]

boun: American Portrait (Boston: Houghton Mifflin Co., 1951); Richard N. Current, *John C. Calhoun* (New York: Washington Square Press, 1966); and Charles M. Wiltse, *John C. Calhoun*, 3 vols. (Indianapolis: Bobbs-Merrill Co., 1944–51).

39. Dumas Malone, *The Public Life of Thomas Cooper* (New Haven: Yale University Press, 1926), p. 309.

40. Freehling, *Prelude to Civil War*, pp. 136–37; Robert V. Remini, "Martin Van Buren and the Tariff of Abominations," *American Historical Review* 63 (1958): 903–17.

In the summer of 1828 Calhoun returned home puzzled and somewhat frightened. A legislative committee headed by William C. Preston requested him to formulate a protest against the tariff. Calhoun well knew the direction in which events were tending. He hoped his state would "not be provoked to step beyond strict constitutional remedies," but he acknowledged that the new duties "must lead to defeat to opposition or resistence [sic], or the correction of what perhaps is a great defect in our system; that the seperate [sic] geographical interests are not sufficiently guarded." Facing a Carolina constituency united in their anger toward the federal government, Calhoun realized "that the system is getting wrong and if a speedy and effective remedy be not applied a shock at no long interval may be expected." Looking beyond the interests of his own state to the needs of his section—with both the section's economic condition and his own political condition doubtless in mind—and trying to reconcile those needs with his genuine love of the Union, Calhoun groped for a response.[41]

Like Madison and Jefferson in 1798, like the Hartford Convention in 1814, Calhoun turned to the doctrine of state interposition or, as he called it, Nullification. He was not the first Carolinian to espouse the doctrine in opposition to the tariff, but he was by far the most eloquent. By the autumn of 1828, as Calhoun was winning reelection to the vice presidency, this time with Jackson, his essay, entitled the *South Carolina Exposition and Protest*, was ready. It argued that "imposing duties on imports,—not for revenue, but for the protection of one branch of industry at the expense of others,—is unconstitutional, unequal, oppressive, and calculated to corrupt virtue and destroy the liberty of the country. . . ."

Adducing import and export figures and applying the tariff schedule, Calhoun concluded that Southerners "are the serfs of a system,—out of whose labor is raised, not only the money paid into the Treasury, but the funds out of which are

41. Calhoun to James Edward Calhoun, August 27, 1827, Calhoun to James Monroe, July 10, 1828, *Calhoun Correspondence*, pp. 251, 267.

drawn the rich rewards of the manufacturer and his associates in interest." If the high tariff persisted, "the last remains of our great and once flourishing agriculture must be annihilated. . . ." Lest his audience miss the point, he elaborated upon the "hazardous extremity" of abandoning "our ancient and favorable pursuit, to which our soil, climate, habits, and peculiar labor are adapted. . . ."

There must, he argued, be a mechanism for the oppressed minority to protect its rights. Whenever "a majority of the States, through the General Government" threatened to "usurp powers not delegated" by the Constitution "and by their exercise, increase their wealth and authority at the expense of the minority," an aggrieved state had the right to call a state convention. The convention then would determine whether the act in question constituted—and here the precedents of 1798 and 1814 asserted their usefulness—"a violation so deliberate, palpable, and dangerous, as to justify the interposition of the State to protect its rights." Delighted, Preston delivered the *Exposition* to the legislature in December, and that body, though failing to adopt it, ordered several thousand copies to be printed and circulated.[42]

The circular had great impact. Though Calhoun, who submitted the *Exposition* anonymously, wrote the essay as a warning rather than as a statement of present policy, a number of South Carolinians seized upon it as a formidable intellectual justification for a policy of immediate resistance to the general government. While Calhoun labored for the next several years to avoid a confrontation between his state and the federal authorities, other Carolinians spoke of "revolution." What Calhoun saw as a means of preserving the Union he loved—he neglected to address all the ramifications of this theory—some of his fellow citizens viewed as a way of restoring their influence and fortune in a new, independent government.

There soon developed in South Carolina three political

42. Richard K. Crallé, ed., *The Works of John C. Calhoun*, 6 vols. (New York: D. Appleton and Co., 1855) 6: 2, 10, 12–13, 50, 45.

factions. One group, who called themselves Unionists, opposed the tariff but denounced Nullification as the proper remedy. This group, comprising mostly merchants of Charleston and farmers of the upcountry, was led by a group of Charleston aristocrats who were tied to the lowcountry planting circle. Among the leaders of this group were men like Hugh Swinton Legaré, Daniel Huger, James Petigru, Langdon Cheves, Henry Middleton, William Elliott, and William Drayton. Calm and conservative, pillars of distinctive Charleston society, such men were appalled at what they considered as the demagogic excesses of the Nullifiers. With a stake of many generations in the preservation of their way of life, they were opposed equally to tariff and Nullification and preferred to work through the normal channels of government to win redress. "Let us consider the *issue*," begged Legaré. "Let us *weigh and consider*." If the tariff really meant emancipation to these men, they concealed their fears and suppressed them well. A more likely explanation of their opposition to Nullification was their conservative unwillingness to change and their desire not to risk their own high position in society. Two remarks suggest this very outlook. Huger, asked in the state legislature what the people of his district thought of a particular bill, haughtily answered, "Think! They will think nothing about it—They expect me to think for them *here*." Petigru, looking down disdainfully at the "nullies," called them "little men . . . crowing on their own dunghill. . . ."[43]

Petigru was partly correct, but he failed, like most of his colleagues, to distinguish between the two wings of the Nullification movement. One wing followed Calhoun. Differing only in temperament from the Unionist leaders, the leaders of the Calhoun group—among them Henry Laurens Pinckney, Stephen D. Miller, William Harper, and Robert Turnbull—

43. Freehling, ed., *Nullification Era*, p. 134; John B. O'Neall. *Biographical Sketches of the Bench and Bar of South Carolina*, 2 vols. (Charleston: S. G. Courtenay, 1859), 1: 181; James L. Petigru to James Chesnut, December 9, 1834, Williams–Chesnut–Manning Papers, South Caroliniana Library, University of South Carolina.

generally came from the lowcountry aristocracy. They saw in Calhoun's theory a means both of preserving the Union and, perhaps, of thwarting for all time any efforts to tamper with slavery, which was the basis of their distinctive style of life. They spoke harshly but, like Calhoun, never of disunion. The most radical pronouncement any of them ever made was an Independence Day oration by Turnbull in 1832. He mentioned a "Southern Confederacy," but in his view even this extreme version of Southern unity would remain a part of the Union.[44]

For most of these Nullifiers, the tariff was merely a symbol of an incipient federal campaign to abolish slavery. Since most of these leaders were from the lowcountry, where economic dislocation had been relatively insignificant, they had little reason to react so violently to the tariff. In fact, they were reacting not to the tariff at all, but to abolition. For example, in 1827 Turnbull issued an inflammatory pamphlet indicating the true nature of the confrontation. "It is not," he wrote, "whether we are to be taxed without end [but] . . . whether the institutions of our forefathers . . . are to be preserved. . . ." Harper called the tariff "the symptom instead of the disease" and predicted a federal attempt "to relieve . . . your free negroes first; and afterwards your slaves." Pinckney believed that if South Carolina should cease "opposition to the tariff . . . abolition will become the order of the day. . . ." Yet none of these men wished to dissolve the Union. "The principle we contend for would . . . promote harmony and tend to the perpetuation of the Union," asserted Harper. "Nullification is the conservative principle of the Union," echoed Pinckney.[45]

44. Robert J. Turnbull, *An Oration, Delivered in the City of Charleston, Before the State Rights and Free Trade Party, The State Society of Cincinnati, The Revolution Society, The '76 Association, The Young Men's Free Trade Association, and Several Volunteer Companies of Militia; on the 4th of July, 1832* (Charleston: A. E. Miller, 1832), p. 27.

45. [Robert J. Turnbull], *The Crisis; or Essays on the Usurpations of the Federal Government* (Charleston: A. E. Miller, 1827), p. 64; *Speeches in the Convention, March, 1833*, p. 50; Freehling, *Prelude to Civil War*, p. 256; William Harper, *The Remedy by State Interposition, or Nullification* (Charleston: E. J. Van Brunt, 1832), p. 19; Henry L. Pinckney, *An Oration Before the State Rights and Free*

IV

The other wing of Nullifiers made up in noise what they lacked in numbers. Their leadership was very different from either the Unionists or the Calhounites. These men looked beyond Nullification. They envisioned a separate Southern nation.

From the great mass of materials on the Nullification movement in South Carolina, the names of seven identifiable, unquestionable Southern nationalists emerge. These men may not have mirrored their constituencies. Nor is the list necessarily complete. But each of these men was without doubt a leader in the Nullification campaign. All of them at some point indicated their desire for a separate Southern nation either by action or declaration, and some of them even revealed what kind of a nation they had in mind.[46]

The leader of the group was Thomas Cooper, president of South Carolina College, which was located in Columbia. Short, corpulent, and afflicted with many of the physical burdens of old age, Cooper, born in England in 1759, was a man of great energy, cranky disposition, and highly controversial ideas. He had pursued a number of careers, beginning as a pamphleteer in the 1790's when he dared to applaud Jacobin excesses in France. He came to Philadelphia in 1794, immediately joined the Jeffersonian party, and was imprisoned under the Sedition Act in 1800. He was appointed to the Pennsylvania bench in 1804, but by 1811 his controversial decisions resulted in his being hounded off the court by Pennsylvania Democrats. From 1811 to 1819 he was a lecturer in chemistry at the University of Pennsylvania. In 1820 he left for South Carolina College, where, in 1821, he became president. Finding the style of life in Columbia attractive, Cooper became a

Trade Party, *The State Society of Cincinnati, The Revolution Society, The '76 Association, and the State Volunteers on the 4th of July, 1833* (Charleston: A. E. Miller, 1833), pp. 3, 35.
46. For a discussion of how the list was drawn up, see Appendix V. The list itself is in Appendix II.

staunch defender of slavery and the plantation system. By 1827 he was convinced that the tariff threatened the South with consequences far greater than mere economic inferiority. At a large rally in 1827 he made his famous "value of the Union" speech, in which he charged the North with forcing its will upon the Southern minority.[47]

Except for Cooper, the other six Southern nationalists were young men closely tied to the plantation system. Their average age in 1832 was thirty-seven. Two of them were graduates of South Carolina College. All but one was a lawyer; all, including Cooper, owned some slaves, but only half of them were large slaveholders; all but one was a planter; and, perhaps most striking, all but two were from the upcountry. The typical Southern nationalist, then, was a young, professional man with a stake in agriculture, engaged in a law practice that kept him close to cities or towns, which in turn exposed him to events in the wider world.[48]

These characteristics, however, differed little from those of the leaders of the Union and Calhoun factions. What set the Southern nationalists apart from the other two groups was the recency with which they had attained their present status. The origins of these young, planter-lawyer Southern nationalists were generally humble. Whatever wealth or status they possessed they had earned themselves. It had not been passed to them by distinguished ancestors. For example, George McDuffie was the Georgia-born son of poor Scottish immigrants. Cooper was an immigrant from England. Rhett, who changed his name from Smith, was of noted ancestry, but his parents were so poor that they could not afford to educate him.[49]

---

47. Malone, *Public Life of Cooper, passim.*
48. See Appendix II.
49. Biographical information on the seven Southern nationalists comes from the following sources: Malone, *Public Life of Cooper;* Freehling, *Prelude to Civil War;* O'Neall, *Bench and Bar of South Carolina; Cyclopedia of Eminent and Representative Men of the Carolinas of the Nineteenth Century* (2 vols.; Madison, Wis.: Brant and Fuller, 1892); Edwin L. Green, *George McDuffie* (Columbia: State

All of them rapidly became prosperous during the post-war boom. For example, Pickens moved to upcountry Edgefield and augmented his already sizable fortune. McDuffie practiced scientific agriculture and realized a high income from his productive fields. Rhett, through a propitious marriage to a rice planter's daughter, restored his lost fortunes. Cooper won fame and influence if not fortune at South Carolina College, and he aided E. W. Johnston, who became editor of the influential pro-Nullification *Columbia Telescope*. Warren Davis's law practice in upcountry Pendleton was highly lucrative, and he, too, owned a plantation. Hamilton was as much an entrepreneur as the rest, investing heavily in numerous capitalistic enterprises.

Their quick success made them naturally protective of their newly acquired status, and that status may explain the antagonism between these "little men" and the aristocratic leaders of the Union and Calhoun factions. When economic disaster struck them, their reaction to the high tariff took a predictably extreme form, for the tariff seemed to threaten their economic prosperity. It placed "burden on burden," cried McDuffie, attacking Congress for its "perpetual tampering with the great pecuniary interests of society." Yet the economic crisis does not itself explain why, by 1833, these men had all become convinced of the necessity for separate Southern nationhood. Other upcountrymen did not react so fiercely. In fact, at the outset of the crisis, the distinction between Calhounites and Southern nationalists was unclear. For example, Rhett in 1828 strongly urged Governor John Taylor to summon the legislature and vaguely asked his state to "resist . . . openly, fairly, fearlessly, and unitedly." In 1827 Cooper was calculating the value of the Union. Only after the crisis developed did the difference between those Nullifiers who hoped to preserve the Union and those who wished to disrupt it emerge.[50]

Co., 1936); and Laura A. White, *Robert Barnwell Rhett: Father of Secession* (New York: Appleton–Century–Crofts, 1931).
50. *Charleston Mercury*, June 28, 1828; Freehling, *Prelude to Civil War*, pp. 130, 147.

V

In 1832 the tariff issue came to a head. A new tariff bill, which lowered some rates but maintained others—notably cottons, woolens, and iron—at the old rate, convinced even Calhoun, who had a year earlier resigned the vice presidency when his authorship of the *Exposition* became known, that the time for resistance had arrived. "The question is no longer one of free trade, but liberty and despotism," he stated. "Let every Carolinian do his duty."[51]

In August Calhoun published a letter to Governor James Hamilton offering a firm, detailed, theoretical underpinning for the actions South Carolina should take. The crisis stemmed, he began, from "the radical error" that the general government "is a national, and not, as in reality it is, a confederated Government." If the general government should ever exceed its constitutional powers, which the states granted in 1787, a state convention had the right to nullify the unconstitutional enactment and forbid its enforcement within the state. The general government must then either accept the nullification or submit a constitutional amendment to the states for ratification. If the amendment should not pass, "no alternative would remain for the general government but a compromise or its permanent abandonment" of unconstitutional policy. If, on the other hand, three-fourths of the states should ratify the amendment, the nullifying state must then consider whether or not to continue as a member of the Union. The likelihood of ever reaching that extreme, however, was rare, for the glorious system of American government was structured so as "TO COMPEL THE PARTS OF SOCIETY TO BE JUST TO ONE ANOTHER BY COMPELLING THEM TO CONSULT ONE ANOTHER." Nullification was a means, then, of preserving the Union *"by compelling the agent to fulfill the object for which the agency or trust was created. . . ."* Nullification was not secession; it was, rather "a

51. Freehling, *Prelude to Civil War*, pp. 248–49.

conflict of moral, and not physical force—a trial of constitutional, and not military power. . . ."[52]

The Nullifiers were well organized. Hamilton established
a number of "Associations" around the state to spread the gospel of Nullification. During the 1832 legislative elections, a
vigorous statewide campaign—which included barbecues,
stump speeches, and numerous public gatherings—yielded a
staunchly pro-Nullification legislature representing all portions of the state. That body called a state convention, which
assembled in Columbia on November 19. The Unionist
Legaré lamented that "the South Carolina in which and for
which I was educated has somehow or other disappeared, and
left a *simulacrum* behind of a very different kind—which I don't
understand, neither am understood by it." Meanwhile a new
South Carolina was about to emerge in Columbia.[53]

With the Nullifiers in control, the South Carolina convention quickly did its duty. It nullified the tariff, effective February 1, 1833, over the objection of radicals, who wanted immediate implementation. If Congress chose to employ "military
or naval force against the State of South Carolina" such an act
would be "inconsistent with the longer continuance of South
Carolina in the Union." Finally, the convention prescribed for
all state officeholders a test oath of loyalty to the Ordinance of
Nullification. To the people of South Carolina the convention
announced that "nullification will preserve, and not destroy
this Union" and asked for united support. To the people of the
United States the convention blamed the Northern majority in
Congress for "imposing duties, which are utterly destructive of
the interests of South Carolina" and which "confer enriching
bounties upon their constituents, proportioned to the burthens
they impose upon us." Significantly, the convention claimed
that it acted not for South Carolina alone, but for "the great
Southern section of the Union," which had "suffered for so

---

52. *Calhoun Works* 6: 158, 160, 169, 190, 168, 164.
53. Freehling, *Prelude to Civil War*, pp. 244–54; Hugh Swinton Legaré to
Stephen Elliott, April 14, 1839, typed copy in South Caroliniana Library.

many years" because of the tariff. The convention then adjourned, to reconvene in March 1833.[54]

The great Southern section of the Union was quick to respond, and their message was not encouraging. A scattered few—John A. Quitman in Mississippi, Dixon H. Lewis in Alabama, Robert M. T. Hunter in Virginia—supported Nullification, but in general the Southern response was cautious. North Carolina sympathized with its neighbor's complaint but called Nullification "revolutionary" and "subversive." Alabama, too, understood Carolina's grievance but feared that Nullification would lead "finally to the dissolution of the Union." It was "unsound in theory and dangerous in practice. . . ." Mississippi agreed that the tariff law was unfair to the South but labeled South Carolina's attitude "unwarrantable" and its position "contrary to the letter and spirit of the Constitution. . . ." Georgia recognized the need to lower the tariff but warned South Carolina not to pursue its "mischievous policy."[55]

President Jackson responded with equal swiftness. In December he issued a Nullification Proclamation, declaring South Carolina's action to be "incompatible with the existence of the Union, contradicted expressly by the letter of the Constitution, unauthorized by its spirit, inconsistent with every principle on which it was founded, and destructive of the great object for which it was formed." Nullification, said the President, was "treason against the United States. Treason is an offense against sovereignty and sovereignty must reside with the power to punish it. . . ." Jackson, while calling for tariff reform, promised to enforce the law in South Carolina. To do otherwise would be "to say that the United States are not a nation."[56]

54. *State Papers on Nullification: Including the Public Acts of the Convention of the People of South Carolina, Assembled at Columbia, November 19, 1832 and March 11, 1833* (Boston: Dutton and Wentworth, 1834), pp. 5, 19, 28, 31, 51, 66, 70.
55. *Ibid.*, pp. 201, 222, 230–31, 274; John McCardell, "John A. Quitman and the Compromise of 1850 in Mississippi," *Journal of Mississippi History* 37 (1975): 240–42.
56. *State Papers on Nullification*, pp. 80, 87.

By the time the South Carolina convention reassembled in March, Nullification was in retreat. Supported by the Southern states, a compromise tariff that reduced duties had passed Congress. Within South Carolina, Calhoun had been counseling delay in following through on the threat to secede. A bitter fight over the loyalty oath had destroyed Nullifier unity. With the other states declining to support Nullification, with the tariff reduced, and with internal unity disappearing, the convention rescinded the Ordinance of Nullification and petulantly nullified Jackson's so-called "Force Bill."[57]

The crisis was over, but, paradoxically, the next few months saw the emergence of the influential wing of the Nullification movement dedicated to the creation of a distinct and separate nation. Behind this drive were two forces. One was economic. Between 1831 and 1835 cotton prices doubled to reach almost 20 cents per pound. Economic recovery was slowly but indisputably returning. Their instinct for the main chance stimulated anew, upcountry radicals became even more radical on the subject of the tariff, which seemed to impede the recovery of their slowly returning fortunes.[58]

The second force was social. On January 1, 1831, Garrison published the first issue of his *Liberator* antislavery journal. In August of that year, Nat Turner, a charismatic Virginia slave, led a bloody uprising in Southampton County, a tidewater county where blacks outnumbered whites. Meanwhile, in South Carolina, a series of hideous and threatening upcountry episodes in 1832 seemed to confirm the lowcountry's oft-repeated warnings about abolitionism. In Lancaster district a slave murdered his master's daughter. In Sumter a black cook served poisoned food to an Independence Day banquet. A number of guests died and several hundred became extremely ill.[59]

For the first time an awareness of the dangers of abolitionism penetrated to the upcountry, where most of the incipient

57. Freehling, *Prelude to Civil War*, pp. 286–96.
58. Gray, *History of Agriculture* 2: 1027.
59. Freehling, *Prelude to Civil War*, pp. 250–51.

Southern nationalists lived. Their spirits, already troubled by an unpredictable economy, became further disturbed as the social consequences of abolition became more vivid and the threat of social upheaval seemed more immediate. The resulting strain which, they thought, was making their existence unbearable, forced them to make connections and discern patterns that had hitherto gone unnoticed. Their perception of their worsening plight became for them the reality, and the intensity of their response matched what they believed to be the seriousness of their predicament.

One by one they made the linkage of tariff and abolitionism. Hamilton "looked to the present contest with the general government, on the part of the Southern States, as a battle at the out-posts. . . ." To lose this battle would "authorize the federal government to erect the *peaceful* standard of servile revolt. . . ." McDuffie saw "the irresistible tendency of this protecting system" to be "the abolition of slavery. . . ." Warren Davis announced, "Our situation is peculiar," and attacked the "nefarious" tariff. Rhett warned, "Every stride of this Government, over your rights, brings it nearer and nearer to your peculiar policy." Pickens compared nullification of the tariff to the earlier nullification of Adams's decree concerning Negro seamen. Cooper as early as 1826 wrote a pamphlet attacking both the tariff and abolition. Johnston's *Telescope* accused Charleston of being "a colony of Yankee speculators, cherishing not a spark of Southern feeling." The *Telescope* also published numerous tracts, among them one linking the tariff and abolition, in order to show the consequences of Northern domination. Carolinians must decide whether their children "shall be the free and undisputed heirs of the liberty and the land which our fathers bequeathed, or the dastardly and hereditary drudges of imperious taskmasters."[60]

60. *Ibid.*, pp. 256, 257, 207; *Register of Debates in Congress*, 22 Cong., 2 sess., p. 1769; White, *Robert Barnwell Rhett*, p. 27; Malone, *Public Life of Cooper*, pp. 288–89; Thomas Cooper, *On the Constitution of the United States and the Questions that have Arisen Under It*, rev. ed. (New York: DaCapo Press, 1970); *Columbia Telescope*, February 5, 1830, quoted in Freehling, *Prelude to Civil War*, p. 178;

Southern nationalists soon made their statements of conversion. "We have the right of glorious rebellion and I am prepared to go into it," cried Pickens. Hamilton, calling secession a last resort, issued a pamphlet declaring that "the day of salvation NOW IS," that "all argument is now at an end," that "the Planting States" must join South Carolina to "cut up the Tree of Discord by the Roots." Johnston's *Telescope* published the document, and Johnston himself soon afterward advocated a Southern convention as "the certain forerunner of secession." Davis, an avowed secessionist, called the Union *"a thing that creeps and licks the dust!!!"* McDuffie termed "the Union, such as the majority have made it . . . a foul monster" and later prophesied "the organization of a new and separate Government." The South faced "independence on the one hand or subjection on the other," said Cooper, making his preference clear by supporting Johnston's convention call. Rhett wished for "a Confederacy of the Southern States" as a "happy termination . . . of our long struggle for our [constitutional] rights."[61]

These Southern nationalists, like the less radical Nullifiers, sought to return government to its constitutional moorings. Their recurrent theme was that the present Union was incorrigibly hostile to Southern interests, that only a Southern nation could restore government as it was originally conceived. A South united in the pursuit of agriculture and its need for slave labor had interests that were incompatible with those of the manufacturing, abolitionist North. Nowhere were the causes and aims of Southern nationalism better stated than in the 1832 "Address to the People of the United States by the Convention of the People of South Carolina," which, though written by Calhoun, was revised by McDuffie:

An Appeal to the People on the Question What Shall We Do Next? (Columbia: Telescope Office, 1832), p. 12.
61. Freehling, *Prelude to Civil War*, pp. 268, 325, 176, 206; *What Shall We Do Next?*; Green, *George McDuffie*, pp. 110, 116; Malone, *Public Life of Cooper*, p. 386; White, *Robert Barnwell Rhett*, p. 27.

> . . . South Carolina now bears the same relation to the manufac-
> turing States of this confederacy, that the Anglo American Colo-
> nies bore to the mother country. . . . [T]he majority of Congress
> [are] our inexorable oppressors. . . . They are tyrants by the very
> necessity of their position.
>
> With us, it is a question involving our most sacred rights—those
> very rights which our common ancestors left to us as a common
> inheritance. . . . It is a question of liberty on one hand, and slav-
> ery on the other.[62]

Certain features of this kind of appeal Southerners undoubtedly found attractive. The emphasis on minority rights
was especially compelling to the tidewater Virginians, who
very recently had seen their leadership of both their state and
the nation slip away. They had employed a similar vocabulary
in their constitutional convention. Not surprisingly, the
Virginia legislature, while offering to mediate, passed resolutions endorsing both the principles of 1798 and the right of
secession. Nullification likewise had some appeal to political
minorities in other states who, like the Virginians, had had to
surrender their disproportionate legislative influence in constitutional revisions, which occurred in almost every Southern
state. Yet most Southern state legislatures were controlled by
ardent supporters of Jackson. Understandably they stood by
the president in his determination not to permit Nullification,
and they agreed with him that the tariff should be reduced.
Thus, while sympathizing with South Carolina's problems,
the rest of the South repudiated Nullification.[63]

Though only a handful of Nullifiers adopted Southern nationalism, the tariff crisis did produce a new awareness of

---

62. *State Papers on Nullification*, pp. 66–67, 71.
63. Freehling, *Prelude to Civil War*, pp. 292–94; *State Papers on Nullification*, pp.
328–31. Cleo Hearon, "Nullification in Mississippi," *Publications of the Mississippi Historical Society* 12 (1912): 37–72 gives a good view of the impact of the
tariff crisis on another Southern state. Mississippians who lost legislative influence through reapportionment tended to become (sometimes extreme) exponents of Nullification.

shared and distinct Southern interests. This Southern sectionalism in turn inspired efforts throughout the South to emphasize and promote things peculiarly Southern. The Nullification controversy provided a basis for all of these movements, for it fostered a feeling in the South of being a "conscious minority," a minority different from the Northern majority. This consciousness lay at the heart of the plantation myth, which first emerged during the 1830's. The image of a genteel, noncompetitive way of life, where old families ruled, old values were retained, loyal slaves performed their happy tasks, and culture and chivalry abounded, was the offspring of Nullification. It had, of course, its ugly Northern counterpart, best expressed by one of the radical Nullification pamphleteers:

> The present contest has arisen from the low-minded, minute attention to dollars and cents, that our oppressors have been bred up to consider as the great business of life, as the one thing needful, as the summum bonum of this world. . . .
>
> We have to oppose the groveling maxim of senseless ignorance and shop-keeping vulgarity! . . .
>
> In that sink of prostitution—in that public bear-garden of republican America—in that hot-bed of corruption, venality, rapacious speculation . . .—where public virtue is laughed to scorn, . . . the moneygrasping band has succeeded.[64]

It was indeed ironic that the most vigorous spokesmen of this viewpoint were entrepreneurial, parvenu planters, whose own "minute attention to dollars and cents" helped lead them to conclude that a continuation of the Union was no longer possible.

The Nullification crisis revealed the incompleteness of the American nation. Still unresolved was the question of a state government's rights and the national government's authority; still undetermined was the compatibility of sectional interests and national policy. Some Southerners were already convinced, however, that the interests of their section could be protected only in a separate nation.

64. *What Shall We Do Next?*, p. 5.

CHAPTER TWO

The Great Distinguishing Characteristic

Between 1830 and 1860, Southern nationalism found expression in a variety of ways. One of the most important elements in the growth of the idea of a Southern nation was the new emphasis Southerners placed on their peculiar institution of slavery. Although the proslavery argument first took a cohesive form during the 1830's, many of its ideas had been expressed long before. Most Southerners in one way or another had always defended slavery, whether they held that slavery was a necessary evil, that it was required for social control, or that it was the basis of Southern society.[1]

To support slavery, then, did not alone make a man a Southern nationalist. But Southern nationalism, as a political movement, did require the exploitation of the proslavery argument. Exploitation, in turn, required ever more vivid methods of demonstrating the benefits of the peculiar institution. As a result, Southern nationalism eventually became associated with the most extreme and, at the same time, the most apparently convincing strain of the proslavery argument.

The emergence of a coherent proslavery argument coincided with the shift of Southern leadership from the divided

1. William S. Jenkins, *Pro-Slavery Thought*, pp. 76–77; Carpenter, *South as a Conscious Minority*, pp. 7–21; Robert McColley, *Slavery in Jeffersonian Virginia*, *passim*, but esp. pp. 182–89.

and demoralized state of Virginia to the homogeneous, cotton growing state of South Carolina. Beginning about 1820 with the debates over the admission of Missouri as a slave state and continuing to the 1830's with the protracted struggle over the tariff, the view that slavery was a positive good was systematized. A growing number of defenders adduced scriptural and historical evidence to support their belief that slavery was a paternalistic institution benefiting master and slave alike. This view of the proslavery argument tended to emphasize slavery both as a means of organizing society and as a distinctive feature of a South that was developing a conscious sense of sectionalism, of shared interests. Not all, of course, who held these positions were Southern nationalists, but virtually all Southern nationalists adhered to these views.[2]

A second version of the proslavery argument appeared in the late 1840's, when the leadership of the South was shifting from the older, more stable seaboard to the dynamic, adaptive interior. This version minimized the sociological and Biblical defense of slavery and justified it primarily on grounds of the Negro's alleged racial inferiority. As defenders of slavery sought to establish fundamental differences between the white and black races, this version of the proslavery argument accompanied a concerted effort by a group of Southerners to emphasize similarly irreconcilable differences between North and South. Even conservative Virginians like George Fitzhugh finally accepted the racist argument and, at the same time, became Southern nationalists. While some racist defenders remained Unionists to the last, virtually all Southern nationalists by 1860 had come to accept the racial argument.[3]

2. Eugene D. Genovese, *The World the Slaveholders Made* (New York: Pantheon Books, 1969), p. 98; John W. Walker to Charles Tait, February 11, 1820, quoted in Jenkins, *Pro-Slavery Thought*, p. 69; *Annals of Congress*, 16 Cong., 1 sess., pp. 268, 279.

3. George Fredrickson, *The Black Image in the White Mind: The Debate on Afro-American Character and Destiny, 1817–1914* (New York: Harper and Row, 1971), pp. 61–70. Fredrickson implies that the two strains of the proslavery argument, which he labels "paternalistic" and "*herrenvolk* democratic," were mutually exclusive. I accept his distinctions but question the notions that

I

Governor John Floyd addressed a tense Virginia legislature in December 1831. He called their attention to the "inflammatory pamphlets which the meek and charitable of other States have seen cause to distribute as firebrands in the bosom of our society," and he urged them to take action "to preserve in due subordination, the slave population of our State."[4] It was a message suffused with fear and determination.

As they had been divided in 1829 over the issue of representation, Virginians in 1831 were divided over the question of slavery. Slaveowners still formed an important interest in the Old Dominion, and most planters were unwilling to part with their human property. Their reluctance was strengthened by fears of racial strife, which stemmed from the abortive insurrection of the charismatic slave, Nat Turner, earlier in 1831 in predominantly black Southampton County. It was reinforced by the fact that Northern abolitionists like William Lloyd Garrison were attacking the state and its institutions. Moreover, the patriarchal social view of the tidewater planters, who had been so recently assailed by the reformers in the constitutional convention, had increased their awareness of their vulnerability as it hardened their resistance to further change. On the other hand, many planters had a lingering humanitarian hostility to slavery. Declining agricultural output was compelling some planters to consider how to get rid of their unprofitable slaves. The nonslaveholders of the western counties, too, remained implacable foes of slavery.[5]

Southerners were either paternalists or *herrenvolk* democrats; both strains were present in the slavery writings of virtually every apologist, and classification, then, becomes a matter not of exclusion but of emphasis.

4. E. Griffith Dodson, *The Capitol of the Commonwealth of Virginia at Richmond* (Richmond: privately printed, 1937), pp. 22–23, 31; *Journal of the House of Delegates of the Commonwealth of Virginia, 1831–32*, pp. 8ff., quoted in Theodore M. Whitfield, *Slavery Agitation in Virginia, 1829–1832* (Baltimore: Johns Hopkins University Press, 1930), p. 67.

5. Charles Henry Ambler, *Sectionalism in Virginia*, p. 158; Joseph Clarke Robert, *The Road from Monticello: A Study of the Virginia Slavery Debate of 1832*, His-

The debates in the Virginia legislature in 1831 and 1832 gave a thorough airing to all these views, both for and against slavery. The advocates of reform were not lacking spokesmen. The arguments advanced by the emancipationists closely resembled the arguments employed by the trans-Allegheny nonslaveholders against the tidewater aristocrats in 1829, when to speak of representation was in reality to speak of slavery. Henry Berry of Jefferson County in the northern Shenandoah Valley declared slavery to be "a grinding curse upon this state." His western colleague Charles J. Faulkner called the institution "that bitterest drop from the chalice of the destroying angel." Thomas Marshall, son of Chief Justice John Marshall and a master of a central Virginia plantation of forty-five slaves claimed that "slavery . . . retards improvements—roots out an industrious population—banishes the yeomanry of the population. . . ." According to Marshall, slavery was "ruinous to the whites."[6]

But these Virginia opponents of slavery ran into two obstacles. The first was the opposition of the slaveholding minority, for whom emancipation portended not merely financial ruin but social chaos. J. H. Gholson, a young slaveholder from Brunswick County in the tidewater region, where blacks outnumbered whites by two to one, took the lead in organizing opposition to change. Urged by Gholson to "rise up, almost as one man, against" any scheme of emancipation, the slaveholders voted as a bloc against all change.[7]

Second, advocates of emancipation were divided. No delegate advocated unconditional emancipation; the foes of slavery could not agree upon the conditions to be imposed. How were the deprived property holders to be compensated for their sizable losses? What was to become of the free black pop-

---

torical Papers of the Trinity College Historical Society, series 24 (Durham: Duke University Press, 1941), pp. 8–11. An excellent recent study of the slavery debates is Freehling, "Drift Toward Dissolution."

6. Jenkins, *Pro-Slavery Thought*, pp. 83–84; Robert, *Road from Monticello*, p. 115.

7. *Richmond Enquirer*, January 21, 1832.

ulation? Were they to be colonized, and if so, where? At whose expense? There was no consensus.[8] Divided among themselves and facing a united opposition, the emancipationists were defeated on every attempt.

Yet many Virginia slaveholders still harbored sincere doubts about slavery. A typical remark was that of a tidewater delegate, J. Thompson Brown, who, though unconvinced "that slavery, as it exists in Virginia, is either criminal or immoral," claimed to be "no advocate of slavery in the abstract." In fact, the man who dared to regard slavery as intrinsically good was likely to be attacked. When W. D. Sims made such an "unfortunate" avowal, the *Richmond Enquirer* charged that he "differ[ed] from every gentleman who had spoken on the subject."[9]

Not long after the conclusion of the debates, a young professor of political economy at the College of William and Mary, Thomas R. Dew, reviewed the debates of the recent legislative session in a detailed and widely circulated essay. Dew, a lanky, personable bachelor, clumsy in movement though not in thought, was the son of a successful Virginia planter. He had himself acquired a slave late in 1831, doubtless as a symbol of status to his academic colleagues, most of whom, like Dew, were comfortable but hardly wealthy on the salary of $1,000 a year. Previously known chiefly as an opponent of protective tariffs, Dew did not confine himself to an objective summary of the recent debates in the legislature. Instead, he saw in those discussions the shape of the future: either eventual abolition of slavery and the vexing problem of race adjustment or continued slavery.[10] If Virginia chose the

8. Jenkins, *Pro-Slavery Thought*, pp. 85–86; Robert, *Road from Monticello*, pp. 24–27.

9. Jenkins, *Pro-Slavery Thought*, p. 87; *Richmond Enquirer*, January 28, 1832.

10. Broadus Mitchell, "Thomas Roderick Dew," *Dictionary of American Biography*, Allen Johnson and Dumas Malone, eds. (New York: Charles Scribner's Sons, 1943) 5: 266–67; Stephen S. Mansfield, "Thomas Roderick Dew: Defender of the Southern Faith" (Ph.D. diss., University of Virginia, 1968), pp. 2–24.

road to abolition, "every year you would hear of insurrections and plots, and every day would perhaps record a murder; the melancholy tale of Southampton would not alone blacken the page of our history. . . ." Virginians must support the continuance of slavery.

Dew's essay did not confine itself to a discussion of the necessity of retaining slavery; it argued rather that slavery was intrinsically good. The professor scoured the past for evidence to buttress his arguments. He relied chiefly on Biblical and historical references to support his case. The Bible endorsed slavery. It was "established and sanctioned by divine authority among even the elect of heaven, the favored children of Israel. Abraham, the founder of this interesting nation, and the chosen servant of the Lord, was the owner of *hundreds* of slaves." Likewise "the children of Israel, under the guidance of Jehovah, massacred or enslaved their prisoners of war." Clearly, the slaveholder had the Bible—or at least the Old Testament—on his side.

So, too, did "profane history" sanction slavery. "The historical view of the origin and progress of slavery," Dew wrote, "shows most conclusively that something else is requisite to convert slavery into freedom than the mere enunciation of abstract truths. . . ." Greece and Rome, Carthage and Phoenicia, were slaveholding societies. Every continent in the modern world as well was populated by slaveholders. Unquestionably, "slavery has been, perhaps, the principal means of impelling forward the civilization of mankind." Debtors, losers in war, criminals, were all at one time or another sentenced to slavery instead of put to death. Slavery was, then, an enlightened and compassionate institution.

The evidence of the past showed that slavery was not reserved for any one race. Why, then, were Virginia's slaves all black? As a matter of fact, Americans had erred in not enslaving Indians. "A much greater number of Indians, within the limits of the United States, would have been saved, had we rigidly persevered in enslaving them, than by our present policy." According to Dew, societies tended to evolve through stages—from primitive to savage to civilized—and Africans and Indians had not yet reached the civilized stage. These races needed slavery to bring social order. Eventually, they would reach the civilized stage. But until that time they should remain enslaved. Americans had thus enslaved the black, "savage" population, which needed to be regulated for its own good. Slavery was, then, a natural, sociological condition for a certain variety—not necessarily race—of men. The Negro race met the qualifications for slavery; but slaves need not necessarily be black.

Slavery benefited free society, too. Dew attempted to demonstrate the commonality of interest in slavery shared by slaveholder and nonslaveholder alike. "The institutions of property and the existence of slavery" worked together to advance civilization. Imposing slavery upon the "savage element of the population" tended to raise the level of the rest of society.

> It is a singular fact [Dew continued], that the two extremes of society are most favorable to liberty and equality—the most savage, and the most refined and enlightened—the former, in consequence of the absence of the institution of slavery, and the latter from the diffusion of knowledge, and the consequent capability of self-government. The former is characterized by a wild, licentious independence, totally subversive of all order and tranquillity; and the latter by a well-ordered, well-established liberty, which, while it leaves to each the enjoyments of the fruits of his industry, secures him against the lawless violence and rapine of his neighbors.

Thus, "wealth and talent must ever rule," and "the property, talent, concert, and, we may add, habit, are all with the whites, and render their continued superiority absolutely certain, if they are not meddled with." Slavery permitted the best men to rule while at the same time it imbued the black with "the principles, the sentiments, and feelings of the white." Slavery and democracy were not, therefore, incompatible. The benefits of the peculiar institution were universal.

Even to contemplate the abolition of slavery was to threaten the very existence of Virginia.

> It is, in truth, the slave labor in Virginia which gives value to her soil and her habitations; take away this, and you pull down the Atlas that upholds the whole system; eject from the State the whole slave population, and we risk nothing in the prediction that on the day in which it shall be accomplished, the worn soils of Virginia would not bear the paltry price of the government lands in the West, and the Old Dominion will be a 'waste, howling wilderness;'—the grass will be seen growing in the streets, and the foxes peeping from their holes.

And not Virginia alone, but the entire South must oppose any scheme of emancipation, for it would threaten "the whole Southern country with irremediable ruin." The general government must not promote abolition or offer funds to aid in the deportation and colonization of slaves. "The South hitherto has had nothing to ask of the Federal Government," and it must beware, lest "the *emancipating* interest . . . be added to the *internal improvement* and *tariff* interests, and Virginia can no more array herself against the torrent of Federal oppression."[11]

Dew's essay committed Virginia to the South by stating clearly that slavery was a predominant sectional interest which ordered society as it controlled the black race. Though most of Dew's arguments had been made before, he presented the defense of slavery with a cogency and coherence never previously attained, and the essay gained added influence because of its author's position at the prestigious College of William and Mary. Widely circulated throughout the South, the essay was repeatedly quoted and paraphrased by the Southern press as abolitionist attacks mounted.[12]

11. "Professor Dew on Slavery," *The Pro-Slavery Argument* (Charleston: Walker, Richards, and Co., 1852), pp. 295, 306, 325, 297–301, 355, 332, 300, 465, 463, 358, 288, 449.
12. W. E. Dodd, *The Cotton Kingdom: A Chronicle of the Old South*, vol. 27 of *The chronicles of America*, ed. Allen Johnson and Allan Nevins, 55 vols. (New Haven: Yale University Press, 1921), pp. 49–53; Jenkins, *Pro-Slavery Thought*, p. 88; Robert, *Road from Monticello*, p. 48. For a dissenting view, see Clement

II

While Virginians agonized over the future of slavery in their state, South Carolinians were contemplating the future of the South in the Union. Where the legislators in the Old Dominion were still thinking primarily in terms of problems confronting an individual state, the Palmetto State's most agitated citizens were beginning to speak in terms of regional grievances and regional remedies. They were angered that fellow Southerners—and Virginians in particular—failed to understand the significance of the struggle against the tariff. Standing alone in defiance of the federal government, the Carolinians warned their fellow Southerners of the real meaning of the tariff confrontation. "Do they not know," asked an anonymous pamphleteer, "that what is *her* fate today may be theirs tomorrow—that after the Tariff comes the question of *Emancipation!*"[13] At least a few Nullifiers were beginning to emphasize the South's common stake in the preservation of slavery.

It was into this highly charged atmosphere that Dew's essay emerged with such impact. Leading periodicals took up the argument. Charleston's widely read *Southern Quarterly Review* recognized the South's indebtedness to "Professor Dew, for the first clear and comprehensive argument on the subject of slavery," and proceeded to reiterate that "slavery is consistent with [C]hristianity" and that "the cultivation of the South requires the preservation of the only species of labor which she is able to command, and, without which, our fields would be abandoned." A. P. Upshur, a leading Virginia conservative, in an article written for the prestigious *Southern Literary Messenger* in 1839, derived from Dew's "able pamphlet" his conclusion that "slavery is the great distinguishing characteristic of the

Eaton, *The Freedom-of-Thought Struggle in the Old South*, rev. ed. (New York: Harper and Row, 1964), p. 30, which seems to ignore the evidence to the contrary.

13. Freehling, *Prelude to Civil War*, *passim*, but esp. pp. 288–90; A South Carolinian, *Remarks on the Ordinance of Nullification* (Charleston: A. E. Miller, 1833), p. 67.

Southern states, and is, in fact, the only important institution which they can claim peculiarly as their own." James D. B. DeBow proclaimed somewhat later in his *Review* that Dew's "able essay on the institution of slavery entitles him to the lasting gratitude of the whole South."[14]

Political figures, too, turned to Dew. Chancellor William Harper of the South Carolina Supreme Court cited Dew to prove that slavery had beneficent moral influences on master and slave. John C. Calhoun, who had devised the theory of Nullification, declared in 1837—as Dew had done earlier—that slavery was a "positive good." The Virginia agricultural reformer Edmund Ruffin read and reread Dew. He termed slavery historically and scripturally justified, the basis of the South's superior civilization. All seemed to agree with James H. Hammond of South Carolina, another of Dew's admirers, who claimed that slavery was "the greatest of all the great blessings which a kind Providence has bestowed upon our glorious region."[15]

Finally Dew influenced a number of Virginians who conversed with him at William and Mary, of which he was named president in 1836. William A. Smith, a Methodist clergyman as well as a trustee and later president of Randolph–Macon College, demonstrated Dew's influence in his published *Lectures on the Philosophy and Practice of Slavery*. Thornton Stringfellow, also a clergyman, wrote numerous defenses of slavery on scriptural grounds in the Dew spirit. And Dew's colleague, Nathaniel Beverley Tucker, declared that "it is on this point of

14. E. Gridley, "Slavery in the Southern States," *Southern Quarterly Review* 8 (1845): 317–60; A. P. Upshur, "Domestic Slavery," *Southern Literary Messenger* 5 (1839): 677–87; Mitchell, "Thomas Roderick Dew," p. 266.

15. William Harper, "Slavery in the Light of Social Ethics," in *Cotton Is King, and Proslavery Arguments,* ed. E. N. Elliott (Augusta, Ga.: Pritchard, Abbott, and Loomis, 1860), p. 576; *Congressional Globe,* 24 Cong., 2 sess., p. 158; Avery O. Craven, *Edmund Ruffin, Southerner: A Study in Secession* (New York: D. Appleton Co., 1932), p. 133; James H. Hammond, "Speech on the Justice of Receiving Petitions for the Abolition of Slavery in the District of Columbia," *Selections from the Letters and Speeches of the Hon. James H. Hammond of South Carolina* (New York: J. F. Trow and Co., 1866), p. 34.

the necessity of forcing those to labor who are unable to live honestly without labor, that we base the defense of our system."[16]

The reception accorded Dew's essay suggests that sectional tension hardly slackened even after the compromise that lowered the tariff and gained South Carolina's compliance. Abolitionism was on the rise throughout the Northern states, and this movement, more than the tariff, opened Southern eyes to the dangers predicted by the Nullifiers. A group of Nullifiers in Mississippi established a State Rights Party in 1834. They seemed less concerned with the tariff than with slavery. "How long will it be," they asked in an address to their fellow citizens, "before the South will be compelled to yield up her peculiar domestic institutions . . . or incur the deep hazard of resistance to the law?" Their leader, John A. Quitman, threatened that "should we ever live to see the proud institutions of our country overthrown . . . the last retreat of freedom will be in the South. . . . I think I can demonstrate that our institution of domestic slavery is in harmony with, and almost indispensable to, a constitutional republic." The *Southern Advocate* of Huntsville, Alabama, charged that "the discussion of the matter is *forced* upon the South, and the South must meet it in a free, fearless, unblenching spirit. She must place herself in an attitude of rightful, self-preserving, and constitutional defence."[17] From a newly strengthened Virginia came a stern warning:

> We hold in utter contempt the designs of such fanatics as Garrison . . . —but they are not the oracles of the Northern People.

16. William A. Smith, *Lectures on the Philosophy and Practice of Slavery, as Exhibited in the Institution of Domestic Slavery in the United States: With the Duties of Masters to Slaves* (Nashville: Stevenson and Evans, 1856), esp. pp. 192–209; Thornton Stringfellow, *Slavery and Government* (Washington: n.p., 1841); N. B. Tucker, "Note to Blackstone's Commentaries," *Southern Literary Messenger* 1 (1835): 230.

17. Hearon, "Nullification in Mississippi," p. 65; John A. Quitman to F. Henry Quitman, October 17, 1835, in J. F. H. Claiborne, *Life and Correspondence of John A. Quitman*, 2 vols. (New York: Harper Brothers, 1860), 1: 139; *Huntsville (Ala.) Southern Advocate*, August 4, 1835.

Should it ever come to be so, and *their* designs carried out, then indeed we should admit the die was cast, and we should bid 'a long farewell' to the Union of these States. The whole South, to a man, would never hesitate in their choice between an immediate Dissolution, and an Union, the essential principles of which were so grossly and flagrantly violated.[18]

The center of agitation, however, remained South Carolina, which assumed after Nullification the leadership of a newly conscious South, a role for which the homogeneous Palmetto State was peculiarly fitted. Among the many Carolinians who made names for themselves during the Nullification crisis, two young, ambitious men—James H. Hammond and Robert Barnwell Rhett—played major roles in linking Dew's version of the proslavery argument to Southern nationalism. Each emerged from the Nullification experience not merely a loyal Carolinian but a devout Southerner. Their subsequent careers and ideas served to define two possible courses available to the South in the post-Nullification period.

Both Hammond, born in upcountry Newberry in 1807, and Rhett, born in lowcountry Beaufort in 1800, were native South Carolinians. Hammond's father, a nonslaveholding merchant and teacher, was a native of Massachusetts and a descendant of Benjamin Hammond, who had landed in Boston in 1634. Rhett, too, was the offspring of respectable though impoverished parentage and was a distant relative of the eminent Massachusetts Adamses.[19]

Their early years doubtless influenced the development of

18. *Richmond Enquirer*, May 21, 1833.
19. The only (and inadequate) published biography of Hammond is Elizabeth Merritt, *James Henry Hammond, 1807–1864* (Baltimore: Johns Hopkins University Press, 1923). A better life is Robert C. Tucker, "James H. Hammond, South Carolinian" (Ph.D. diss., University of North Carolina, 1958). A penetrating short sketch may be found in Clement Eaton, *The Mind of the Old South*, rev. ed. (Baton Rouge: Louisiana State University Press, 1967), pp. 44–68. The best (and quite good) biography of Rhett is Laura A. White, *Robert Barnwell Rhett*.

their personalities. Between Hammond's graduation from South Carolina College in 1825 and his entry into the Nullification battle in 1830 had intervened five years of failure and despair. First he tried teaching school, where he failed completely. Then he turned to the law, at which he was never very successful because of what a friend cryptically referred to as "interfering wishes." In 1826 Hammond confessed to a correspondent that "my soul pants to throw off the weight of mortality." Then came the Nullification battle, and Hammond found a purpose at last. Freed from the dull practice of law, he realized influence as editor of the pro-Nullification *Southern Times*. A year later Hammond married the daughter of a wealthy Charleston merchant and slaveholder. Hammond resigned his editorship and removed with his bride to Silver Bluff, a Savannah River plantation owned by his father-in-law. Well educated and physically handsome, articulate and socially charming, Hammond had the potential of becoming a great leader. Yet so much of what he possessed was given to him, so little was earned, that his public manner was frequently haughty and his private conduct occasionally scandalous. He was given to regular bouts of melancholia and constantly complained about his health.[20]

Rhett, on the other hand, was an aggressive, impulsive young man. Tall and often smiling, Rhett was described by his daughter as "nervous and mercurial" in temperament, "quick in movement and quick-tempered." Another contemporary described him as "all passion, excitement, and fire." Rhett's family could not afford to educate him beyond his seventeenth year. Therefore, he began the self-study of law and commenced practice in 1821, shortly thereafter moving to the neighboring Colleton district. Rhett's standard of living was modest, and he continued a rigorous program of study and reading. In 1827, soon after his election to the South Carolina legislature, he married Elizabeth Washington Burnet, ward of

20. Merritt, *James Henry Hammond*, p. 12; Eaton, *Mind of the Old South*, p. 47.

a well-to-do family, and his fortunes began to rise. Rhett was devoted to his family, which grew rapidly, and they in turn helped to buoy his spirits in moments of defeat in later life.[21]

Increasingly conscious of their social position, both Hammond and Rhett became interested in their ancestry. The new aristocrat Hammond was hardly ensconced in his new mansion when he commissioned a genealogist to travel to England to discover the noble branches of the Hammond family tree. The investigator returned to report the disheartening news that Hammond was descended not from nobility but from simple yeoman stock. Enraged, Hammond refused to pay the investigator's fee and had all the documents destroyed. Rhett, too, took pride in his distinguished forebears, among whom were great planters, governors, and military heroes. In 1837 he officially changed his surname from the commonplace Smith to the more distinguished and illustrious Rhett.[22]

Editor Hammond favored Nullification but opposed disunion. His editorials were tightly reasoned attacks on the tariff that emphasized that Congress had no constitutional power to enact such a law. "If the [tariff] law be constitutional," he wrote, "what right have we to speak of resistance?" Congress had, however, exceeded its powers, and South Carolina, by nullifying the illegal act, was working to preserve both the Union and the Constitution. The idea of disunion made Hammond's blood "run . . . cold with apprehension." The true policy was resistance within the Union.[23]

While Hammond was asserting a moderate position like Calhoun's, Rhett was openly declaring for secession. In 1830 he avowed that "Washington was a disunionist, Samuel

21. B. F. Perry, *Reminiscences of Public Men* (Philadelphia: J. D. Avil and Co., 1883), p. 131; Elsie Rhett Lewis to Laura A. White, 1912, quoted in White, *Robert Barnwell Rhett*, p. 7.
22. Eaton, *Mind of the Old South*, p. 48; *Charleston Mercury*, September 25, 1851; White, *Robert Barnwell Rhett*, p. 34.
23. *Southern Times*, January 29, February 4, February 27, 1830, quoted in Merritt, *James Henry Hammond*, p. 15.

Adams, Patrick Henry, Jefferson, Rutledge, were all disunionists and traitors . . . and for maintaining the very constitutional principles for which we contend . . . shall we temble at epithets . . . ?" In the 1832 state convention, Rhett spoke out unequivocally in favor of a Southern nation.[24]

Neither Hammond's keenly intellectual arguments against the tariff nor Rhett's bombastic polemics in favor of Southern nationhood dealt very much with slavery specifically. But in 1835 Hammond was elected to Congress, where slavery was emerging as an explosive national issue. In his maiden speech, Hammond vehemently opposed the acceptance of petitions for the abolition of slavery. He warned that "the moment this House undertakes to legislate upon this subject, it dissolves the Union." Angrily waving a sheaf of abolitionist circulars, Hammond bellowed, "Sir, while we are discussing the question of the reception of these petitions, movements are making at the north" that threaten slavery. "Our last thought will be to give up our Institutions. We were born and bred under them, and will maintain them or die in their defence."[25]

As Hammond left Congress for reasons of health in 1837, Rhett arrived, now himself a planter and slaveholder. He, too, had managed to ally himself with the powerful political faction led by Calhoun, who admonished the youthful firebrand to curb his rhetoric. Yet in 1838, as the flood of abolition petitions swelled, Rhett spoke out, warning that if slavery was not kept out of congressional debates, "it will conclusively prove to the south that the Union ought to be dissolved. We can hold no terms of alliance with deliberate, open enemies. . . ." Like his mentor Calhoun, Rhett called for Southern congressmen to unite to seek a constitutional amendment barring abolition petitions. As an alternative he proposed a Southern convention to demonstrate "that we are united and determined upon this

24. *Charleston Mercury*, October 19, 1830; White, *Robert Barnwell Rhett*, p. 77. See Chapter One, note 61.
25. *Letters and Speeches of Hammond*, pp. 31, 27, 35, 49.

great subject; and this is all that is necessary to give us peace."[26]

The controversy over the petitions taught Southern leaders a lesson. So long as there was a threat to slavery most Southern congressmen stood together. With virtual unanimity men of both parties backed a so-called "gag rule," which provided for the automatic tabling of all abolitionist petitions.[27]

No other issue, they discovered, could produce such sectional unanimity. In 1844 when Rhett tried, by organizing a movement in Bluffton, South Carolina, to renew the old Nullification arguments against the recent higher tariff enacted by Congress, his organization quickly collapsed. Not even Calhoun, who thought the movement untimely and a threat to his own presidential aspirations, supported it, and Rhett's move attracted few followers in other states. One participant in the Bluffton conference came away with a clear recognition of the obstacles to Southern unanimity. It was, he wrote, "clear to my mind that the whole South must go together or we can do nothing. The whole South will not go together, except upon the slave question, and this will never be put in such shape by the Government, as to be so clear as to unite the South."[28]

Therefore, the Southern nationalists must stake all not on tariffs or vague constitutional theories, but on slavery. It was impossible to convince the Southern public that a tariff posed any real threat. Slavery was the only issue that could unite the South, and yet it was the weakest position—morally and politically—possible. Southerners were also Americans, yet slavery and Americanism, as a growing number of Northerners believed, were morally incompatible. The apparent irreconcilability of slavery with morality defined by an increasingly hostile Northern majority did nothing to alleviate the tensions

26. White, *Robert Barnwell Rhett*, pp. 32–34; R. B. Rhett, *Address to the People of Beaufort and Colleton Districts Upon the Subject of Abolition, January 15, 1838* (n.p., 1838), p. 8.

27. *Congressional Globe*, 25 Cong., 3 sess., pp. 21–28.

28. R. W. Singleton to George Frederick Holmes, August 6, 1844, George Frederick Holmes Letterbook, Duke University.

building in the South. It seemed possible through the party system and political influence to keep other sectional goals in line with national policy. But slavery, the one truly distinguishing feature of Southern life, must not be tampered with. In fact, the whole subject must be suppressed in the councils of the general government.

While Rhett was still trying to unite a Southern nation on the tariff, Hammond, elected governor of South Carolina in 1842, was reinforcing his belief that the true source of regional solidarity within the Union was slavery. Yet other problems interrupted his thoughts. In November 1844 Hammond had had a bitter fight with the Calhounites in the legislature over his proposal to arm the state to resist the 1842 tariff. Hammond's action was an outgrowth of Rhett's Bluffton Movement, of which he approved. He recommended in addition that the legislature call a convention of the Southern states. His proposals were soundly defeated in December 1844 and, disgusted, he left office shortly thereafter. His breach with the Calhounites would never be healed.[29] Even though Hammond's clearly developed views on slavery and the South were closer to Calhoun's than were the occasional and belligerent views of the tariff oriented Rhett, and although Bluffton temporarily placed Rhett and Calhoun at bitter odds, Hammond never gained admission to the inner circle.[30]

In addition, though Rhett was at times difficult to control, his intellectual and leadership capacities were inferior to Hammond's. Rhett probably posed less of a threat to Calhoun's own ambitions, and his skills at arousing the emotions of Carolinians made him a valuable ally. A member of the South Carolina leadership described Rhett unfairly and with disdain in 1844 as "useful as a whipper in, but fit for nothing else. . . . He is too hot-headed, too rash, too hasty, and too heedless to be placed in any office of . . . uncontrolled influence. . . . But we should wish to see him always in a subordinate capacity, in

29. Merritt, *James Henry Hammond*, pp. 68–71.
30. *Charleston Mercury*, December 2, December 4, December 8, 1843; Eaton, *Mind of the Old South*, p. 51.

which he might stimulate to action, but never direct it."[31]
Such a role was hardly possible for the aloof, intellectual Hammond.

At the close of Hammond's term in 1845 he wrote two letters on slavery addressed to the British abolitionist Thomas Clarkson, which argued, much in the manner of Professor Dew, that slavery was "a moral and humane institution, productive of the greatest political and social advantages. . . ." Hammond examined scripture, history, and the present situation. Slavery was not sinful. It had many historical antecedents. While it necessarily created a class of "the poorest and most ignorant," it permitted the free members of society to be "higher toned and more deeply interested in preserving a stable and well ordered Government, than the same class in any other country." He fearfully cited the French Revolution, that "rash experiment upon social systems," as a warning to all abolitionists of the consequences of their activities.

Balancing this sociological argument, Hammond turned to race in order to explain why slavery was reserved for Negroes. Blacks and whites "differ essentially, in all the leading traits which characterize the varieties of the human species, and color draws an indelible and insuperable line between them." Any plan to emancipate slaves was a "diabolical design."

In a second, more truculent letter, Hammond asserted his and the South's devotion to the Constitution, *such as it came from the hands of our fathers.*" He followed with a warning that

> the South is under no such delusion as to believe that it derives any *peculiar* protection from the Union. On the contrary, it is well known we incur peculiar *danger*. . . . The apprehension is also fast fading away that any of the dreadful consequences commonly predicted will necessarily result from a separation of the States. And, *come what may*, we are firmly resolved that OUR SYSTEM OF DOMESTIC SLAVERY SHALL STAND.

Hammond's view of Southern society was similar to Dew's. Under slavery the South had realized a high level of

31. Holmes to Joseph Daniel Pope, August 20, 1844, Holmes Letterbook.

civilization. In the South "intelligence and wealth" succeeded "in keeping in check reckless and unenlightened numbers." In the North, however, the ignorant white masses were "rapidly usurping all power . . . and threatening a fearful crisis in republican institutions. . . ." The Southern nonslaveholder, though not as wealthy or as well educated as the slaveholder, was nonetheless equally "interested in preserving a stable and well ordered government. . . ." The Northern workingman, whose "spirit of discontent" was "rampant and combative," required—as the black slave did not—"a strong government, after some of the old fashions. . . ." Reiterating, Hammond insisted that "stability and peace are the first desires of every slaveholder, and the true tendency of the system."

Here, then, was the most comprehensive view to date of Southern slavery, written by a man who, like Dew, had himself not been a slaveholder for very long. Though containing some racism, it was mostly a paternalistic, conservative argument which claimed for the slaveholding minority a nobility of character, a breadth of vision, and a loftiness of purpose. "It is a wretched and insecure government," wrote Hammond, "which is administered by its most ignorant citizens, and those who have the least stake under it." Like the Virginia conservatives, Hammond disliked the idea of "universal suffrage, . . . a necessary appendage to a republican system," which placed government "in the hands of a numerical majority; and it is hardly necessary to say that in every part of the world more than half the people are ignorant and poor." To a seaboard slaveholding minority still reeling from constitutional concessions, these words from aristocratic Carolina must have sounded both appealing and reassuring. To the newer, younger members of the slaveholding class throughout the South, of whom Hammond was one, the Clarkson letters surely glorified their newly acquired station as it provided them with a rebuttal to abolition attack.[32]

The impact of the Clarkson letters was immediate and electrifying. The Charleston newspapers reprinted them, and

32. *Letters and Speeches of Hammond,* pp. 115, 123–25, 127, 170, 171, 192–93, 126, 128.

the *Mercury* office was flooded with requests and printed fifteen thousand additional copies. Leading Carolinians such as
the novelist William Gilmore Simms and Chancellor Harper
sang their praises. Hammond himself received almost a
hundred letters of support. In later years the Clarkson letters
were republished in *DeBow's Review*, whose editor called them
"admirable and unanswerable," and they appeared in all the
important proslavery anthologies of the 1850's.[33] If Hammond's purpose had been to bring Southerners to a common
ground, he had not failed.

The Clarkson letters were written in January and March
1845, just after Hammond concluded his turbulent and unsuccessful term as governor. His defeats in the legislature and os-
tracism from the leadership councils had certainly influenced
his thinking. At the same time he was writing his letters on
slavery, he was mourning that "the heroic age is past. . . . The
first rate men of our country whose tastes or stars lead them to
pursue public life permanently must content themselves with
being patriot martyrs." This despairing reference to himself
was followed by an even more revealing statement. "Such is
the fate of Mr. Calhoun," wrote the man who would very
much have liked a share of the power and influence of the senator who had so often thwarted him.[34] The Clarkson letters,
then, were the musings of an embattled and embittered politician who believed himself entitled to a kinder fate. They were
as much an effort to understand as to be understood.

In 1845 Hammond was not yet a Southern nationalist. He
still favored united action of all the Southern states to achieve
their rights within the Union, though he did foresee secession
as a last resort to be avoided as long as possible. Here, again,
he stood closer to Calhoun than did Rhett. Hammond still op-

33. William Gilmore Simms to James H. Hammond, July 10, 1845; A. P.
Aldrich to Hammond, July 1, 1845; J. L. Clark to Hammond, June 27, 1845,
James Hammond Papers, Library of Congress; *DeBow's Review* 7 (1849): 249;
Merritt, *James Henry Hammond*, pp. 76–77.
34. Hammond to Armistead Burt, March 18, 1845, Armistead Burt Papers,
Duke University.

posed individual state action, whether Nullification, which he now thought futile, or secession, which he believed should be done only jointly. In short, he was wavering, and his position on slavery, elegantly balanced between paternalism and racism, made him one of the South's foremost spokesmen on the subject. Yet, although Hammond returned to Washington as a fire-eating senator in 1857, his role was largely fulfilled. It had been his function to emphasize Southern similarities of interest, to conceive and present a view of Southern society; it fell to others to demonstrate how Southern interests differed from those of the North.

Rhett, meanwhile, continued to labor as the "whipper in," capitalizing at random on potentially divisive issues. He spoke out in Congress in favor of "Southern rights" in the territories, a term that meant the right of Southerners to take their human property where they wished. When Rhett did actually speak out on slavery, he made no general theoretical argument but came, as always, straight to the point. In 1848 he claimed to have been the earliest prophet of the effects of abolitionism. "In 1828 I declared . . . that if we yielded on the Taxing power, the next stride would be against our slave institutions; and that I was for fighting on the Tariff the battle which must otherwise be fought on slavery." Continuing, he claimed, "I said the same thing in 1844. . . . Now you have this great question of Slavery upon you; and my counsel is as of yore— meet the question at once, and forever." Again, in 1850, he bluntly asserted that "of all the races of man, the negro race is the most inferior," and thus had to be retained in bondage. For Rhett, while slavery may have been one element of Southern unity, other issues—tariffs, public land policies—served a similar purpose in creating a sense of Southern nationalism.[35] Systematic thought was not necessary for the "whipper in."

35. *Charleston Mercury,* September 29, 1848; White, *Robert Barnwell Rhett,* p. 106; R. B. Rhett, "Oration Before the Legislature of South Carolina, November 28, 1850," *The Death and Funeral Ceremonies of John Caldwell Calhoun* (Columbia: A. S. Johnston, 1850), p. 151; *Charleston Mercury,* September 8, October 11, 1851.

The difference between Hammond and Rhett was more than merely a matter of temperament, intellect, or political success. As the breezes of Southern nationalistic feeling picked up, South Carolina served as the wind vane. Leadership of the South and the country had once been Virginia's, but as time passed, so did Virginia's influence, and South Carolina became the most influential Southern state. Soon, however, the balance of power tipped again, this time westward. The conservative politics and social views of the seaboard began to be overwhelmed by a vibrant, powerful, forward-looking new attitude that was changing both politics and society.

Rhett caught the spirit of the new politics; Hammond failed. As Hammond repeated and expanded the conservative Virginia attitude toward slavery, Rhett, who took over the editorship of the *Charleston Mercury* in 1852, mastered the new political techniques and adapted to the new outlook, which placed a higher premium on rhetoric and symbol than on logic and substance. While Hammond wrote and thought in the tradition of Leigh, Upshur, and Dew, Rhett preferred the company of William Lowndes Yancey, John A. Quitman, and other practitioners of mass politics. "When the people speak we should hear," Rhett proclaimed, while encouraging them to think and speak correctly from the political stump and the columns of the *Mercury*. Such sentiments and such tactics ought to have been equally palatable to Hammond, who was, like Rhett, perhaps to his discomfort, recently a man of the people. But Rhett was politically astute enough to recognize the trend of the time, while the intellectual Hammond, having at last achieved the status of slaveholder, held to the views of a still useful but dying past. Hammond could write eloquent and detailed defenses of slavery as a Southern sectionalist. But he lacked the requisite ability to make of slavery the symbol of Southern nationalism.[36]

Meanwhile, one thing certainly was clear. The proslavery

36. White *Robert Barnwell Rhett*, p. 61. The generalizations about antebellum campaign methods are developed at length in Chapter Seven.

arguments expressed by Dew and reiterated by Hammond in relentless logic were now, in the less able hands of Rhett and his colleagues, no longer merely the basis of Southern sectionalism. Rather, they were giving to every issue a new significance as the idea of a Southern nation began to spread. In 1852 there appeared an anthology of writings in defense of slavery. Entitled *The Pro-Slavery Argument* and published in Charleston, the volume included selections by Dew, Harper, Hammond, and William Gilmore Simms. All four authors had written in the paternalistic vein, and the publication of the book seemed to indicate that there was nothing more to be said on the subject of slavery.[37]

III

Just as the earlier version of the proslavery argument received its definitive embodiment, there was rising in the west a proslavery argument with a new emphasis. Western writers stressed the racial characteristics of slavery and placed less emphasis on its value as a means of societal organization. This new argument attempted to depict the North and the South as fundamentally different. It bespoke an increasing sense of urgency on the part of Southerners. Though the new argument claimed to be "scientific," it was, ironically, less rational and more emotional than the patriarchal view; the rhetoric was less controlled and more passionate than that of earlier defenders. And the new doctrine was contagious. By 1860 even the once moderate, Richmond-based *Southern Literary Messenger* was arguing that "in the long duration of negro life, not one single ray of civilization has appeared to lighten its gloomy past. . . . The highest point in the scale of civilized being to which they have attained . . . has been in slavery to the white

37. The full title of the volume was *The Pro-Slavery Argument; as Maintained by the Most Distinguished Writers of the Southern States, Containing the Several Essays, on the Subject, of Chancellor Harper, Governor Hammond, Dr. Simms, and Professor Dew* (Charleston: Walker, Richards, and Co., 1852).

races."[38] Soon after making this avowal, the *Messenger* declared for Virginia's secession.

The declension of the proslavery argument paralleled the passing of Southern leadership from the seaboard to the interior. The drain of population and wealth that had begun to affect Virginia and South Carolina during the 1820's siphoned off much of their spirit as well. After Calhoun's death in 1850, the leadership of the Southerners in Congress passed to such men as Jefferson Davis of Mississippi and John Slidell of Louisiana. The racist premises of the proslavery argument found liveliest expression in the pseudo-scientific writings of the Alabama physician Josiah Nott and the sociological treatises of Mississippian Henry Hughes.

The leading journal of the South during the 1850's was the New Orleans-based *DeBow's Review*, edited by the feisty disciple of Southern economic independence, James D. B. DeBow. It became the principal outlet for proslavery writers. It carried contributions from all over the South, but it gave special prominence to the writings of westerners who endorsed slavery not as a paternalistic system but as a necessary condition for an inferior race. Appealing to white racial pride and economic self-interest, DeBow himself periodically wrote hard-headed editorials explaining why all whites had a stake in slavery and making overt kinds of appeals to the selfish instincts hitherto muted in the proslavery tracts.[39]

The western defender of slavery differed in outlook and circumstances from his seaboard counterpart in fundamental ways. Both easterner and westerner, of course, shared the belief that slavery was the cornerstone of Southern civilization. But economic conditions, political exigencies, and psycholo-

---

38. "The Negro Races," *Southern Literary Messenger* 21 (1860): 3.

39. Otis C. Skipper, *J. D. B. DeBow, Magazinst of the Old South* (Athens: University of Georgia Press, 1958), is an adequate biography of DeBow. The best, though not the only, example of DeBow's polemical skill in the proslavery argument is his "The Non-Slaveholders of the South," in *Slavery Defended: The Views of the Old South*, ed. Eric L. McKitrick (Englewood Cliffs: Prentice–Hall, 1963), pp. 169–77.

gical needs combined to make the new defense of slavery rely upon racism and also to become an argument for Southern nationalism.

So rapid had the economic development in the southwest been that by the 1850's a genuine shortage of black labor occurred. Land was still abundant and relatively cheap. Uncleared, rich Mississippi bottom land sold in 1850 for $12 to $20 per acre, and the price of improved cotton plantations— sometimes as much as $100 per acre—was no higher than it had been in 1819. Moreover, less choice but still good land in well settled parts of upland Georgia and Alabama sold for only $5 to $25 per acre, and further west, on the vast Texas frontier, the richest, most improved cotton growing land in 1857 was selling for less than $10 per acre. Yet labor was in short supply and the cost of a prime black field hand, for whom a planter might have paid $1,000 in 1835, had jumped to an average price of $1,800 by 1860. Even in Virginia a planter lamented that "while landholders . . . cannot do without negroes, they sell so high that few persons in Virginia can afford to *keep them*, much less to buy." A noted historian of the antebellum Southern economy has correctly noted that "the real economic scarcity of the section [during the 1850's] was in labor and capital, not in land."[40]

In addition to the high cost of slaves, another and more ominous result of the labor shortage was a growing fear of social stratification. During the 1830's, as a Mississippian commented, "a plantation well stocked with hands [was] the *ne plus ultra* of every man's ambition who [resided] at the South." Indeed, in the fluid society of Jacksonian America—North and South—there was a widely shared belief that anything was possible. "No matter how one might begin," the South Carolina poet William J. Grayson explained, "as lawyer, physician, clergyman, mechanic, or merchant, he ended, if prosperous, as proprietor of a rice or cotton plantation." Slaveholder and

40. R. T. Hubard, November 28, 1859, Hubard Family Papers, Southern Historical Collection; Gray, *History of Agriculture* 2: 642–43, 666.

nonslaveholder alike, then, as Hammond and Dew had
argued, had a stake in slavery as an index of economic and
social progress. But the heightening demand for slave labor
and the inflated prices for that labor caused a concern, expressed by a New Orleans paper, that "the present tendency of
supply and demand is to concentrate all the slaves in the hands
of the few, and thus excite the envy rather than cultivate the
sympathy of the people." The result, as a contributor to *De-
Bow's Review* predicted, might be a *"great upbearing of our
masses."* It was this, he announced, *"that we are to fear, so far as
our institutions are concerned."* In 1856 DeBow rejected for publication an article submitted by R. B. Brashear of Louisiana,
who described "much of the Southern excitement as artificial,
as belonging to the class of editors and politicians. . . ." In a
nasty letter attacking DeBow the frustrated contributor
challenged, "Well, admit the 2,000,000 interested in slavery—
shall they give the law to the other Twenty odd Millions? Are
not the rights of majorities as sacred as minorities?"[41]

At the very same time, Southern political power in Washington seemed to be on the wane. Southern senators had been
unable to defeat the 1850 Compromise, and each succeeding
territorial decision seemed only to guarantee permanent
Southern minority status in Congress. As the free state population continued to grow and expand, the population of the
slaveholding South remained confined by barriers both natural
and legal and new fears surfaced. The *Richmond Enquirer* asserted, "We must *reinforce the powers of slavery as an element of political control.* . . ." The admission of California in 1850 upset
the political balance between North and South in the Senate,

41. Joseph H. Ingraham, *The South-west, By a Yankee*, 2 vols. (New York:
Harper and Brothers, 1835), 2: 84; William R. Taylor, *Cavalier and Yankee:
The Old South and The American National Character* (New York: Harper and
Row, 1961), p. 156; *New Orleans Daily Delta*, April 3, 1858, quoted in
Ronald T. Takaki, *A Pro-Slavery Crusade: The Agitation to Reopen the African
Slave Trade* (New York: Free Press, 1971), p. 63; J. H. Taylor, "Manufactures
in South Carolina," *DeBow's Review* 8 (1850): 25; R. B. Brashear to J. D. B.
DeBow, February 8, 1856, J. D. B. DeBow Papers, Duke University.

and with that act, claimed an Alabama congressman, the South became "a fixed, dreary, hopeless minority in the face of a growing aggression which threatens our very existence."[42]

For a slaveholder who seemed to be losing control there were several responses. One was to continue to push for territorial expansion into Latin America to add new slave states to the Union. Another was to agitate for a reopening of the African slave trade, which would both ease the labor shortage and increase the population and, hence, congressional representation. In both cases the center of activity was the southwest, where the labor problem was most acute, the social structure most fluid, and Democratic politics most skillfully practiced.[43]

To ensure the continued support of slavery among poorer whites required in part a shifting of the terms of the proslavery agrument. If the slave shortage threatened to pit white against white, the paternalistic, hierarchical defense of slavery would hardly suffice. If slavery was a "positive good," then to deny it room to expand was to deny its benefience. If expansion into the Caribbean was necessary to restore a balance in Congress, the consequences of restriction must be pictured with the typically vivid exaggeration of stump speaking at its best. Whether slavery had to expand or die was less important than making the Southern people perceive the necessity of expansion, the perils of confinement. The result was a changing of the emphasis of the proslavery argument from class to race in order to reinforce the belief that all white men had an equal stake in the peculiar institution. Since 51.1 percent of the population of Mississippi, 47.3 percent in Louisiana, and 44.4 percent in Alabama were slaves compared to 33.2 percent each in Virginia and North Carolina, it was not surprising that the new, racial terms of the argument emanated from the west.[44]

More important, though, than the economic, social, or

42. Carpenter, *South as a Conscious Minority*, p. 179; *Congressional Globe*, 31 Cong., 1 sess., pp. 358–59.
43. Southern attitudes toward territorial expansion receive full treatment in Chapter Six. The reopening of the slave trade is discussed in Chapter Three.
44. Gray, *History of Agriculture* 2: 656.

political concerns in effecting a change in the proslavery argument were the intellectual currents of the southwest in the
1850's. The ideological baggage of the two Southern regions
and the differences in time when the two forms of the argument were advanced were highly significant. In the east, even
as late as the 1830's, the legacy of the Enlightenment, with its
emphasis on rationalism, progress, and perfectibility, was
widely held. The essence of Dew's argument was that civilization was advancing to a constantly higher state and that slavery
was a contributor to the general progress of all mankind. In the
southwest of the 1850's, on the other hand, such notions were
almost heretical. Organic thinking was rampant, environmentalism dominant, and fundamentalist religious orthodoxy
had replaced rationalism. Absolutes had replaced intellectual
shading; intolerance and extroverted self-confidence had replaced liberal thinking and quiet introspection.

By the 1850's, then, both the media and the molders of
Southern opinion had a decidedly western look. Yet while the
westerners emphasized the racist aspect of the proslavery argument, they did not originate these theories, nor were they the
only ones who held them. All the earliest Southern nationalists
emphasized white supremacy. Rhett often spoke in terms of a
Southern nation, with "the African for the laborer,—the
Anglo-Saxon for the master and ruler." Virginian Beverley
Tucker, who believed that the black belonged to a different
species from the white, urged in his 1836 novel, *George Balcombe*, that Negroes be left "in their humility, their grateful affection, their self-renouncing loyalty."[45]

The westerners were, however, responsible for infusing
proslavery racism with scientific respectability. The formula-
tors of the new doctrine were hardly intellectual lightweights.
George R. Gliddon of Mobile was a renowned authority on
Egyptian archaeology. Dr. Samuel Cartwright of New Or-

45. Rhett, *Address to the People of Beaufort and Colleton*, p. 13; Quitman to Col.
Brush, August 23, 1823, in Claiborne, *Life and Correspondence of Quitman* 1:
84–85; Taylor, *Cavalier and Yankee*, p. 306; N. B. Tucker, *George Balcombe*
(New York: Harper and Brothers, 1836), 2: 165.

leans earned praise for his valuable investigations into cholera and yellow fever. Northerners, too, contributed their findings. Samuel G. Morton's research in craniology and Louis Agassiz's work in the field of zoology gave added strength to the arguments of the scientific racists.[46]

But the chief participant in the scientific defense of slavery, or "niggerology," as he called it, was tall, slender, white-haired Josiah Nott, whose influence upon the course not only of proslavery thought and Southern nationalism but also of American science has been neglected. Like so many molders of Southern opinion, Nott was born in South Carolina in 1804 and graduated from South Carolina College in 1824, one year ahead of Hammond. His father, Abraham Nott, was a native of Connecticut who had moved to South Carolina via Georgia in 1789 and who served as a Federalist congressman in the Sixth Congress. Young Josiah left his Columbia birthplace to study medicine, first in New York and then at the prestigious University of Pennsylvania, where he stayed on as lecturer in anatomy after graduation in 1827. He returned to Columbia in 1829 to begin private practice, went to Europe in 1835 to study in Paris, and resumed his medical work in Mobile, Alabama, in 1836. Nott's gray eyes sparkled as the young, aggressive Alabamian reported to a friend in 1836 that he was "going ahead very cleverly & I think next year I shall make from 8 to 10 thousand dollars." He helped organize the Mobile Medical Society in 1841 and soon thereafter began to publish numerous articles on surgery, hypnotism, and yellow fever. Nott has been credited with advancing the important theory that yellow fever was transmitted by flying insects. His intensive study of that dreaded disease was inspired at least in part by the deaths of four of his eight children during the Mobile yellow fever epidemic of 1853.[47]

46. Jenkins, *Pro-Slavery Thought*, p. 261; "Samuel A. Cartwright," *Appletons' Cyclopedia of American Biography* 1: 545; William Stanton, *The Leopard's Spots: Scientific Attitudes Toward Race in America, 1815–59* (Chicago: University of Chicago Press, 1960), *passim*, but esp. pp. 27–32, 100–101, 104–109.
47. George H. Ramsey, "Josiah Clark Nott," *Dictionary of American Biography* 13: 582; Stanton, *Leopard's Spots*, p. 66.

Nott's greatest influence, however, lay in his publications in the field of ethnology. These studies indicated—as they reinforced—a shift in the proslavery argument. The paternalistic argument generally explained the suitability of the Negro for slavery on the basis of God's curse upon Canaan, "a *judicial* act of God," according to one such explanation.[48] The ethnologists, led by Nott, advanced a more scientific argument. In 1844 Nott delivered a pair of lectures in Mobile in which he contended that his careful comparative study of the two races proved that the Negro was of a separate and inferior species.

Nott realized that his argument was a novel and even dangerous one to make in the South, which was becoming increasingly fundamentalist in theology. His theory ran directly counter to the account of Creation in Genesis, but he did not hesitate to advance it nevertheless. He chided others who declined to follow his lead in testing the validity of scriptural truths. Nott argued that

> if there be several *species* of the human race—if these species differ in the perfection of their moral and intellectual endowments—if there be a law of nature opposed to the mingling of white and black races—I say if all these things be true, what an unexplored field is open to the Philanthropist!! Is it not the *Christian duty* to inquire into this subject?[49]

Privately, Nott was more blunt. His goal, he wrote, was to "just get the dam'd stupid crowd safely around Moses & the difficulty is at an end."[50]

---

48. Josiah Priest, *Bible Defense of Slavery, or The Origin, History, and Fortunes of the Negro Race* (Louisville: W. S. Brown, 1851), p. 104.

49. Josiah C. Nott, *Two Lectures on the Natural History of the Caucasian and Negro Races* (Mobile: n.p., 1844), pp. 33–34. Scathing reviews of Nott's writings emanated chiefly from the Eastern States, where conservative clergymen undertook to discredit the attackers of holy writ. For example, John Bachman of Charleston argued vociferously that the paternalistic, scriptural defense of slavery provided "all the strong arguments" in favor of slavery. See John Bachman, "Types of Mankind," *Charleston Medical Journal* 9 (1854): 627–59.

50. Josiah C. Nott to Hammond, July 25, 1845, Hammond Papers, Library of Congress.

One of Nott's most interested readers was Hammond, who, in sullen retirement in 1845, was writing defenses of slavery. "I wish I had your knowledge of comparative anatomy & physiology," wrote Hammond. "Such knowledge is at the bottom of all great investigations in modern times." Continuing, he inquired, "Have your Science and Philosophy of man furnished you with any *certain knowledge* of the causes which enable the negro to stand heat better than the Caucasian . . . ?" Nott responded negatively, but commended Hammond for his efforts, adding in a subsequent letter that "the nigger business has brought me into a large and heterogeneous correspondence."[51] The South was clearly interested.

In 1848, as the guest of DeBow in New Orleans, Nott delivered two lectures at the University of New Orleans on the Biblical and natural history of man. "The Almighty in his wisdom has peopled our vast planet from many distant centres, instead of one," he claimed, "and with races or species originally and radically different." Pronouncing that any attempt to defend slavery with Biblical references necessarily required "forced constructions of the Old and New Testaments," Nott declared that his purpose was "to cut loose the natural history of mankind from the Bible, and to place each upon its own foundation, where it may remain without collision or molestation."

Nott then proceeded, by a tactic that would soon become familiar, to demolish the Biblical proofs for unity of the races. Citing not his own work but that of Gliddon, Nott said that Egyptian monuments revealed the existence of two species, "fair and dark . . . as distinctly marked as now," while "the skulls taken from the catacombs of Memphis and Thebes prove beyond dispute that these differences antedate all written records. . . ." Capping his argument, Nott asked, "Where, in the Bible, is there to be found any chronology reconcilable with this early diversity of mankind? Or where, in the whole

---

51. Hammond to Nott, August 3, 1845; Nott to Hammond, August 12, September 4, 1845, *ibid.*

range of history, are to be found facts, of any kind, to explain these difficulties on any other ground than that of *original* diversity?"

The Negro, according to Nott, belonged to one of "the barbarous tribes of the earth." That race's "highest contribution is attained in the state of slavery, and when left to itself, after a certain advance, as in St. Domingo, a retrograde movement is inevitable." Again presenting scientific evidence not his own, Nott pointed out that "Dr. S. G. Morton, by a long series of well-conceived experiments, has established the fact, that the capacity of the Mongol, Indian, and Negro, and all dark-skinned races, is smaller than that of the pure white man." As a result, *"mental cultivation cannot elevate an inferior to the level of a superior race."*

Nott concluded with a warning.

> A fearful crisis must come, sooner or later. With three million negroes crowding down upon the Gulf States, and rapidly increasing—cut off, too, as we are from the sympathies not only of the rest of the world, but of our own government . . . —what then? *Emancipation* must follow. . . .

This would force the South "to carve her way out [of the Union] at any and every hazard, with the sword."[52] Secession and science were finding a common cause.

Nott's thinking interacted with that of DeBow, the youthful Louisiana editor who was at this time formulating his own ideas on the place of slavery in American and Southern life. In his *Review* DeBow called upon his contemporaries "as Southerners, as *Americans*, as MEN" to make "no *explanation* . . . no apology" for slavery. "It is sufficient that we, the people of a State, we the people of half the States of this Union, in our sovereign independence of all other people or peoples upon earth, of all mortal men, have decreed our institutions as they are, *and so will dare maintain them."*[53]

52. Josiah C. Nott, *Two Lectures on the Connection Between the Biblical and Physical History of Man* (New York: Bartlett and Welford, 1849), pp. 5, 7, 35–37, 18.
53. *DeBow's Review* 3 (1847): 421.

Nott was rapidly coming to a more extreme conclusion, and finally—in December 1850, before the Southern Rights Association of Mobile—he sounded the call for a Southern nation. "Negro slavery," he cried, "has become a part of our very being; our natural prosperity and domestic happiness are inseparable from it." The Negro had never "risen above the grade of mediocrity in the whites;" it was erroneous to assume his lot could be improved, for "no negro race has ever yet invented an alphabet, however rude, or possessed the semblance of literature." Indeed, "the negro races stand at the lowest point in the scale of human beings." Southerners must therefore be made aware that "the *perpetuation* of slavery is no sin." He concluded that "if any man wishes to find the strongest of all arguments for a severance of the Union, and for the formation of a Southern Confederacy, he may deduce it from the chain of facts I have detailed." Significantly, DeBow—still uncommitted to a separate nation—omitted Nott's concluding remark in a reprint of the speech in his *Review* in March 1851.[54]

Nott's harangue was just what the fire-eating citizens of Mobile wanted to hear. They had formed their association to protest the 1850 Compromise measures, and they longed for support from their community leaders.[55] As a leading scientist, Nott surely must have commanded their attention and respect. With the skill of a seasoned agitator, Nott relied upon his scientific prestige to advance the cause of Southern nationalism. There was no logical step from "scientific" racism to Southern nationalism, but such was the character of many Southern nationalists that a predetermined judgment of Negro inferiority, uncritically tested and presented with passion and urgency, could become a strong argument in favor of a South-

---

54. Josiah C. Nott, *An Essay on the Natural History of Mankind, Viewed in Connection With Negro Slavery* (Mobile: Dade, Thompson, and Co., 1851), pp. 8, 24; "Nature and Destiny of the Negro," *DeBow's Review* 10 (1851): 329–32.
55. Clarence P. Denman, *The Secession Movement in Alabama* (Montgomery: Alabama State Department of Archives and History, 1933), pp. 51–55.

ern nation. The Southern nationalists of Mobile on that December night must have been well pleased.

Neither Nott nor the radical Alabamians were alone in their Southern nationalism. A Virginian, contemplating the future of the Union, asked, "Shall the labouring class be an inferior race, so controlled and directed by the superior minds of whites, as continually to progress in material and moral well being, far beyond any point it has ever shown a power of attaining in freedom?" The Mississippi Friends of Southern Rights, dominated by the Southern nationalist element, circulated an Address declaring that "there can be no equality of the races. They cannot live amongst us except as our slaves, or as our masters. . . . We must either maintain our superiority, or surrender the land of our fathers."[56]

Back to their studies the scientists went, led by Nott, who delved with evangelistic zeal into the new field of ethnology that they had opened. "My great object for several years has been to get the world quarreling about niggerology, and I have at last succeeded," he chortled in 1850. Samuel A. Cartwright, chairman of the Medical Association of Louisiana, got a head start and published his amazing findings in the *New Orleans Medical and Surgical Journal* in the winter of 1850–51. "A shade of pervading darkness" present in the Negro's skin was observed as well in "the membranes, the muscles, the tendons and all the fluids and secretions," in the "brain and nerves, the chyle and all the humors." The Negro's bone and skull structure was very different from the white man's and his brain was not only considerably smaller but also "has in great measure run into nerves." The Negro as a result tended to be afflicted with peculiar diseases, among them "drapetomania," which made the slave want to run away, and "dysaethesia," better known as "rascality." Since these diseases were prevalent only

56. [M. R. H. Garnett], *The Union Past and Future: How It Works and How to Save It, By a Citizen of Virginia* (Charleston: Walker and James, 1850), p. 38; *Address of the Committee Appointed by the Friends of Southern Rights to the People of Mississippi, December 10, 1850* (Jackson: Fall and Marshall, 1850), pp. 12–13.

among Negroes, Cartwright solemnly advised that the South be left alone to cope with such maladies.[57]

Others echoed the Louisianian, but none so authoritatively as the irrepressible Nott, who, in collaboration with Gliddon in 1854, published *Types of Mankind,* a collection of the latest ethnological thinking on the subject of slavery. The book rapidly sold out in its first printing, and by 1900 it had gone through nine editions. Nott's own contribution to *Types* was less scientific than polemical. The destiny of the white man, Nott wrote, was "to conquer and hold every foot of the globe where climate does not interpose an impenetrable barrier," to maintain control over the "inferior races" of the world. So great was the success of *Types* that in 1857 Nott and Gliddon published *Indigenous Races of the Earth,* which repeated most of the earlier arguments. Nott's own contribution to this less successful venture was small, mainly because in 1856 he had become involved in the translation and publication of Arthur de Gobineau's *Essai sur l'inegalite des races humaines.* Nott prepared a lengthy appendix to the book reiterating his contentions in favor of racial diversity and white supremacy. Like *Indigenous Races,* the *Essai* contained more rhetoric than reason, more racism than scientific evidence.[58]

Yet the arguments advanced by Nott and his colleagues had caught on with many Southerners and paralleled the rise of secession feeling. DeBow warned in 1851 that "the time has passed when the progress of investigation can be interrupted

57. Nott to E. G. Squier, May 4, 1850, quoted in Jenkins, *Pro-Slavery Thought,* p. 260; Samuel A. Cartwright, "Report on the Diseases and Physical Peculiarities of the Negro Race," *New Orleans Medical and Surgical Journal* 7 (1850–51): 692–96, quoted in John Duffy, "A Note on Ante-Bellum Southern Nationalism and Medical Practice," *Journal of Southern History* 34 (1968): 262; Samuel A. Cartwright, "The Unity of the Human Race Disproved by the Hebrew's Bible," *DeBow's Review* 29 (1860): 130.

58. Stanton, *Leopard's Spots,* pp. 161–63, 174–76; Jenkins, *Pro-Slavery Thought,* p. 262; Josiah C. Nott and George R. Gliddon, eds., *Types of Mankind* (Philadelphia: Lippincott, Grambo, and Co., 1854), p. 79; Fredrickson, *Black Image in the White Mind,* p. 79.

by the spirit which dictated from its haughty tribunal to Co-
pernicus and Galileo. . . ." In 1860, still smarting from the attack leveled against him by Brashear in 1856 and angered by
Hinton R. Helper's recently published *The Impending Crisis of
the South*, which urged nonslaveholders to unite against the
slaveholding minority, DeBow—now a Southern nationalist—published an important essay. Entitled "The Non-
Slaveholders of the South," the article emphasized "the status
of the white man" in the South who "can look down at those
who are beneath him, at infinite remove." The influence of
Nott was apparent. Hammond, at last convinced by the racists, arose in the Senate in 1858 and, after declaring that "cotton is King," said that the Negro "constitutes the very mudsill
of society and of political government" because he possesses "a
low order of intellect and but little skill." Thus, the Negro was
well qualified "to do the menial duties, to perform the drudgery of life." Mississippi Senator Jefferson Davis, with obvious
reference to Hammond, claimed in 1859 that "the lower race of
human beings that constitute the substratum of what is termed
the slave population of the South, elevates every white man in
our community." In 1860 Yancey, long an Alabama secessionist, cried out that in the South "we . . . elevate [the white
man] to a place amongst the master race and put the negro race
to do this dirty work which God designed they should do."[59]
Side by side, racism and Southern nationalism were, in 1860,
triumphant.

59. "Ethnological Researchers—Is the African and Caucasian of Common Origin?" *DeBow's Review* 9 (1850): 243; G. S. Alexander to C. C. Clay, Jr., June 8,
1856, C. C. Clay Papers, Duke University; Hammond, *Letters and Speeches*, p.
318; Dunbar Rowland, ed., *Jefferson Davis, Constitutionalist: His Letters, Papers,
and Speeches*, 10 vols. (New York: J. J. Little and Ives Co., 1923) 4: 49; W. L.
Yancey, *Speech of the Hon. William L. Yancey of Alabama, Delivered in the National
Democratic Convention, Charleston, April 28th, 1860*, William Lowndes Yancey
Papers, Alabama Department of Archives and History.

IV

During the 1850's a commitment to the racist defense of slavery often preceded an advocacy of Southern nationalism. Not every racist defender of slavery was a Southern nationalist; but, because of the exertions of Nott and his associates, racism and Southern nationalism became jointly more fashionable. During the 1850's, more and more Southerners came to rest their advocacy of a Southern nation upon the preservation of slavery and the preservation of slavery upon the doctrine of white supremacy and enhancement at the Negro's expense.

Gradually the seaboard South, accustomed to leading rather than following, fell in line. During the 1850's the leading Virginia writer on slavery was George Fitzhugh, paternalistic defender of slavery, teacher, writer, and— failure. Fitzhugh was born in Prince William County in northern Virginia in 1806, the son of a doctor and small planter of modest means. His father died in 1829, and the Fitzhugh family estate had to be sold to meet debts. In the same year young George married Mary Brockenbrough of Caroline County on the Rappahannock River in eastern Virginia and moved into his bride's home, which was described by a neighbor as a "rickety old mansion, situated on the fag-end of a once noble estate." Caroline County, like the Brockenbrough estate, had been in decline for some time, a fact bemoaned by John Taylor, Caroline's most famous son, in a series of essays published in the early years of the nineteenth century. It was, then, to a region that had seen better days that Fitzhugh came to live in 1829.[60]

Twenty years of frustration followed. Fitzhugh had had little in the way of formal education and no training in the legal profession, and he set up a law practice that proved unsuccessful. Providing for nine children taxed his meager resources to the limit. Most of his time was spent in genealogical research, seeking some evidence of noble ancestry, but the study of his

60. Harvey Wish, *George Fitzhugh, Propagandist of the Old South* (Baton Rouge: Louisiana State University Press, 1943), pp. 1–12.

family tree revealed sturdy, modest limbs rather than noble branches. Until his marriage he was not himself a slaveholder, and even through the Brockenbroughs he acquired only a few slaves. As Fitzhugh's life soured, he turned more and more to his books, reveling in Thomas Carlyle's indictments of abolitionism and his critiques of the new industrial age, which Fitzhugh believed was victimizing men like himself. In other, more stable times, he thought, a Fitzhugh of Caroline County would have been secure financially and respected socially; but the nineteenth century, with its emphasis on equality and "Mammonism," failed to offer the Virginian security and deference.[61]

Embittered, Fitzhugh published a pamphlet in 1850 entitled *Slavery Justified*, which announced that "liberty and equality are new things under the sun." Liberty and free competition produce a society whose Golden Rule is "every man for himself and devil take the hindmost." Fitzhugh's alternative? Plantation slavery, for "at the South all is peace, quiet, plenty and contentment. We have no mobs, no trades unions, no strikes for higher wages, no armed resistance to law, but little jealousy of the rich by the poor." Who was best suited for slavery? Fitzhugh answered the question by asking another in the title of a second pamphlet, *What Shall Be Done with the Free Negro?*, published in 1851. Slavery was "the only condition for which he [the Negro] is suited."[62]

George Fitzhugh was following in the footsteps of Thomas R. Dew and William Harper; he was now a Southern sectionalist. But he was not a Southern nationalist. In fact, he was moving in the opposite direction from other defenders of slavery, who were embracing ethnological arguments. Fitzhugh was becoming a proponent of slavery in the abstract rather than just Negro slavery. In 1854 he published *Sociology for the South*, in which he argued that "a Southern farm is a sort

61. George Fitzhugh, *Cannibals All! or Slaves Without Masters*, ed. C. Vann Woodward, John Harvard Library (Cambridge: Harvard University Press, 1960), p. 67; Wish, *George Fitzhugh*, pp. 10–13.
62. Fitzhugh, *Cannibals All!*, xv–xvi.

of joint stock concern or social phalanstery, in which the master furnishes the capital and skill, and the slaves the labor, and [they] divide the profits, not according to each one's in-put, but according to each one's wants and necessities." Lest anyone doubt his position, Fitzhugh announced that "we abhor the doctrine of 'Types of Mankind'."[63] Class, not race, was the basis of slavery.

Sociology influenced other Southerners in their defense of slavery. The educator and reviewer George Frederick Holmes praised the volume in several periodicals. Edmund Ruffin, the agricultural reformer, Albert Taylor Bledsoe, a Virginia educator, Thornton Stringfellow, a Virginia clergyman, all adopted Fitzhugh's position, and William J. Grayson, the South Carolina poet, eagerly took up Fitzhugh's argument.[64] Understandably Fitzhugh's greatest impact was in the older sections of the seaboard South, where a paternalistic defense of slavery sat well with a region whose leadership role was passing and whose glories were in the past. In the west, only the eclectic DeBow gave support.

For the first time in George Fitzhugh's life, people were listening to him; for the first time he was a man of influence. Jubilantly he claimed he had "revolutionized public opinion in the South on the subject of Slavery." It was no time for doubting the rightness of the cause. Fitzhugh wrote to Holmes, "I see great evils in slavery, but in a controversial work I ought not to admit them."[65] Rather, it was necessary to build upon the foundations of *Sociology* and take the battle into the enemy's camp.

It was an easy step to advance from a paternalistic defense of slavery in the South to an advocacy of slavery's extension to the white workingmen of the North. Fitzhugh did so in *Cannibals All!* published in 1857, urging the Northern states not

63. George Fitzhugh, *Sociology for the South, or the Failure of Free Society* (Richmond: A. Morris, 1854), pp. 48, 95.
64. Wish, *George Fitzhugh*, pp. 113–124.
65. George Fitzhugh to Holmes, March 27, April 11, 1855, Holmes Letterbook.

necessarily to "reduce white men to the state of negro slavery" but to afford "the masses . . . more of protection, and the masses and philosophers equally . . . more of control."[66]

While Fitzhugh was publishing his two books, he was also writing articles to explain the finer points of his theories. Most important were his futile admonitions to his fellow Southerners to defend slavery in the abstract. "Inferiority of race," he warned in *DeBow's* in 1857, "is quite as good an argument against negro slavery as in its favor" because it tends to "beget cruel and negligent treatment in the masters, who naturally feel little sympathy for ignorant, brutal savages." Not to defend slavery in the abstract is to "take the weakest position. . . . We admit it to be wrong, and then attempt to defend it in that peculiar form which has always been most odious to mankind." Though DeBow questioned this more radical position as "a little impractical," and though Fitzhugh's loyal following was limited to a few Virginians and Carolinians, he repeatedly warned the racist Southern nationalists through *DeBow's* that "domestic slavery must be vindicated in the abstract, and in the general, as a normal, natural, and *in general*, necessitous element of civilized society, without regard to race or color."[67]

Fitzhugh at first opposed a growing movement, instigated by younger men, many of whom were Southern nationalists from the western states, to reopen the African slave trade. In *Cannibals All!* Fitzhugh wrote that the slave trade "is the most inhuman pursuit in which man ever engaged." Yet one year later he completely reversed his position, explaining that "the South cannot, consistently, approve the sentence passed by christendom on the slave trade, and yet justify slaveholding." Rebuked for his mildness by DeBow, whose extreme support of the trade persuaded Fitzhugh initially to reverse himself, the Virginian subsequently wrote that "an exasperated South would blow the Union to shivers, if hordes of Northern im-

---

66. Fitzhugh, *Cannibals All!*, pp. 19, 247.
67. George Fitzhugh, "Southern Thought Again," *DeBow's Review* 23 (1857): 451, 347; Wish, *George Fitzhugh*, p. 198.

migrants continue to seize upon and monopolize" the western territories, while the importation of slaves is prohibited. He advised DeBow in 1858 to "stick to the Slave Trade. I am sure it is *now* popular North & South—else why do none but [Senator William H.] Seward and [Congressman Joshua] Giddings oppose it in Congress?"[68] It was a belated and illogical conversion, but George Fitzhugh, reluctant to surrender the influence he had achieved, was taking the first step toward Southern nationalism.

As late as 1860, though, Fitzhugh was opposed to the dissolution of the Union. In an addendum to a later edition of *Cannibals All!* he noted that "a comparison of opinions and of institutions between North and South will lead to kinder and more pacific relations."[69] Indeed, Fitzhugh's continuing purpose was to emphasize not the differences between the Northern and Southern labor systems, but the similarities. It was not surprising that Fitzhugh in early 1861 opposed the secession of Virginia.

Yet in April 1861, while the Old Dominion was calculating the value of the Union, Fitzhugh, still sensitive to the direction of public opinion and desiring not to lose its favor, was calculating too. New York ethnologist John H. Van Evrie had recently published *Negroes and Negro "Slavery,"* which reiterated the tenets of scientific racism and earned plaudits from Jefferson Davis and Alexander Stephens, president and vice president of the new nation Virginia was soon to join. Fitzhugh did not miss the opportunity to associate himself with the popular side. In a review of Van Evrie's book, Fitzhugh admitted that the ethnologist's evidence seemed to prove "that the negro is physically, morally, and intellectually a different being (from necessity) from the white man, and must ever so

68. Takaki, *A Pro-Slavery Crusade*, pp. 9–22; Fitzhugh, *Cannibals All!*, p. 337; George Fitzhugh, "The Conservative Principle, or Social Evils and Their Remedies," *DeBow's Review* 22 (1857): 461; George Fitzhugh, "Wealth of the North and the South," *DeBow's Review* 22 (1857): 592; Wish, *George Fitzhugh*, p. 242.
69. Fitzhugh, *Cannibals All!*, p. 260.

remain. . . ."[70] George Fitzhugh, like his state, was at last converted to Southern nationalism.

V

In 1860 E. N. Elliott of Port Gibson, Mississippi, published a massive collection—comprising over nine hundred pages and weighing several pounds—entitled *Cotton Is King*, which contained virtually all of the proslavery arguments. It went through a number of editions. All of the important writers and positions were either present or represented—Hammond, Harper, Stringfellow, Bledsoe, and Cartwright—and the tome in more ways than one became the last word on the subject. In it one could trace the movement of the argument from legalism to science, from class to race, from Virginia to South Carolina to the west, and from Southern sectionalism to Southern nationalism.

In his introduction, Elliott wrote, "There is now but one great question dividing the American people, and that, to the greater danger and stability of our government, the concord and harmony of our citizens, and the perpetuation of our liberties, divides us by a geographical line.[71] The issue to which he referred was slavery, which by 1860 had become the cornerstone of the ideology of Southern nationalism.

70. George Fitzhugh, "The Black and White Races of Men," *DeBow's Review* 30 (1861): 447.
71. Elliot, ed., *Cotton Is King*, p. 3.

CHAPTER THREE

The Degrading
Shackles of
Commercial Dependence

The proslavery argument emphasized an institution that formed the basis of a distinctively Southern way of life. Southern nationalists tended to use the defense of slavery as a means of pointing out irreconcilable sectional differences between North and South. As it developed, their definition of Southern civilization embraced a whole set of values and beliefs that were rooted in slavery.

Slavery provided the basis for a Southern way of life that was superior in its distinctiveness. But some Southerners believed that distinctiveness had little value so long as the South remained dependent on Northern commerce and industry. Thus, there arose in the South after Nullification an impulse toward economic self-sufficiency, toward independence of Northern influences. Probably the most significant economic manifestation of this impulse was the commercial convention movement, which began in 1837 and continued until 1860.

When the first Southern commercial convention assembled in Augusta, Georgia, in 1837, its business-man–delegates were concerned with little more than economic development through diversification. By the time the last

Southern commercial convention adjourned at Vicksburg, Mississippi, in 1859, its politician–delegates were hopeful of imminent secession and a separate Southern nation. During the antebellum years, then, the commercial conventions became outlets for Southern nationalism.

Though the economy of the nineteenth-century South was primarily agricultural, some Southerners contemplated diversification by encouraging manufacturing and trade. Between 1837 and 1852 Southerners repeatedly convened and resolved to cooperate for mutual economic benefit by encouraging commercial ventures. Though the businessmen who constituted a majority of the delegations acknowledged that agriculture must remain the basis of the Southern economy, they believed that commerce must assume a larger role. Gradually, however, as planter indifference greeted the pronouncements of each convention, it began to appear that Southern economic independence could be achieved only at the expense of Southern agricultural distinctiveness.

Into the vacuum moved politicians, many of them Southern nationalists, who claimed that economic self-sufficiency and sectional distinctiveness were not necessarily mutually exclusive terms. Invoking the image of "King Cotton" and calling for a reopening of the African slave trade, Southern nationalists attempted to show that an agricultural, slaveholding section possessed the potential for economic and, if necessary, political independence. By harnessing the twin impulses of Southern sectionalism, by emphasizing both Southern solidarity as an agricultural region and Southern distinctiveness from the industrializing North, the Southern commercial conventions helped pave the way for a Southern nation.

I

"A Crisis has arrived in the commercial affairs of the South and Southwest," proclaimed a correspondent of *Niles' Register* in July 1837. William Dearing, a concerned Georgian, was circulating a message to Southern merchants urging them, in the depths of the economic depression of 1837, "to attempt a new organization of our commercial relations with Europe." The Baltimore-based *Register*, the most widely read commercial periodical in the South at the time, gave Dearing's compelling message a place of prominence. "We ought to be our own importers and exporters, for . . . we furnish nearly all the articles of export in the great staples of cotton, rice, and tobacco," Dearing wrote. "Yet, with all this in our favor by nature, we employ the merchants of the Northern cities as our agents in this business." It was time to "look to the natural advantages of our situation as Southern men, and take measures to secure to ourselves the full enjoyment of them." The circular from Athens proposed as a remedy "a convention of Southern and Western merchants," to meet in Augusta, Georgia, in October 1837.[1]

The economic crisis to which Dearing referred was, in 1837, less a Southern crisis than a Southern opportunity. Although the Northern states in the late 1830's were in economic distress, the South—which relied, some said, too heavily on staple crops—had rallied from the depression of the late 1820's and was in relatively good condition. Still, this general tendency did not obscure the fact that certain parts of the Southern economy were in a transitional state and facing important decisions about the future.

The booming cotton economy of the southwest had caused great economic dislocation in the seaboard states during the late 1820's and early 1830's. The problem was less one of exhausted soil than of the temptations of the cotton siren, which lured many a Virginian and Carolinian westward. The lure of flush times siphoned off not only the population of the seaboard but also the spirit. In the Old Dominion the emigration problem was compounded by social and political unrest, which had caused many Virginians to question the utility of a

1. *Niles' Weekly Register* 52 (1837): 369; Herbert Wender, *Southern Commercial Conventions, 1837–1859*, Johns Hopkins Studies in Historical and Political Science, series 48, no. 4 (Baltimore: Johns Hopkins University Press, 1930), p. 11.

slaveholding, agricultural economy, a dilemma apparently resolved by the failure of the legislature in 1832 to take steps
toward slave emancipation. On the other hand, South Carolina
and Georgia, because of their soil and climate, were turning to
cotton planting. Though the production of the Carolina and
Georgia plantations hardly matched that of the rich interior
lands, a tie of common economic interest was beginning to
bind the cotton states.[2]

While the economy was in transition, the Nullification
crisis took place and caused a new sectional awareness to
emerge. A few men had gone to the extreme during the tariff
imbroglio and called for the forming of a separate Southern nation. Most, however, although their sectional consciousness
had been aroused, preferred to express their Southern attitudes within the Union. Such expressions appeared to take either of two forms. One might choose to emphasize and defend
elements of Southern life that were distinctive. Or one might
instead envision a need for sectional self-sufficiency. These
two impulses of Southern sectionalism were not, in 1837,
clearly defined, and their compatibility with one another had
yet to be tested. Still, by 1837 such attitudes were beginning to
appear, and their interplay was the central feature of the
growth of economic Southern nationalism.

In 1837 there were several paths of economic development
open to Southerners. They might reinvest their capital in more
land and additional slaves, or they might, instead, look for alternative ventures to support. It was by no means clear in 1837
that the South would continue to be primarily agricultural.
During the 1830's the country was on the brink of a transportation revolution which would contribute, many believed, to
rapid economic diversification and development. Up to this
time both North and South had been equally agricultural. The

---

2. Soil exhaustion as a factor in Southern economic life has perhaps been over-
emphasized. A recent corrective study is Robert W. Fogel and Stanley Engerman, *Time on the Cross: The Economics of American Negro Slavery*, 2 vols. (Boston:
Little, Brown, and Co., 1974), esp. 1: 197–99. The history of cotton expansion
is fully told in Gray, *History of Agriculture* 2: 691–720.

North, however, seemed to be moving toward industrialization. Southerners who grew up during the tariff crisis
believed that the South was already the North's economic vas-
sal, and the likelihood of continued Northern dominance demanded a response.[3]

One such response was the proslavery argument, which
emphasized a distinctive feature of Southern life and made it
the cornerstone of a Southern civilization. By 1837 that response, in its paternalistic form, was already well developed.
The proslavery argument seemed to indicate that the slaveholders, who dominated Southern economic and political life,
preferred to accentuate the virtues of an agricultural economy.
The planters followed this impulse for good reasons and with
great effect throughout the antebellum period. Though there
were great risks in running a plantation, there were also great
profits to be made. The states of the upper South, which were
moving to grain production, were beginning to restore their
waning economic fortunes. To the west, cotton planting promised large profits. A traveler in Alabama in 1837 was told that
profits regularly reached 35 percent. Such prospects caused
production to soar. Between 1832 and 1842 exports of cotton
from New Orleans increased from 394,000 bales to 873,000
and from 135,000 to 371,000 in Mobile. Between 1834 and
1837 over eighty million dollars were invested in bank capital
in Mississippi, Louisiana, Arkansas, Florida, and Alabama.
Times were flush.[4]

The nature of the plantation economy was such that, as
one historian has written, "no part of the South needed much
of the product of any other part." In an economy existing for
export, there was little widespread demand for a vast transportation network. Of primary concern was a means of getting the
crop to market and then selling it for a good price. Small, un-
connected rail lines and steam boats that could ply the rivers of

3. Taylor, *The Transportation Revolution* is a fine study of the rapid development of transportation in the nineteenth century.
4. Harriet Martineau, *Society in America*, 3 vols. (New York: A. M. S. Press,
1966), 1: 307; Gray, *History of Agriculture* 2: 899–900.

the interior were sufficient. Moreover, the shrewd planter cared not who shipped his crop once it reached the place of export, so long as he received a fair price; and the merchant, equally astute, would deal not with the most patriotic shipper but with the one whose rates were the most economical. Northern shippers, therefore, did a good deal of the business in Southern ports, and the planter compromised his sectional chauvinism for a good price.[5]

With the South seemingly committed to a profitable, slave-holding, agricultural economy, it might have seemed odd that anybody cared very much about commercial development. In fact, some Southerners from the beginning saw the commercial conventions more as a political tool than as an economic necessity. Calhoun, for example, was concerned less with the disposition of excess capital than with uniting the South politically. Taking time out from the vicious debates over the reception of abolition petitions, Calhoun urged "that the meeting in Augusta should be fully attended. Now is the time," he wrote, encouraging his brother to serve as a delegate. "There never was so favorable an opportunity . . . to unite the South. It must not be lost."[6]

But the aim of most of the convention delegates was more modest. Sixty-five Georgians and thirteen South Carolinians assembled on October 17, 1837, in Augusta and elected Charlestonian Ker Boyce, a wealthy cotton merchant, as presiding officer. The delegates then appointed the feisty South Carolina anti-tariff leader George McDuffie chairman of a committee to prepare an address to the public. McDuffie's committee reflected the background and purpose of a majority of the delegates, for it comprised men whose primary concerns were commercial, not agricultural. Among the committee's more influential members were James Gadsden, aged forty-nine, a Charleston-born Floridian and successful soldier,

5. *Southern Literary Messenger* 5 (1839): 3; Sydnor, *Southern Sectionalism*, p. 274.
6. Calhoun to James E. Calhoun, September 7, 1837, October 27, 1837, *Calhoun Correspondence*, pp. 378, 382.

planter, and diplomat who was preparing a return to his native state to serve a long tenure as president of the Louisville, Cincinnati, and Charleston Railroad; and Thomas Butler King, aged thirty-seven, a Georgia lawyer, legislator, and planter who helped found the Brunswick (Georgia) Railroad and Canal Company in 1840.[7]

The Augusta Convention adjourned after resolving "to throw off the degrading shackles of our commercial dependence," to "encourage and sustain importations" through Southern seaports, to call upon the legislatures of Georgia and South Carolina for financial assistance, and, finally, to reconvene in Augusta the following April.[8] The convention's importance lay not in its actions, which were vague and mostly rhetorical, but in its demonstration that Southern men of commerce were concerned about their position and desirous of cooperating for mutual improvement. The convention was not intended to unite the South politically but rather, at most, to unite Southern businessmen in favor of "direct trade," of greater reliance on Southern commercial facilities.

The first convention made an impact, for in April 1838 two hundred delegates representing seven states—Virginia, North Carolina, South Carolina, Tennessee, Georgia, Florida, and Alabama—arrived in Augusta for a second session. King was chosen president, and former Governor Robert Y. Hayne, another South Carolina Nullifier who, in 1836, had helped found the Louisville, Cincinnati, and Charleston Railroad,

7. W. W. Davis, "Ante Bellum Southern Commercial Conventions," *Transactions of the Alabama Historical Society, 1904*, ed. Thomas McAdory Owen (Montgomery: Alabama Historical Society, 1906), 5: 158–59; John G. Van Deusen, *The Ante-Bellum Southern Commercial Conventions*, Trinity College Historical Society (Durham: Duke University Press, 1926), 16: 15; Wender, *Southern Commercial Conventions*, p. 18; Henry Kalloch Rowe, "James Petigru Boyce," *Dictionary of American Biography*, ed. Allen Johnson and Dumas Malone (New York: Charles Scribner's Sons, 1943) 2: 523; J. Fred Rippy, "James Gadsden," *Dictionary of American Biography* 7: 83–84; E. Merton Coulter, "Thomas Butler King," *Dictionary of American Biography* 10: 403.

8. *Georgia Messenger*, October 26, 1837, quoted in Davis, "Ante Bellum Conventions," p. 159.

chaired the resolutions committee. The key resolution of this convention, echoing the desires of the earlier gathering, called for a banking system under which banks in Southern states would honor one another's notes. Speaking in support of the resolution, South Carolinian Christopher G. Memminger revealed the ambiguity of the emerging Southern position. Blaming the tariff and the United States Bank as the twin instruments of Northern economic oppression, Memminger urged his fellow Southerners to invest their capital at home. The implication was that the instruments of commerce were not intrinsically evil. Rather, Southerners, by taking an interest in the advancement of commerce in their own section, might more equitably compete with the North under the existing economic system. To foster commerce, Memminger proposed that parents encourage their sons to enter business, that banks make liberal loans to merchants, and that planters make every effort to deal with Southern mercantile enterprises.[9]

The spirit of this convention, then, was one of sectionalism, of commercial competition with the North on the North's terms, rather than one of Southern nationalism, of disassociation from the North on irreconcilable terms. That this was the prevailing sentiment can be seen most clearly in the banquet toasts proposed on the last day of the convention. "To our country—The whole must prosper when every part takes care of itself," went one. "To the Northern States—Let us show that in honorable enterprise brothers may compete and be brothers still," went another. A third, more sectional toast was offered by McDuffie: to "the Southern and Southwestern States—United in their commercial and political destiny; united they stand, divided they fall."[10]

At least one Southerner saw in McDuffie's toast a potential for discord. Acknowledging that McDuffie's intention was probably harmless, he stated that such rhetoric was "like talk-

9. U. B. Phillips, "Robert Young Hayne," *Dictionary of American Biography* 8: 456–58; Sydnor, *Southern Sectionalism*, p. 269; Van Deusen, *Ante-Bellum Conventions*, p. 16; Wender, *Southern Commercial Conventions*, pp. 22–23.
10. Wender, *Southern Commercial Conventions*, p. 21.

ing to a friend with a bowie knife in your hand just to trim your nails,—it looks ugly, if you don't mean anything by it." In general, however, optimism prevailed and the convention adjourned, determined to reassemble in Augusta in October.[11]

During the summer of 1838 Virginia held its own direct trade convention in Richmond. Though a few North Carolinians were also present, the affair was conducted by Virginians for Virginia. Parochial in nature, the convention was politically divided. An able report, drafted by Francis Mallory but voted down by his political enemies in the convention, was later given wide circulation in pamphlet form. The report reiterated the call made earlier for doing business with home merchants. Yet, because of the internal squabbling in Virginia, Mallory's pamphlet probably made a greater impact outside the Old Dominion.[12]

In October the commercial convention reassembled as scheduled in Augusta. Conspicuously absent were delegates from North Carolina and Virginia. The price of cotton had begun to plummet, perhaps explaining the presence of representatives from Mississippi for the first time. The convention passed a series of resolutions that, though echoing earlier resolves, contained a strikingly new feature. Perhaps encouraged by convention president Gadsden, the committee on resolutions called for the construction of a railroad linking the seaboard with the interior. An additional resolution called upon the individual states to charter railroads with state bank funds. Hammond, a South Carolina delegate, was hesitant to augment the powers of his political foes in the Bank of South Carolina. He protested and the wording was modified as follows:

> . . . that the legislature of each Southern state be recommended to inquire whether there be or not, in each state, a sufficiency of

11. *Charleston Courier*, April 6, 1838.

12. Robert R. Russel, *Economic Aspects of Southern Sectionalism, 1840–1861* (Urbana: University of Illinois Press, 1932), pp. 20–21; *Richmond Enquirer*, June 22, June 26, 1838.

banking capital, and if found insufficient, to provide for its increase in such manner as may be deemed safest and most con-
ducive to the interest of Southern commerce.

Here, then, was a direct call for the states to assist in railroad
construction and a recognition that lack of adequate capital was
a serious problem. The states should step in to do what a planting economy, which was reinvesting surplus capital in land
and slaves, could not or would not do.[13]

On a note of unity, the convention adjourned, resolving to
meet again in Charleston in April 1839. Among the toasts offered at the farewell banquet was one to Northerners, "pioneers in enterprise, most honored when best imitated," and
one to "political and commercial independence—our fathers
fought for one—let their sons work for the other."[14]

The independent Virginians, meanwhile, reconvened in
Norfolk in November 1838. Once again the presence of outspoken agricultural spokesmen such as Edmund Ruffin made
harmony impossible. The result was a good deal of bickering
and several vague resolutions calling for increases of banking
capital.[15] It appeared that Virginia was not quite in step with
its Southern colleagues.

On April 15, 1839, the largest and last of the early conventions assembled in Charleston. Of the two hundred and
twenty delegates present, one hundred and seventy were from
South Carolina and thirty-three were from Georgia. The ex-
tent of the cotton depression—the price had dropped below
8 cents—was reflected in the presence of delegates from Alabama, Mississippi, and Tennessee. But the two seaboard
states, as before, dominated the proceedings.[16]

---

13. *Georgia Messenger*, October, 1838, quoted in Davis, "Ante Bellum Conventions," p. 163.

14. *Niles' Register* 54 (1838): 188, quoted in Wender, *Southern Commercial Conventions*, pp. 23–24; *Charleston Courier*, October 17, 1838.

15. *Richmond Enquirer*, June 19, November 23, 1838, quoted in Russel, *Economic Aspects*, p. 27.

16. Davis, "Ante Bellum Conventions," p. 164; Van Deusen, *Ante-Bellum
Conventions*, pp. 18–20.

Hayne again chaired the resolutions committee, and that group's report was highly significant. Much of the report, of course, represented what had by then become quite common Southern thinking. The committee's report pointed out "that the Southern and Southwestern States, while producing near three-fourths of the domestic exports of the Union, import scarcely one-tenth of the merchandise received in exchange for them." This imbalanced trade, "which derives its existence from the productions of our industry, and which is the unfailing source of so much wealth to others, is carried on by the citizens of other States, causing their cities to flourish, while ours have been falling into decay." Yet the report departed from the Nullification rhetoric to claim that Southerners, by the added burden of the tariff, were forced to "devote themselves *too exclusively* to agriculture." What was lacking was "that DIVERSITY IN THE PURSUITS OF THE PEOPLE," so that profits might be invested in something other than "land and negroes . . . the acquisition of more land and the production of more cotton."

Hayne recognized three needs for the South: capital, a home market, and steamships. To provide the necessary capital, Hayne proposed that planters "set apart a portion of their annual surplus and invest it in commerce." The legislatures might support this effort by authorizing co-partnerships, "by which means the opportunity is afforded to every one, of investing such portion of his capital as he may think proper . . . without incurring a risk of losing . . . more than the amount so invested." In addition, Hayne urged banks to extend credit more liberally and called for efforts to obtain foreign investment.

To encourage and then to satisfy a Southern home market, Hayne endorsed the existing "schemes of improvement, all having in view the extension and connection between . . . commercial cities and the inhabitants of the interior." The goal ought to be "ONE GRAND SYSTEM" of transportation, "which, like links in a common chain, may tend to bind together all of its parts."

Finally, capital once created should be used to build a line of steamers *"promptly* and *strenuously."* The ships would carry Southern goods both to the North and to the rest of the world and would terminate the South's dependence on Northern shippers. By following these guidelines, Hayne argued, commercial independence would be assured.[17]

The convention adopted a series of resolutions that embodied all of the report's proposals. In addition the delegates resolved "to adopt proper means for introducing commercial education among the youth of the South" and "to revive the 'Southern Review'," a periodical that had failed for want of subscribers, "and dedicate it to the defence and development of Southern institutions." The traditional closing dinner, lubricated by an abundance of spirits, bespoke the feeling of unity and success as toast after toast was drunk to the South, the North, and the United States; to free trade, steamboats, and railroads; to William Harper, the ladies of Charleston, and the Emperor of Russia; and to England, Prussia, and France. Thoroughly spent in their celebration of Southern prospects, the delegates departed Charleston with unbridled optimism.[18]

But nothing happened. It is impossible to attribute a single initiative to the commercial conventions. Those enterprises that had been undertaken earlier—canals, railroads, and turnpikes—proceeded at a more or less constant pace, but no grand new projects were ever attempted. Several years later a pensive Southerner, re-reading the Charleston proceedings, wistfully remarked that he "turned over their pages with great interest and marveled that a movement begun in such a spirit and prosecuted for a time with so much vigor, could have at last been suffered to die away, and pass, as it were, from memory."[19] The Charleston convention had decided to reassemble the following May at Macon, Georgia; the Norfolk convention planned a session for Raleigh, North Carolina, in November 1839. Neither convention ever met.

17. *DeBow's Review* 4 (1847): 341–56.
18. Wender, *Southern Commercial Conventions*, p. 42.
19. *DeBow's Review* 3 (1847): 558.

The vicissitudes of the Southern economy and the backgrounds of many of the convention delegates provide clues as to the reasons for both the rise and fall of the commercial convention movement. After 1838, as cotton prices started to collapse, the states of the southwest had begun to face the same choices that were confronting the seaboard: land and slaves or commerce and diversification, Southern distinctiveness or Southern self-sufficiency. The men of the east who had first raised the questions and stimulated the convention movement were mostly city dwellers with a personal economic stake in the development of Southern commerce. Economic conditions throughout the South were forcing a reexamination of profits and prospects, and the urgings of men like Dearing and Hayne, expressed in sectionalist rhetoric, made the questions even more compelling. It was not surprising that as the entire region reached the economic crossroads drawn by the spreading depression of the 1830's, more and more states joined the convention movement.

Yet the conventions produced nothing, and the explanation was planter resistance. Confronted by hard economic choices, the planter found the impulse to Southern distinctiveness stronger than the idea of diversification. To build railroads, to encourage commerce, even to contemplate manufacturing, was to copy the "Yankee," the epitome of everything evil, grasping, and non-Southern. The Yankee, an editor wrote,

> . . . would kiss a queen till he raised a blister,
> With his arm around her neck and his felt hat on,
> Would address the king with the title of mister,
> And ask him the price of the throne he sat on.[20]

Indeed, wrote a Georgian, "the strength and durability of the Southern States [dwells] in the planters of the country. . . ."

20. Quoted in Weymouth T. Jordan, *Rebels in the Making: Planters' Conventions and Southern Propaganda*, no. 7, *Confederate Centennial Studies*, ed. William Stanley Hoole (Tuscaloosa: Confederate Publishing Co., 1958), p. 21. This is a brilliant book on an interesting and neglected subject.

They were "the true conservatives"—the pillars on which rested the South's "prosperity and perpetuity." Pragmatic planters readily recognized how hollow the resolutions adopted by the commercial conventions were. When the Augusta convention urged Southerners "not to freight Northern vessels when they can freight Southern, unless the Northern are the cheapest," a Richmond commentator was reminded of the oath Neptune demanded of sailors crossing the equator: "never to eat brown bread when one could get white, unless he preferred brown. . . ."[21]

The convention proclamations were not only viewed by planters as emptily rhetorical; they were also either incorrect or intrinsically unrealistic. Take, for example, the Hayne report. It claimed that the tariff forced Southerners to rely "too exclusively" on agriculture. In fact, commerce and manufacturing did not flourish in the South for very different reasons. The plantation economy, with its widely dispersed population, was to blame. The Southern home market, which Hayne hoped to stimulate, was inaccessible and probably too small to sustain large scale commodity output. The inadequacy of the rural market in turn prohibited both urbanization and industrialization. The Southern population was neither large enough nor dense enough to support Hayne's proposals.[22]

Moreover, in the midst of deepening depression, the planter was more concerned with recovery than with innovation, and the reason was clear: profits. The sinking price of cotton in 1839 does not tell the whole story about the state of the Southern economy. Maryland, Virginia, North Carolina, Kentucky, and Tennessee were not much affected by cotton prices. In 1839 they were the leading producers of grain in the

21. *Georgia Telegraph*, November 25, 1841; Wender, *Southern Commercial Conventions*, p. 25; *Southern Literary Messenger* 5 (1839): 3.
22. Eugene D. Genovese, *The Political Economy of Slavery: Studies in the Economy and Society of the Slave South* (New York: Vintage Books, paperback ed., 1967), pp. 167–72. Fogel and Engerman, *Time on the Cross* 1: 250–57, takes statistical issue on this point with Genovese. These authors tend to underemphasize the accessibility of the market.

South, and the prices of these crops showed nothing like the kind of drop experienced by cotton. These states had completed their transitional phase and were making money. From South Carolina westward, the cotton states were indeed undergoing hardship, but the psychological attractiveness of plantation life combined with the memory of recent good fortune to produce a response not toward diversification but away from it.[23]

As the full force of the cotton plunge struck the lower South, the interest in commercial conventions evaporated. South Carolina and Georgia had been in transition, but now their link with the cotton kingdom became inextricable. In the summer of 1839 two bankers, John G. Gamble of Florida and James Hamilton, Jr., of South Carolina, composed a circular calling a convention of Southern cotton planters to meet in Macon in October 1839. The signers of the circular represented every state in the lower South. The Macon convention proposed that planters deal with only one London merchant house and that banks advance cash to planters at the high rate of 12½ cents per pound of cotton. Southern businessmen, to whom the financially oppressed planters were indebted, vigorously opposed the platform, and bankers noting the desperation of the gathering immediately began calling in loans.[24]

The Macon convention seemed to confirm that the concerns of the planter ran counter to the concerns of the businessman. It helps explain why the commercial convention movement achieved so little; the impulses to Southern distinctiveness and Southern economic self-sufficiency were

23. Gray, *History of Agriculture* 2: 1042.
24. Weymouth T. Jordan, "Cotton Planters' Conventions in the Old South," *Journal of Southern History* 19 (1953): 322; Thomas P. Govan, "An Ante-Bellum Attempt to Regulate the Price and Supply of Cotton," *North Carolina Historical Review* 17 (1940): 306. The signers were N. A. Ware and J. J. Hughes of Mississippi, John G. Gamble and D. K. Dodge of Florida, Thomas E. Turtt, W. H. Pratt, J. L. Hunter, and Henry W. Hilliard of Alabama, D. P. Hillhouse and A. B. Davis of Georgia, Nathan McGehee of Louisiana, George McDuffie and James Hamilton, Jr., of South Carolina, and J. Branch of North Carolina.

apparently incompatible. Moreover, the Macon convention revealed that there was emerging among the planters of the deep South both an awareness of a shared economic plight and a renewed commitment to the soil. It was uncertain if the commercial convention movement was dead or merely dormant; but if planter opposition to the aims of the commercial conventions was not yet, in 1840, widespread or irrevocable, it was nonetheless powerful enough to demonstrate the apparent antagonism between the Southern man of agriculture and the man of commerce.

II

In 1839 a contributor to Richmond's *Southern Literary Messenger* voiced the disillusionment of Virginians when he characterized the commercial conventions as willing only "to resolve and re-resolve to meet again." He spoke with the wisdom of bitter experience. Preceding the struggle over Nullification, the agricultural depression of the 1820's had hit the Old Dominion especially hard. Staggering under burdens of the soil's declining relative productivity, deserted farms, and a depressed economy, Virginians during the 1820's had been forced to face questions avoided for two centuries and, as a consequence, began diversifying their one-crop economy. The attractiveness and high productivity of the western cotton lands in the 1820's and 1830's had, lamented a Virginian, enticed "our most hardy and energetic" citizens away. "If there had been no western country," claimed another, "Virginia would already have reached a high state of agricultural improvement and prosperity." Virginia soil, by contrast with the cotton belt, seemed inferior since the value of its yield could not match that of the southwest. Careless agricultural practices had, of course, exhausted some of the soil, although recent studies have indicated that such complaints (the farmer, for example, who asserted, "Ask those who have gone, or are going West, why they have left, or intend to leave their native hills, and they will tell you 'the soil is worn out' ") were probably exaggerations. The movement of Southern agriculture westward was due more, as another recent study has shown, "to the increase in the demand for products whose relative advantage was on western rather than eastern soils" than to soil exhaustion. As late as 1859 the Old Dominion's exhausted soil continued yielding tobacco crops of sufficient size to maintain Virginia's position as the leading tobacco producing state, and the price of the "infernal weed," despite fluctuations, tended ever higher from 1820 to 1860.[25]

The problem, then, was not so much exhaustive agricultural practices as it was the danger of reliance on a single crop, tobacco, which influenced the economic well-being of every Virginian in some way. Of course, there had been earlier warnings issued by men who saw the inevitable result of tobacco farming. From Robert Beverley to John Taylor of Caroline, criticisms had been leveled at the evils of a one-crop economy. To Beverley, Virginians' reliance upon tobacco was a "Drudgery" and a "Disease," which indicated a tendency "aiming more at sudden Gain, than to form any regular Colony, or establish a Settlement in such a Manner, as to make it a lasting Happiness to the Country." Likewise Taylor assailed unscientific agriculture, proposing crop rotation, a shift away from tobacco to corn and wheat, and experimentation with fertilizers. In Taylor's famous collection of essays, *Arator*, published in 1818, he admonished that "agriculture must be a politician." Taylor opposed not an agricultural economy but a thriftless agricultural economy which weakened his native state.[26]

Young Edmund Ruffin, born in 1794, read Taylor eagerly, and—likewise a believer in the virtues of agriculture—determined to become the savior of his state and its way

25. Craven, *Soil Exhaustion*, pp. 91–121; Fogel and Engerman, *Time on the Cross* 1: 199; Gray, *History of Agriculture* 2: 765.
26. Robert Beverley, *The History and Present State of Virginia*, ed. Louis B. Wright (Charlottesville: University of Virginia Press, Dominion Books ed., 1968), pp. 70–71, 55; Gray, *History of Agriculture* 2: 801; John Taylor, *Arator* (Petersburg: Whitworth and Yancey, 1818), p. 19.

of life. It was not an easy task for the young, wealthy Virginian, whose sense of *noblesse oblige* typified the attitude of the Virginia gentry of an earlier generation. Ruffin later recalled that during the 1810's "there was scarcely a proprietor in my neighborhood . . . who did not desire to sell his land, and who was prevented only by the impossibility of finding a purchaser, unless at half of the then very low estimated value. All wished to sell, none to buy." At first he, too, following Taylor's scientific farming suggestions, failed. Then, after experimenting with marl, or fossil shells, on the theory that "vegetable acids" affected soil productivity, Ruffin witnessed a miracle: his marled soil produced a larger corn crop than ever before. Happily astounded, Ruffin began to spread the word of his success. Before his county agricultural society in October 1818, he delivered a paper—later published in his pivotal, revolutionary *Essay on Calcareous Manures* in 1829—which called for new agricultural methods. Here was a man and an idea to be reckoned with.[27]

Yet few Virginians took Ruffin very seriously. His neighbors jeered at "Ruffin's Folly," and other farmers scoffed at the young upstart. In 1823 he began a four-year term in the Virginia Senate, but his constituents criticized his failure to advocate their interests and he lacked both oratorical ability and political tact. Frustrated by his treatment, he resigned his seat in 1826 and never again held public office. "It was not because I was devoid of ambition," he later wrote, but because "I had no talent for oratory" and was unwilling to pay "the necessary price for popularity." His ideas scorned and his ambitions thwarted, a dejected Edmund Ruffin resumed experimentation determined to advance his agricultural theories.[28]

From Shellbanks, Virginia, in 1833 Ruffin published the first issue of the *Farmer's Register*, a monthly journal dedicated at its founding to the cause of scientific agriculture. The first

27. Craven, *Edmund Ruffin*, pp. 52–56; Edmund Ruffin, *An Essay on Calcareous Manures*, ed. J. Carlyle Sitterson, John Harvard Library (Cambridge: Belknap Press of Harvard University Press, 1961), pp. vii–xxxv.
28. *Farmer's Register* 8 (1841): 609–10, quoted in Craven, *Edmund Ruffin*, pp. 58–59, 39–41.

volume of the *Register* carried an anonymous poem indicative of the state of Virginia agriculture:

> . . . Tillage Old Virginia knows,
> Which cheats with hope the husbandman who sows;
> . . . .
> With crops immense no barn here ever cracks;
> The wheat comes always badly from the stacks.
> The corn falls ever most immensely short
> Of vague conjecture and of false report. . . .

This poetaster recognized two needs for Virginia farmers: they must diversify their agricultural production and they must increase the yield from their soil so that barns would "crack" with large crops of corn and wheat. The farmer, not the soil, was to blame.[29]

In fact, the mournful verse from the *Register* was an inaccurate portrayal of the state of Virginia agriculture in 1833. By that time Virginia farmers were already well along in production of grain and their profits were increasing. Ruffin's purpose likely was not to bewail the present situation but to spur Virginians further along the path they had already chosen.

It was exceedingly difficult for the concerned Virginia farmer of the 1830's to stay removed from politics. Indeed, Ruffin concurred with Taylor that agriculture "must be a politician." For Ruffin, now wholly devoted to agricultural improvement, the temptation to mix politics and farming in the *Register*, for which he himself wrote nearly half the articles, was irresistible. Ruffin provided the Virginia farmer with a villain in the form of banks. As subscriptions to the journal waned during the early 1840's, Ruffin escalated his political rhetoric in an attempt to secure new patrons. Failing, he angrily suspended publication of the *Register* in 1842 and accepted an offer from Governor Hammond of South Carolina to make a detailed study of the soil and topography of the Palmetto State.[30]

In 1842 Ruffin was not a Southern nationalist. His year in

29. *Farmer's Register* 1 (1833): 551.
30. *Farmer's Register* 9 (1842): 163, 618; Craven, *Edmund Ruffin*, p. 79.

South Carolina, however, not only confirmed his belief that the South must improve itself agriculturally but also exposed him to some of the more ardent Carolina planter–secessionists. As he made the rounds with Hammond, talking farming and politics with the governor and the planters, Ruffin began to alter his thinking. He was becoming less of a Virginian and more of a Southerner. More important, he was coming to believe that an agricultural society could and should be independent as well. Admiring Hammond's attack on the Bank of South Carolina, laboring without stint among the receptive South Carolinians, reveling in the respect and deference shown him, Ruffin spent a joyful year preaching the gospel of marl.[31]

Ruffin returned to Virginia in 1843 with fond memories of his year in South Carolina, a new awareness of the common problems faced by Southern men of agriculture, and an abiding bitterness toward those who had ridiculed him in earlier years. He moved to a new plantation, appropriately named Marlbourne, in tidewater Virginia. As Ruffin again increased the productivity of his soil, the newly formed Virginia State Agricultural Society in 1845 named him its first president. Curtly declining the offer, Ruffin replied that "any compliments and honors offered" by the state that had for so long mistreated him were *"too late."*[32]

The bitter Virginian continued to follow events in South Carolina and correspond with his friend Hammond. Shortly after the Bluffton Movement, Ruffin wrote to Hammond that he supported Carolina's tariff resistance. Regretfully he added that "though part of our people would be as zealous and determined as yours, unfortunately we are divided. . . ." At the same time the budding Southern nationalist declared his "general dislike of all Yankees."[33]

31. Craven, *Edmund Ruffin*, pp. 81–82; William K. Scarborough, ed., *The Diary of Edmund Ruffin, Volume I, Toward Independence, October, 1856–April, 1861* (Baton Rouge: Louisiana State University Press, 1972), p. xix.
32. Craven, *Edmund Ruffin*, p. 88.
33. Edmund Ruffin to James H. Hammond, July 6, 1845, September 7, 1845, Hammond Papers.

Like the Virginia economy twenty years earlier, Edmund Ruffin's life was in transition. Changes now came rapidly. Some were tragic: his wife died in 1846. Some were pleasant: he was invited to contribute a series of articles to a Richmond newspaper, a belated though genuine recognition of his importance. And some were of national significance. The Wilmot Proviso, introduced in the Congress in 1846, urged the prohibition of slavery in all newly acquired territories. Alerted by Hammond and his other South Carolina friends to this new threat from the general government, Ruffin feared that the South was declining in infuence and threatened from without. The South needed a savior and a spokesman. If it would but listen, Ruffin was ready to lead.[34]

Bursting into print with the zeal of an evangelist, Ruffin began attacking the North and calling for a Southern nation. In the *Richmond Enquirer* and the *Charleston Mercury* he repeatedly advised the dissolution of the Union and the formation of a Southern Confederacy. Why was a Southern nation necessary? First, because the North threatened to abolish slavery. This threat caused Ruffin to reconsider the justifications for the peculiar institution. He added to the paternalistic arguments of Dew by turning to racism. A defense based on assumptions of class and hierarchy lacked the persuasive power of an argument that vividly described the consequences of abolition. If the South remained in the Union, Ruffin announced, it faced "the extinction of the white race" by "the brutal barbarism of the [emancipated] black."[35]

More important, though, Ruffin saw a Southern Confederacy as necessary to save the farmers of the region from the evil Northern manufacturing interests. A "separation from, and independence of, the present Union" was economically necessary to end the unfair system by which "hundreds of millions . . . have . . . been drawn from the South . . . to pamper the prosperity of the North." But more insidious still

34. Craven, *Edmund Ruffin*, pp. 107–109.
35. *Richmond Enquirer*, *passim*, quoted *ibid.*, pp. 112–13. The articles were reprinted in the *Mercury*.

were the "Yankee" influences upon Southern character and distinctiveness. Ruffin described the rules of free society:

> When the greatest possible amount of labor is thus obtained for the lowest amount of wages that can barely sustain life and strength for labor, there has been attained the most perfect and profitable condition of industrial operations for the class of capitalists and employers, and also the most rapid increase of general and national wealth.

In the South, on the other hand, where slavery "immeasurably exalted" every white man, society rested upon openness, generosity, and trust. So basic were these values that Ruffin thought they excused all the failings of his native region—even those against which he had earlier railed. He explained:

> I would not hesitate a moment to prefer the entire existing social, domestic, and industrial conditions of these slave-holding states, with all the now existing evils of indolence and waste, and generally exhausting tillage and declining fertility, to the entire conditions of any other country on the face of the globe.

"God forbid," he concluded, "that we should deem the accumulation of wealth" a "compensation for the loss or deterioration of the mental and moral qualities of Southern men" that the abolition of slavery would inevitably bring.

Beneath these statements lay a fear that Southerners, pursuing profits, might emulate Northerners. Ruffin had opposed commercial ventures as early as 1838, and by the late 1840's he was convinced not only that the South must cut loose from the nefarious Yankees, but also that a nation of farmers should be independent. He attacked the Virginia legislature for "squandering thousands, perhaps millions, for private interests and visionary schemes, and even jobs for selfish and predatory individual interests, under the specious but deceptious [sic] guise and name of public improvements. . . ." It was up to "the great agricultural community" to resist such activities while promoting "the great and noble object" of agriculture, preferably in a Southern nation. In Ruffin's mind there was no doubt that an agricultural South could be independent, for separate nationhood "would redound as much to the wealth, strength and political safety of the southern States, as the federal protective and bounty system has heretofore operated in opposite directions. . . ." The old Virginian was attempting to harness the twin impulses of Southern sectionalism. He had convinced himself; now he must convince the South.[36]

III

By 1845 Virginia and the upper South were well along the road to economic recovery. The prices of corn and wheat were beginning a steady climb, and even tobacco prices were rising. Per capita income, too, was increasing. The upper South, turning to grain, had renewed its commitment to both farming and slavery. The transition was complete and successful. It was no wonder that Ruffin so strongly believed that agriculture—at least as he knew it—could support an independent nation.[37]

Yet between 1841 and 1845 the cotton economy was in a state of collapse, and the price reached a low of 5½ cents in 1844. Railroad ventures, begun in the 1830's with such optimism, went bankrupt as loans came due. From Charleston the *Southern Quarterly Review* commented that "at no period of our history, from the year 1781, has a greater gloom been cast over the agricultural prospects of South Carolina, than at the present time." Calhoun acknowledged in 1844 after Bluffton that "cotton still continues to fall. . . . The effect will be ruinous in the South, and will rouse the feeling of the whole section."[38]

36. *Ibid.*; Edmund Ruffin, "The Political Economy of Slavery," in McKitrick, ed., *Slavery Defended*, p. 78; Edmund Ruffin, *Address to the Virginia State Agricultural Society* (Richmond: B. D. Barnard, 1853), pp. 1, 8; Edmund Ruffin, *Slavery and Free Labor Described and Compared* (n.p., n.d.), p. 16.

37. Gray, *History of Agriculture* 2: 1039–41; Fogel and Engerman, *Time on the Cross* 1: 248.

38. *Southern Quarterly Review* 8 (1845): 118; Calhoun to Thomas C. Clemson, December 27, 1844, *Calhoun Correspondence*, p. 635; Russel, *Economic Aspects*, p. 34.

The prediction was on the mark. The situation called for action, and the call came most loudly from the planting west. Perhaps agriculture needed an industrial complement. *"We must go to work,"* wrote a Mississippian. "We must establish every description of manufacturing & of the mechanic arts that we possibly can. We must have better highways, have turnpikes, railroads, & canals." South Carolinian William Gregg, probably the most successful cotton manufacturer in the South, published in 1844 a number of articles under the general title *Essays on Domestic Industry*. The articles were reissued in pamphlet form and appeared in many newspapers in Alabama and Georgia. Gregg called for the creation of joint stock companies to construct factories in the South.[39]

But the final spur to action came when a Captain Bingham of Arkansas presented to a committee of Memphis citizens a proposal to build a plank road to the Indian territory. The commitee held a public meeting on the plan and so enthusiastic were the Tennesseans on the subject of internal improvements that they called a convention to meet in Memphis in November 1845. Calhoun and Henry Clay were extended special invitations. At last, perhaps, the South would act.[40]

The Memphis convention bore some resemblance to its predecessors in Augusta and Charleston, though it was not a sectional gathering. Delegates came from the growing non-slaveholding states of Ohio, Indiana, Illinois, and Iowa Territory, as well as from Pennsylvania. The leaders of the convention were men of mature age who mostly lacked politicaal experience. Virtually all of the delegates who can be identified were lawyers, and many were merchants and businessmen as well. A decided minority were farmers and planters. And of the entire group of leaders, only five—Calhoun, C. C. Clay of Alabama, A. C. Dodge of Iowa Territory, J. C. Jones of Tennessee, and James Guthrie of Kentucky—held or would hold

39. William M. Rives to John A. Quitman, August 18, 1844, J. F. H. Claiborne Papers, Mississippi Department of Archives and History; Russel, *Economic Aspects*, p. 40; Broadus Mitchell, *William Gregg, Factory Master of the Old South* ((Chapel Hill: University of North Carolina Press, 1928), pp. 16–18.
40. Van Deusen, *Ante-Bellum Conventions*, p. 21.

national political office. Henry Clay declined the invitation. A few others were members of state legislatures, but on the whole, the leadership at Memphis was in middle age and non-political.[41] Clearly, the purposes of the convention were to be national and unifying.

Calhoun, aging but hoping for one more chance at the presidency, saw the convention as an ideal opportunity to present his views and enlarge his constituency. Hoping to forge a bond between South and West, Calhoun accepted the Memphis invitation and was elected its president.[42] Thus, the leading Southern sectionalist had a forum and control.

As the nearly six hundred delegates settled down, Cal-

41. I have consulted a large number of sources in compiling the information on the convention leadership at Memphis in 1845, including *Appletons' Cyclopaedia of American Biography; Dictionary of American Biography; The Biographical Directory of the American Congress, 1774–1971* (Washington: Government Printing Office, 1971); Thomas McAdory Owen, *History of Alabama and Dictionary of Alabama Biography* (Chicago: The S. J. Clarke Publishing Company, 1921), 4 vols.; Henry S. Marks, *Who Was Who in Alabama* (Huntsville: Strode Publishers, 1972); David Yancy Thomas, *Arkansas and Its People, A History, 1541–1930* (New York: American Historical Society, 1930), 4 vols; L. L. Knight, *A Standard History of Georgia and Georgians* (Chicago and New York: Lewis Publishing Co., 1917), 6 vols.; William J. Northen, *Men of Mark in Georgia,* reprint ed. (Spartanburg, S.C.: Reprint Co., 1974), 7 vols.; John M. Palmer, ed., *The Bench and Bar of Illinois* (Chicago: Lewis Publishing Co., 1899), 2 vols.; Edward H. Stiles, *Recollections and Sketches of Notable Lawyers and Public Men of Iowa* (Des Moines: Homestead Publishing Co., 1916); William B. Allen, *A History of Kentucky* (Louisville: Bradley and Gilbert, 1872); *The Biographical Cyclopedia of Representative Men of Maryland and the District of Columbia* (Baltimore: National Biographical Publishing Company, 1879); Dunbar Rowland, *Courts, Judges, and Lawyers of Mississippi, 1798–1935* (Jackson: Hederman Brothers, 1935); *The Biographical Encyclopedia of Pennsylvanians of the Nineteenth Century* (Philadelphia: Galaxy Publishing Co., 1874); John A. May and Joan R. Faunt, *South Carolina Secedes* (Columbia: University of South Caroline Press, 1960); Emily B. Reynolds and Joan R. Faunt, *Biographical Directory of the Senate of South Carolina, 1776–1964* (Columbia: South Carolina Archives Dept., 1964); Chalmers Davidson, *The Last Foray: The South Carolina Planters of 1860* (Columbia: University of South Carolina Press, 1971); Will T. Hale and Dixon L. Merritt, *A History of Tennessee and Tennesseans* (Chicago and New York: Lewis Publishing Co., 1913), 8 vols.; L. G. Tyler, *Encyclopedia of Virginia Biography* (New York: Lewis Publishing Co., 1915), 5 vols.

42. Coit, *John C. Calhoun*, pp. 416–18.

houn, taking charge, delivered the opening address. It was a temperate, relevant effort, interrupted repeatedly by applause and once by the eviction of an intoxicated delegate. The South Carolinian encouraged the convention to deliberate on three major topics: improvement of the Mississippi River, development of a transportation and communication link between the seaboard and the interior, and strengthening of the naval defenses along the Gulf Coast.

To the surprise—and dismay—of some of his listeners, Calhoun called upon the federal government to undertake improvements on the Mississippi. Referring to the river as an "inland sea," Calhoun equated its defense and improvement with similar efforts already made on the Atlantic and Gulf coasts, the Chesapeake Bay, and the Great Lakes. He admitted that most improvements should be made by the individual states but pointed out that, since the various states lacked the resources to maintain the "inland sea," Congress was obligated to appropriate federal funds.

To foster economic growth, Calhoun stated the need for a railroad to link—not surprisingly—Memphis, Charleston, and New Orleans. Additional lines might then be built to form a great rail network. To placate the Northern delegates, Calhoun also supported the creation of a canal linking the Mississippi Valley with the Great Lakes.

Concluding, Calhoun envisioned the future of the South and West. "In less than one generation," he prophesied, "should the Union continue, and I hope it may be perpetual . . . you will . . . become the centre of commerce of the world, as well as that of our great Union, if we shall preserve our liberty and free institutions." On this somewhat ominous note, Calhoun took his seat.[43]

Immediately the interstate squabbling began, demonstrating the illusory nature of Southern unity on commercial matters. Every delegate had a pet project, and there was no procedure to determine the convention's priorities. The least

43. *Calhoun Works* 6: 284.

tributary of the "inland sea" had its advocate. One delegate later recalled that "there were those who would fain have played their oratory upon the rippling stream, which almost noiselessly wends its course by the side of their native village." To restore order, Calhoun had all proposals referred to a resolutions committee comprised of one delegate from each state.[44]

The committee, whose typical member was a middle-aged man of affairs, reported eighteen resolutions. Five concerned various aspects of Mississippi River improvements, such as the need for federal funds to deepen the river's mouth, construct levees, and remove obstacles. Five dealt with matters of Gulf defense, including the construction of lighthouses, a national armory, marine hospitals, and a dry dock. Three resolutions discussed railroads, urging that state legislatures act quickly to issue charters and provide funds and calling upon the general government "to consider the equity of granting the right of way and alternate sections, in aid of the works so situated." This was the same kind of proposal that Stephen A. Douglas and other Illinois railroad supporters would later advocate for the Illinois Central, and it would later serve as the precedent for the building of the Union Pacific. Additional resolutions called for a canal to the Lakes, the use of western waters to reinforce the Navy, improved mail service, and a national military road from Memphis westward. The resolutions were adopted with hardly any debate.[45]

Yet little happened as a result of the Memphis deliberations. Before adjournment Calhoun appointed a committee of five to present the resolutions to Congress and another committee of five to prepare a public address. The congressional response, generally, was to ignore or reject outright the Memphis petitions. Nor was there agreement among the Southern states on future cooperation. Louisianians feared the siphoning off of trade from New Orleans by an east–west railway. The

---

44. *DeBow's Review* 1 (1846): 10.

45. *Ibid.*, p. 17; Robert W. Johannsen, *Stephen A. Douglas* (New York: Oxford University Press, 1973), pp. 306–17; John F. Stover, *History of the Illinois Central Railroad* (New York: Macmillan Publishing Co., 1975), pp. 16–22.

western states were annoyed by the failure of Congress to act.
The purpose of the Memphis convention had been to consoli-
date a Southern–Western alliance on a program of economic
diversification through internal improvements. But the plan
failed.[46]

To many Southern nationalists the Memphis convention,
with its promises of diversification of the economy, seemed a
betrayal of the idea of Southern distinctiveness. Strong criticism of both Calhoun and the convention emanated from
South Carolina. The *Charleston Mercury* spoke for the Carolina
Southern nationalists in attacking Calhoun's conciliatory posture. The staunchly agricultural *Southern Quarterly Review* remarked acidly in Charleston: "The Mississippi River an inland
sea! . . . A sea is a sea and a river is a river, whether a long or a
short one, a broad or a narrow one. . . ." The *Review* claimed
that "we, of the South . . . are busy with our planting interests. . . . Let the Western States, then, depend on their own
irrepressible energies." Virginians had earlier broken off from
the commercial convention movement, and proving the Old
Dominion's relatively unchanged attitude was the fact that
only Iowa, Pennsylvania, Texas, and North Carolina sent
fewer delegates to Memphis. While Virginia newspapers and
Richmond's *Southern Literary Messenger* did give the convention
notice, they offered little encouragement or support.[47]

At the same time the seaboard was criticizing the southwest's contemplated withdrawal from agriculture, the northwest was turning its attentions eastward. By 1847, at a Chicago internal improvements convention, it was becoming clear
that Calhoun's efforts had failed. The political skills of Daniel
Webster, who played an active role in the Chicago affair, and
Stephen A Douglas, who arranged a similar northwestern
railroad convention for St. Louis in 1849, were binding the
northwest to the nonslaveholding states. The legacy of Mem-

46. Van Deusen, *Ante-Bellum Conventions*, p. 24.
47. *Charleston Mercury*, November 29, December 2, 1845; *Southern Quarterly
Review* 9 (1846): 267–68, 272; *Southern Literary Messenger* 11 (1845): 577.

phis was not Southern solidarity; it was Southern division and isolation.[48]

IV

Despite the collapse of Calhoun's grand scheme, a few Southerners still clung to the idea of a South united and self-sufficient through diversification. For one young South Carolinian, the Memphis convention of 1845 was a momentous experience. James Dunwoody Brownson DeBow of Charleston, aged twenty-five, believed he had found a cause at last. Reflecting upon Memphis, DeBow wrote dreamily of "the whole south and west" that "their destinies are one." He rejoiced to "see the Palmetto State and the time-honored Dominion, sending their sons to shake hands with the hearty pioneers of the distant Arkansas." As a result of the "beautiful commingling . . . on the high bluffs of the father of rivers," DeBow foresaw "happy union and cooperation . . . and when the south and the west are interested, we will ever feel that we are brothers all—all citizens of one GLORIOUS UNION!" Despite the inaccuracy of his observations, the young Carolinian set himself to the task of fulfilling the promise of Memphis. He moved to New Orleans and there established *DeBow's Review*, which proclaimed on its cover, "Commerce is King." An important career was about to begin.[49]

For J. D. B. DeBow nothing had come easily. Born in Charleston in 1820, DeBow was the son of a once prosperous merchant who had come South from his native New Jersey. James's father went bankrupt in 1825 and died a year later, and the young boy attended public schools on borrowed money while working part-time as a clerk in a Charleston wholesale grocery. When his mother died of the cholera in 1836, James soon afterward removed—now orphaned—to Greenville in the upcountry, where he began to work as a teacher. A voracious

48. Van Deusen, *Ante-Bellum Conventions*, pp. 25, 29–30.
49. *DeBow's Review* 1 (1846): 20–21.

reader, DeBow disliked "keeping school" for the "brats" of the Carolina hills. Trying to escape, he applied to Senator Calhoun for a position at West Point but was refused. So he decided to enter the Cokesbury Institute in Abbeville, where, according to a biographer, he "received a thorough training in the classics and even more exacting training behind the plow." After graduation in 1839 DeBow entered the College of Charleston, from which he received, as class valedictorian, his degree in 1843.[50]

In his early years DeBow was a rudderless, impoverished, and not very attractive young man. His hair was unkempt, his beard heavy, and he had a long nose and a protruding lower lip and chin. As poverty continued to haunt him in college the ugly student tried his hand at poetry and prose that exuded both amateurishness and bitterness. Recurrent themes in his compositions were the lamentation of his lot as a needy lad descended from undistinguished stock and the portrayal of himself as an enemy of "pomp and luxury and the friend of virtue." Trying to rise in the confining social and intellectual atmosphere of Charleston, DeBow read law for a year and was admitted to the bar in 1844. He published occasional essays in the *Southern Quarterly Review* and, as a result, in October 1845 was named by a Charleston convention to attend the Memphis meeting. That experience changed the course of his life, and he set about organizing his *Review* with ardor.[51]

At the outset, *DeBow's* reflected the sectional views of Calhoun, who advocated Southern solidarity as a means of strengthening the Union. Early numbers of the journal reiterated the theme. "We cherish Maine and Louisiana as sisters," DeBow wrote in 1847, rejoicing in the North's progress

50. Broadus Mitchell, "James Dunwoody Brownson DeBow," *Dictionary of American Biography* 5: 180–82; Skipper, *J. D. B. DeBow*, pp. 5–11; Diffee William Standard, "*DeBow's Review*, 1846–1880, A Magazine of Southern Opinion" (Ph.D. diss., University of North Carolina, 1970), pp. 10–13; Robert F. Durden, "J. D. B. DeBow: Convolutions of a Slavery Expansionist," *Journal of Southern History* 17 (1951): 441–61.

51. Skipper, *DeBow*, p. 10.

"in wealth, enterprise, population, intelligence, and resources.
. . . But let us," he warned, "imitate as well as admire. . . . It
is time that the South *should* be understood correctly, and as-
persions be forever silenced." DeBow was not, in 1847, a
Southern nationalist, although he distinctly perceived the existence of a "South" that was "distinguished from our Northern
confederates by peculiar domestic and civil institutions, which
are inseparably identified with our great staple productions.
. . ." For this reason, the South should carry on its own commerce and eschew dependence on Northern merchants, pa-
tronizing instead "those who have an interest in the preservation of our institutions, and who, in case of a political
convulsion, would seek no distant refuge or separate destiny."
The position, even the ominous speculation, was pure Calhoun.[52]

Unlike those Carolinians and Virginians, however, whose
paradigm of the ideal society lay in the maintenance of an agricultural system, DeBow's vision, personal as well as regional,
turned toward diversification. While agriculture might remain
the dominant form of livelihood in the South, DeBow called
for diversity of pursuits, for more railroads; in short, for *"action!* ACTION!! ACTION!!!—not in the rhetoric of Congress, but
in the busy hum of mechanism, and in the thrifty operations of
the hammer and the anvil." If the South would "construct its
railroads, extend its commerce, build up its manufactures,
protect its arts, endow its universities and colleges, provide its
schools," then it might "increase its strength and weight in this
Union."[53]

DeBow was a staunch defender of slavery. During the
early years of the *Review*, DeBow published the essays of Dew,
Hammond, and Harper. From the outset, however, he wore
their borrowed ideas about the patriarchal basis of slavery with
a difference. His own view was that slavery had reached its
natural geographical limits. It need not, however, expire be-

52. *DeBow's Review* 4 (1847): 210–11, 219.
53. *Ibid.* 9 (1850): 120; 13 (1852): 571; 4 (1847): 211.

cause it was contained, since he believed that slavery and diversification were compatible. Southern blacks, "properly organized and directed, can be as effective as the ignorant and miserable operatives of Great Britain." Slaves might be readily employed in railroad construction work as well. Indeed, slavery promised "much clear gain to the wealth of the country."[54]

The *Review* was not well received at first. Contributors were few and subscribers fewer. Nor was DeBow much aided by notices such as that in the *Jackson Mississippian* in July 1847, which criticized a recent article on railroads. *"We are not shown whereby the means to construct the roads are to be obtained,"* its editor complained. "It strikes us that this same lack of the most essential information characterizes all the reports, memorials, resolutions, and speeches, which we usually meet with in the South." By December 1848 DeBow's money had run out and publication was suspended. From South Carolina Hammond wrote to DeBow that "it is a disgrace to the South that it [the *Review*] should be allowed to fail."[55]

But DeBow was by now accustomed to hard times, and he set about obtaining new subscribers. More important, Maunsel White, a wealthy New Orleans sugar planter and merchant, lent money to the young editor and promised him more if needed. Working, eating, and sleeping in a single room provided by a New Orleans bookseller, DeBow resurrected his *Review* in July 1849 "upon a far better basis than ever, with an increased subscription list," as he reported in the first revived issue. Publication continued uninterrupted until the Civil War, though the fact that most issues had to be printed in New York or some other Northern city that had the proper facilities was a concealed source of embarrassment.[56]

The sectional crisis of 1850–51 aroused the young Louisianian to a more vocal expression of sectionalism. DeBow

54. Skipper, *DeBow*, p. 62; *DeBow's Review* 7 (1849): 289–97, 377, 490–501; 8 (1850): 232–43, 339–47; 10 (1851): 658–65; 12 (1852): 461; 13 (1852): 13–19.

55. *Jackson Mississippian*, July 30, 1847; James H. Hammond to J. D. B. DeBow, May 4, 1849, J. D. B. DeBow Papers, Duke University.

56. Skipper, *DeBow*, pp. 25–26; *DeBow's Review* 7 (1848): 101.

warned that "the agitation of this *slave question*" might well lead to "a *separate confederation*" of Southern states. Specifically, he proposed in 1851 a Southern convention to "lay down in distinct and unmistakable terms, what will constitute . . . a ground for *resistance*, or for the establishment, should necessity demand even that extreme, of a separate Confederation." He declared that "common interests and common dangers should unite us." In addition DeBow urged the assembling of a Southern mercantile convention and a Southern manufacturing convention. Finally he called for increased use of Southern watering spots, universities, and journals. Still he stopped short of actually endorsing Southern nationalism, and by 1852, when the crisis seemed to have passed, he had returned to his advocacy of emulating the North in order to compete with it in the Union.[57]

DeBow was always interested in statistics, which were a major feature of the *Review*. In 1852 he began an ambitious project by issuing the first of three volumes entitled *The Industrial Resources, Statistics, Etc. of the United States and More Particularly of the Southern and Western States*, a compendium of statistical data and articles from early numbers of the *Review*. The publication of *Industrial Resources* led, in 1853, to DeBow's being appointed superintendent of the seventh (1850) census— at a salary of $3,600 a year—by President Franklin Pierce. Although the data were already gathered, DeBow was to direct their organization and publication. The result was the most detailed and informative census that had heretofore been published.

While performing his census duties in Washington, DeBow for the first time was able to make an intensive, comparative study of economic statistics. He discovered that cotton was by far the country's primary export and that its lead was increasing over lumber, which ran a distant second. He noticed, too, that the price of cotton in 1850 had climbed back to 11.7 cents, that the prices of corn and wheat were rising ever

57. *DeBow's Review* 10 (1851): 161, 107–108; 13 (1852): 571.

higher, and that production of all three crops was increasing to meet the heavier and heavier demand. He found per capita income throughout the agricultural, slaveholding South rising at a higher average annual rate than in the North. Yet he saw that the North was outstripping the South in railroad building, that New York alone between 1840 and 1850, by building almost one thousand miles of railroads, had exceeded the progress made by all the slaveholding states combined. The fascinating, mind-expanding work took more than two years, during which DeBow earned a reputation as "perhaps the most eminent statistician" in the country. When the time came for him to resume his editorial duties in mid–1855, the man—and his journal—had changed.[58]

DeBow returned to New Orleans famous and—because of his government salary, which was a sum far in excess of any income he had previously earned—financially secure. He was now also a champion of agriculture. In 1855 he launched *DeBow's Agricultural Journal* as a complement to the *Review*. Though the *Journal* had a short life span, its contributors began to turn up in the pages of the *Review*. Edmund Ruffin became a regular, and more and more articles on agriculture found their way into a journal that once proclaimed the superiority of commerce. In 1856 DeBow purchased two farms in Mississippi and became, for the first time, a slaveholder. At the same time the *Review* stopped supporting federal promotion of internal improvements.[59]

But, most important, from 1855 on the parvenu editor and novice planter was an unrelenting champion of separate Southern nationhood. He called for a "hearth and home party" to support and defend Southern rights and institutions. Setting the example, DeBow presented his vision of the necessity and prospects of a Southern nation. The South's devotion to the Union was "the result of Revolutionary struggles" which

58. Skipper, *DeBow*, pp. 69–80; Taylor, *The Transportation Revolution*, pp. 71, 189; Gray, *History of Agriculture* 2: 1027; Fogel and Engerman, *Time on the Cross* 1: 248.
59. Skipper, *DeBow*, pp. 79, 115.

produced a Constitution of "fundamental purity." But the antislavery Republican party threatened "the existence of the South as an inhabitable, productive region" by an "unlawful and tyranical purpose, . . . slavery extinction." The abolition of slavery would cause

> . . . a degradation greater than has ever yet fallen to the lot of a free and enlightened people, and one from which they could not escape, but by fleeing the homes of themselves and their ancestors, and by abandoning their country to its former slaves, to become the permanent home of disorder, anarchy, poverty, misery, and ruin.

The beginning slaveholder knew "poverty, misery, and ruin" well enough and wanted no part of it.

The South possessed both "rights more to be valued . . . than any . . . sentiments about Union" and "resources . . . sufficient . . . to establish a separate confederation. . . ." The South boasted unity through its "homogeneity in pursuits, tastes, inclinations, manners, modes of life. . . ." And because Northerners—not merely Republicans—"in their pulpits, in their press, at their hustings, in their parlors and schools, on their streets, in their legislative halls, on the floors of Congress, menace us with insurrection and civil war," it was time for the South to demand its rights: "the right of regulating [its] own affairs" and "the right of expansion and development . . . under due protection of law." And, failing, it should dissolve the Union.[60]

DeBow believed reconciliation was impossible. "Let the South assume her stand among the nations," he cried. He endorsed the forming of state rights associations in Southern counties to agitate for secession and welcomed contributions from Southern nationalists in the *Review*. The Louisianian also had specific ideas. He supported expansion into the Caribbean and the reopening of the slave trade; he condemned universal suffrage and government by simple majority; he called for

60. "The Rights, Duties, and Remedies of the South," *DeBow's Review* 23 (1857): 225–38.

Southern books and Southern publishers, for a Southern university, and even for a Southern language, which Northern
emphasis on phonetic pronounciation threatened to destroy.
These sentiments laced DeBow's speeches and articles on secession, which was now an all-consuming cause. Because of his
efforts, the idea of a Southern nation was receiving greater attention. DeBow had longed for a better life. He had achieved
it. And he became one of its most vigorous defenders. Now
wealthy and prominent, DeBow gave the idea of a Southern
nation new respectability.[61]

V

Meanwhile, the commercial conventions continued to meet
through the 1850's. These sessions, like DeBow, underwent a
change in outlook. The conventions that met irregularly between 1845 and 1853 were at first devoted almost exclusively
to railroads. Southern railroad conventions met in 1849 at
Memphis and in 1851 at New Orleans.[62] Both were dominated
by representatives from the southwest, and each was called to
agitate for constructuon of a trans-continental railway via a
southern route. In 1852 a group of Baltimore businessmen invited Southern delegates to a convention which turned out to
be little more than an advertising campaign for the advantages
of that city. The following year Memphis again held a convention, which reiterated earlier resolves for railroads, direct
trade, and economic diversification.[63]

These conventions, primarily economic in purpose, effected little in the way of economic diversity or regional unity.
While many Southerners were interested in railroads, there
was little agreement and much conflict over the routes such
vehicles of progress should take. Little Rock's *Arkansas Gazette*

61. Skipper, *DeBow*, pp. 114–15; Standard, *"DeBow's,"* pp. 127, 222; *DeBow's
Review* 25 (1858): 377.
62. In addition, national railroad conventions met in 1847 at Chicago and 1849
at St. Louis, to which a few Southern states sent a handful of delegates.
63. Davis, "Ante Bellum Conventions," pp. 170–78; Van Deusen, *Ante-Bellum
Conventions*, pp. 26–35; Wender, *Southern Commercial Conventions*, pp. 70–100.

insisted the proposed railway pass in its direction. New Orleans interests, ever wary, declared that "South Carolina has already insidiously extended her hand into the Tennessee Valley, and will shortly snatch from New Orleans all the trade of North Alabama and Tennessee. She is pushing the same grasping hands" to Kentucky and the Ohio. Charleston feared losing trade to Savannah; Richmond suspected the motives of Baltimore; Mobile demanded consideration. The conventions succeeded in stirring interest, at the same time inciting an intense rivalry.[64]

Exacerbating the growing tension was the lack of any real progress on a regional basis. No railroad was ever constructed with an eye toward Southern betterment. Though individual states inaugurated numerous projects, hardly any extended beyond the initiating state's borders. In 1860, to travel from Charleston to Philadelphia by rail one had to make eight different transfers. Only one rail line—and that one built with an endless variety of track gauges—linked east and west, Memphis and Charleston. It is no wonder that the lack of adequate, modern transportation facilities was a major cause of the defeat of the Confederacy.[65]

Nor is it any wonder that by 1852 businessmen and other interested Southerners were becoming disheartened about the value of the commercial conventions. An 1853 article in the *New Orleans Weekly Picayune*, published by F. A. Lumsden, an active delegate at Memphis in 1845, charged that "speeches and reports, however able and convincing, produce no immediate influence on public affairs unless accompanied by active organization and strengthened by cordial cooperation and followed by continuous effort."[66] Even DeBow acknowledged "that in practical results the Convention has fallen short of the

64. *Arkansas Gazette*, May 3, 1850; *DeBow's Review* 10 (1851): 465; 12 (1852): 315; 14 (1853): 373–79.
65. Taylor, *The Transportation Revolution*, pp. 82, 86; Clement Eaton, *A History of the Southern Confederacy* (New York: Macmillan Co., 1954), pp. 253–59. In addition, lines would not permit the cars of competitors to use their tracks.
66. *New Orleans Weekly Picayune*, June 13, 1853; Van Deusen, *Ante-Bellum Conventions*, pp. 43–44.

fond expectation and hopes of many. . . ." The more important Southern industrialists, men like William Gregg and J. R.
Anderson of Richmond's Tredegar Iron Works, had little to do
with the conventions after 1853, but worked quietly and pro-
ductively to build up their isolated operations. Anderson's efforts in addition to the iron works were limited to occasional
fairs held in conjunction with the Virginia Agricultural Society. Gregg helped organize the South Carolina Institute for the
encouragement of mechanic arts in 1849, favored a high tariff,
and opposed the haphazard railroad schemes of the state legislature. Although both had supported secession in 1860, neither
had agitated for it.[67]

While efforts at diversifying the Southern economy were
coming to naught, Southern agriculture was entering another
boom period, which seemed to occur just often enough to
make agriculture irresistibly attractive. The price of upper
South corn and wheat steadily increased and reached record
heights. After dropping to 7.4 cents in 1851, cotton began a
steady, sustained rise in price. Between 1850 and 1859, production doubled while the price remained stable and ever so
slowly increased. There was no problem of glutting the market. The challenge was, rather, improving production to keep
profits high. Planters strove with considerable success for
greater efficiency. Per capita income in the South by 1860 was
fifty percent higher than in 1840. The Southern planter was
making money.[68]

Attracted by the prospect of profit and beguiled by the
image of plantation life, Southerners turned even more than
formerly toward agriculture and rejected further efforts to diversify their economy. "I do not care for the general introduc-

67. Kathleen Bruce, *Virginia Iron Manufacture in the Slave Era* (New York: The
Century Co., 1931), pp. 259–334; Charles B. Dew, *Ironmaker to the Confederacy: Joseph R. Anderson and the Tredegar Iron Works* (New Haven: Yale University Press, 1966), Mitchell, *William Gregg*, pp. 164–82; *DeBow's Review* 23
(1857): 232.
68. Gray, *History of Agriculture* 2: 1026–27, 1039; Fogel and Engerman, *Time
on the Cross* 1: 191–200.

tion of manufacturing into the South," wrote a Louisiana sugar planter in 1856. More to the point was a contributor to the *Southern Quarterly Review* in 1854. "If the dreams of the Southern commercial conventions should ever be realized," warned the writer, "the planter society would perish at once." Frustration with the failures of the convention combined with a resurgence of agricultural prosperity caused even Southern businessmen to lose interest in further moves for economic diversification. After all, some of the leading figures in the early commercial conventions—men like Ker Boyce and Daniel Pratt of Alabama—had always been both planters and industrialists. Now growing agricultural prosperity caused them to drop their pleas for industrializing the South and discountenance further commercial conventions.[69]

Nowhere was the growing strength of Southern agriculture more apparent than in the new militancy of the planters' conventions. For a number of years since 1839, cotton planters had been convening regularly to discuss means of upholding the price of their crop. These conventions, whose membership was at least as regular and ongoing as the membership of the commercial bodies, encouraged establishment of country agricultural societies and generally provided for planters what the commercial conventions provided for merchants and businessmen—an opportunity to meet, chat, and plan ways of mutual progress.

In the early 1850's the concerns of the planters' conventions became more than merely economic. In 1852, after the sectional crisis over the 1850 Compromise, the convention met in Macon in order to "unite and combine the energies of the slave-holding States; . . . to establish and fortify a public opinion within our own borders in antagonism to that without. . . ." Before the 1853 session in Montgomery, the official organ of the convention, the *Soil of the South*, launched a series of attacks against "abolitionism, with all its sanctimonious

69. Genovese, *Political Economy of Slavery*, p. 182; *Southern Quarterly Review* 26 (1854): 431.

ravings and appeals. . . ." The North "misrepresented and abused" the South. The journal declared that it was time "to fortify ourselves against such faithlessness, by providing for our own wants. . . ." A committee of correspondence planned the convention agenda, which included a discussion of Southern education and direct trade. At the convention the planters proposed new and specific measures such as "common school instruction" and "a great Southern Medical Association" as well as continued efforts to improve agriculture. Most important, however, a group of planters—mostly Alabamians—established the Agricultural Association of the Planting States, which planned to work to improve the "wealth, power, and dignity" of the South on a wide range of fronts, including science and education.[70]

If anyone doubted the Association's purpose, its well circulated proclamation in the fall of 1853 made it very clear:

> The Agricultural Association of the Planting States has, for its object, the diffusion of knowledge as it appertains to all branches of agriculture and of our peculiar institutions. We desire a closer bond of fellowship that we may develop our resources and be united as one man in our interests.
>
> It has been said that 'the world is against us.' Be it so. The world, we know, is dependent on us, and we glory in our position.[71]

Among the fifty-seven founders of the Association were a number of prominent men who played important roles in the South in the late 1850's: Senator Robert Toombs of Georgia and Yancey, both of whom would later lead the South out of the Union; former Governor H. W. Collier of Alabama, a strong opponent of the 1850 Compromise; and avowed secessionists such as M. A. Baldwin, W. M. Mason, George Goldthwaite, and Congressman S. W. Harris, all from Alabama, and J. A. Whetstone, a rabid fire-eater from Louisiana. Many

---

70. Jordan, *Rebels in the Making,* p.82; *American Cotton Planter* 1 (1853): 186; *Soil of the South* 2 (1852): 324–25; 3 (1853): 426–27, 497.
71. *American Cotton Planter* 1 (1853): 186–87, 275–76.

of these men were newcomers to the planters' conventions. Instrumental in organizing the Association was Dr. Noah B. Cloud, editor of the *American Cotton Planter* and long an advocate of Southern rights and scientific agriculture. Cloud viewed the Association as a means of achieving *"union among ourselves."*[72]

The planters' conventions and the commercial conventions were moving in the same direction. In 1853 at a meeting in Columbia, the planter delegates (one of whom was DeBow) echoed the call of the Memphis commercial convention for "education of . . . our youth at home." In 1854 the organizers of the Charleston commercial convention issued the following resolution:

> Whereas, the objects and aims of the Southern Agricultural Convention coincide with those of the Southern and South-western [i.e., the commercial] Convention; and whereas, also, the annual assemblage of each, in an independent organization, is attended with some inconvenience; therefore,
>
> *Resolved*, That the Southern Agricultural Convention be, and is hereby respectfully invited, upon such plan as may seem to that body most expedient, to unite with this convention as one body, in the promotion of Southern and South-western agriculture and commerce.

The offer was accepted, and from that time on a prominent and at times dominant element of the commercial conventions were the planters, many of them Association members.[73]

In fact, the Charleston convention of 1854—attended by leading Southerners of all persuasions—represented less a takeover from businessmen by planters than a takeover from both planters and businessmen by politicos and agitators, who turned the convention into a political forum. It was to be the last commercial convention for most of the businessmen but

72. Denman, *Secession Movement in Alabama*, pp. 16–17, 56–59, 92, 163.
73. Jordan, *Rebels in the Making*, pp. 86, 89; Craven, *Edmund Ruffin*, p. 160. This merger goes unnoticed in all previous accounts of the commercial conventions and receives only passing mention by Jordan. Its influence in the radicalization of the commercial conventions during the 1850's was probably decisive.

the first for the disaffected politicians and members of the radical Agricultural Association. Rhett and Gregg, Ruffin and Unionist Benjamin F. Perry—all were present. From that time on
the purpose of the commercial conventions changed.

Over the six-day meeting period, the convention passed
thirty-five resolutions. While twenty-seven dealt with matters
of commerce, eight appeared to be the work of the newer
members. Of these eight, six involved education. Southerners
were urged to send their children to Southern colleges, to establish normal schools, and to read books "by their own citizens, scholars, printers, and publishers." A seventh resolution
called for "each of the Southern States having a seaport, to
adopt the most efficient measures for the protection of the slave
property of each State, against abduction by sea or otherwise."
The final resolution made a contribution to the Calhoun Mon-
ument Fund. The convention then adjourned.[74]

At least one Southerner feared that the planters, in accepting the invitation to the Charleston convention, were
abandoning the ideal of Southern distinctiveness and were ca-
pitulating to the drive for Southern self-sufficiency through
diversification. The convention's performance was not an encouraging sign. A contributor to the *Southern Quarterly Review*
warned:

> Let every Southern man solemnly decide for himself whether
> our civilization is worth preserving; if he is satisfied with it, then
> let him act on the defensive, and resist the efforts of those who,
> dazzled by the splendors of the Northern civilization, would en-
> deavor to imitate it. . . . Nothing maintains slavery but the influ-
> ence extended upon it by the dominant class of the South. It is
> right because the ruling class declare it to be right. . . . Let the
> planter class feel itself inferior to the merchant and the manufac-
> turer and it will no longer dare to defend an institution con-
> demned by them.[75]

74. *DeBow's Review* 16 (1855): 632–41.
75. *Southern Quarterly Review* 26 (1854): 431. This attack on the Charleston proceedings, which is rebuffed by the *Quarterly*'s editor, is cited by Wender incor-
rectly as evidence of planter discontent with the conventions of the 1837–39
period. See Wender, *Southern Commercial Conventions*, pp. 45–47.

But the writer had little to worry about. Though the sessions continued with regularity, they avoided a choice between Southern distinctiveness and Southern self-sufficiency. Instead they covered over the antagonism between these two goals by arguing, more generally, for Southern nationalism. In 1855 the convention met at New Orleans, but only two hundred delegates attended and little of importance took place.[76] In 1856 a circular announcing the Savannah meeting proclaimed:

> It is impossible to resist the evidence that these Conventions . . . stimulated and deriving renewed activity from the insolent and aggressive spirit exhibited at times by the free States . . . have contributed largely to a consolidation of Southern sentiment, to a better understanding of our condition and necessities. . . .[77]

Almost one thousand delegates from ten states, mostly from Virginia and Georgia, answered the summons. Lawyers and planters again constituted the leadership. Meeting after a bitter presidential election campaign, in which the antislavery Republican party had run extremely well, and fearing the outcome of civil strife now raging between slaveholders and non-slaveholders in Kansas, the convention passed thirty-nine resolutions. At least fifteen implied, if they did not openly avow, Southern nationalism. In addition to the ritual calls for direct trade and railroads, the convention asserted the South's "equal rights in the Territories," called again for home publishers and education, and encouraged investigation of the reopening of the African slave trade.[78]

VI

The slave trade resolution suggested that by 1856 Southern nationalism was the major concern of the commercial–planters' conventions. Reopening the slave trade obviously appealed to

76. Van Deusen, *Ante-Bellum Conventions*, pp. 49–52; Wender, *Southern Commercial Conventions*, p. 148.

77. *Southern Convention, At Savannah, Georgia* (n.p., 1856), p. 2.

78. *DeBow's Review* 22 (1857): 81–105, 216–24, 307–18.

advocates of Southern distinctiveness, for extending the peculiar institution would make the South even more unlike the rest
of the United States. The resolution also appealed to advocates
of Southern self-sufficiency, who believed that a larger,
cheaper labor force would permit economic independence
through diversification. DeBow, who always seemed to be
running with the current of Southern opinion, was a reliable
indicator. During the first six months of 1857, his *Review* welcomed George Fitzhugh, no friend of industry or the North, as
a regular contributor and ran articles on such subjects as "Agricultural Features of Virginia and North Carolina" by Ruffin,
"Management of a Southern Plantation," and "Agricultural
Associations and Universities." Alongside these new subjects
ran more typical *Review* articles on such topics as "Ocean
Steamers from New Orleans to France," "Louisiana and the
Texas Railroad," and "Will the Southern Cotton Planters Manufacture Their Own Cotton?"[79]

It appeared that the slave trade might be the issue on
which the advocates of distinctiveness and self-sufficiency
could find a common purpose. In many a Southern heart the
South's sustained agricultural prosperity during the 1850's encouraged a confidence bordering on arrogance and a belief in
the distinctive Southern economy's superiority. "Our Cotton
is the most wonderful talisman in the world," proclaimed a
member of the Agricultural Association in 1853. "By its power
we are transmuting whatever we choose into whatever we
want. . . ." Another immodestly declared, "The sun does not
shine on a land so teeming with God's choicest gifts, which He
has placed here for us, as He has placed us here for them. . . ."
Rising in the Senate in 1858, Hammond placed the capstone
on the argument with his famous, ringing pronouncement to
his Northern enemies: "No, you dare not make war on cotton.
No power on earth dares to make war upon it. Cotton *is*
king."[80]

79. *Ibid.*, pp. 38–44, 318–24, 387–402, 432–38, 462–79, 495–505.
80. *American Cotton Planter*, 2 (1854): 33–38, 222; *Congressional Globe*, 35 Cong.,
1 sess., p. 961.

To keep the king on the throne, to maintain and increase Southern distinctiveness, required the reopening of the slave trade. Leonidas Spratt, a nonslaveholding South Carolinian who had first raised the issue in 1853, argued that the time had come for Southerners, if they truly accepted slavery as a positive good, to prove their integrity and consistency by demanding reopening of the slave trade. Breaking with a longstanding Southern opposition to the trade, Spratt occupied new ground in foreseeing "the time . . . when we will boldly defend this system of emigration. . . . *It is time to think for ourselves.*" He predicted "a great destiny" for the distinctive, slaveholding "chosen people" of the South.[81]

Other Southerners soon indicated an interest in the Spratt proposal. The *Charleston Mercury*—long an organ of secession under Rhett, its editor—seconded Spratt's emphasis on Southern distinctiveness in 1854, calling the slave trade one of "those mysteries which, however repulsive to fastidious eyes, are yet, in the hands of God, the instruments of man's progress." Later the *New Orleans Delta*, echoing the belief that all white Southerners had a stake in slavery, averred that enabling more people to hold slaves would increase Southern distinctiveness. "We would reopen the African slave trade," it stated, "that every white man might have a chance to make himself owner of one or more negroes."[82]

81. *Charleston Southern Standard*, June 25, 1853, quoted in Takaki, *A Pro-Slavery Crusade*, p. 1. Other useful studies of this campaign are Barton J. Bernstein, "Southern Politics and Attempts to Reopen the African Slave Trade," *Journal of Negro History* 51 (1966): 16–32, which argues persuasively that political exigencies forced Southerners to back away from supporting reopening; Jack K. Williams, "The Southern Movement to Reopen the African Slave Trade, 1854–1860: A Factor in Secession," *The Proceedings of the South Carolina Historical Association* (1960), p. 23–31, which unintentionally shows that the slave trade was not a factor in secession; and Harvey Wish, "The Revival of the African Slave Trade in the United States," *Mississippi Valley Historical Review* 27 (1941): 569–88, which suggests but does not always develop fully the political implications of reopening.

82. *Charleston Mercury*, November 9, 1854; Wish, "Revival of the Slave Trade," p. 571.

The issue was equally appealing to those proponents of Southern self-sufficiency. Reopening would increase the size of the labor force. While land and capital were abundant, the price of slaves had soared during the 1850's. The longstanding ban on the trade was viewed by many Southerners as merely another artificial barrier the unfriendly government had erected to impede economic freedom. Though the ban, which took effect in 1808, had been enacted by Congress in conformity with a specific provision in the Constitution, many Southerners agreed with Yancey, who wanted the ban put "where the Constitution left it, to be governed by the law of supply and demand." Governor James Adams of South Caroline announced that "our true purpose is to diffuse the slave population" for different kinds of projects. "Give us more and cheap operatives," demanded a Tennessee editor, "and we would not only have the will, but be enabled to diversify our labor and improve our country." DeBow was even more specific, predicting that the importation of Africans would enable the South to make the internal improvements necessary for the attainment of economic independence.[83]

Although not all slave trade advocates were Southern nationalists, most Southern nationalists, hoping to unite the South, supported repeal of the trade ban in the mid-1850's. Spratt's proposal was "to render the South *sui Juris* upon the subject of domestic slavery . . . by demonstrating the fact that the Union is inconsistent with our objects." Yancey concurred, hoping that "in agitating the question . . . there would be one link more between Southern men—one link more snapped between Southern men and Northern men."[84]

There was a difference, however, among Southern nationalists over how far they should press their claims. While some believed reopening inexpedient at the moment, all con-

83. *DeBow's Review* 24 (1858): 586; 16 (1854): 612; 27 (1859): 364; Van Deusen, *Ante-Bellum Conventions*, pp. 56–57; Takaki, *A Pro-Slavery Crusade*, p. 41.
84. Leonidas Spratt to William Porcher Miles, February 12, 1859, William Porcher Miles Papers, Southern Historical Collection; *DeBow's Review* 24 (1858): 587.

tended that the congressional jurisdiction over the importation of Africans must end. The more prominent advocates, men like Quitman, Yancey, and Rhett, stopped short of endorsing immediate reopening. "I, sir, am not prepared to advocate the reopening of the slave trade," said a South Carolina congressman, "but I am prepared to advocate with all my mind and strength, the sweeping away from our statute-book of laws which stamp the people of my section as pirates, and put a stigma upon their institutions." These men had a coterie of younger, less prominent allies who desired to reopen the trade at once. The difference between those who favored the trade in principle and those who desired its actual reopening made unity tenuous.[85]

This distinction drove a wedge between the two groups who favored removing the ban. The rising young fire-eaters had a more urgent desire to reopen the trade immediately. Some appealed to purely economic instincts. "Remove the restrictions upon the Slave Trade, and where is there a poor man in the South who could not become a slaveholder?" asked one. Another claimed that failure to reopen would "put it out of the power of common farmers to purchase a negro" and would "make him an abolitionist at once." Others argued that to import more blacks would enable Southerners to compete for western territories and would increase their representation in Congress.

The older, more prominent leaders, however, stopped short. They were, of course, already established and secure themselves but, more important, they were beginning to reenter politics after a period of exile. Acutely sensitive to the mood of the electorate and wishing not to divide the Southern people, these men quickly realized the divisive nature of the slave trade issue. Thus, they backed away from reopening as inexpedient.[86]

85. Van Deusen, *Ante-Bellum Conventions*, p. 76; Wender, *Southern Commercial Conventions*, p. 187.
86. For a thorough discussion of the pros and cons of reopening, see Takaki, *A Pro-Slavery Crusade*, pp. 23–85.

Between 1856 and 1859 the battle over the slave trade was waged primarily on the floor of the commercial conventions. At Savannah in December 1856 the Southern nationalists were in general agreement as to the propriety of discussing the issue. At Knoxville in 1857 the planter–lawyer–politician delegates elected DeBow to preside. In his acceptance speech the Louisianian cried that the South was able "to exist without the Union and to maintain the rank of a first class power whenever it shall be deemed necessary to establish a separate confederation." The convention went on to call for repeal of Article Eight of the Webster–Ashburton Treaty, which required that the American Navy patrol the African coast to prevent slave trading.

At Montgomery in 1858, "every form and shape of political malcontent was there present, ready to assent in any project having for its end a dissolution of the Union . . . ," claimed one Montgomery editor. A Georgia editor remarked that "when the South gets ready to dissolve the Union, all she has to do is, to reassemble the Southern Commercial Convention which met at Montgomery." A group of delegates presented a resolution declaring that "slavery is right, and that being right there can be no wrong in the natural means to its formation," and, therefore, "that it is expedient and proper the foreign slave trade should be reopened . . ." The votes of upper South delegates narrowly defeated this resolution.[87]

As the conventions threatened to take more radical stands, upper South delegations began to shrink, so that by 1859 only the most hardened secessionists from the deep South bothered to attend. At Savannah as at Montgomery it had been the votes of upper South men that tabled all slave trade resolutions. When the convention assembled at Vicksburg in 1859, Maryland, Virginia, and North Carolina were unrepresented. As a result the convention resolved that the African slave trade should be reopened.[88]

87. Russel, *Economic Aspects*, p. 143; *DeBow's Review* 24 (1858): 491; Takaki, *A Pro-Slavery Crusade*, p. 153.
88. Takaki, *A Pro-Slavery Crusade*, pp. 152–53; Wender, *Southern Commercial Conventions*, p. 228.

It was a hollow triumph, for many Southerners by 1859 had drifted away from the slave trade issue. The first defector was Rhett, who early in 1857 perceived that the issue was too divisive and would retard progress toward secession. Virginian Roger A. Pryor, editor of the *Richmond South*, in 1858 declared that other and better reasons than the slave trade might be found for secession. In Alabama, Yancey, seeking election to the Senate in 1858, was warned by his advisors to retreat from the slave-trade issue. Until his death in 1858, Quitman continued to distinguish between the principle of removing the ban and the practice of reopening.[89]

The actions of the various states confirmed that the slave trade was not to be the pivotal issue for Southern resistance. The Louisiana Senate defeated a bill to import 2,500 African "apprentices" in 1858. The Mississippi Democratic party press claimed that the slave trade divided the South "when she has need to stand as one man in view of the darkening future which lies before her." The Alabama legislature voted down a resolution on reopening the trade, and the Georgia legislature refused to strike a prohibition of the trade from the state's constitution. The Texas gubernatorial campaign of 1859 was waged over the trade, and Sam Houston, who opposed reopening, won election. In short, the deep South largely concurred with the border states in opposing reopening of the African slave trade.[90]

To the end, however, both DeBow and Ruffin—exponents respectively of self-sufficiency and distinctiveness—persisted in their advocacy of the slave trade, lending their voices to a campaign that events were dooming to defeat. So closely tied were they to the extremist conventions, so divorced were they from the political exigencies of the time, that these two leading Southern economic spokesmen were unable to detect shifting Southern opinion during these years. After Vicksburg DeBow, now wholly caught up in the move-

89. White, *Robert Barnwell Rhett*, p. 140; *DeBow's Review* 24 (1858): 580–84; Claiborne, *Life and Correspondence of Quitman* 2: 231–35.
90. Bernstein, "Southern Politics," pp. 31–34.

ment, announced the forming of an African Labor Supply Association to propagandize for the slave trade. He voted for the Vicksburg resolutions and then rushed back to his *Review* to inform Southerners that the convention vote proved widespread Southern agreement on the advisability of reopening. Ruffin, too, long separated from politics, had not the ability to notice the contradiction between the impulses to self-sufficiency and distinctiveness.[91]

The Louisianian and the Virginian, an improbable pair, standing together though virtually alone, rejoiced when secession at last occurred in 1861, though the new nation's constitution forbade the slave trade. These men, who in their early years had yearned for distinction and a cause, were justifiably proud of their roles in effecting secession, though the underlying antagonism between their positions would form one of the central themes in Confederate history. Yet when the Southern government took shape, DeBow and Ruffin played insignificant roles. Though loyal Southerners, they proved too extreme for the moderate government organizing in 1861. In the cause of Southern nationalism they had done so much; for the Southern nation they would do little.[92]

91. Craven, *Edmund Ruffin*, p. 164; Skipper, *DeBow*, p. 93; Takaki, *A Pro-Slavery Crusade*, pp. 156–57; Wish, "Revival of the Slave Trade," p. 587; *De-Bow's Review* 25 (1858): 116; 27 (1859): 120–21.
92. Craven, *Edmund Ruffin*, pp. 235–44; Skipper, *DeBow*, pp. 140–50.

CHAPTER FOUR

A Southern Republic
of Letters

The quest for a national literature was one of the most significant movements in nineteenth-century American intellectual history. Inspired by repeated calls to develop an independent and peculiarly American literature, American writers took up their pens and began to follow instructions, writing about what they knew best, their own surroundings. In New York, James Fenimore Cooper produced exciting novels of frontier life. In Massachusetts, Nathaniel Hawthorne, Ralph Waldo Emerson, Henry David Thoreau, and Henry Wadsworth Longfellow set their tales in their familiar New England. In the South, John Pendleton Kennedy and William Gilmore Simms among others wrote historical, frequently sentimental romances of plantation days. In the Southwest, young humorists produced delightful stories of life in the backwoods. In the Northwest, James Hall and Henry Schoolcraft wrote tales of life in the Mississippi Valley. Regional journals were founded. Some, like the *Southern Literary Messenger*, the *North American Review*, and Cincinnati's *Western Monthly Magazine*, had relatively long lifespans. Others, launched with much optimistic fanfare, struggled for a time for adequate patronage and passed quietly from the scene.[1]

1. Spencer, *Quest for Nationality*, pp. 73–90; David Donald and Frederick A. Palmer, "Toward a Western Literature," *Mississippi Valley Historical Review* 35

Although all regions knew both success and failure in their literary endeavors, by the 1840's it was becoming clear that the Northeast, which was also emerging as the dominant region economically, was setting the nation's literary standards as well. Publishing houses and successful literary journals became centered in Boston, New York, and Philadelphia. These, in turn, issued and promoted primarily the work of Northern writers. Of course the best writers anywhere in the country, men such as Simms, Hall, and Schoolcraft, were assured an outlet in the prestigious and efficiently modern Yankee houses. Others, however, had to rely on the erratic presses and languishing journals of their own regions.[2]

The results were predictable. As Northeastern literature emerged as the American literature, more and more the voices from the hinterlands cried for regional literature and regional publishers, regional writers and regional journals. An Ohioan warned that "the people of the West will win scornful censure, unless they encourage, with pen and purse, and good will and good words, instrumentalities which are competent to individualize a Western literature." The *Richmond Enquirer* announced that "Southern men owe it to themselves to . . . support home literature. . . ."[3]

Offended by the tone of moral superiority that pervaded such Eastern works as James Russell Lowell's *Biglow Papers*, John Greenleaf Whittier's poetry, and Charles Sumner's oratory, Southerners mounted an intense and bitter literary coun-

---

(1948): 413–28 is a suggestive study of the tribulations of Western writers. It is reprinted without notes in David Donald, *Lincoln Reconsidered: Essays on the Civil War Era* (New York: Alfred A. Knopf, 1956), pp. 167–86. For a similar study on the South see Jay B. Hubbell, "Literary Nationalism in the Old South," *American Studies in Honor of William K. Boyd*, ed. David Kelly Jackson (Durham: Duke University Press, 1940), pp. 175–220.

2. Spencer, *Quest for Nationality*, pp. 143–50.

3. Donald and Palmer, "Toward a Western Literature," p. 419; *Richmond Enquirer*, June 19, 1854; Spencer, *Quest for Nationality*, pp. 264–66; Lewis Simpson, *The Man of Letters in New England and the South: Essays on the History of the Literary Vocation in America* (Baton Rouge: Louisiana State University Press, 1968), pp. 201–22.

teroffensive. "It is all important that we should write our own books," admonished George Fitzhugh. "It matters little who makes our shoes." A fearful Mississippian lamented that "at present all the Slave States are flooded with Yankee schoolbooks. . . ."[4]

Behind the Southern sectionalists' call for an indigenous literature lay a grave concern that an insidious "Yankeeness" was undermining the distinctively Southern way of life.[5] The result was a redoubled effort to emphasize those aspects of Southern life that distinguished the South from the rest of the country. Just as arguments that slavery was a socially useful institution became shrill assertions that the peculiar institution was the best system of labor, just as claims that the Southern agricultural way of life had distinctive merits became asseverations that the plantation economy was the best and most natural basis for society, so calls for a distinct Southern literature degenerated into increasingly shrill announcements of sectional superiority. In literature as in economics and race relations, Southern sectionalism soon became Southern nationalism.

I

"To be *national* in literature, one must needs be *sectional*," declared William Gilmore Simms, the antebellum South's leading novelist. "No one mind can fully or fairly illustrate the characteristics of any great country; and he who shall depict *one section* faithfully, has made his proper and sufficient contribution to the great work of *national* illustration." The great New England writer Hawthorne agreed, admitting that "New England is quite as large a lump of earth as my heart can really

---

4. *DeBow's Review* 23 (1857): 341; C. K. Marshall to S. A. Cartwright, October 23, 1854, Cartwright Family Papers, Louisiana State University, Baton Rouge.
5. Taylor, *Cavalier and Yankee* brilliantly discusses this idea for the states of the seaboard South.

take in."[6] Devotion to the nation stemmed from loyalties that were immediate and local.

After 1815, stimulated by widely held emotions best expressed in Channing's Harvard speech in 1818, Americans set about creating a national literature. There were but two rules, as Channing himself stated, by which literary nationalists should be guided. One was to emphasize those aspects of American life that were fresh and distinctive. The other was to break away from reliance on European—particularly English—models. "Let the American Scholar turn homeward," Channing urged, and "let our own rivers and mountains and valleys and forests be as holy in his fancy and bring to his mind as burning and rapid associations, as the classical regions." The South was a full partner in the enterprise. The *Southern Literary Messenger* in Richmond announced its intention of working toward "building up a character of our own. . . ." American literature was to be both distinctive and independent.[7]

Although the *Messenger* looked toward an American rather than a Southern "character," the years following the Nullification crisis witnessed the emergence of a dual purpose for American writers living in the South. On the one hand they were fervent disciples of American literary nationalism; on the other they were strong in the belief that a Southern sectional literature was a necessary component of the American national literature they envisioned. At least up to the late 1840's, the aims of Southern writers were compatible with the purposes of literary nationalists elsewhere in America.

One way in which American literary nationalism expressed itself in the South was in the founding of a number of regional periodicals. One student of Southern literature has

6. William Gilmore Simms, *The Wigwam and the Cabin* (New York: A. C. Armstrong and Son, Redfield ed., 1882), p. 4; Jay B. Hubbell, *The South in American Literature, 1607–1900* (Durham: Duke University Press, 1954), p. 450.
7. Channing, "Literary Independence," p. 4; *Southern Literary Messenger* 1 (1834): 2.

counted at least thirty such journals in the antebellum period with the word "Southern" in their title. For instance, the *Southern Review* was founded in 1828 by a group of leading Charlestonians who regretted "the state of mental dependence on our brethren of the East and North, in which we have so long contentedly remained." Among its contributors were Thomas Cooper and Hugh Swinton Legaré. Legaré undertook the magazine's direction "because of its epithet 'Southern,' which awakens in my mind the proudest, fondest, sweetest recollections." In 1835 the *Southern Literary Journal* appeared in Charleston hoping "to breathe a Southern spirit, and sustain a strictly Southern character."[8]

But the journals also made their nationalistic purposes quite clear. The *Southern Literary Messenger* "embarked on the cause of *Southern* literature . . . with perfect amity to all sections. . . ." The editor of *Orion* in Charleston eschewed the phrase "Southern literature," preferring to talk of "literature in the South." In the 1830's sectionalism and nationalism reinforced one another.[9]

Probably the most exuberant early advocate of a literature at once sectional and national was the South Carolinian Simms. From the outset of his long career, Simms was as much a Southerner as Hawthorne, Emerson, or Lowell were New Englanders, and his notion of a "South," though variously expressed, was the one constant of his turbulent and tragic life. His loyalties never changed.[10] In 1832 he opposed

8. Hubbell, "Literary Nationalism," p. 203; Robert Y. Hayne to Warren R. Davis, September 25, 1827, Robert Y. Hayne Papers, South Caroliniana Library; Frank Luther Mott, *A History of American Magazines*, 4 vols. (Cambridge: Harvard University Press, 1930–57), 1: 573–75; Hugh Swinton Legaré to J. B. Harrison, November 3, 1828, Legaré Papers, South Caroliniana Library; *Southern Literary Journal* 1 (1835): 58.

9. Spencer, *Quest for Nationality*, p. 269.

10. Jon L. Wakelyn, *The Politics of a Literary Man: William Gilmore Simms*, Contributions in American Studies, no. 5 (Westport, Conn.: Greenwood Press, 1973) is a useful biography that greatly improves upon William P. Trent, *William Gilmore Simms*, American Men of Letters Series, ed. Charles Dudley Warner (Boston: Houghton, Mifflin, and Co., 1892), though Wakelyn concen-

Nullification not because of a belief in the supremacy of the national government but because otherwise his state would "be run over by the U. States; her name & star place, blotted out, and her territory divided among the contiguous and more loyal states." In 1859 a friend accurately recited Simms's consistency: "—the consciousness of having been true to the Penates, of having illustrated, as none other has, the *genius loci*. . . ." First, last, and always, Simms was a Southerner.[11]

Simms's loyalty was deeply rooted. Born in Charleston in 1806, he was the son of a Scotch–Irish immigrant merchant who went bankrupt in 1807 and, after the death of his wife soon thereafter, removed to Mississippi to start life anew as a planter. Young William, meanwhile, was left in Charleston, in the care of a grandmother. In 1824 after a short, distasteful stint as a druggist's apprentice and a visit to his father's plantation, Simms was told by his father to decide between living in Mississippi or Charleston—the first of many geographical choices he would be forced to make during his lifetime. Answering that he wished to return to Charleston to take up the practice of law, young William was met with strong parental remonstrances—"Why should you return to Charleston, where you can never succeed in any profession, where you need what you have not, friends, family, and fortune?" Remaining insistent, however, he returned to a city whose inner social circle seldom had room for druggists who were sons of bankrupt immigrants.

Having freely chosen Charleston, Simms was ever after bound by the conservative tastes—literary and otherwise—of that most conservative of cities. Yet he found the atmosphere challenging rather than stifling and soon adapted to his sur-

---

trates more on Simms's political activities than on his fiction. John W. Higham, "The Changing Loyalties of William Gilmore Simms," *Journal of Southern History* 9 (1943): 210–23 remains helpful.

11. William Gilmore Simms to James Lawson, November 25, 1832, *The Letters of William Gilmore Simms*, ed. Mary C. Simms Oliphant et al., 5 vols. (Columbia: University of South Carolina Press, 1952–56), 1: 47; Paul Hamilton Hayne to Simms, January 14, 1859, quoted in Trent, *Simms*, pp. 16–17.

roundings. His love for South Carolina was strengthened as he studied law and was admitted to the bar. In 1828 Simms assisted in the publication of the *Southern Literary Gazette,* and in 1829 he took over the editorship.[12]

As early as 1828 Simms was a staunch American literary nationalist. In the *Gazette* he condemned imitation of European forms and lauded those American writers who had forsaken British models for local themes and characters. Simms advised his countrymen to study German literature in order both to sever the British connection and to discover how other nations developed their own literary traditions.[13]

But he was also a sectionalist. Southerners, Simms claimed, were "taunted by Englishmen and Northernmen" as intellectually inferior. Since a people's literature "depends upon their manners and civil institutions," Simms desired that the *Gazette* encourage Southern writers employing Southern themes, and he advocated the establishment of a publishing house in Charleston to make Southern literature truly independent. At the age of twenty-two, then, Simms was able to reconcile the conflicting demands of section and nation.[14]

Yet Simms's sectionalism had another side that developed only over a long period of time. During the Nullification crisis there first emerged the Cavalier–Yankee antithesis, which many Southerners adopted to explain their peculiar needs and distinctive traits. To most Southerners the epithet "Yankee" was derisive, meaning crude, brutal, unscrupulous, acquisitive, and demagogic. Young Simms employed the terminology but for a different purpose. To Simms "Yankeeness" meant adaptability, cleverness, and both economic and social advancement. In short, it meant the very qualities by which

12. Wakelyn, *Politics of a Literary Man,* pp. 3–18; Trent, *Simms,* p. 17.
13. John C. Guilds, Jr., "Simms's Views on National and Sectional Literature, 1825–1845," *North Carolina Historical Review* 34 (1957): 395, 399; C. Hugh Holman, *The Roots of Southern Writing* (Athens: University of Georgia Press, 1972), pp. 16–18, 23.
14. Guilds, "Simms's Views," p. 399; Wakelyn, *Politics of a Literary Man,* pp. 12–13.

Simms had gained a toehold in Charleston. He openly admired the Yankee:

> The Yankee is the man who first hung out the banner of liberty . . . and determined to be free. . . . It is his Genius which has contrived the great system of manufactures which however extravagant and unjust their demands upon us, we must nevertheless admire. . . .[15]

Simms's life soon endured a series of jolts. The *Gazette* collapsed financially in 1829. Simms then edited the *Charleston City Gazette*, through which he attacked the Nullifiers but affirmed his belief in states' rights. That paper failed in 1832. Not long after, within the span of a year, Simms's wife and grandmother both died. Alone but for a young daughter and virtually penniless, Simms left Charleston first for New York, where he became friends with the poet William Cullen Bryant, and then for New Haven, where he wrote his first novel, *Martin Faber*, a Gothic tale. In 1834 and 1835 he published *Guy Rivers*, a romance about the settlement of Georgia in the 1820's, *The Yemassee*, a novel dealing with a 1715 South Carolina Indian war, and *The Partisan*, the first of a series of romances on the Revolutionary War in the South.

Upon Simms's return to Charleston in 1835 better times followed. He remarried in 1836. His bride, Chevillette Roach, was the daughter of a wealthy planter whose palatial mansion, Woodlands, near the Savannah River in the upcountry became the Simms's new home. At Woodlands between 1836 and 1843 Simms continued to write romances and short stories. Many were set on the southwestern frontier, where the author's father had settled. *Richard Hurdis* dealt with the rough-and-tumble life in frontier Alabama; *Border Beagles* continued the story in Mississippi; and *Beauchampe*, set in Kentucky, was a sensational tale of murder, seduction, and unrequited love. But Simms continued his interest in South Carolina, writing *Melli-*

15. Quoted in Higham, "Changing Loyalties of Simms," p. 211.

champe and *The Scout*, which continued the story of the Revolution begun in *The Partisan*. [16]

Through all these books ran a common theme and an implicit warning. The theme was nationalism, illustrated most clearly in *Mellichampe*. Ernest Mellichampe is a young nobleman who quarrels with Thumbscrew Witherspoon, his yeoman scout, over the rightfulness of avenging the murder of Mellichampe's father. Mellichampe hotheadedly avers that "not to be quick when one is wronged is to invite injustice," to which Witherspoon replies tartly, "My idee is, that true fightin' is the part of a beast-brute, and not for a true-born man, that has a respect for himself and knows what's good-breeding." As the story unfolds, Mellichampe adopts Witherspoon's position and thereby comes to realize that the larger cause of the Revolution is more important than his personal desires. The warning—for impulsive abolitionists and Nullifiers alike—was clear enough. The ideal society of Revolutionary days was cooperative and orderly; the Yankee and the aristocrat were equally admirable, mutually dependent—like North and South—and were unable to succeed without one another. [17]

Into the 1840's Simms's sectionalism reinforced his intense American nationalism. In 1842 he wrote to George Frederick Holmes, the Virginia critic and educator, that he was "an ultra-American, a born Southron. . . ." Dividing his time equally between New York and Charleston, he was generally acknowledged to be the South's leading man of letters. Critics praised his efforts. In those heady days he allied himself with the Young America movement, a group of Democrats mostly in the North, whose platform included a call for a national literature. He had earlier edited the short-lived though critically acclaimed *Magnolia* magazine in Charleston in 1841–42 and

16. Wakelyn, *Politics of a Literary Man*, pp. 51–79.
17. William Gilmore Simms, *Mellichampe* (New York: Harper and Brothers, 1836), p. 34 *et passim*; J. V. Ridgely, *William Gilmore Simms* (New York: Twayne Publishers, 1962), pp. 72–73.

there published several essays on "Southern Literature," reiterating his belief that "the literature of a nation is, in plain
terms, the picture of its national character," and that a sectional literature was the best way to define that character. In
1845, while serving in the South Carolina legislature as a supporter of his neighbor, Governor Hammond, against Calhoun
and the state bank, Simms found time to publish *Views and
Reviews*, which contained essays extolling "Americanism in
Literature" and proclaiming the greatness of James Fenimore
Cooper. In addition he published a two-volume history of
South Carolina and reissued several volumes of poetry.
Throughout this incredibly sustained period of hard labor, the
theme of Southernness as Americanness persisted.[18]

In his novels—in a setting far removed from the present,
in a genre dependent upon the author's imagination—Simms
readily coped with the duality of sectionalism and nationalism.
In his essays, writing of an unknown future, he could easily
join these two elements in imagining the coming of a national
literature. Like other Southern writers who set their works in
either the distant past or the equally distant future, Simms
could vividly portray his vision of an ideal society. Forced,
however, to explore the present, the Southern writer had difficulty. Only once in his early years was Simms so forced, and
his response was portentous.

In 1837 the *Southern Literary Messenger* invited Simms to
review Harriet Martineau's travel saga, *Society in America*. Miss
Martineau was British and an abolitionist, and Simms's review, "Miss Martineau on Slavery," was both a strong defense
of a distinctive Southern civilization and a biting attack on ex-
ternal critics. He was annoyed that Miss Martineau spent most
of her essay on—and none of her traveling time in—South

18. Simms to George Frederick Holmes, November 18, 1844, *Simms Letters* 1:
442; Perry Miller, *The Raven and the Whale: The War of Words and Wit in the Era
of Poe and Melville* (New York: Harcourt, Brace, and Co., 1956), *passim*, but
esp. pp. 106, 108–109; Simms Letters 1: 207; *Magnolia* 4 (1842): 251; Wakelyn,
Politics of a Literary Man, pp. 86–87; Holman, *Roots of Southern Writing*, pp.
25–31.

John C. Calhoun
THE NATIONAL ARCHIVES

Defenders of Slavery

Thomas R. Dew
THE COLLEGE OF WILLIAM
AND MARY IN VIRGINIA

Robert Barnwell Rhett
LIBRARY OF CONGRESS

Josiah C. Nott

James Henry Hammond

*Economic
Spokesmen*

James D. B. DeBow

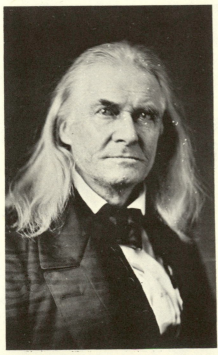

Edmund Ruffin

*Southern
Literary
Nationalists*

Nathaniel Beverly Tucker

William Gilmore Simms

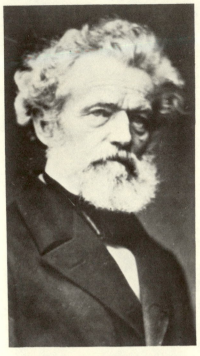

*Advocates
of Southern
Expansion*

John A. Quitman (*left*)
THE NATIONAL ARCHIVES
Pierre Soulé (*below left*)
LIBRARY OF CONGRESS
William Walker (*below right*)
LIBRARY OF CONGRESS

*Leaders
in Religion
and Education*

Bishop James O. Andrew (*right*)
LIBRARY OF CONGRESS
Bishop Leonidas Polk (*below left*)
THE NATIONAL ARCHIVES
George Frederick Holmes (*below right*)
DUKE UNIVERSITY LIBRARY

*Political
Antagonists
of the 1850s*

William Lowndes Yancey
ALABAMA DEPARTMENT
OF ARCHIVES AND HISTORY

Jefferson Davis
THE NATIONAL ARCHIVES

Carolina. He declared that the Negro was much better off in the South than in the North, and he claimed for his section a superior system of societal relationships. Simms also argued that because of the "immoral and animal and irresponsible" nature of the Negro, the slaveholders were "the great moral conservators, in one powerful interest, of the entire world." Finally he claimed that the agricultural system of the South was the basis of the nation's economic strength.

Yet in Simms's defense of slavery there were some striking admissions, which he did not expunge when the essay, revised, was republished in 1852 in *The Pro-Slavery Argument* anthology. He acknowledged Miss Martineau's references to "the abuses, among slaveholders, of the institution of slavery, . . . the illicit and foul conduct of some among us" as "full of truth." His explanation of this startling concession was that such unfortunate activities occurred on "the borders. They belong to that period in the history of society, when civilization sends forth her pioneer to tame the wilderness." By contrast, "your well-bred city gentleman"—perhaps Simms himself—"is no pioneer—he belongs to a better condition of things and to after times."

In his review Simms faced the difficult task of defending not only America from British slurs but also the South from abolitionist attacks. In 1837 it was still possible for Simms to defend slavery as an American institution, to criticize British outsiders for their condescending and divisive interference, and to rationalize the behavior of the frontier Southern slaveholder. At the same time, there was in Simms's review at least a hint of sectional defensiveness. Even while admitting that slavery was accompanied by abuses and brutality, he challenged Miss Martineau to prove that crime among white laborers in New York was less frequent than among Southerners. His was a difficult position to maintain.[19]

Simms's difficulty was not unique. Out of the Nullifica-

19. [William Gilmore Simms], "Miss Martineau on Slavery," *Southern Literary Messenger* 3 (1837): 641–57; cf. David Donald, "The Proslavery Argument Reconsidered," *Journal of Southern History* 37 (1971): 3–18.

tion turmoil there emerged other Southern writers who, like Simms, attempted to employ regional characters and themes. They too wrote of the plantation ideal and the Cavalier Southron—as well as the antithetical Yankee. Though these writers, like Simms, believed that a sectional literature would contribute to the creation of a national literature, they preferred to explore those aspects of Southern life that they believed to be unique.

Most of the writers who pursued the Cavalier–Yankee theme were Virginians, who watched with dismay the decline of their state's influence during the 1820's and early 1830's. They reflected the bitterness of such rising young political figures as William C. Preston who, on a trip to England in 1817, had declared himself not a Yankee but a Virginian. "To us you are all Yankees," was the reply, "rascals who cheat the whole world." Preston never forgot this insult, and when he returned to America he moved to South Carolina, where the gentleman planter seemed still to be flourishing and where democracy, which was sweeping Virginia, was still under control. Twenty years later on the floor of the United States Senate, Preston fearfully mourned "that the public mind is . . . active, and stirred up, and agitated beyond all former example." Another Virginian, no friend of democracy, deplored the prevalence in political discourse of "scurrilous epithets, impotent threats, and low abuse, such as men of decency and sense should scorn to use."[20] If Simms, in his exuberant nationalism, was the epitome of optimism, the Virginians viewed the tendencies of American life with gloom and foreboding.

Curiously, those writers who responded most strongly to the decline of the tidewater aristocracy were not members of the planter élite. William Alexander Carruthers was the son of a merchant; Philip Pendleton Cooke lived west of the Blue Ridge and his father had been a leading proponent of constitutional revision; and John Pendleton Kennedy was only nominally a Virginian. Yet these men were the creators of an endur-

20. Taylor, *Cavalier and Yankee*, pp. 47, 63–64.

ing literary tradition that many Southerners—and Northerners as well—readily accepted.[21]

The early career of Kennedy, the writer most responsible for fixing American attitudes toward the plantation, represented the problems these writers faced. Born in Baltimore in 1795, the son of an immigrant merchant of Scotch–Irish descent, Kennedy began law practice in his native city in 1816. As a young man he prescribed for himself a program of study on "how to become a gentleman before dawn." The young parvenu surely had himself in mind when he observed that "success depends so much upon present manners and tact in the affairs of life, and often, so little upon scholarship and acquirement." After the failure of several literary ventures, the death of his first wife, and the unpromising development of his law practice, Kennedy began to work on a novel. A second marriage, to the daughter of a successful textile manufacturer, occurred in 1829, providing him with financial security.[22]

Kennedy's first novel, *Swallow Barn*, appeared in 1832. It extolled a Virginia plantation modeled on a Shenandoah Valley farm that Kennedy's maternal ancestors once owned. Swallow Barn "is an aristocratical old edifice which sits, like a brooding hen, on the southern bank of the James River." The descriptive vocabulary for the mansion—"time-honored," "ancient," "aristocratical"—suggests Kennedy's own fascination with the past. The salutary effect of life at Swallow Barn is described by an enchanted narrator:

> There is a fascination in the quiet, irresponsible, and reckless nature of these country pursuits, that is apt to seize upon the imagi-

21. *Ibid.*, pp. 150, 165, 205–209; Francis Pendleton Gaines, *The Southern Plantation: A Study in the Development and Accuracy of a Tradition* (New York: Columbia University Press, 1924), pp. 18, 22.

22. Charles H. Bohner, *John Pendleton Kennedy: Gentleman from Baltimore* (Baltimore: Johns Hopkins University Press, 1961), pp. 1–71; Taylor, *Cavalier and Yankee*, pp. 188–90. See also J. V. Ridgely, John Pendleton Kennedy (New York: Twayne Publishers, 1966); Edward M. Gwathmey, *John Pendleton Kennedy* (New York: Thomas Nelson and Sons, 1931), pp. 11–56; and Mary Wilhelmina Williams, "John Pendleton Kennedy," *Dictionary of American Biography* 10: 333–34.

> nation of a man who had felt the perplexities of business. Ever since I have been at Swallow Barn, I have entertained a very philosophical longing for the calm and dignified retirement of the woods. . . . I only want a thousand acres of good land, an old manor-house, on a pleasant site, a hundred negroes, a large library, a host of friends, and a reserve of a few thousands a year in the stocks. . . .

Clearly Virginia represented an alternative to the acquisitive, Yankee "perplexities of business" in the nineteenth century.[23]

While *Swallow Barn* was most significant for its idealization of plantation life, it was also acclaimed as a major contribution to the national literature. Kennedy, a staunch supporter of Henry Clay and an advocate of internal improvements, was a vocal young nationalist. Critics praised the novel. One asserted that "the distinguishing feature of *Swallow Barn* is its pure Americanism." Another called the book "a valuable addition to our little, very little, stock of really national literature." Meanwhile, Kennedy was hard at work supervising the construction of a $15,000 mansion in Baltimore and working on a second novel.[24]

The experiences of Simms and Kennedy suggest that for the dozen or so years after Nullification, sectionalism—while a compelling attitude—was not incompatible with nationalism. These men, who were themselves "Yankeeish" in their calculating rise from low beginnings to higher social status, both glorified a way of life which they had only recently attained and contributed to the growing store of national literature at once distinctly Southern and wholly American. At least until the mid-1840's, Southerners joined with Americans everywhere else in the quest for nationality in literature.

23. John Pendleton Kennedy, *Swallow Barn, or a Sojourn in the Old Dominion*, vol. 22, Hafner Library of Classics, intro. and notes by William S. Osborne (New York: Hafner Publishing Co., 1962), pp. 27, 451–53.
24. Bohner, *Kennedy*, p. 88; Hubbell, *South in American Literature*, p. 485.

II

"The South don't care a d—n for literature or art," wrote Simms disconsolately in 1847. While editing may have been prestigious, in the antebellum South it was seldom remunerative, and while the thrill of publication could be exhilarating, it often failed to produce much in the way of royalties. Despite his massive labors, Simms in 1847 was a depressed and pessimistic man. To Hammond he drearily recited the woeful tale of continual setbacks:

> I am greatly behind with my publishers. I have numerous tasks before me which I cannot neglect. On the performance of these tasks depend my resources, which, to deal with you frankly, are small & diminishing. My residence in South Carolina, is unfavorable to me as an author. I lose $2000 per annum by it. Our planting interests barely pay my expenses and my income from Literature which in 1835 was $6000 per annum, is scarce $1500 now, owing to the operation of cheap reprints. . . . To earn this $1500 I have to labor constantly.[25]

Simms's discouragement stemmed from a variety of sources. Abolitionism was spreading in the North and attacks on the South were increasing in number and bitterness. Growing ever more conscious of the South's minority status, literary men revealed their alienation from national literary advancement. A new sensitivity to every suggestion of Southern inferiority pervaded the writings of many Southerners. "Twenty years ago it was scornfully asked in England, 'who reads an American book?' " stated the *Southern Literary Messenger*. "This same question is doubtless now asked in the North concerning Virginia." DeBow mimicked the derisive Northern critic: "Who of the North 'reads a Southern book'—they have said this themselves sneeringly. . . ." A contributor to *DeBow's* declared that "the pure stream of literature has been corrupted by

25. Simms to James H. Hammond, December 24, 1847, *Simms Letters* 2: 385–86.

the turbid waters of Abolition, and it has, at last, become a *necessity* to the South to have a literature of her own."[26]

As it was becoming apparent that Northern political doctrines were becoming majority opinion, so did it seem increasingly obvious that Northern literary standards were becoming the measure of American literature. Proximity to large cities, where modern printing facilities and efficient marketing techniques abounded, gave writers in the North a decided edge over their Southern counterparts. The novels published by Simms in New York or Philadelphia invariably sold better than those issued from Charleston. Only in New York could DeBow find satisfactory facilities for publishing his *Review*. Only after strong pressure from the local newspaper did the University of Mississippi decide to have its catalogue printed in Charleston instead of New York. The young Southern poet Henry Timrod summed up the dilemma. A writer, he said,

> . . . publishes a book. . . . Probably the book is published by a Northern house. Straightway all the newspapers of the South are indignant that the author did not choose a Southern printer, and address himself more particularly to a Southern community. He heeds their criticism, and of his next book—published by a Southern printer—. . . he finds that one half of a small edition remains upon his hands. . . . The North is inattentive or abusive and the South unthankful, or, at most, indifferent.[27]

The power of the press carried with it the power of editorial discretion. Though New York's Harper and Brothers happily and profitably published A. B. Longstreet's *Georgia Scenes* in 1840, they returned two anti-abolition pamphlets written by Longstreet several years later with silent promptness. The *Southern Quarterly Review* muttered that this action was "a sufficient commentary on the boasted freedom of speech and opinion at the North." Hinton R. Helper's *The Impending Crisis*

26. *Southern Literary Messenger* 13 (1847): 438; *DeBow's Review* 12 (1852): 500; 24 (1858): 305–306.
27. Hubbell, *South in American Literature*, pp. 363–64; Skipper, *DeBow*, pp. 25–26; *Charleston Mercury*, July 19, 1858; *Russell's Magazine* 5 (1859): 386.

found a Northern outlet because of its appeal to abolitionists, but no Northern press would touch any of Helper's other essays that had anything favorable to say about slavery. The *Northern Christian Examiner* made arbitrary deletions and revisions in a Southern physician's proslavery retort to an abolition article. DeBow angrily reprinted both the original and the altered version.[28]

Yet Southerners continued to subscribe to Northern periodicals and patronize Northern authors while neglecting their own sectional publications. The editor of the *Southern Literary Messenger* described the situation:

> . . . if the angel Gabriel had gone into the very heart of the South, if he had even taken his seat on the top of the office of the *Charleston Mercury* and there proclaimed the immediate approach of the Day of Judgment, that would not have hindered the hottest secessionist from buying the *New York Herald* and subscribing to *Harper's Magazine*.

The short life span of Southern periodicals was well known. One Charleston journal after another failed during the 1830's. Simms accurately prophesied the fortunes of yet another attempt, the *Magnolia*, begun in 1840. In a letter to the journal's founders, Simms predicted that it

> . . . will go into operation, progress twelve or eighteen months, and expire because subscribers won't pay, though dunned from the first number to the last. . . . You have run up to five hundred [subscribers] so fast that you'll almost wish you had made three thousand the minimum—from five hundred to seven hundred you'll begin to think the prospectus has not been half circulated, from seven hundred to a thousand you'll begin to fret about the lack of public spirit in the South, and between a thousand and fifteen hundred it will gradually ease out of notice.

The prophecy was fulfilled; in 1843 the *Magnolia* expired.[29]

The problem of the journals as well as the novels was two-

28. Hubbell, *South in American Literature*, p. 365; *Southern Literary Review* 13 (1848): 257; Hubbell, "Literary Nationalism," p. 199; *DeBow's Review* 20 (1856): 87–96.

29. *Southern Literary Messenger* 33 (1861): 237; Mott, *American Magazines* 1: 699.

fold. First, the inaccessibility of the Southern market made circulation of literature, like marketing of home manufactures, difficult and unprofitable. Simms alluded to the problem of selling subscriptions and then collecting payments "over an extensive tract of interior country, from a community scattered 'broad-cast' over thousands of miles."

But Northern publications seemed not to have this problem. For one thing their circulation was nationwide, owing to a more sophisticated marketing system employed by the publishers in the Northern cities. The cities themselves afforded a built-in mass market easily reached. The real problem, hinted at by Simms and others, was the generally inferior quality—both in form and in content—of Southern publications. Simms admitted that the inability to collect payments forced "the printer, who is not a capitalist" to issue the work "on villainous paper, 'but half made up'. . . ." In fact, "our printing in the South, is not generally so well considered, and carefully managed as in the North." Northern publishers employed proof-readers; "such an officer is particularly needed in the printing offices of the South."

But if the quality of Southern printing was bad, the quality of Southern literature generally was worse. Except for the works of Simms, Kennedy, Edgar Allan Poe, and a handful of others, Southern literature, said Simms, was "usually furnished by young Misses from their school exercises" or by "men, generally, in our country, devoted to other professions" whose work, "good, bad, or indifferent," the editor was "compelled to publish. The constant drain upon himself, enfeebles his imagination and exhausts his intellect. He has little time for thought, and no opportunity for the exercise of taste and fancy." Pressed by men like Alexander B. Meek, the Alabama jurist and poet, who believed that a true Southern journal would be better to "be stupid and original than possess all the commonplace excellence of the *North American*," and who claimed that "something we cannot get elsewhere, whether that something be good, bad, or indifferent, is what we want," the Southern editor was doomed to failure in the unbreakable cycle of poor production and poor support.[30]

Added to the inferior quality of Southern printing and the thinness of Southern literary output was yet another problem that caused Simms in particular unending difficulty. Since the early 1840's he had been a vigorous advocate of a copyright law. British publishers were one target, but American houses, which in 1834 issued only nineteen original novels and ninety-five cheap reprints of English and American works—for which the author received no compensation—were mostly to blame. The practice of reprinting flooded the book market with poorly bound, hastily printed works that competed with the more expensively published new volumes of contemporary writers. In addition, authors like Simms often had their books pirated. The result was that the more an author produced and the more fame he won, the more desirable his works became and, thus, the more likely he was to suffer a severe reduction in royalties by competing, in effect, against himself.[31]

Since virtually all major publishing houses were located in the North, it was hardly surprising that Simms gradually came to generalize about all Northerners from his dealings with unscrupulous publishers. Bitterly he recalled:

> I have been as great a simpleton, dealing with publishers, as any man I know; and I have been wronged, robbed, cheated and abused by them in due degree with my good nature and simplicity. I have done more gratuitous work than any man I know, and I have never been, in any way made aware, that I had even the gratitude of the parties . . . to whom the service has been rendered. Briefly, the moral of the whole country of trade is essentially base.

30. Simms to P. C. Pendleton, December 1, 1840, March 10, 1841, *Simms Letters* 1: 196–97, 238, 239; Alexander B. Meek to Simms, February 20, 1849, Alexander B. Meek Papers, Alabama Department of Archives and History.
31. Edd Winfield Parks, *William Gilmore Simms As Literary Critic*, University of Georgia Monographs, no. 7 (Athens: University of Georgia Press, 1961), pp. 98–99.

To Simms's mind, at least half of the editors at Northern presses were

> . . . lyars and knaves and dastards; who will stab at you from behind & skulk beneath your eye. For thirty years, my experience has been uniform to this effect, and to him who knows . . . the conditions & history of social growth in this country, it cannot be otherwise.[32]

Beset by personal financial woes, discouraged by repeated literary failures, and alarmed by the growing sectional tension between North and South, Simms's alienation from American literary nationalism was beginning.

Simms's intellectual progress was not unique but shared by a growing number of writers from the seaboard South. For many years these authors had indirectly defended their region by writing of the West with regret or disdain. Thus Longstreet in Georgia had made a name for himself with his delightful tales of the crudities of frontier life. But after he became a Methodist minister, sorely troubled by that church's schism over slavery in 1845, Longstreet transferred his hostility from the West to Massachusetts, which was "responsible for the ills of an otherwise happy nation." The abolitionists of New England "had engendered a disease, which by [their] quackery, [they] had turned into a cancer." As Longstreet's biographer has perceptively noted, "the Yankee type and the Georgia [frontier] type were . . . nearly one. . . ."[33]

Other writers who had earlier poked fun at the frontier yeomanry likewise transferred their criticism to Northerners. Johnson Jones Hooper of Alabama had, during the 1840's, published a volume of stories ridiculing life on the frontier. A conservative, North Carolina-born editor, Hooper wrote convincingly of the unforgettable Simon Suggs, a man "ready to

---

32. Simms to E. A. Duyckinck, March 18, 1859, *Simms Letters* 4: 137.
33. A. B. Longstreet, *A Voice from the South: Comprising Letters from Georgia to Massachusetts, and to the Southern States* (Baltimore: Samuel E. Smith, 1848), letter 1· John Donald Wade, *Augustus Baldwin Longstreet: A Study in the Development of Culture in the South* (New York: Macmillan Co., 1924), p. 165.

cope with his kind . . . in all the arts by which men *'get along'* in the world." Suggs's motto, "It is good to be shifty in a new country," served him well. Hooper, an opponent of democracy and a strong advocate of minority rights, turned in the late 1840's to political writing. Like Longstreet he changed targets, proclaiming from the masthead of his *Montgomery Mail* his advocacy of *"State Rights, Without Abatement"* and announcing in the editorial column that he and his associates had "been in minorities during all their political lives. . . . If the Union is worth more than the institution of slavery . . . Lord forbid that we should be Union men."[34]

The alienation from seemingly Yankeeish America was seen most clearly in the career of Nathaniel Beverley Tucker of Virginia. Born in 1784 in slaveholding Chesterfield County, Tucker graduated from the College of William and Mary in 1801 and for the next eight years was an unsuccessful lawyer. In 1809 he moved to "Roanoke," the home of his half-brother John Randolph, who supported him financially and nourished him intellectually. Six years later Tucker departed for Missouri, where he served as a circuit court judge. He deplored the immigration of nonslaveholding Northerners to Missouri and ridiculed their attitudes and mannerisms. Tucker vehemently opposed the Missouri Compromise in 1820. In that campaign he became one of the earliest Southern nationalists.[35]

The rude life of the frontier reinforced Tucker's love for Virginia. He returned to a vastly changed Old Dominion in

34. W. Stanley Hoole, *Alias Simon Suggs: The Life and Times of Johnson Jones Hooper* (University, Ala.: University of Alabama Press, 1952), pp. 15–46, 100, 102; Eaton, *Mind of the Old South*, p. 140; Hubbell, *South in American Literature*, p. 674.

35. Robert J. Brugger, "A Secessionist Persuasion: The Mind and Heart of Beverley Tucker of Virginia" (Ph.D. diss., Johns Hopkins University, 1974); Gerald Lee Wilson, *Nathaniel Beverley Tucker, "Aristocratic Paternalist": The Search for Order and Stability in the Ante-Bellum South* (Chapel Hill: University of North Carolina Press, 1975); Maude H. Woodfin, "Nathaniel Beverley Tucker: His Writings and Political Theories, With a Sketch of His Life," *Richmond College Historical Papers* 2 (1917): 9–34.

the winter of 1833–34. Like that of his contemporary in up-state New York, James Fenimore Cooper, Tucker's home as found was not at all to his liking. Democracy had invaded his native state, changed its political character, led to a serious discussion of emancipation, and, as a result, had prostrated Virginia in the midst of what Tucker regarded as the most serious sectional controversy yet, the Nullification crisis. As a professor of law at William and Mary, Tucker vented his anger in the classroom and in books and letters. For the rest of his life Tucker waged a lonely war against democracy and in favor of a Southern nation.

In 1836 Tucker published two novels. The first, *George Balcombe*, was a mystery romance set in Virginia and Missouri. The description of frontier life in Missouri suggests a view similar to that of Longstreet, Hooper, and Baldwin. Slavery is portrayed as a kindly institution, and George Balcombe, who seems to be the personification of Tucker, periodically discourses on matters of politics and society with a pronounced conservatism. *George Balcombe* earned flattering reviews as a "bold, highly spirited, and very graceful border story, . . . a fine picture of society and manners on the frontier."[36]

Also in 1836 Tucker published *The Partisan Leader: A Tale of the Future*. The book was issued under a pseudonym and carried the date 1856. The story takes place in 1849. Martin Van Buren, in his fourth term, is trying to prevent Virginia from joining other Southern states in a new confederacy. The cause of secession is not slavery but an oppressively high tariff. The new Southern nation is pure, agricultural, and non-democratic. The Virginians, gentlemen "of good breeding," rise up to defeat the Federal invasion and, presumably, secure the independence of Virginia and the South. The Yankee–Democrat is the villain, whose "calculating selfishness" in a society of "wolf eat wolf and Yankee cheat Yankee" leads him to elect a president "to whom habitual intercourse with the base"

36. Hubbell, *South in American Literature*, p. 429; *Southern Literary Messenger* 3 (1837): 58.

was routine. Such practices "encouraged the unwashed artificer to elbow the duke from his place of precedence. . . . While the sovereignty of numbers was acknowledged, the convenience of the multitude had set the fashions." Though Tucker's book was neither an artistic nor a financial success, its message was powerful.[37]

Except for *Gertrude*, a nondescript novel serialized in the *Southern Literary Messenger* in 1844, Tucker's literary career began and ended in 1836. His influence thereafter was exerted in the classroom and in his private conversation and correspondence. In a remarkable series of letters between 1836 and 1851 to Hammond, Tucker unburdened himself. The United States was nothing but "a mere creature of convention, the despotism of which will restore nature to her rights, and give us leave to regard as enemies those who hate us and whom we hate," namely, "Yankeys." As for the South, "we are homogeneous & united in one common interest," slavery. Yet Tucker feared that "the craven spirit of the Virginia delegation" in Congress during Nullification "caused the day to pass by us. Had Virginia been true to herself, the Union would have dissolved peaceably." But his home state no longer commanded his allegiance. "Nothing would gratify me more," he wrote Hammond, "than to have some member of your delegation consider me as one of his constituents." Only in South Carolina had "the *Gentleman* . . . not lost his proper weight and influence." In Virginia, "Pennsylvanians and Yankeys" in the western part of the state "have changed her constitution, and make a display of numerical power and the will to abuse it."[38]

Tucker's last public appeal for a Southern nation came at the Nashville convention in 1850. Prophesying the glories of a Southern confederacy, Tucker declared that "there is no reason to apprehend such a step as secession would mean war." A year later he charged Hammond to "give yourself, mind and

37. Nathaniel Beverley Tucker, *The Partisan Leader: A Tale of the Future*, 1861 ed. (New York: Rudd and Carleton, 1861), pp. 205, 253, 141, 134.
38. N. B. Tucker to Hammond, February 18, 1836, March 15, 1851, March 13, 1847, Hammond Papers, Library of Congress.

heart, to the great interests now at stake. . . . [A] Southern Confederacy is the one thing needful, and for God's sake, let not any personal or other consideration turn away the thought . . . from that great object! Stand! Stand!! Stand!!!"[39] Only two months after this impassioned plea, his dreams unrealized, the Old Virginian's tormented soul at last found rest.

Simms's slow transition from American literary nationalist to Southern literary nationalist was more typical of Southern writers than Tucker's instant conversion. The frustrations of the 1840's caused Simms to break with Young America and the Democrats in 1848 to support General Zachary Taylor, a slaveholding Whig, for the presidency. The election of Taylor brought dreams not only of Southern safety but also of personal prestige. Both were evanescent. Simms expected a diplomatic appointment in return for his service during the campaign, but he failed to secure a position. At the same time Taylor, the slaveholder, moved to organize California as a free state to prohibit slavery in the territory recently acquired from Mexico. Alarmed, Simms wrote to Hammond that "only by calling in the Sister States to council" could the South mount a "successful resistance to adolition."[40]

Yet although Simms's attitude toward the North was ambivalent, he was not yet a Southern nationalist. As editor of the *Southern Quarterly Review*, a position in which he served from 1849 to 1854 without compensation, he showed that his sentiments were still wavering. Early in 1849 he revealed to a friend his assessment of the relationship between North and South. "We have long since been satisfied," he remarked, "that the North was the maggot in the brain of the Elk feeding on his vitals, yet destroying his benefactor." But he was not yet pre-

---

39. For a sample letter to Simms, see Trent, *Simms*, pp. 184–88; *Speech Delivered by the Hon. Beverley Tucker of Virginia in the Southern Convention Held at Nashville, Tenn., April 13th [sic], 1850*, p. 19; N. B. Tucker to James H. Hammond, June 23, 1851, Hammond Papers.

40. Miller, *Raven and the Whale*, p. 194; *Charleston Mercury*, September 16, 1848, quoted in *Simms Letters* 2: 446; Simms to Hammond, November 11, 1848, *Simms Letters* 2: 453.

pared to convert the *Quarterly* into an organ of sectional conflict. In a brief letter to Kennedy, a staunch Unionist, he promised to avoid "as a matter of policy, all vexing questions which may more properly be left to other channels of publication." In a much longer letter to Tucker, meanwhile, he wrote that

> . . . as an organ of opinion and education at home, and for all the Southern States—having for its objects in politics—the promotion of Free Trade,—the maintenance of State Rights—the arrest of centralism,—and the assertion of our Institutions, morally as well as socially—the Southern Quarterly is one of those agencies in a wholesome and necessary work.[41]

This inconsistency was not duplicitous but was indicative of the uncertainty that was plaguing Simms at the time. In *Katherine Walton*, published in 1850, Simms further indicated his wavering views. The theme of *Katherine Walton* is the conflict of loyalties in the Revolution, and the author—portraying extreme patriots and loyalists unsympathetically—concentrates on a man, General Andrew Williamson, caught in the middle. Williamson changes sides several times. After a stinging defeat and capture he joins the Tories. Then he becomes a spy and returns to the patriots. Finally the patriots court-martial him "for his desertion of the American cause." Williamson replies, "I never deserted it until it had deserted me. . . . [O]ur troops were scattered—we had no army left. . . . Congress would, or could, do nothing for us. . . ." Like Simms and like a growing number of Southern writers, Williamson had changed allegiances only after "it was no longer possible to offer defence."[42] To break away from old associations was risky and painful but, when confronted by a hostile power that threatened to overwhelm, necessary.

41. Simms to Lawson, February 5, 1849; Simms to John P. Kennedy, February 12, 1849; Simms to Tucker, March 15, 1849; all in *Simms Letters* 2: 475, 479, 498.
42. William Gilmore Simms, *Katherine Walton* (Philadelphia: A. Hart, 1851), p. 163; Holman, *Roots of Southern Writing*, pp. 35, 37, 41; Ridgely, *Simms*, pp. 93–96.

III

In the South during the 1850's Southern literary nationalism supplanted American literary nationalism. It was the publication of Harriet Beecher Stowe's *Uncle Tom's Cabin* in 1852 that was the catalyst in transforming Americanism into Southern literary nationalism. James P. Holcombe, a professor of law at the University of Virginia, announced, "Literature alone can dispossess the demon of fanaticism. . . . Let us appeal to her varied forms . . . to enter every cottage in the land, and disperse delusions which invest this whole subject of domestic slavery." Mrs. Stowe's reviewers echoed this cry. A review in the *Southern Literary Messenger* blamed the Southern people, who had

> . . . underrated and disregarded all productions of Southern intellect; and now, when all the batteries of the literary republic are turned against them, and the torrent of literary censure threatens to unite with other agencies to overwhelm them, it is in vain that they cry in their dire necessity, 'Help me, Cassius, or I sink.'[43]

Within two years of the appearance of *Uncle Tom*, at least fourteen novels by Southern writers were published in rebuttal—all either in New York or Philadelphia. Their subtitles made their purpose plain: "Southern life as it is," "a tale of real life," "a fair view of both sides of the slavery question," "Uncle Robin in his cabin and Tom without one in Boston." The recurrent theme in all these novels is the goodness and gentility of life in the plantation South as opposed to the savagery of life in the capitalistic North. Gone are any admissions of doubt about slavery. The Cavalier–Yankee antithesis receives full, aggressive development. Each novel contains a debate over slavery between a Southerner and a Northerner, and the former always wins out. The Northerner is constantly portrayed either in "a constant depression of spirits" as a victim of

43. Hubbell, "Literary Nationalism," p. 206; *Southern Literary Messenger* 18 (1852): 724–25.

capitalism or as *"a hypocrite and liar."* One novelist concludes, "If from the ruin and degradation of our Northern land I shall have succeeded in drawing forth one human soul and in having restored it to its original brightness and purity, I shall not have written, nor you read in vain. . . ."[44]

Though most of these feeble attempts were predictably ineffectual, Simms, sweeping away the doubts of *Katherine Walton*, published his memorable *Woodcraft*, another Revolutionary romance, called by the author "probably as good an answer to Mrs. Stowe as has been published." The central character in *Woodcraft*—probably Simms's best creation—is Captain Porgy, a corpulent, Falstaffian figure who represents the best and worst aspects of the Southern planter. It is Porgy who, having squandered his inheritance on hedonistic pursuits, is chastised for his wastefulness by a blunt, nonslaveholding sergeant named Millhouse. Porgy acknowledges:

> . . . that our fathers lived too well, were too rapidly prosperous. . . . We were to be affluent in what they should leave us—enough, in God's name, if we could keep it—but it is very sure that the best way to teach one to value and keep what he gets, is just to teach him how to get it himself.

In this passage Simms clearly summarizes his own changing ideas. Reviewing Miss Martineau he had conceded certain elements of brutality, of Yankeeness in Southern society; here he recognizes the tendencies of Southern society toward consumption and even dissipation rather than production and thrift.

Mrs. Stowe had, however, struck a raw nerve, and Simms's response—through Porgy's squandering his fortune and suddenly realizing his loss—is shrewd. The complementary figures of Porgy, the newly wise aristocratic planter, and Millhouse, the gruff yeoman, serve several purposes. They illustrate Simms's belief that Mrs. Stowe's depiction of Southern society was inaccurate, for the evils she revealed were nei-

44. Jeanette Reid Tandy, "Pro-Slavery Propaganda in American Fiction of the Fifties," *South Atlantic Quarterly* 21 (1922): 41–50, 170–78.

ther new—*Woodcraft* is set in 1782—nor bad, for out of Porgy's loss rises a new sense of responsibility. His renewal is possible only in an interdependent, organic, inherently superior society which can by its very nature overcome Yankee tendencies. When Tom, the loyal slave, refuses Porgy's offer of freedom by declaring, "Ef *I* doesn't b'long to *you, you* b'longs to *me!*", the portrait is complete.[45]

For Simms, as for most other Southern writers, the ideal society was not in the present but in the past. During those happy times, when classes were interdependent, when benign masters and loyal slaves toiled on a happy plantation, and when the grand ideals of the Revolution were honored by Americans everywhere, the South was flourishing and strong. Men like Porgy—and Simms—had glory and influence. But in the present, whatever shortcomings existed in the South were the result of an unfriendly and unequal Union. Whatever Yankeeness there was in the South was the fault of the accelerating social and political changes that Northern society was doing so much to promote. If the frontiersman abused his slave, it was only because the South was trying to keep up with the abusive, aggressive times. As Porgy discovers the singular virtues of Southern society anew, so does Simms begin to acknowledge the incompatibility of North and South. During this time Simms wrote to a friend of "the distinction between a determined advocacy of Southern mind . . . and . . . hostility to Northern mind" that was the difference between sectionalism and Southern nationalism. And not long afterwards Simms and other Southern writers became Southern nationalists.[46]

As they had earlier defended a settled, established society

---

45. S. P. C. Duvall, "W. G. Simms's Review of Mrs. Stowe," *American Literature* 30 (1958): 107–17; J. V. Ridgely, "*Woodcraft:* Simms's First Answer to *Uncle Tom's Cabin*," *American Literature* 31 (1960): 421–33; William Gilmore Simms,*Woodcraft*, reprint ed. (New York: W. W. Norton and Co., 1961), pp. 206, 509; Ridgely, *Simms*, pp. 99–104; Taylor, *Cavalier and Yankee*, pp. 287–90. The original title of *Woodcraft* was *The Sword and the Distaff*.
46. Simms to Richard Henry Wilde, August 11, —, quoted in *American Literature* 44 (1972–73): 670.

against the disruptive influences of the frontier, so now did Southerners, defending a deferential social order, attack the Yankees of the North. A Southern literature was no longer in existence to contribute to an American literature. It would, rather, help form a Southern nation. "Now we must have Southern authors & indeed we have them & we must raise up Southern teachers—we must print & publish our own books & maintain the ancient renown and dignity of the South. . . ," announced a Mississippi educator. The *New Orleans Delta* called for "a Southern republic of letters. . . ." Another Southerner warned that "so long as we depend upon the North for books to read and cloths [*sic*] to wear, we may expect to have our literature poisoned with fanaticism, and our purses emptied of their contents." Southern literary nationalism was replacing American literary nationalism.[47]

A war between Northern and Southern periodicals broke out in the mid–1850's. The *Southern Literary Messenger* charged the newly founded *Atlantic Monthly* in Boston with attempting "to wage war upon Southern society." The *Atlantic* had inquired tauntingly, "What book has the South ever given to the libraries of the world? What work of art has she ever given to its galleries?" Southerners gave as they got. "What, but the persistent efforts of Yankee periodicals," asked one, "could have given the prosaic Longfellow a wider circle of readers on this side of the Atlantic than Tennyson, Campbell, or Burns?" Reviewing an issue of New York's *Putnam's Monthly*, Charleston's *Russell's Magazine* pointed out that forty years earlier England "sneered at American literature. The North was indignant. . . . But now the North has turned sneerer, and sneers at Southern literature."[48]

In the vanguard of Southern literary nationalism were the

---

47. J. M. Wesson to J. F. H. Claiborne, August 11, 1858, J. F. H. Claiborne Collection, Mississippi Department of Archives and History; *New Orleans Delta*, undated clipping [1857], Henry Hughes Scrapbook, Mississippi Department of Archives and History.

48. *Southern Literary Messenger* 25 (1857): 472; *Atlantic Monthly* 1 (1857): 244; *DeBow's Review* 31 (1861): 357, *Russell's Magazine* 1 (1857): 83.

Southern Quarterly Review and the *Southern Literary Messenger*. The *Quarterly* had begun in New Orleans in 1842 under the editorship of Daniel K. Whitaker, a Massachusetts native and Harvard graduate. After a year in New Orleans, Whitaker moved the *Quarterly* to Charleston, which was even then known as a graveyard of magazines. By 1847 Whitaker, under the usual burdens of debt and overwork plus the added one of Northern birth, was ready to sell. The purchaser was J. M. Clapp, junior editor of the Southern nationalistic *Charleston Mercury*. Clapp in 1849 appointed the energetic though disillusioned Simms as editor.[49]

Over the next several years the *Quarterly*, with Simms slowly making up his mind, gradually became an organ of Southern nationalism, often preferring the partisanship of a contribution over its quality. Virtually every issue contained a defense of slavery. In one such article in 1853, Simms called the South "a people, a nation. . . ." At the same time, the *Quarterly* was a strong supporter of agriculture, especially cotton planting. Agriculture was "the noblest of human avocations." It bred men who were satisfied with a "quiet, contemplative life." By contrast the North was full of cities that were "the mere sinks and sewers of civilization" and people who were skilled in "the art of making money out of small things." Indeed, South and North possessed different "national characteristics" which were neatly summarized in a classic appeal to Southern nationalism in 1853:

> Whenever any one people, in the progress of their career, shall become different from all others in essential, moral, and physical respects—when they shall arrive at such form, outline, and material, as to possess for themselves a figure of individuality, and attain a sufficient degree of civilization for the purpose of self-

49. Mott, *American Magazines* 1: 722–27; Frank W. Ryan, Jr., *"The Southern Quarterly Review*, 1842–1857: A Study in Thought and Opinion in the Old South" (Ph.D. diss., University of North Carolina, 1955); *Southern Quarterly Review* 9 (1846): 523; Trent, *Simms*, p. 165.

government, . . . they then either are, or should be—and per-
force, will be—a separate political community. . . .[50]

After a brief revival under Simms, the *Quarterly* began to
decline. In 1854 Simms resigned after the journal was sold to a
Northerner, Charles Mortimer, under whose direction its
quality and patronage continued to deteriorate. Mortimer
transferred the comatose journal to Columbia in 1856 and appointed the Reverend James Thornwell, president of South
Carolina College, as editor, but the disease was terminal and
the *Quarterly* expired in 1857. Its demise was considered a
"disgrace" by at least one subscriber. "We of the South must to
Europe, continue to appear inferior to the North in intellectual
cultivation," he asserted.[51]

The jewel of Southern periodicals was the *Southern Literary Messenger*, which emanated from Richmond from its founding in 1834. In 1847 the *Messenger* was purchased by John
Reuben Thompson, a young Richmond lawyer. At the outset
of his tenure, which was to last thirteen years, Thompson
vowed "to show our Northern brethren that Southern learning
can think for itself." This statement he made without rancor
since the *Messenger* already had a distinguished reputation for
promoting Southern literature as American literature. Reso-
lutely refusing to meddle in political questions, Thompson
helped secure the *Messenger*'s position as the South's leading periodical.[52]

To ease its self-doubts, the *Messenger* occasionally ran supportive endorsements from all over the country. For example,
in June 1848 there appeared on the cover favorable comments

50. Trent, *Simms*, pp. 173–74; *Southern Quarterly Review* 8 (1853): 419–20, 540;
2 (1850): 197; 10 (1854): 441; 7 (1853): 180.
51. Mott, *American Magazines* 1: 726–27; Samuel Tyler to James H. Thornwell, July 13, 1857, James Henley Thornwell Papers, South Caroliniana Library.
52. Shanks, *Secession Movement in Virginia*, p. 74; Benjamin Blake Minor, *The
Southern Literary Messenger, 1834–1864* (New York: Neale Publishing Co.,
1905); Mott, *American Magazines* 1: 636–39, 645–47.

from newspapers in Washington, D.C.; Norfolk; Savannah; Raleigh; Pickens, Alabama; and Jackson, Missouri. In December endorsements were added from St. Louis; Memphis; Tuskegee, Alabama; Brandon, Mississippi; Minden, Louisiana; and even the *Northern Literary Messenger* in Meriden, Connecticut. All concurred with the *Pickens Republican* that the *Messenger* was the "first rate monthly periodical, published at the south. . . ."[53]

Since the *Messenger* dominated its field, and since it was generally fiscally sound and under uninterrupted management, it was an accurate barometer of changing feelings in the South toward the Union.[54] Southern sectionalism did not emerge as a theme in the *Messenger*'s articles until 1851, after the passage of the 1850 Compromise (See tables in Appendix IV). Even when the *Messenger* turned to Southern sectionalism, it continued to be primarily a literary journal; its advocacy of the South usually appeared not in fictional or critical articles but rather in clearly labeled articles on politics. Its greatest outbursts of sectionalism coincided with the moments of greatest national political tension: in 1851 after the Compromise, in 1854 during the debates over the Kansas–Nebraska Act, in 1856–57 during the Kansas warfare and the Dred Scott controversy, and in 1860 during the presidential election campaign.

A recurrent theme in the *Messenger* articles that exude Southern sectionalism is concern over "Yankeeness," over apparent differences between North and South, that often ends with an appeal for Southern unity. For instance, in March 1851 the *Messenger* ran a lengthy review of New York Senator William Seward's speech invoking a "higher law" than the Constitution in attacking the Fugitive Slave Bill. Viciously damning Seward, the critic charged that "this age is the age of progress and improvement; and it is not to be denied, that the

---

53. *Southern Literary Messenger* 14 (1848): *passim.*
54. I have explained the methodology behind this analysis in Appendix VI. The tables may be found in Appendix IV.

senator from New York . . . has . . . discovered that the violation of an oath may be made the means of political advantage."
It was the acquisitive lust for glory that led Seward er-
roneously to argue the "absurd" idea "that *all creatures are equal*
by nature." As response to such Northern notions, the *Messenger* endoresed the formation of Southern Rights Associations
in Virginia to demonstrate to the "Yankee pedlers" the seriousness of the times.[55] Sectionally oriented articles were
few in 1852 and 1853, but in 1854 the Kansas–Nebraska Act
brought a resurgence of anti-Yankee rhetoric.[56] Controversy in
the *Messenger* articles then again briefly diminished, but it
peaked once more in 1856–57. In a typical article the *Messenger* attacked "Northern politics and corruption," which made
life in the Northern capitalistic system "savage, heartless, destructive, and suicidal . . . ," though it again expressed hope
that a united South might preserve the Union.[57]

A gradual ebbing of sectionalism in 1858 and 1859 preceded a most intense outburst of sectional articles in the *Messenger* in 1860. Thompson resigned his editoship in May 1860 to
accept a position elsewhere, and his successor, George W.
Bagby, had no aversion to meddling in politics. Under Bagby's
editorship the *Messenger* pictured the North as the scene of
"revolutions, disorders, and violence," of "aggressive im-
pudence and vulgarity of sentiment." It was only a small step
to the advocacy of Southern nationalism after the election of
Lincoln, the candidate of the North, which sought "self interest" and "aggrandizement" at the expense of the "conservative"
South.[58]

With the North ascendant and the South threatened, with
the "bold, hardy" Yankee apparently ready to subjugate the
"courteous and gentle" South, the *Messenger*'s decision was
clear: "the time for our separation has come."[59]

55. *Southern Literary Messenger* 17 (1851): 132, 179.
56. *Ibid.* 20 (1854): 181, 187, 327, 514, 524.
57. *Ibid.* 25 (1857): 88, 84–85, 93, 326.
58. *Ibid.* 31 (1860): 345, 349.
59. *Ibid.* 32 (1861), 2–3, 86.

Though the *Messenger*, like most Southerners, did not embrace Southern nationalism until 1860, Simms had much earlier made up his mind. Mrs. Stowe had convinced him that sectionalism and nationalism—Southernism and Yankeeism—were incompatible. Although he added two more novels to his series of Revolutionary romances, most of Simms's efforts were devoted not to literature but to politics. "Let all your game lie in the constant recognition & assertion of a *Southern Nationality!*" he implored a friend in 1857. More clearly than ever before Simms drew the distinctions between North and South. Southerners, as agriculturalists, were "not accustomed to that constant attrition of rival minds & interests which sharpens the wits, & makes daring & eager the enterprises of all commercial people." The Union was "hostile, & denies us the exercise of independent action of every kind." Referring to the Southerner's "Norman appetite for the possession of domain," Simms—the Scotch–Irish immigrant's son—warned the North not to enact restrictions on the spread of slavery westward. Hoping that territorial limitations passed by a Northern majority in Congress might spark secession, Simms looked toward a Southern nation that restored constitutional rights. To the North he cried, "you . . . ban our institutions;—your flag shelters not our property, and we know the nation only as the antagonist. . . ." Only a Southern nation could make final a break with the "nation of mercenaries" in the "ignorant, impudent, dishonest" North.[60]

IV

As late as 1850 most Southerners who thought at all about such matters probably would have agreed with Daniel Whitaker's observation:

60. Simms to William Porcher Miles, *Simms Letters* 3: 518; Wakelyn, *Politics of a Literary Man*, pp. 224, 238–42; Simms to Hammond, January 28, 1858, June 11, 1858; Simms to Duyckinck, March 18, 1859; all in *Simms Letters* 4: 17, 25, 26, 65, 137.

> There can be no national, without a sectional, literature, for a nation, like the human body, is made up of parts and members. . . . A Southern book is both southern and American, as Charleston is both a southern and an American city; and literature, in general, does not lose its sectional character because it is national, nor its national character because it is sectional.[61]

As those words were being written some Southerners were beginning to have difficulty reconciling their sectional literary concerns with national literary and political developments. The most probing questioners were men like Tucker and Simms who, having achieved their fame by a customarily "Yankeeish" route—a profession, a good marriage, a contribution to the public—did the most to create and glorify a mythical, cavalier past when men like Porgy (and themselves) were recognized for their accomplishments.

Depressed and disheartened by the trends of nineteenth-century American life—trends all too obvious to them on the frontier even in their beloved South—these writers found their paradigm of the perfect society lay either in the Revolutionary past or in an imagined revolutionary future. For Simms, Arcadia was the American Revolution, when deference and respect, hierarchy and stability seemed to reign. For Tucker, the ideal society lay in the not-too-distant future, when the South, led by a reinvigorated Virginia, would restore its lost grandeur in a Southern nation. These men and others yearned for a return to simpler days. "We have lost some of those moral restraints," wrote Simms sadly in 1856, "which might have kept many of us virtuous. . . . [S]ome of the coarseness of modern taste arises from the too great lack of that veneration which belonged to, and elevated to dignity, even the errors of preceding ages."[62]

Whether ignored, rejected, or swindled by the Southern reading public and Northern publishers, or displaced by yeoman, nonslaveholding Democrats, Southern writers projected

---

61. Whitaker quoted in Hubbell, "Literary Nationalism," p. 219n.
62. Simms, *The Wigwam and the Cabin*, pp. 1–2.

their prejudices and anxieties onto the "Yankee" figure, which came to represent a cluster of negative values—the opposite both of what they longed for and of what they wished they were. As these feelings grew in intensity, as Southern political, economic, and intellectual influence declined, many Southern writers came to advocate a separate Southern nation in order to recover the lost influence and the lost virtues. Southern literary nationalism represented an attempt by frustrated pseudo-Southrons to restore order and purpose to an increasingly Yankee world.

CHAPTER FIVE

Northern Domination in Our Schools and Pulpits

During the 1830's the Southern states began to experience the same forces of accelerating social and political change that were altering the rest of American society. New settlers streamed into the western states. The population of Alabama and Mississippi doubled between 1830 and 1840. Significant though less striking leaps in population also occurred in Georgia, Tennessee, and Louisiana. Mass migration and the opening of new lands made for a disordered and unpredictable way of life, not only in the new states trying to cope with a burgeoning population but also in the older states, which attemptd to restore order to a fragmented society.[1]

In these times of uncertainty, Southerners turned to two institutions—the church and the school—in their search for stability. By 1845 religious activity had reached new heights and so had higher education. Orthodoxy was ascendant; more and more Southerners were attending services; and almost every Southern state had at least one church-affiliated college. Hand-in-hand, religion and education were helping to create a sense of order.

1. Sydnor, *Southern Sectionalism*, pp. 3–4, 255–59.

The year 1845 saw the emergence of Southern nationalism in the areas of religion and education. The slavery issue
split both the Baptists and the Methodists, which between
them comprised almost three-fourths of the Southern population, into separate Northern and Southern branches. Shortly
thereafter, and not coincidentally, appeals in behalf of Southern education began to change from a competitive denomina-
tionalism or state chauvinism to a hostile and urgent Southern
nationalism. Educational and religious Southern nationalism
began to spread, reaching its fusion and fulfillment on a Tennessee mountaintop in October 1860. In preparing the Southern mind for separate nationhood, religion and education were
of crucial importance.

I

Why mayn't our Southern Clime the
    race of learning run?
Is it because we're burnt beneath
    a scorching sun?
Beneath those rays how rich our
    vegetations rise!
And may not *mind* attain to equal size?

So rhymed Rev. Samuel J. Cassels of Georgia in 1838.
Like Southern planters, Southern merchants, and Southern
writers, the Georgia minister saw his section lagging behind
the North in scope and quality of education. Something must
be done.[2]

Curiously, widespread concern for education in the South
focused not on elementary or secondary education but rather
on liberal arts or professional training of older children. This
emphasis was due at least in part to the wide dispersal of the
Southern population in comparison, for instance, to that of
New England, where the town system of government and a

---

2. Samuel J. Cassels quoted in John S. Ezell, "A Southern Education for
Southrons," *Journal of Southern History* 17 (1951): 305.

mercantile economy encouraged areas of more concentration. In general, the primary and secondary educational needs of the South were served by private academies and, later in the antebellum period, free schools for the less well-to-do who were willing to make a declaration of poverty. In 1850 the South boasted two thousand private academies, with over thirty-two hundred teachers and seventy thousand students. Among the more distinguished academies were Concord and Hanover in Virginia, and Willington, run for many years by Moses Waddel, mentor of a host of distinguished South Carolinians. During the 1840's some of the larger cities—including New Orleans, Nashville, Charleston, Memphis, and Mobile—were beginning programs of public school education. The education of young children was hardly neglected.[3]

Colleges and universities, however, stirred the greatest interest. The state universities were first into the field, beginning with the chartering of the University of Georgia and continuing with the chartering of the Universities of North Carolina, Tennessee, Virginia, and Alabama, and South Carolina College.

Before 1830 there were only three church colleges in the whole South: the Presbyterian-controlled Hampden–Sydney in Virginia, founded in 1783; Centre in Kentucky, founded in 1819; and Washington in Tennessee, founded in 1795. Between 1830 and 1844, however, a great flurry of educational activity took place, led by the three major religious denominations in the South—the Baptists, the Methodists, and the Presbyterians. The Baptists established Richmond College in

3. Albea Godbold, *The Church College of the Old South* (Durham: Duke University Press, 1944) is the best survey of denominational institutions, while E. Merton Coulter, *College Life in the Old South*, rev. ed. (Athens: University of Georgia Press, 1951) remains the best general account of life in the state universities. A good general survey of antebellum Southern education is *Social Life of the South*, vol. 10 of *The South in the Building of the Nation*, ed. Samuel Chiles Mitchell (Richmond: Southern Historical Publishing Co., 1909), pp. 184–429. Not to be overlooked is Edgar W. Knight, ed., *A Documentary History of Education in the South before 1860*, 5 vols. (Chapel Hill: University of North Carolina Press, 1953).

Virginia, Wake Forest in North Carolina, Mercer in Georgia, and Howard in Alabama. The Methodists could claim Randolph–Macon and Emory and Henry in Virginia, Emory in Georgia, and Centenary in Louisiana. The Presbyterians established in this period Oglethorpe in Georgia, Davidson in North Carolina, Erskine in South Carolina, and Cumberland and Tusculum in Tennessee.[4]

The proliferation of church colleges during these years reflected an intense interdenominational competition to save the souls of Southerners. Church-related colleges were not primarily inculcating Southern sectionalism or nationalism; they were instead fighting one another for sectarian supremacy. The Baptist founders of Richmond College pointed out that "other denominations are paying the most careful, devoted attention" to education. South Carolina Methodists in 1835 noted "the pains beginning to be taken by different denominations to bring education back to sound principles. We may not, we cannot, linger behind all others." Reacting to the impending financial collapse of Oglethorpe College in 1841, the Presbyterian founders appealed to their brethren for support "in view of what sister denominations are doing, and of the deep and lasting blot which a failure in this enterprise would fix upon us."[5]

Denominational leaders wanted their own colleges for several reasons. Only church-affiliated colleges could teach denominational values and virtues. A speaker before the Randolph–Macon Alumni Association in 1844 declared that "the connection between religion and education is a natural one. . . ." The Baptist *Christian Index* newspaper agreed that "Christianity has always been the friend and prompter of

---

4. Clement Eaton, *A History of the Old South*, 2d ed. (New York: Macmillan Co., 1966), p. 422. Georgia actually opened in 1801, North Carolina in 1795, Virginia in 1825, Alabama in 1831, and South Carolina in 1805. See also Donald G. Tewksbury, *The Founding of American Colleges and Universities Before the Civil War* (New York: Arno Press, 1969), pp. 211–20; James B. Sellers, *History of the University of Alabama* (University, Ala.: University of Alabama Press, 1953), pp. 7–27. See also Table 1, Appendix V.
5. Quoted in Godbold, *Church College*, pp. 67–68.

learning. . . ." Nor were the denominations unaware of the need to educate ministers. A Baptist writer in 1832 wondered, "How is it possible for a man to teach those already better taught than himself?"[6]

Colleges were likewise necessary to make education more accessible to the common man. The trustees of Randolph–Macon announced their intention "to reduce the expenses of obtaining a liberal and finished education. . . ." Wake Forest advertised itself as "a good cheap school." Mercer College in 1838 was intended to make "intelligent lawyers, physicians, merchants, and planters" as well as to "do more toward the spread of Baptist influence, than by the efforts and preaching of all the ministers at present living in our country combined."[7]

The rivalry among Baptists, Methodists, and Presbyterians underscored a movement in the South away from Jeffersonian rationalism toward religious orthodoxy and fundamentalism. Their battle for sectarian ascendancy was rooted in disagreements over both belief and practice—the frequency of sacramental rites, the kind of baptism, or the need for an educated ministry—but the debates had a greater significance than mere theological hair-splitting. While it was necessary to maintain denominational influence through the church colleges, it was even more important to preach and enforce the letter of scripture in matters of personal conduct. Rapid change was causing old values and beliefs to be questioned. A society in a state of flux needed rules, and preachers, turning to the scriptures, wielded tremendous influence in defining a rigid code of right and wrong, heaven and hell. From William and Mary Professor Dew reflected the new orthodoxy when he wrote that "he who obtrudes on the social circle his infidel notions, manifests the arrogance of a literary coxcomb, or that want of refinement which distinguishes the polished gentleman."[8]

6. Quoted *ibid.*, pp. 49–51.
7. Quoted *ibid.*, pp. 55, 56, 64.
8. Eaton, *Mind of the Old South*, p. 220; Walter B. Posey, *Frontier Mission: A History of Religion West of the Southern Appalachians to 1861* (Lexington: University

Gradually fading after 1830 were the fine and genuine distinctions of denominational ritual and diversity; waxing were the shared notions of piety and uniformity. Though they squabbled with one another, the church colleges agreed that their existence was vital to counter the influence of the supposedly "Godless" state universities. Founded in the heady days of Jeffersonian liberalism, the state universities appeared to Baptists and Methodists to be bastions of immorality and faithlessness. Though the complaints were aimed partly at the considerable Presbyterian influence (because of their educational standards) in the state schools, they were mostly caused by what seemed to be a lack of piety in the university environment. A Baptist minister in Kentucky called on his counterparts in other denominations to "abandon your sectarianism, meet on the holy Scripture, and bear with one another's infirmities. . . ." All denominations must join because "your schools, your colleges, are full of skepticism. The great majority of your educated men are infidels. . . ."[9]

As orthodoxy grew in strength the universities were forced to compromise. In 1834 the South Carolina legislature ousted Cooper, as free a thinker on religion as he was on the value of the Union, from the presidency of South Carolina College. His religious views, claimed the legislature, were "dangerous to the youth and abhorrent to the feelings of the great mass of the community." Only Cooper's strong support of Nullification kept him in power for so long. In his place the legislature installed Robert W. Barnwell, a noncontroversial Episcopalian whose sectional views were "correct" and whose religious position was neutral. At the University of Virginia politics and orthodoxy combined to initiate regular chapel services in violation of a Jeffersonian dictum. At the University of

---

of Kentucky Press, 1966), pp. 327–51; Eaton, *Freedom-of-Thought Struggle*, pp. 300–334; *Southern Literary Messenger* 2 (1836): 768.

9. *A Debate Between Rev. A. Campbell and Rev. N. L. Rice on the Action, Subject, Design, and Administrator of Christian Baptism*, quoted in Eaton, *Freedom-of-Thought Struggle*, pp. 311–12.

Georgia the denominations struggled for control of an institution that had previously tolerated all sects.[10]

In the years following Nullification the new orthodoxy in
religion had its political counterpart with the emergence of the
proslavery argument and a new emphasis on things Southern.
As a result, the churches occasionally made appeals dealing
with the intrinsic value of an education that was both Southern
and denominational. A professor at Furman Theological Institute wrote in 1838 that he hoped his school might "hold out
such advantages and inducements to young brethren . . . as to
supersede the necessity of going North for study." A Georgia
female seminary appealed in 1838 "to parents wishing to educate their daughters thoroughly and at home" not to send them
to "Northern Seminaries." The University of Alabama's
trustees declared that "our sons should be educated in our
own State."[11]

By 1840 religious orthodoxy—with education as its vehicle—was clearly ascendant in the South. Fusing with sectionalism, orthodoxy faced the North with a defense of slavery
based on a strict interpretation of the Bible. Within the South
orthodoxy demanded and often got a rigid conformity of behavior and belief. Southern Christians were beginning to reach
a consensus on certain basic values—chiefly the question of
slavery—and they differed from their Northern brethren in
fundamental ways.

II

"Of all the systems of iniquity that ever cursed the world, the
slave system is the most abominable," asserted the Maine Baptist Association in 1836. Abolition sentiment was on the rise in

---

10. Eaton, *Freedom-of-Thought Struggle*, pp. 300–312; Malone, *Public Life of Cooper*, pp. 254–67; Eaton, *Mind of the Old South*, p. 201; Coulter, *College Life*, pp.
158–65.
11. Quoted in Godbold, *Church College*, pp. 74–75; Alma Foerster, "The State
University in the Old South" (Ph.D. diss., Duke University, 1939), p. 417.

New England, and the churches, arbiters of good and evil, were taking unequivocal stands against slavery. In 1837 the New England Anti-Slavery Society resolved overwhelmingly in favor of "excommunication of slaveholders, and a solemn consideration of the question whether the churches remaining obdurate, it is not the duty of the advocates of truth and righteousness to come out from among them and be separate." By 1839 a national abolitionist convention urged the secession of antislavery churchmen from their national organizations.[12]

Southerners responded in kind. Many Southern churchmen—clergy and congregation—were slaveholders or aspiring slaveholders and had a stake in the peculiar institution. In addition to devising a comprehensive Biblical defense of slavery, Southern spokesmen answered the abolitionist attack with a matching bitterness and intractability. The Presbyterian *Southern Christian Herald* warned "our orthodox brethren at the north [to] let the subject of slavery alone." The Georgia Methodist Conference unanimously resolved in 1837 "that slavery, as it exists in the United States, is not a moral evil . . . and we view slavery as a civil and domestic institution." The Alabama Baptist Association resolved in 1840 "to resist all interference of Northerners in our domestic relations." The feeling existed even at the lowest levels. A devout North Carolina farmer wrote in 1840 that "untill I am convinced that slavery is sinfull & whilst it is sanctioned by the civil government under which I live, no Ecclesiastical tribunal shall deprive me of the use of them."[13]

The issue of slavery arose at the General Assembly of the Presbyterian church that met in Pittsburgh in 1835. Ostensi-

12. William Warren Sweet, *The Story of Religions in America* (New York: Harper and Brothers, 1930), p. 426. A magisterial study of American religious history is Sydney Ahlstrom, *A Religious History of the American People* (New Haven: Yale University Press, 1972).

13. C. Bruce Staiger, "Abolitionism and the Presbyterian Schism of 1837–1838," *Mississippi Valley Historical Review* 36 (1949): 404; Posey, *Frontier Mission*, pp. 353, 364–65; John Ruff to John S. Martin, March 25, 1840, John S. Martin Papers, Southern Historical Collection.

bly the conflict was between the so-called Old School Presbyterians, located mostly in the states south of New York, who
believed that man's will was bound by his predestination and
that salvation was limited to the elect, and the New School
churchmen of the midwest and northeast, who held to "the
sufficiency of human reason in matters of religion." The
staunch South Carolina Old School Presbyterian James H.
Thornwell recognized the insidious threat of New School rationalism which "made the prophets and apostles succumb to
philosophy and impulse" and which therefore might lead to
"serious disasters, not only to the religious, but likewise the
political interests of the country." The logical extension of
New School theology was that slavery was a sin. The Old
School idea that it was "infinitely more important that the
slaves be delivered from the bondage of sin and Satan than
from temporal slavery" was clearly in jeopardy.[14]

The behavior of Northern Presbyterians and Congregationalists confirmed these vague Southern fears. During the
late twenties and early thirties the dynamic preacher Charles
Grandison Finney had sparked revivals across upstate New
York and through Ohio that were accompanied by a blaze of
reformist zeal. Moved by the revivalist impulse, the wealthy
merchant brothers Lewis and Arthur Tappan of New York,
who sponsored educational reform and temperance legislation,
helped found the American Anti-Slavery Movement. In all
these developments Presbyterian ministers in the North
played a small but influential role. Their influence was especially visible at both Lane Theological Seminary, founded in
Ohio in 1832, and Oberlin College, where Theodore Dwight
Weld, a Finney convert and a man of unusual qualities, labored among his fellow seminarians to bring them to an abolitionist position. As the converts went forth to spread their

14. William Goodell, *Slavery and Anti-Slavery: A History of the Great Struggle in
Both Hemispheres* (New York: W. Harned, 1852), p. 152; Posey, *Frontier Mis-
sion*, p. 339; Staiger, "Abolition and the Presbyterian Schism," pp. 393–94;
Jenkins, *Pro-Slavery Thought*, p. 237.

message, New School Presbyterian clergy opened their churches to mass abolition meetings.[15]

The threats to slavery came to a head at Pittsburgh, where for the first time there was a sufficient number of abolitionists present to place the slavery question on the Assembly agenda. Weld happily reported that the number of delegates "believing slavery a *sin* and *immediate emancipation a duty* . . . constitute nearly *one-fourth part* of the Assembly." Southern delegates joined with Northern moderates to forestall debate by assigning a committee to study the issue and report back at the 1836 Assembly. By that time the majority of representatives were New School and unity among Presbyterians was a hollow term. That Assembly voted to establish Union Theological Seminary in New York to train New School clergy but, because moderates still prevailed, resolved to postpone the subject of slavery indefinitely.[16]

But the issue could not so easily be ignored. The *New York Evangelist*, a leading Presbyterian organ, exclaimed that "the recent agitations have brought the true question to light.—IS SLAVERY SIN?—On this the whole matter turns, and here the churches, and particularly the Presbyterian churches are to be tried and perhaps divided asunder." A Kentuckian wrote, "Look! The Northern Abolitionists and the Southern Spirits of Violence! Are they not together hastening on a crisis, the most tremendous? . . . Separation! Separation!! This fearful note is already being sounded by the *Northern* Section

15. William Warren Sweet, *The Presbyterians, 1783–1840*, vol. 2 of *Religion on the American Frontier*, 4 vols. (New York: Harper and Brothers, 1936), pp. 114–17; Ernest T. Thompson, *The Presbyterians in the South*, 3 vols. (Richmond: John Knox Press, 1963), 1: 377–94; Gilbert H. Barnes, *The Anti-Slavery Impulse, 1830–1844* (New York: Appleton–Century Company, 1933), pp. 79–87.

16. Margaret B. Deschamps, "The Presbyterian Church in the South Atlantic States, 1801–1861" (Ph.D. diss., Emory University, 1952), p. 182; Staiger, "Abolition and the Presbyterian Schism," p. 397; Gilbert H. Barnes and Dwight Dumond, eds., *Letters of Theodore Dwight Weld, Angelina Grimké Weld, and Sarah Grimké*, 2 vols. (New York: D. Appleton–Century Co., 1934) 1: 224; Posey, *Frontier Mission*, pp. 342–43.

of the Church." The Charleston Presbytery threatened to withdraw from the national Assembly rather than "be associated with a body of men who denounce the ministers and members of southern churches as pirates and man stealers, or cooperate with those that thus denounce them."[17]

Before the 1837 Assembly in Philadelphia a caucus of Old School delegates plotted strategy. These conservative churchmen tried to find "effectual measures for putting an end to the contentions. . . ." The first move was to overturn the Plan of Union with the New England Congregationalists, who tended toward the New School. The Plan had been in effect since 1801. That done, all synods—ecclesiastical districts equivalent to the Methodist Conference or the Episcopal Diocese—not organized under strict Presbyterian rules were exscinded. As a result four troublesome synods—three in upstate New York and one in Ohio, which were not so organized—were cast out.[18]

Slavery was never mentioned, but it was responsible for the successful purging of the reformers. Northern and Southern Old School delegates could stay united only by ignoring the issue of slavery. While it was clear that the Old School placed harmony above sectionalism in 1837, it was also clear that slavery lay not far below the surface. The North Carolina Synod, for example, acknowledged that the Old School strategy was to make the case for excision on grounds other than abolition. "As it [abolition] was not alluded to in the debate [the Synod] believe[s] it had little or no influence in bringing about the decision, but [it believes] the question was honestly debated and decided on its merits." It was equally clear that had the first plan failed, the slavery question would have been introduced and the separation would have been a good deal less peaceful. Slavery was on the Carolinians' minds; it was doubtless on others' as well. Thereafter, Old School and New

17. *New York Evangelist*, November 21, 1835, quoted in Staiger, "Abolition and the Presbyterian Schism," p. 398; Sweet, *The Presbyterians*, p. 120.
18. Sweet, *The Presbyterians*, pp. 120–22.

School Presbyterians existed separately—and practically equal in size—until 1861.[19]

Less successful in handling the slavery issue were the Baptists, who constituted about one-third of the Southern population. The Baptist church was loosely organized. Each congregation was an autonomous body often served by a minister who farmed for six days of the week and preached on the seventh. There was no desire to change this arrangement, but by the 1830's church officials were beginning to see the value of unity. They organized state conventions in many states over vigorous local opposition. The Mississippi Convention gave a typical warning to the advocates of church hierarchy, vowing that it would "never possess a single attribute of power or authority over any church or association."

Still lacking a formal organization, various groups of Baptists had organized a number of boards over the years to direct denominational activities. One, formed in 1814 with headquarters in Boston, was the Foreign Mission Board; another, the Home Missionary Society, had been founded in New York in 1832. Together these two bodies constituted the Triennial Convention, which served as the sole national and unifying force among Baptists.

A number of Southern Baptists had long believed that the Northern-based Home Society gave insufficient support to activities in the South and West. In 1837 a Nashville Baptist publication announced "that the only way to produce effort in the south must be brought about by the formation of a Southern Baptist Home Mission Society." Another journal, employing familiar anti-tariff rhetoric, was more specific: "The South is sustaining missions in the Eastern and Northern States. . . . The domestic missions of the South can be better sustained in our separate existence." Still another charged Maine, New Hampshire, Vermont, and Michigan with "hostility to the South. . . ; yet these states, while supplying thousands of emigrants to the West, have never collectively given half as much

19. Posey, *Frontier Mission*, pp. 148–50.

in one year to the Home Mission Society, as has been contributed by Virginia in the same space of time."[20]

   To remedy the charges of inequity, which were
unfounded, the call arose for the organization of a separate
Southern Baptist convention. The desire was rooted in the
belief that the decentralized nature of the denomination
needed to be replaced by a more formal organizational structure, and it was advocated by the educated leadership of the
church, not by its less well informed rank-and-file membership. This feeling, which underlay the paternalistic defense
of slavery, was far stronger in the South, where a dispersed,
isolated population was prone to the erratic and omnipotent
behavior of an often illiterate and independent ministry. A
Louisville minister demonstrated this concern when he envisioned "a great national association" where "we might display our national motto *e pluribus unum. . . .*" If Northerners
continued to prefer a less organized system, Southerners
would set up their own separate hierarchy. In the meantime,
Southern Baptists began to intensify their efforts to organize
state conventions to bring greater unity to their scattered
flock.[21]

   The injection of the slavery issue gave an added impetus
to the search for order among Southern Baptist leaders. Like
the Presbyterians, the Baptists tried to avoid discussing slavery
in their national meetings. In 1837 only the Methodists, who
owned an estimated 220,000, held more slaves than the Baptists, who owned 115,000. The *Baptist Magazine* refused to open
its pages for debate on the subject. But in 1834 a group of English Baptist ministers addressed a letter to "the Pastors and
Ministers of the Baptist denomination throughout the United
States of America." The letter spoke of British efforts recently
completed to abolish slavery in the West Indies and suggested

---

20. William Wright Barnes, *The Southern Baptist Convention, 1845–1953* (Nashville: Boardman Press, 1954), pp. 12–16.
21. *Ibid.*, p. 10; A. H. Newman, *A History of the Baptist Churches in the United
States,* vol. 2 of *American Church History,* ed. Rev. Philip Schaff et al., 13 vols.
(New York: Christian Literature Co., 1894), pp. 433–37.

that American Baptists might begin to labor for similar results. The Boston office of the Foreign Board responded by politely but firmly pointing to present unity among American Baptists and urging the British not to interfere. In response the English Baptist Union sent delegates to America in 1835 determined, they asserted, "to promote most zealously, and to the utmost of their ability, in the spirit of love, of discretion, and fidelity, BUT STILL MOST ZEALOUSLY to promote the sacred cause of negro emancipation." The English delegates attended the 1835 Triennial Convention held in Richmond, and, though silent on the convention floor, they met privately with a number of sympathizers and later attended a Baptist meeting in New Hampshire to make a vocal attack on slavery. The English Baptist Union continued to correspond with its American friends during the 1830's.[22]

The Richmond Convention was the last peaceful gathering of Baptists. Southerners—desiring a tighter organization, aware of the British efforts, and surely cognizant of growing abolitionism in America—made their position clear. The Charleston Baptist Association in 1835 stated that "the Divine Author of our holy religion . . . found slavery a part of the existing institutions of society, with which, if not sinful, it was not his desire to INTERMEDDLE. . . ." The Goshen (Virginia) Baptist Association upheld the rights of its members to hold slaves. *The Baptist* in Nashville vowed that Southerners alone would determine the future of slavery. The *Southern Watchman*, far ahead of its readers, called Southerners "a distinct and separate people" who had "their domestic institutions to protect and vindicate in conformity with the word of God."[23]

22. Sydnor, *Southern Sectionalism*, p. 299; Sweet, *Story of Religions*, p. 428; Goodell, *Slavery and Anti-Slavery*, pp. 493–96; Mary B. Putnam, *The Baptists and Slavery* (Ann Arbor: University of Michigan Press, 1913), pp. 10–13. See also Table 2, Appendix V.

23. Goodell, *Slavery and Anti-Slavery*, p. 184; Posey, *Frontier Mission*, p. 337; *Southern Christian Advocate*, December 1, 1837, quoted in Donald G. Mathews, *Slavery and Methodism: A Chapter in American Morality, 1780–1845* (Princeton: Princeton University Press, 1965), p. 207.

The sections were growing further apart. In April 1840 the National Baptist Anti-Slavery Convention was organized in New York "for the purpose of considering the connection of the denomination with slavery, and inquiring 'What could be done?' " The convention issued an inflammatory *Address to Southern Baptists*, which evoked a quick and bitter response. The Alabama Baptist Association resolved in October 1840 "to resist all interference of Northerners in our domestic relations." The Savannah River Baptist Association encouraged Southern delegates to the Triennial Convention of 1841 scheduled for Baltimore, "to DEMAND of our northern brethren WHETHER THEY CAN ACKNOWLEDGE THOSE [abolitionist] FANATICS AS THEIR CO-WORKERS IN THE GREAT WORK OF EVANGELIZING THE WORLD, and to state fully to them the impossibility of our further co-operation, UNLESS THEY DISMISS SUCH FROM THEIR BODY."[24]

Southerners pretty much had things their way in Baltimore in 1841. Northern moderates joined with Southerners to remove Elon Galusha, an active abolitionist, as vice president of the Foreign Board, replacing him with Richard Fuller of South Carolina. Contented with their influence in the expanding role of the national body, the Southerners agreed not to press the slavery question and the convention adjourned on a hopeful note.[25]

But the abolitionists were outraged, not only at the removal of Galusha in favor of the slaveholder Fuller but also at the agreement to suppress discussion of slavery. "Like all compromises," muttered one abolitionist, "it gave all to slavery." A Vermont Baptist antislavery meeting attacked slaveholders as "these despoilers of God's image—these robbers of earthly interests—these destroyers of souls" and vowed to "withdraw from cooperation with slave-holders and their supporters." In 1843 Baptist abolitionists organized their own Free Missionary

24. Goodell, *Slavery and Anti-Slavery*, p. 496; Posey, *Frontier Mission*, pp. 364–65.
25. Sweet, *Story of Religions*, pp. 428–29; Posey, *Frontier Mission*, p. 365.

Society in Boston to operate independently from the Foreign Board.[26]

A year later, in 1844, the Triennial Convention assembled in Philadelphia. Only about one-fifth of the delgates present were Southerners. Each board confronted a decision that was inseparable from slavery. The Home Society met to consider the nomination of a Georgia slaveholder, James E. Reeves, as a missionary. Georgia Baptists urged his selection "as it will stop the mouths of gain-sayers. . . ." The society rejected Reeves, the first slaveholding candidate since the compromise, claiming that his nomination would, by introducing the slavery question, violate earlier agreements.[27]

The Foreign Board was also facing the same irrepressible question. An angry group of Alabama Baptists had addressed a letter to the board demanding "the distinct and explicit avowal that *slaveholders* are eligible and entitled to . . . receive any agency, *mission*, or other appointment. . . ." When the board replied that "if . . . anyone should offer himself as a missionary, having slaves, and should insist on retaining them as his property, we could not appoint him."[28]

With that answer dissolution became inevitable. The Virginia Baptist Foreign Missionary Society called a convention of Southern Baptists to meet at Augusta in May 1845. Three hundred and seventy-seven delegates from eight Southern states reluctantly resolved there to make the "painful division" and set up a separate Southern Baptist "provisional government." The Southerners emphasized without malice that "the constitution we adopt is precisely that of the original union. . . . Thrust from the common platform of equal rights, between the Northern and Southern churches, we have but

26. Goodell, *Slavery and Anti-Slavery*, pp. 498–99; *Address to the Baptist Anti-Slavery Convention Held At Waterbury* [*Vt.*] *on the 29th and 30th of September, 1841* (n.p., 1841).
27. Posey, *Frontier Mission*, p. 367; Sweet, *Story of Religions*, pp. 430–31.
28. Goodell, *Slavery and Anti-Slavery*, pp. 500–501; Newman, *History of Baptist Churches*, pp. 446–47; Posey, *Frontier Mission*, pp. 365–66; Sweet, *Story of Religions*, p. 431.

reconstructed that platform. . . ." Indeed, but for the tolera-
tion of slavery, the Southern Baptist Convention was a more
highly centralized duplicate in doctrine of the convention from
which it had seceded, and it remained so. "We do not regard
the rupture as extending to foundation principles," the Southerners declared. But the slavery issue had interfered with their
efforts to strengthen the church hierarchy. When that hierarchy began to assert itself as Southerners had long desired, the
South quickly realized the double-edged sword they had fash-
ioned. "Fanatical attempts have indeed been made . . . to exclude us of the South from Christian fellowship," the Southerners stated, but at heart "Northern and Southern Baptists
are still brethren." There is no evidence to suggest that the advocacy of a centralized organization was a cover for a conspiracy to win church sanction of slavery. Rather, the slavery issue
gave an added charge to efforts in creating the desired structure, for such desires preceded the intrusion of slavery into the
convention. Resolving to "go everywhere preaching the gospel," the Southern Baptist Convention began its career.[29]

At almost the same time the Methodist were suffering a
similar ordeal. Although early on that denomination had advocated emancipation, by 1800 Methodism had abandoned all
antislavery efforts. By 1824 the church rules or *Discipline*—the
religious code for the thirty-seven percent of the Southern
population who called themselves Methodists—were changed
for the last time until 1860. The *Discipline* prohibited slaveholders from holding church positions in states having emancipation laws; state laws were to take precedence over church
laws with regard to emancipation; and slaves were to receive
regular religious instruction.[30]

29. Newman, *History of Baptists*, pp. 451–452; Sweet, *History of Religions*, pp.
432–33; Ahlstrom, *Religious History*, p. 664.
30. Lewis M. Purifoy, "The Methodist Episcopal Church, South, and Slavery" (Ph.D. diss., University of North Carolina, 1965), p. 325; William Warren Sweet, *The Methodist Episcopal Church and the Civil War* (Cincinnati: Methodist Book Concern Press, 1912), p. 19; William Warren Sweet, *The Methodists*,
vol. 3 of *Religion on the American Frontier*, p. 233. See also Table 2, Appendix
V.

Concession and compromise bespoke a prevalent desire to avoid disruption over the slavery issue. The General Conference held in Cincinnati in 1836, though challenged by a British delegate to take a stand favoring emancipation and annoyed by the address of two New Hampshire delegates to a local antislavery society, tried to maintain a conciliatory spirit. The conference adopted by a vote of 120 to 14 a Pastoral Address declaring that "the question of slavery in the United States, by the constitutional compact . . . is left to be regulated by the several State Legislatures themselves; and thereby is put beyond the control of the general government, *as well as of all ecclesiastical bodies*. . . ." At the same time the conference, seeking to placate abolitionists, rejected the nomination of William Capers, a South Carolina slaveholder, for bishop and instead elected three nonslaveholders, two Northerners and one Southerner.[31]

After the so-called compromise, neither side was satisfied. William Lloyd Garrison cried that "all genuine Methodists . . . will loathe and abhor the pro-slavery doings of the Cincinnati Convention, and ascribe them to Satanic influences." Orange Scott, a leading New England Methodist minister, traveled from Maine to Ohio addressing many local conferences on abolition, advocating "conference rights" to oppose the Cincinnati declaration and charging repeatedly that "the *professed* Christians of the South, together with their *apologists* in the North are the *main supporters* of slavery. . . ." Scott and his sympathizers during 1837 and 1838 launched a number of abolition newspapers and organized Methodist antislavery conventions throughout the northeast.[32]

Southerners responded predictably, terming the defeat of

31. John Nelson Norwood, *The Schism in the Methodist Episcopal Church, 1844: A Study of Slavery and Ecclesiastical Politics* (Alfred, N.Y.: Alfred Press, 1923), pp. 26–27; Posey, *Frontier Mission*, p. 332; William Warren Sweet, *Methodism in American History* (Cincinnati: Methodist Book Concern, 1933), p. 237; Mathews, *Slavery and Methodism*, pp. 139–47; Sweet, *Story of Religions*, p. 433.

32. Goodell, *Slavery and Anti-Slavery*, pp. 145–46; Mathews, *Slavery and Methodism*, pp. 148–49, 157; Sweet, *M.E. Church and the Civil War*, p. 21.

Capers a "proscription" and an "insult." William A. Smith, later a leading proslavery writer, urged the formation of a separate Southern General Conference if "these men" continued their efforts to "reduce the whole southern portion of the church. . . ." Capers himself claimed for the South a superior civilization, attacked Northern church editors for supporting congressional acceptance of abolition petitions, and argued that opposition to slavery was "foreign alike from the constitution and aims of the Methodists as applied to the South." William Winans of Mississippi pointed out that "the South has its chivalric notions in regard to foreign interference in domestic concerns." The Georgia Conference in 1837, promising to shed "the last drop of blood that warmed their hearts before submitting to the doctrines of Northern fanatics," charged the abolitionists with "perverting" the church *Discipline*. "It is the sense of the Georgia Annual Conference," the disturbed ministers declared, "that slavery, as it exists in the United States, *is not a moral evil.*"[33] Rapidly dawning was the belief that Southern Methodists shared ideas that were incompatible with the thinking of their Northern brethren.

The raising of the slavery issue brought to the surface another Southern concern. In the highly structured Methodist organization—which ranged from the General Conference, which was the national organization, to the bishop, to the presiding elder, to the local conference, to the local congregation—Southerners wished settled the issue of conference jurisdiction. Since 1836 bishops and presiding elders had regularly rejected abolitionist petitions. This practice of local censorship prevented the petitions from reaching the agenda of the annual local conferences. Abolitionists argued that such local censorship eroded the authority of the General Conference. Southerners, on the other hand, contended that slavery was not a matter over which the church had any jurisdiction. Emphasizing the need for separating affairs of church and state, Southerners urged the General Conference to uphold the ac-

33. Mathews, *Slavery and Methodism*, pp. 177–78, 181, 189–90; Goodell, *Slavery and Anti-Slavery*, p. 149.

tions of the censoring officials and warned against "improper
intermeddling with the subject of slavery." The issue of conference authority did not emerge until the slavery question
arose. There is no evidence that a genuine Southern concern
for General Conference powers existed before the question of
slavery appeared.[34]

The 1840 General Conference gathered in Baltimore with
all the antagonists—Scott, Capers, Smith—present but with
moderates still in control. The local conferences had earlier
been asked to vote on a change in the *Discipline* proposed by the
New England Conference to prohibit "the buying or selling, or
holding [of] men, women, or children as slaves, or giving them
away except on purpose to free them." Only New Hampshire
voted for the change, though several conferences had sizable
minority votes. The General Conference rejected a number of
abolition petitions and censured the New Englanders for
threatening church unity. Finally it endorsed the actions of
those bishops who had blocked discussion of abolition in the
local conferences. These leaders had a right, resolved the conference, "to decline putting a question, which . . . did not
relate to the proper business of the annual conference." The
conference therefore upheld the Southern argument favoring
the power of the local conferences. No new bishops were elected, since the moderate majority feared a repetition of the 1836
episode. In response frustrated abolitionists refused to make a
routine donation to the Methodist church in Natchez, Mississippi—which had been destroyed by fire—believing that to
contribute would be to give approval to slaveholding. Contented slaveholders, apprehensive moderates, and angry abolitionists left Baltimore in 1840 with the future of their national
organization in peril.[35]

34. Sweet, *Methodism in American History*, pp. 239–40; Mathews, *Slavery and Methodism*, p. 188.
35. Sweet, *M.E. Church and the Civil War*, p. 22; Charles Baumer Swaney, *Episcopal Methodism and Slavery; With Sidelights on Ecclesiastical Politics*, reprint ed. (New York: Negro Universities Press, 1969), pp. 93–99; Sweet, *Methodism in American History*, p. 240.

Radical Northerners spoke of secession. In 1841 a small group of Michigan Methodists organized themselves as Wesleyan Methodists, splintering from the General Conference. Orange Scott called a convention of antislavery men to meet in Albany, New York, late in 1842, where secession was consummated. In May 1843 these dissidents also adopted the name of Wesleyan Methodists, and within six months the new organization claimed a membership of fifteen thousand from Maine to Michigan.[36]

Southerners tactlessly failed to conceal their glee. Smith with his venomous pen attacked the "New England enemies" of the South. Needlessly exacerbating tensions, the editors of other Southern journals belittled "yankees" and described Southern Methodism as "calm and placid" in contrast to Methodism in the North, which was "like an ocean in the uproar and rage of the storm." While moderate men, whose numbers were declining, feared further schism, William Wightman, editor of the Charleston-based *Southern Christian Advocate*, wanted to press for the election of a slaveholding bishop at the 1844 General Conference. "The dodging or refusing such an election," he raged, "endorses on the part of the General Conference the calumnies of the abolitionists. . . ."[37]

Bishop James O. Andrew of Georgia became the focus of debate as the 1844 General Conference assembled in New York on May 1. Andrew, a gentle, quiet man—and a nonslaveholder—had been a bishop since his unopposed election in 1832. In 1844, after the death of his first wife, Andrew remarried. Since his second wife had inherited slaves from the estate of her first husband, he immediately initiated legal proceedings renouncing personal ownership of the black laborers. When a number of antislavery delegates, including many moderates who were offended by Southern attacks and feared further Northern defections, informed Andrew they would vote to

---

36. Sweet, *Methodism in American History*, pp. 241–42; Mathews, *Slavery and Methodism*, pp. 230–32; Norwood, *Schism in the M.E. Church*, pp. 50–56.
37. Mathews, *Slavery and Methodism*, pp. 236, 242–43.

remove him from office, the moderate Georgian agreed to re-sign his position.[38]

But the Southern delegates would not permit him to re-sign. Fearing his acquiescence represented a "fatal conces-sion," Southerners took to the floor to defeat his removal, argu-ing that the General Conference had no authority in the case of a bishop, who was an officer of the conference. The episcopacy and the conference were consubstantial; to allow the suspen-sion of Andrew was to deny the principle of local conference rights, the belief in separation of church and state, and—more important—-the morality of slavery. As in the case of the Bap-tists, the search for clarification of the structure's workings proved divisive in the end. "The southern ministry at large," claimed one delegate, had a vital interest in the outcome of the case. Throughout the month of May the debate raged, attract-ing thousands of curious New Yorkers who wanted to witness a slavery debate for themselves. Smith argued that the General Conference had no power to decide the issue, since the confer-ence was merely a creation of the local conferences, which had jurisdiction in such cases. Winans, declaring himself "a South-ern man—an extreme Southern man," concurred. G. F. Pierce of Georgia called the move to unseat Andrew "an infraction of Southern rights."[39]

Finally, on June 1, the issue came to a vote. It was clear that most of the moderates, who had so long sympathized and sided with the South, were repelled by Southern intransigence in refusing to accept Andrew's resignation and calm a troubled church. By a vote of 110 to 69 it became "the sense of this Gen-

38. Wilbur Fisk Tillett, "James Osgood Andrew," *Dictionary of American Biog-raphy* 1: 277–79; Sweet, *Methodism in American History*, p. 246; Mathews, *Slav-ery and Methodism*, pp. 246–57.

39. Mathews, *Slavery and Methodism*, pp. 258, 262; George G. Smith, *The Life and Letters of James Osgood Andrew* (Nashville: Southern Methodist Pub. House, 1883), pp. 336–37; *New York Herald*, May 25, 1844; Norwood, *Schism in the M.E. Church*, p. 74; *The Debates of the General Conference of the Methodist Episcopal Church, May, 1844* (New York: L. J. McIndoe, Printer, 1845), pp. 181, 74, 146.

eral Conference that [Bishop Andrew] desist from the exercise
of his office so long as this impediment [slaveholding] remains." Thirteen Northerners joined a solid and unanimous
bloc of Southerners in the minority.[40]

The Southern delegates then met and decided unanimously to withdraw to set up the Methodist Episcopal
Church, South. They explained their decision on the grounds
that

> the Constitution of the Church, like the Constitution of the
> United States, was framed and adopted in the spirit of compro-
> mise. There were, in the Convention, slaveholders, and there
> were men who were opposed to slavery. These all agreed to offer
> up their respective peculiarities on one common altar, for the
> glory of God and for the good of his Church.

More than seventy churches scattered throughout the South
voiced their approval immediately, and in May 1845 delegates
from fifteen Southern conferences convened at Louisville.
They voted officially to sever ties with the General Conference, thereby freeing "the minority of the South from the
oppressive jurisdiction of the majority in the North." The
Methodist church ceased to be national.[41]

In a pamphlet the founders of the new church contended
that

> the Methodist Episcopal Church, as an organized body, is but an
> association of individuals, voluntarily united for specific pur-
> poses. . . .
>
> The Northern Methodist Church . . . is so mixed up with
> the whole machinery of abolition and anti-slavery agitation and
> invasion, by its recent proclamation of hostility to the South, in
> so many forms of bitter and malignant assault, that its own cho-

---

40. *Debates*, p. 280. Actually, one Texas delegate, who had recently removed
from the North, did not vote with the South. The Baltimore Conference, in
the dilemma of a border state, split 5–5. See *Debates*, pp. 278–79.
41. Alexander McCaine, *Slavery Defended from Scripture, Against the Attacks of
the Abolitionists* (Baltimore: William Woody, 1842), p. 27; Mathews, *Slavery and
Methodism*, pp. 277–79; Posey, *Frontier Mission*, p. 359.

sen colors will not allow us any longer to distinguish it from the common enemy. It has become a pander to political agitation. It is an *Abolition* church.

Preaching a "states' rights" gospel, the Methodists explained their separation.[42]

Thus, by 1845 the Baptists, Methodists, and Presbyterians had each confronted the slavery issue. Defining the position of a church, like defining the position of a nation, on an issue expressed in moral terms made conflict irrepressible, despite the best efforts of moderate men. Southern churchmen seceded reluctantly only after they became convinced that the existing relationship posed a threat both to themselves as slaveholders and, thus, to their section. After 1845 the three-fourths of the population of the slaveholding states who were Baptists or Methodists were forced to recognize the distinctiveness they shared with others who weekly joined them in worship at the new, Southern branch of their church. After 1845 to be an upright Baptist or Methodist one also had to be an upright Southerner.

III

The effect of the separations of the churches was powerful and catalytic. Senator Clay of Kentucky mourned that the rupture was "fraught with imminent danger" to the Union. Calhoun, considering the schisms "very important . . . in a political as well as in a religious view of the subject," summoned a group of Methodist ministers to tell him the details. Hammond, praising the "patriotic Methodists of the South," provided land on his plantation for the construction of a "handsome" church, which he himself financed. "Nor will I fail," he added, "to

42. H. B. Bascom, A. L. P. Greene, C. B. Parsons, *Brief Appeal to Public Opinion, In a Series of Exceptions to the Course and Action of the Methodist Episcopal Church, From 1844 to 1848, Affecting the Rights and Interests of the Methodist Episcopal Church, South* (Louisville: Morton and Griswold Printers, 1848), pp. 11, 61.

make up any pecuniary losses that may accrue to them from this *Secession*. . . ." The *Charleston Mercury*, calling the schisms the "most ominous event of our times," noted that

> in this content of religion we have an entire and remediless sever-
> ance of the Union—a division that henceforth creates in the two
> most numerous denominations of the country a Northern and a
> Southern religion and this separation brought about by no ac-
> cident, no heat of the moment, but after much deliberation and
> unwearied efforts to reconcile the dissention—efforts that
> yielded only to a settled conviction that reconciliation was impos-
> sible.[43]

The timing of the divisions made it difficult to disentangle the issues at stake in the churches from the events then in prog-ress on the political stage. The religious schisms coincided with the Bluffton Movement in South Carolina against the tar-iff in 1844, which briefly revived the antagonisms and argu-ments of Nullification. The year 1844 was also a presidential election year. The issue on which the campaign turned was the annexation of Texas as a slaveholding state.[44]

Meanwhile, Southern churches began to emphasize their new concern for things Southern. Nowhere were these feel-ings more intensely expressed than in the various churches' new attitude towards education. Southern Methodists received a "Pastoral Address" from their General Conference in 1846 that emphasized "the necessity of seeking to become less de-pendent upon others for the lights of knowledge, and the aids of virtue, as found in the department of education." Before 1844 "others" would have meant Baptists or Presbyterians; now it meant Northerners. In 1856 the Southern Methodists organized an "Educational Institute" with the idea of improv-

43. Calhoun to Hammond, July 7, 1845, *Calhoun Correspondence*, p. 666; Math-ews, *Slavery and Methodism*, p. 282; Hammond to Calhoun, August 18, 1845, *Calhoun Correspondence*, p. 1049; *Charleston Mercury*, June 14, 1844; Putnam, *Baptists and Slavery*, p. 88.
44. Eaton, *History of the Old South, pp.* 325–28; Lee Benson, *The Concept of Jack-sonian Democracy: New York as a Test Case* (Princeton: Princeton University Press, 1960), pp. 131–33.

ing "the character of text-books and to adapt them to the circumstances of the South . . . by the dissemination of right
ideas. . . ."[45]

The other denominations did not hold back in the educational campaign. The North Carolina Presbyterian Synod acknowledged that "we have been too much accustomed to look
abroad," with the result that "we have fallen insensibly into a
most helpless and humiliating condition. . . ." Of ministers,
the synod declared that "we must 'rear them at home.' " Baptists encouraged their fellow churchmen to patronize Wake
Forest because it was not only a Baptist but also "a Southern"
college.[46]

A second wave of church colleges, often founded explicitly in response to the recent schisms, soon followed. The Baptists established Baylor, Southwestern, Furman, and Bethel
Colleges. The Methodists took over Trinity in North Carolina
and founded Wofford College and Southern University. The
Presbyterians, still exercising influence in the state universities, established Austin College. James C. Furman, a delegate
to the 1844 Triennial Convention and an avowed secessionist,
strongly encouraged the South Carolina Baptist Association to
charter Furman College after the 1844 split "because of the importance of bringing the strongest influence to bear upon the
process of education." The vociferous Methodist separatist
William Wightman of Mississippi was named the first president of both Wofford and, later, Southern. In his Wofford inaugural Wightman attacked the "hard, money-getting, money-
hoarding age" and promised to show no denominational dis-
crimination "to any of the South of this country who may
apply for admission. . . ." The *Charleston Courier* published in
1859 an announcement by Southern claiming for itself the title
of "*the* Southern University."[47]

45. Godbold, *Church College*, p. 73; Knight, ed., *Documentary History* 4:
456–57.
46. Godbold, *Church College*, pp. 73–74.
47. *Ibid.*, *passim*, but esp. p. 29; Furman quoted in Robert Norman Daniel,
Furman University: A History (Greenville, S.C.: Furman University, 1951), p.

The budding educational nationalism of the churches had its secular counterpart. State universities were chartered by the legislatures of Mississippi and Louisiana in 1844 and 1848 respectively. Governor Albert G. Brown of Mississippi championed his state university as a protection from "false prejudices against home institutions and laws." DeBow urged "planters in [Louisiana] and the neighboring States . . . to consider the advantages" of the University of Louisiana, adding that it would surely attract "students from half the Confederacy," the Southern half. Alonzo Church, president of the University of Georgia, published an article in 1849 entitled "We Should Cherish Our Own Institutions of Learning." During the sectional crisis of 1850 a friend wrote to President Thornwell of South Carolina College:

> I find these important questions of the times draw my heart away too much from the greater concerns of the Soul & the ministry of reconciliation. . . . Latterly, say within 2 months, I find myself unable to pray except as a *partisan*. I can not help feeling that we are in a contest, & praying that God would give *us* the Victory.

A group of students at the University of Virginia in 1851 formed a Southern Rights Association and issued an address urging their fellows at other Southern schools "to prepare for the contest. We believe, moreover," they declared, "that our rights and liberties can only be preserved by firm, decisive, and united action. . . ." Over one hundred students at South Carolina College formed a similar association and held campus demonstrations.[48]

46; Joseph H. Parks and Oliver C. Weaver, Jr., *Birmingham-Southern College, 1856–1956* (Nashville: Parthenon Press, 1957), pp. 32–33; Knight, ed., *Documentary History* 4: 370–71; *Charleston Courier*, September 24, 1859. See also Table 1, Appendix V.

48. Brown quoted in Foerster, "State Universities," p. 417; *DeBow's Review* 7 (1849): 188–89; Alonzo Church, "We Should Cherish Our Own Institutions of Learning," in *Southern First Class Book*, comp. by M. M. Mason (New York: Pratt, Woodford, and Co., 1849), p. 114; John B. Adger to James H. Thornwell, September 30, 1850, Thornwell Papers, South Caroliniana Library; *Address, 1851, of the Southern Rights Association of the University of Virginia to the*

The growing sectional consciousness in the colleges was closely linked to a more general awareness of Southern educational needs. "All true friends of the South should give freely to endow Southern institutions of learning, and then follow their benefactions, by sending to them their sons and wards," declared Robert L. Stanton in his inaugural address as president of Mississippi's Oakland College. Biloxi, Mississippi, established a new high school in 1852 and one of the founders wrote to Thornwell for recommendations of teaching candidates. "Our main reason why we wish to obtain a teacher from your State," he explained, "is the fact that we wish to keep rid of northern influence as much as possible." The *Richmond Enquirer* avowed in 1854 that "if Southern gentlemen would not be instrumental in the political prostitution of their sons, they should not send them to Harvard for law or to Yale for science." C. K. Marshall, a Mississippi clergyman and commentator on education, bewailed in 1855 that "our sons and daughters return to us from their schools and colleges in the north with their minds poisoned by fanatical teachings and influences against the institution of slavery. . . ." Such "education" threatened to loose "the flesh-eating, blood-drinking, gluttonous, lazy, debased, brutal, ignorant hordes" from slavery. Southern educational nationalism, too, had its racist streak.[49]

Yet few of the campaigners were very specific about just what Southern education should be. The feeling was widespread that young Southerners ought not to be educated in the Northern "hot-bed of political heresy and 'higher law,' " where education "ruins the mind for agricultural life, begets

---

Young Men of the South (n.p., 1851); James S. McLure to William McLure, March 10, 1851, James Stringfellow McLure Papers, South Caroliniana Library.

49. *Addresses, Delivered on Thursday, December 18, 1851, on the Occasion of the Inauguration of Rev. Robert J. Stanton as President of Oakland College, Miss.* (New Orleans: T. Rea, 1852), p. 21; J. B. Finlay to Thornwell, October 16, 1852, Thornwell Papers, South Caroliniana Library; *Richmond Enquirer*, January 14, 1854; *DeBow's Review* 18 (1855): 431, 666.

contempt for home usages, and returns to the roof-tree an ex-
pensively-dressed, 'dandified' boy-man. . . ." Equally strong
was the belief that "southern life, habits, thoughts, and aims,
are so essentially different from those of the North, that here a
different character of books, tuition, and training is absolutely
required. . . ." The Southern alternative, however, was unclear. Concrete proposals rarely derived from vague ideas
about inculcating "fundamental principles upon which the
whole superstructure of the [Southern] society . . . is based."
Typical was the remark of a Southern commentator who, after
belaboring the need for southern education, announced that he
"purposely avoided any exhibition of the details. . . ." He
never revealed what his purpose was.[50]

At bottom was a conviction infrequently expressed but
deeply held that, as a contributor to *DeBow's* admitted, "our
institutions of learning are inferior in endowment and celeb-
rity, and for argument, even inferior in scholastic attainments
and merit. . . ." This belief underlay the longstanding, disin-
terested campaign in behalf of Southern education advanced
all through the early nineteenth century, chiefly by the
churches. But it was also a strong force on which Southerners
with other purposes might capitalize. The difference was between distinction, for which educators such as Thornwell and
Marshall strove, and distinctiveness, which men outside the
field of education such as DeBow and Brown emphasized. Occasionally educators might play upon sectional chauvinism in
appealing for support, and just as often editors and politicians
might write or speak in vague generalities about educational
improvement. But the very different and apparently irreconcilable aims of the two groups help explain why, on the one
hand, educational innovations and improvements went largely
unheralded and, on the other hand, why the most strident calls
for "Southern education" were completely lacking in substance.[51]

50. *DeBow's Review* 10 (1851): 362–63; 13 (1852): 260, 265.
51. *Ibid.*, 13 (1852): 260–61.

The difference was apparent in the rising clamor for Southern school books. Southern educational nationalists repeatedly lamented the biases of the Northern texts they were forced to use. Histories written in the North attacked "the state of manners and morals" in the South and called slavery "that stain on the human race, which corrupts the master as much as it debases the slave." Southerners who attempted to write alternative texts, however, showed equal bias. For example, D. H. Hill, a mathematics professor at Davidson College, published *Elements of Algebra* in 1857. Problems required students to calculate the rate at which Indiana volunteers deserted a battlefield, the profits earned by Yankee traders who adulterated meat, milk, and nutmegs, and the accident rate on Northern railroads. An acid review by Thornwell, to whom distinction and distinctiveness were not interchangeable terms, termed the book fit only for use in military schools.[52]

After the schisms, with the Southern sectional consciousness aroused, a new and very different kind of orthodoxy arose, which severely inhibited the thoughts and actions of some of the men who might have come forth with plans for improving and distinguishing Southern education. Religious orthodoxy, which had earlier made encroachments on state universities, was now supplanted by a more virulent sectional orthodoxy, which inflexibly distrusted all things and all men not Southern. Professor Francis Lieber of South Carolina College, probably the most distinguished American political scientist of the day, came under fire because of his "unsound" beliefs not only on religion but also on slavery. "I deeply regret," he wrote, "that when my country is in danger I live in South Carolina. I am a *Pan American;* I profess it, I teach it, I preach it and of course I isolate myself. The time may come when I shall be called a traitor." For such traitorous notions, expressed in his condemnatory resolutions against joining the

52. *Ibid.*, p. 259; Ezell, "Southern Education," 315–16; Hal Bridges, *Lee's Maverick General, Daniel Harvey Hill* (New York: McGraw-Hill Book Co., 1961), p. 26; D. H. Hill to Thornwell, December 13, 1857, Thornwell Papers, South Caroliniana Library.

Southern Rights Association in 1851 and in his refusal to contribute to the proslavery argument, Lieber was denied the presidency of the college in 1855. "He that is not for us is against us, and should be so treated," cried a legislator, and Lieber departed Columbia for the North.[53]

Other deviants were similarly treated. In 1849 Howard Malcolm, a Northern native who was president of Kentucky's Georgetown College, was forced by the trustees to resign after voting for an antislavery delegate to the state constitutional convention. The distinguished professor of mathematics at the Universities of Alabama and Mississippi, Frederick A. P. Barnard, a Massachusetts native but a Southerner and a slaveholder since 1838, was also suspect. Some time after his election in 1854 to the presidency of Mississippi, while investigating a student's assault on one of his black female servants, Barnard, contrary to state law, accepted the Negro's version of the story as testimony. Though "cleared" by the university trustees, Barnard remained troubled by the unseemly affair and left Mississippi for New York's Columbia College in 1861. In 1858 a Montgomery newspaper called for the ouster of Nathan Green, president of Cumberland University in Tennessee and a former justice of the state supreme court, for publicly branding slavery as evil.[54]

Meanwhile, educational zealots defended slavery. William A. Smith, president of Randolph–Macon during the 1850's, published in 1856 a long proslavery volume in which he urged that "the poison . . . must be distilled" from college

53. Francis Lieber quoted in Eaton, *Freedom-of-Thought Struggle*, p. 58; Lieber to George Hillard, August 11, 1850, Francis Lieber Collection, South Caroliniana Library; Daniel Walker Hollis, *University of South Carolina*, 2 vols. (Columbia: University of South Carolina Press, 1951), 1: 177–93; Frank Freidel, *Francis Lieber, Nineteenth Century Liberal* (Baton Rouge: Louisiana State University Press, 1947), esp. pp. 133–39.
54. Eaton, *Freedom-of-Thought Struggle*, p. 233; Allen Cabaniss, *The University of Mississippi: Its First Hundred Years* (Hattiesburg, Miss.: University and College Press of Mississippi, 1971), pp. 35–48; W. P. Bone, *A History of Cumberland University, 1842–1935* (Lebanon, Tenn.: By the Author, 1935), pp. 80–83.

textbooks. Albert T. Bledsoe of the University of Virginia issued an *Essay on Liberty and Slavery* in 1857 which urged the morality of slavery. In a pseudonymous response published in Boston, one of his colleagues accurately described the state of paranoia then prevalent. "No person," he wrote, "can safely reside in the South who is suspected of liberal views on the subject of slavery."[55]

In churches and schools, then, Southerners were searching for order in the seeming chaos brought about by rapid social and economic change. The confluence of religious orthodoxy, sectional orthodoxy, and Southern chauvinism, to which Southerners were turning in growing numbers, is clearly revealed in the career of George Frederick Holmes. Born in British Guiana in 1820, Holmes began his education in England at the University of Durham, but he abruptly left in 1837 for Canada and then moved to South Carolina, where he settled in 1841. Describing his condition in those days as "a foreigner—friendless—fundless," the tall, lanky, and often sloppily dressed Holmes began a brief and undistinguished career as a member of the South Carolina bar. Bored and less than successful, he married the daughter of John Floyd, former governor of Virginia, and became the owner of four slaves.[56]

As a young man Holmes was, according to his biographer, "an enthusiastic and outspoken devotee of the Enlightenment" and no friend of organized religion. He found his intellectual sustenance in the writings of Bacon, Locke, and Hume, empiricists all. Holmes established himself in the pages

55. William A. Smith, *Lectures on the Philosophy and Practice of Slavery*, p. 29, [Charles B. Shaw], *A Reply to Professor Bledsoe*, both quoted in Eaton, *Freedom-of-Thought Struggle*, p. 226.

56. Samuel Chiles Mitchell, "George Frederick Holmes," *Dictionary of American Biography* 9: 164; Leonidas Betts, "George Frederick Homes: Nineteenth Century Virginia Educator," *Virginia Magazine of History and Biography* 76 (1968): 472–75; Neal C. Gillespie, *The Collapse of Orthodoxy: The Intellectual Ordeal of George Frederick Holmes* (Charlottesville, Va.: University of Virginia Press, 1972), pp. 3–32.

of the *Southern Literary Messenger* and the *Southern Quarterly Review* as one of the South's leading essayists on history and political thought. In one representative effort, he characterized the early 1840's as permeated by "an anxious, restless, feverish spirit of inquiry, which would sift all knowledge, rake over the soil at the root of all opinions, examine and scrutinize all received truths . . . in order to abstract from the mass whatever may escape uninjured through the ordeal." And, he added, "this is all well."[57]

Such views made life in orthodox, provincial South Carolina more and more uncomfortable. Failing several times to secure a position at South Carolina College, Holmes, never wealthy, increased his poverty by accepting a position at Baptist Richmond College in 1845. Unhappy there, he enlisted the support of his good friends William Harper and William Gilmore Simms in South Carolina and Senator R. M. T. Hunter and former President John Tyler of Virginia to secure the chair of political economy at William and Mary recently vacated by the death of Professor Dew. After receiving the appointment Holmes boasted that "this Professorship has magnified me into something of a big fish."[58]

Holmes's tenure at Williamsburg was brief. His opposition to the appointment of a second-rate Dew protégé to the faculty was part of a general struggle going on within the school's administration, which was concerned over declining enrollments and reduced funds. When a trustee roundly condemned "the pernicious influence of these damned foreigners," Holmes promptly resigned.[59]

57. Gillespie, *Collapse of Orthodoxy*, p. 40; George Frederick Holmes to Letitia Preston Lewis, March 26, 1849, George Frederick Holmes Papers, Duke University; Harvey Wish, "George Frederick Holmes and Southern Periodical Literature of the Mid-Nineteenth Century," *Journal of Southern History* 7 (1941): 343–48; [George Frederick Holmes], "Whewell on the Inductive Sciences," *Southern Quarterly Review* 2 (1842): 195.

58. Gillespie, *Collapse of Orthodoxy*, pp. 20–24; Holmes to Lavalette Holmes, March 1, 1847, Holmes Papers, Duke University.

59. Gillespie, *Collapse of Orthodoxy*, pp. 25–28.

Soon thereafter the University of Mississippi asked Holmes to become its first president. In his inaugural address in 1848 he declared his hope of building up a "society of gentlemen." Well aware of the purposes for which the university was established, Holmes asserted that the forces of ignorance and radicalism were loose in the North and in Europe, threatening "the whole fabric of the social system." He attacked "the hazardous, expensive and humiliating experiment" of sending young men "abroad, to imbibe at the North delusive views which will infect their minds during their whole life."[60]

Despite Holmes's best efforts to maintain the sectional spirit at Mississippi, his task proved too arduous. He taught natural philosophy to a poorly prepared class and later wearily recounted how one student, "with concurrence of others, expressed an anxious desire that the Professor would perform 'a few more of them tricks'—thus designating the scientific experiments." Moreover, Holmes's reputation as a religious skeptic had preceded him, and the fact that he was named president instead of the popular A. B. Longstreet, a writer and Methodist minister, offended a number of upright Protestant trustees. When Holmes turned out to be a lax administrator whose simple honor code of conduct was insufficient for the unruly sons of frontier planters, he was dismissed. A failure at the age of twenty-nine, Holmes returned to his Virginia farm to sort out his thoughts with, as he said, "nothing else to do except write articles."[61]

The rustication lasted eight years. Life had gone quickly sour, and Holmes searched for order out of the wreckage of his first twenty-nine years. It was a time, he recorded, of "pov-

60. Neal C. Gillespie, "The Spiritual Odyssey of George Frederick Holmes: A Study of Religious Conservatism in the Old South," *Journal of Southern History* 31 (1965): 296–97; Gillespie, *Collapse of Orthodoxy*, pp. 32–33.

61. John N. Waddel, *Memorials of Academic Life: Being an Historical Sketch of the Waddel Family, Identified Through Three Generations with the History of Higher Education in the South and Southwest* (Richmond: Presbyterian Committee of Publication, 1891), p. 267; Holmes to Lavalette Holmes, December 4, 1850, Holmes Papers, Duke University; [George Frederick Holmes], "Sir William Hamilton's Discussions," *Southern Quarterly Review* 24 (1853): 318.

erty, struggles, and debts, and embarrassments," though he retained his slaves and a modicum of dignity. His son died in 1848, causing "dull, aimless agony." Holmes subscribed to two agricultural journals and studied farming closely, but even in that he failed. Cabbages came up radishes; his livestock died off; insects were a constant problem; cold weather reduced his harvests; and debts continued to mount. Even so, he became even more determined to hold onto his slaves and remarked stoically that "the uncertain fluctuation of fortune, without affording any guarantee for the future, seems to predestine me to an agricultural life. . . . Happily, I have always been fond of the country, and adverse to the cities and the life of crowds."[62]

Tragedy and hardship slowly but inexorably effected a new viewpoint in Holmes's intellectual outlook. As he perused his Aristotle, he confided in a letter to Thornwell, "the less necessity do I discover for any other philosophy than modernized and Christianized Peripateticism." His son's death removed "some of the greatest difficulties of Christianity" from his thinking, that of admitting faith as well as reason. In 1851 Holmes began daily Bible readings, and by 1855 he was regularly practicing "diligent and beseeching prayer. . . ." He read Aquinas faithfully, and his religious readings after 1856 were entirely by Catholic writers. It was not surprising that Holmes later destroyed many of his papers from the years 1839 to 1844 because of their "impropriety and infidelity."[63]

At the same time Holmes was observing the trends of Northern and Southern society. Physical science—technology—in which Holmes the young rationalist had trusted seemed now, in Northern hands, to be destroying society:

---

62. Betts, "George Frederick Holmes," p. 477; Holmes to Thornwell, January 21, 1857, Thornwell Papers, South Caroliniana Library; Gillespie, *Collapse of Orthodoxy*, pp. 84–85.
63. Holmes to Thornwell, September 16, 1856, quoted in Gillespie, "Spiritual Odyssey of Holmes," p. 298; [George Frederick Holmes], "Latter Day Pamphlets," *Southern Quarterly Review* 15 (1850): 336; Gillespie, *Collapse of Orthodoxy*, pp. 103, 155.

> . . . physical sciences have by their discoveries multiplied in-
> calculably our powers, our resources, our knowledge, our com-
> forts, and our wealth—. . . . But notwithstanding these proud
> achievements, there are urgent questions of the gravest impor-
> tance, which no light from Physical science will enable us to
> solve.[64]

Holmes was becoming convinced by events in the North that society was on the verge of disintegration. In his view, "a more profound study of the laws and mechanisms of communi-ties"—or social science—was required in order to "probe the wounds of society and discover medicaments." To apply the scientific method rigorously to a study of past and present societies would help to answer the vexing questions of contem-porary societal disintegration. Increasingly as Holmes studied, he believed that "the doctrine of perfectibility was a dream of the last century; it is a folly in this." Combining this belief with his growing religious orthodoxy, Holmes turned to the South and to slavery as the only place and the only institution which made possible "an equal chance . . . of acquiring every-thing that can minister to the propriety, comfort, prosperity, and happiness of life" by the removal of "factious restraints." The South might prevail not by "imitating, aping, borrowing and rivalling" the manufacturing North, but by relying on ag-riculture and slavery.[65]

Out of Holmes's trials emerged a sense of Southern na-tionalism as well. A watershed in this development was his review in 1852 of *Uncle Tom's Cabin*, which moved Holmes to a vigorous defense of the South and of slavery. John R. Thomp-son of the *Southern Literary Messenger* chose Holmes to prepare a review "as hot as hell-fire, blasting and searing the reputation of the vile wretch in petticoats who could write such a volume—I would have it burn like a stick of lunar caustic.

64. [George Frederick Holmes], "On the Importance of the Social Sciences in the Present Day," *Southern Literary Messenger* 15 (1849): 78.
65. *Ibid.*, p. 77; Harvey Wish, "George Frederick Holmes and the Genesis of American Sociology," *American Journal of Sociology* 46 (1941): 698–707; Gille-spie, *Collapse of Orthodoxy*, p. 197.

. . ." Complying, Holmes excoriated Mrs. Stowe, who "shattered the temple of feminine delicacy and moral graces." For the origins of slavery the North was to blame, as "nearly five-sixths of the slave vessels sail from Baltimore, and the Northern ports of the righteous free States, and none from the more Southern harbors." Praising agriculture, Holmes accused Mrs. Stowe of giving a vivid picture "of graver miseries, worse afflictions, and more horrible crimes" than could ever exist in the South, but which were quite familiar "to the denizens of our Northern cities, and incident to the condition of those societies where the much lauded white labor prevails." After blasting the "willful slander" of *Uncle Tom*, Holmes proceeded to lambaste—perhaps with his early career in mind—"the neglect, injustice, and illiberality of Southern communities" for the "Southern author." It was time to support periodicals and men "for the development of Southern intellect, for the defence of Southern institutions, for the creation of a Southern literature. . . ."[66]

During the years of seclusion Holmes had formulated ideas on how Southerners might be educated. "The Universities and Colleges of the present century neither supply the wants of the time nor render any satisfaction comparable to the expenses of their endowment and continued maintenance," he wrote. He accused "Yankee academies" for placing too much emphasis on the sciences, which aroused "a lively and not always liberal curiosity." Such schools were "a half-way measure, serving Mammon and fawning to God." Holmes believed that Northern schools emphasized the practical at the expense of the liberal. He held that "a liberal education is essential to a really practical one, and is requisite for the fullest efficiency of technical or professional pursuits." Only in the South, where

66. John R. Thompson to Holmes, August 24, 1852, in William R. Manierre, "A Southern Response to Mrs. Stowe: Two Letters of John R. Thompson," *Virginia Magazine of History and Biography* 69 (1961): 85; [George Frederick Holmes], "A Key to Uncle Tom's Cabin," *Southern Literary Messenger* 19 (1853): 322; George Frederick Holmes, "Uncle Tom's Cabin," *Southern Literary Messenger* 17 (1852): 729, 724–26.

slavery served as a barrier to social disintegration, did there exist the possibility for such an education.[67]

Holmes's belief that Southern society offered the possibility of salvation reinforced his notion that slavery was in general a positive good and brought him into agreement with Fitzhugh, who was also exploring the new field of sociology. To both men abolitionism represented "malignity, hypocrisy, fraud, fanaticism, false philanthropy, and imbecility." Comparing Northern and European capitalists, Holmes declared, "The Pharisees of Northern Abolitionism are taught a pleasant escape from the consciousness of their own inequities . . . by magnifying the supposed guilt of their neighbors." They were like the "greedy capitalists of England," who, "wringing profits or selfish gratifications from the agonies of famished labor . . . thank Heaven that they are not as Southern men are." The rise and spread of radical reform movements in the North promised "complete disorganization and decay." The cause of this "social apoplexy" was "a rabid fury to make money," which, of course, had long motivated Holmes as well. On the other hand, slavery in the South was "one of the principal and most enduring arrangements of humanity," a just, benevolent, conservative institution.[68]

Having reached that position, Holmes was ready to become a Southern nationalist. In 1856 "Southron," writing to the *Richmond Enquirer*, recommended Holmes for a position at the University of Virginia. Holmes was no "half-way abolitionist," not an "apologist," but a "champion." One year later, his conversion complete and his soul at peace, Holmes—at the astoundingly high annual salary of $2,500—began a long career as professor of history and general literature at Charlottesville.

67. [George Frederick Holmes], "Universities and Colleges," *Southern Literary Messenger* 20 (1854): 650, 579, 609; Holmes, "Hamilton's Discussions," p. 318, 309.
68. [George Frederick Holmes], "Observations on a Passage in the Politics of Aristotle Relative to Slavery," *Southern Literary Messenger* 16 (1850): 193; [George Frederick Holmes], "Slavery and Freedom," *Southern Quarterly Review* 21 (1856): 81, 75; George Frederick Holmes, "Key to Uncle Tom," p. 324.

There is little information about Holmes's early years at Virginia, where he would remain until his death in 1897. One of the members of his history class in 1860 later recalled how Holmes often "gave his fancy free rein, and indulged in excursions and digressions. . . . The personality of the man dominated all. . . . History was his forte, but his foible was omniscience." Holmes was, too, a close friend of Bledsoe, a colleague at Mississippi and long a member of the Virginia faculty. Bledsoe was a vociferous exponent of Southern nationalism in the classroom. It is quite probable that among Holmes's "excursions and digressions" were speculations if not outright advocacy of a Southern nation, for in 1861 he was a strong supporter of secession.[69]

So fully did Holmes give himself to his new duties, so determined was he to succeed, that he abandoned his diary, published only one article until 1866, and at last found some satisfaction in life. His financial, intellectual, and personal burdens gone, George Frederick Holmes emerged from his long ordeal an orthodox Christian and an equally unswerving Southerner.

IV

"The South needs, more than ever," the pamphlet exclaimed, "men of the very highest education, who shall prove, by their ripe scholarship, that our institutions are not adverse to the loftiest culture. . . ." Early in 1859 the trustees of the planned University of the South were both determined and optimistic. Their determination, while longstanding, had been reinforced by the events of the turbulent 1850's which, according to one of the university's advocates, "forced the Southern mind back upon itself. It has been and is being drawn from the North . . . especially for the means of educating the young. . . ." Their optimism stemmed from the unbelievable financial response to

69. *Richmond Enquirer*, June 4, 1856; Henry E. Shepherd, "George Frederick Holmes," in *Library of Southern Literature*, ed. Edwin A. Alderman and Joel Chandler Harris, 16 vols. (New Orleans: Martin and Hoyt Co., 1907–13), 6: 2465–88; Philip A. Bruce, *History of the University of Virginia, 1819–1919*, 5 vols. (New York: Macmillan and Co., 1921), 3: 260–67.

their appeals by Southern men who, by August 1859, had subscribed $478,000 to the project.[70]

The dream of a central Southern university was not a new one. As early as 1835 in a letter to his Southern colleagues Bishop James Hervey Otey of the Episcopal Diocese of Tennessee unveiled his vision of a "theological and Literary Institution . . . to be situated somewhere near the boundary line between the State of Tennessee and Mississippi." Though Otey's primary purpose was "to supply to some degree the deficiency [of clergymen] . . . by providing a domestic nursery for ministers of the Gospel," he revealed his sectional leanings by emphasizing the need for such an establishment in the South, "a most interesting portion of the Union."[71]

The major obstacle to a regional institution was financial. The state governments, already committed to their own schools, were neither willing nor able to join in any effort of cooperative sponsorship. The two leading religious denominations, though after 1845 quite sectional in their inclinations, likewise were already committed to the several institutions they had established in various states. Only the Episcopal church—uniquely organized into dioceses that followed state boundaries—might, said a Southern bishop, "carry all our points to the satisfaction of all fair and reasonable expectations for the Church as well as the State" in founding the long desired university.[72]

Indeed, for inculcating Southern principles the Episcopal church seemed ideally suited. Though Episcopalians comprised a little more than four percent of the Southern population they often occupied the highest positions in government

70. *Address of the Commissioners for Raising the Endowment of the University of the South* (New Orleans: B. M. Norman, 1859), p. 4; Leonidas Polk to Stephen Elliott, August 30, 1856, quoted in William M. Polk, *Leonidas Polk, Bishop and General*, 2 vols. (New York: Longmans, Green, and Co., 1915), 1: 241; Arthur B. Chitty, Jr., *Reconstruction at Sewanee* (Sewanee, Tenn.: University Press, 1954), p. 50.
71. James Hervey Otey Diary, February 16, 1835, James Hervey Otey Papers, Southern Historical Collection.
72. Polk to Elliott, August 30, 1856, quoted in Polk, *Leonidas Polk* 1: 242.

and society. One historian has remarked that "although there may be other roads to the Celestial City, no gentleman would choose any but the Episcopalian way." While Methodists and Baptists actively competed to save the souls of frontiersmen, the Episcopalians were content to remain in the larger towns, welcoming the successful to their ranks.[73] Moreover, adhering to a strict separation of church and state, the conservative Episcopalians were never deeply agitated by the slavery question. If any denomination should be able to launch a sectional university to teach the Southern gospel of slavery, agriculture, and gentlemanly decorum it was the Episcopalians, who had both the background and the means.

It was just such a purpose that motivated Bishop Leonidas Polk of Louisiana to circulate a proposal among his fellow prelates during 1856. "The Baptists and Methodists have not the bearing or the social position or prestige, required to command the public confidence," he wrote, but the Episcopal church did. The state legislatures by themselves could "not expect to do more than to provide for their several states. . . ." The state universities "have not the claims nor the prestige of anything like nationality about them." Because "a movement of some kind is indispensable to rally and unite us," it was necessary to "rise above diocesan considerations, and look to the good of the whole." In July 1856 Polk distributed a pamphlet to the Bishops of Tennessee, North Carolina, South Carolina, Georgia, Florida, Alabama, Mississippi, Arkansas, and Texas. The pamphlet observed that "our children are expatriated or sent off to an inconvenient distance, beyond the reach of our supervision or parental influence, exposed to the rigors of an unfriendly climate, to say nothing of other influences not calculated. . . ." That October the Southern bishops agreed to meet and lay their plans during the church's general convention in Philadelphia.[74]

73. Dodd, *The Cotton Kingdom*, p. 99; Ahlstrom, *Religious History*, p. 667. See also Table 2, Appendix V.
74. Eaton, *Mind of the Old South*, p. 213; Polk to Elliott, August 30, 1856, July 23, 1856, quoted in Polk, *Leonidas Polk*, pp. 241, 237; David Greene Haskins,

Though Polk seemed to have a willing group of colleagues, he needed tact and forbearance to realize his goal. His
own purpose he made clear in a letter to Bishop Stephen Elliott
of Georgia. "We are afraid," he wrote, "of Northern domination in our schools and pulpits of the South, [of] 'these Northern men with Southern principles. . . .' " In addition Polk
feared that abolitionism would sweep through the Northern
church, that secession was certain to come eventually, and that
it was the duty of the bishops to prepare for that day. Yet to retain the support of all his cantankerous colleagues, Polk was
forced to moderate his tone. The venerable Otey, for example,
received repeated assurances from Polk that the purposes of
the university were not secessionist or even sectional, and in
good faith he conveyed that message while raising funds in
various parts of the South.[75] Bishop Nicholas Cobbs of Alabama, insistent on building the university in his state, threatened the unity of the group. For whatever reason, Bishop
Thomas Davis of South Carolina did not attend a single meeting of the bishops, and his diocese was not listed among the
original contributors to the enterprise.[76]

In dealing with such a diverse group, Polk excelled. He
was "a man whom noble men might love and meaner men
might fear," tall, formidable, energetic, with flowing gray
hair, piercing eyes, and a prominent nose. Born in Raleigh,

A Brief Account of the University of the South (New York: E. P. Dutton and Co.,
1877), p. 26; Knight, ed., *Documentary History* 4:462–66.

75. Polk to Elliott, August 20, 1856, Leonidas Polk Papers, Southern Historical Collection. See, for an example of Otey's position, his address in Montgomery in 1858: "Why should this enterprise be deemed sectional, rather than
national? Is it because we have used the name of 'University of the South'?
The name is one of convenient description; it is no party war cry, no sectional
pass-word. All such interpretations we utterly disclaim," quoted in William
Mercer Green, *Memoir of Rt. Rev. James Hervey Otey, D.D., LL. D., The First
Bishop of Tennessee* (New York: James Pott and Co., 1885), p. 64.

76. Chitty, *Reconstruction at Sewanee*, p. 76. For biographical and professional
data on the bishops involved, see Herman Griswold Batterson, *A Sketch-Book of
the American Episcopate During One Hundred Years, 1783–1883* (Philadelphia:
J. B. Lippincott and Co., 1884), *passim*.

North Carolina, in 1806, Polk graduated from West Point in 1827, resigned his commission a year later, and entered the Virginia Seminary at Alexandria. After ordination to the Episcopal priesthood in 1830 he served as an assistant rector in Richmond, but poor health forced him to give up his ministerial career. He made a tour of Europe and returned to begin life anew as a planter in Tennessee, where he gradually regained his health. Much to Polk's surprise he was appointed as missionary bishop of the southwest in 1838 and spent three arduous years preaching, baptizing, confirming, and establishing churches. In one year alone he "travelled 5,000 miles, preached 44 sermons, baptized 14, confirmed 41, consecrated one church and laid the cornerstone of another." In 1841 Polk was named bishop of Louisiana. He decided that he would be most effective among his new parishioners if he became a planter. Mrs. Polk had recently been offered as an inheritance the choice of either a large sum of money or four hundred slaves. The bishop, a true Southerner, opted not for the cash but for the slaves and soon thereafter took up his twin duties as bishop and sugar planter.[77]

Polk's view of slavery was benevolent and paternalistic. Concerned for both the physical and spiritual welfare of his black laborers, he was a benign master whose idea of discipline was, for example, to make a chicken thief stand for an afternoon with a chicken tied around his neck. He viewed the Negro as essentially childlike and strongly believed in encouraging piety among his slaves. Still he was a firm supporter of the peculiar institution and regarded abolition activities with contempt:

> Talk of slavery! Those madcaps at the North don't understand the thing at all. We hold the negroes, and they hold us! They are at the head of the ladder! They furnish the yoke and we the neck!

---

77. W. S. Perry, *History of the American Episcopal Church*, 2 vols. (Boston: J. R. Osgood and Co., 1885), 2: 563, quoted in Robert Douthat Meade, "Leonidas Polk," *Dictionary of American Biography* 15: 40; Polk, *Leonidas Polk* 1: 159; Eaton, *Mind of the Old South*, pp. 210–12.

My own is getting sore, and it is the same with those of my neighbors in Church and State.[78]

To be at once successful as planter and prelate was not easy. Polk adhered to the fourth commandment—even in the grinding season when no time could be wasted—and therefore he did not prosper financially. His attention to church affairs meant neglect of the day-to-day operation of his estate, and he preferred to spend his time at home conducting services for his slaves. At the same time he endured a period of ill fortune: cholera almost wiped out his work force in 1849, a tornado devastated his $75,000 sugarhouse in 1850, and early frost destroyed that year's crop. Beset with dismal prospects and by now heavily in debt, Polk sold his plantation and moved to New Orleans where, frustrated, he viewed with growing alarm the events that seemed to be dividing North and South.[79]

Polk expressed his fears and hopes in a letter in August 1856 to Stephen Elliott, the erudite and eloquent Bishop of Georgia, whom Polk much admired. Conflict was raging in Kansas Territory between slaveholders and nonslaveholders, and the bloody business genuinely alarmed many Southerners. Polk, doubtless influenced by "the signs of the times," predicted that "what is now [a] shadowy phantom" would soon become "an embodied and living and impressive reality." Slavery obviously was threatened and, as a result, "we in these dioceses [are] cut off in feeling, and sympathy, and in fact from the dioceses of the North with a wall as high as the heavens between us. . . ." If Polk was not speaking Southern naitonalism, he was very close to doing so. To prepare the South for the coming separation, it was necessary to encourage Southern education:

78. Eaton, *Mind of the Old South*, p. 212; Polk to Elliott, August 30, 1856, Polk Papers, Southern Historical Collection.
79. Polk, *Leonidas Polk* 1: 181–209; Meade, "Leonidas Polk," *Dictionary of American Biography* 15: 39; Eaton, *Mind of the Old South*, p. 170.

> Educational establishments in all departments are the universally
> recognized arsenals whence available armor is to be drawn. . . ,
> and a sorry plight we shall find ourselves in presently, cut off
> from those whence we have been accustomed to draw, with no
> alternative of our own in reserve.[80]

These concerns underlay Polk's desire to establish a
Southern university. The Southern bishops convened in Philadelphia in October 1856 and decided to reassemble at Lookout
Mountain, near Chattanooga, Tennessee, on July 4, 1857. In
the meantime they issued a joint letter declaring that "at no
time in all the past, have we been so threatened with the spread
of the wildest opinions in religion and government" and urging
support for their endeavors.[81]

Events then proceeded rapidly. At the July meeting the
bishops and selected lay representatives charted the new university's course. They established an administrative hierarchy,
determined the composition of the board of trustees, and decided not to begin construction until they had raised $500,000,
the interest of which would sustain the university while the
principal remained untouched. The plans were ambitious.
The new university would begin with an endowment half the
size of two-hundred-year-old Harvard College. Still unnamed
and unlocated, the university, it was decided, "shall be as central to all the contracting Dioceses as shall be consistent with
the necessary conditions of location." Polk was placed in
charge of site selection and instructed to report his findings
when the group reconvened in Montgomery in November.
Before adjourning to a soirée provided by the city of Chattanooga—whose citizens hoped to secure the university for
their home town—the bishops and laymen assembled on the
mountaintop for a brief service, which included an address by
Bishop Otey, the senior trustee and the staunchest of Unionists. He asserted "that our aim is eminently national and patriotic . . . not of political schism. . . . We contemplate no strife,

---

80. Polk to Elliott, August 30, 1856, Polk Papers, Southern Historical
Collection.
81. Knight, ed., *Documentary History* 4: 466–72.

save a generous rivalry with our brethren, as to who shall furnish to this great republic the truest of men, the truest Christians, and the truest patriots." While he spoke the American
flag, held by a young boy standing nearby, was wafted by the
breeze, wrapped itself around the expansive prelate, and temporarily, according to one observer, "arrested his discourse."[82]

Polk immediately set about his sensitive task of finding a
suitable site. He desired a central location within an area
bounded north and south by Knoxville, Tennessee, and
Huntsville, Alabama, and east and west by Atlanta, Georgia,
and McMinnville, in central Tennessee. He engaged Colonel
Walter Gwynn, a geologist and engineer for the Blue Ridge
Railroad, to investigate climate, accessibility, elevation, proximity and cost of building materials, suitability for agriculture,
and to give a general description of each proposed site. It was a
demanding task because so many groups were actively seeking
the university for their locale. Huntsville offered $100,000 and
two sites, McMinnville $40,000 and 2,000 acres, Chattanooga
$50,000 and Lookout Mountain, and Cleveland, Tennessee,
1,200 acres and free use of its nearby marble quarry. In addition Polk received written proposals that he did not investigate
from Greenville, Athens, Tullahoma, Franklin, and White's
Creek Springs in Tennessee; Gordon Springs, Dalton, and
Griffin in Georgia; Jacksonville, Alabama; and Corinth, Mississippi.[83]

82. Chitty, *Reconstruction at Sewanee*, pp. 50–51; "Declaration of Principles Set
Forth and Subscribed by the Trustees in Convention Assembled," in *Address of
the Commissioners*, pp. 7–8. The administrative organization, first planned at
Philadelphia and enacted at Lookout Mountain, was as follows: a board of
trustees comprising the Diocesan Bishops *ex officio* and one clergyman and two
laymen from each diocese, a treasurer in each diocese, and a general treasurer
elected by the trustees. The senior bishop served as president, and all measures acted upon required a two-thirds vote by both the bishops and the
clergy/lay trustees. See also Seymour E. Harris, *Economics of Harvard* (New
York: McGraw–Hill, 1970), p. 340. Harvard's endowment did not top $1
million until 1854.
83. *Address of the Board of Trustees of the University of the South to the Southern
Dioceses* (Savannah: George N. Nichols, Printer, 1858), pp. 5–6; Chitty, *Reconstruction at Sewanee*, pp. 52–54.

And then there was Sewanee, Tennessee. The most isolated of all the prospective locations, Sewanee was situated at the end of a rough wagon trail atop a thousand foot high mountain, five miles from the nearest railroad spur line. Sewanee offered no cash but, according to a university historian, "5,000 acres of land, a million feet of pine timber on adjacent land, free transporation of 20,000 tons of freight, . . . and 2,000 tons of coal." Polk, to whom land had always been more important than cash, was convinced that Sewanee, inaccessible though it was, was the logical choice. He managed to persuade his fellow trustees at their November meeting, but only after "long balloting, not unaccompanied by prayer for Divine guidance."[84]

More than a few were appalled at the choice. The *Charleston Mercury* declared that "if this is to be a great sectional institution, identified with the institutions and civilization of the South, then, we think, it should be located in the heart of the South—in a state where slavery is indispensable. . . ." The citizens of Chattanooga angrily denounced the decision and were in turn attacked by Polk as "a repulsive set of vulgarians." Bishop Cobbs of Alabama led a faction preferring Huntsville that demanded a new vote at the trustees' next meeting in July 1858, but Sewanee was reconfirmed.[85]

To calm the uproar the trustees published a pamphlet which claimed that "could we have found . . . a city of from fifty to one hundred thousand inhabitants, combining with the refinement of large towns the facilities which cities afford for the conduct of life, and offering the University undoubted healthfulness," they would have taken it. They envisioned a bright future for their mountaintop which would "be covered over with villas, and cottages, and watering places, and [would] teem with the most refined society of the South and West." Sewanee would become "the place of meeting of the South and West, and Wilmington, Charleston, and Savannah will here shake hands with Mobile, New Orleans, Nashville, and Mem-

---

84. Chitty, *Reconstruction at Sewanee*, pp. 53–54; *Address of the Board of Trustees*, p. 4.

85. *Charleston Mercury*, January 12, 1858; Eaton, *Mind of the Old South*, p. 172; Chitty, *Reconstruction at Sewanee*, p. 56; *Address of the Board of Trustees*, p. 7.

phis. . . ." It would "exhibit the same aspect as West Point does in the summer. . . ."[86]

The trustees then called upon "the men of the South to rally around us; not upon churchmen only, but upon all good men and true of whatever name and profession!" Rally they did, with the dioceses of Louisiana, Alabama, and Tennessee leading the way. A contributor to *DeBow's Review* cited the *"political* necessity for the establishment" of the university "around which shall cluster the hopes and the pride of the South, . . . one pledged to the defence and perpetuation of that form of civilization peculiar to the slaveholding States. . . ." Thus educated, the graduates will "return home to their native States . . . not a whit the less Kentuckians, or Georgians, or Texans, but more thoroughly Southerners." By the time the trustees reassembled on their mountaintop in August 1859 they had raised $478,000 and were prepared to begin construction.

Solicitation of funds continued while the trustees met early in 1860 to draw up the constitution for the University of the South, revealing ambitious plans. Just as the reliance on a large endowment anticipated the course of educational finance in the late nineteenth century, so the planned curriculum was far in advance of that at other colleges. Thirty-two departments or "schools" were planned, each to be headed by a full professor and staffed by assistant professors and tutors. In addition to the traditional Greek, Latin, and mathematics courses, innovative subjects such as the theory and practice of agriculture, American history and antiquities, law, and medicine were also included. Another innovation, which the trustees hoped would attract the flower of Southern society, required students to be housed with neighboring families, who would undoubtedly build homes near the university. Still, many elements of the university organization tied it to the past. Though there were no religious requirements for faculty or students, all the trustees by statute had to be Episcopalians.

86. *Address of the Board of Trustees*, pp. 6, 10, 14.

Moreover, the trustees retained for themselves the right to hire and discharge all faculty and, thus, to screen instructors for "correct" Southern thinking.

The university undoubtedly was designed to cultivate true Southrons. If there were any doubts, the unique provision for a three-month winter vacation and the explanation behind it should have dispelled them. During vacations the student would be able to "engage in the sports which make him a true Southern man, hunting, shooting, riding. . . ."[87] In another appeal for funds the trustees again emphasized the need for such a university:

> The world is trying hard to persuade us that a slaveholding people cannot be a people of high moral and intellectual culture. Because for the last seventy years, in the necessity which was laid upon us for hewing down our forests, and settling our wildernesses, we have been neglectful of the details of our literature, the world has come to suppose, and has worked the impression in among ourselves, that our institutions are unfavorable to literary development. Never was there a grosser error than this.[88]

Brimming with justifiable optimism, the bishops of the South looked forward eagerly to the consummation of their dream of a Southern university.

V

With a trembling hand Bishop Otey recorded in his diary the dreadful yet vicariously happy news. It was December 2, 1859, and Otey wrote, "This day fixed for the execution of Jno. Brown—fanatic—Traitor—and murderer." Three weeks later a train arrived in Richmond from Philadelphia carrying over two hundred medical students who had withdrawn from

87. *Ibid.*, pp. 6, 15; *DeBow's Review* 23 (1857): 491, 502; *DeBow's Review*, 25 (1858): 479. In one year Louisiana, under Polk's watchful eye, contributed over $264,000, Alabama $52,250, Tennessee, $28,480; Chitty, *Reconstruction at Sewanee*, p. 71.
88. *Address of the Commissioners*, p. 11.

the University of Pennsylvania in protest over John Brown's raid. They were welcomed by a large crowd, including the Southern Rights Association and Governor Henry A. Wise, who cried, "Let Virginia call home her children!"[89] The idea of a Southern nation had a new power.

In October 1860 a large crowd gathered on the mountaintop at Sewanee to witness a great event for the University of the South—the laying of the cornerstone. "You will not have it up a whit too soon," a friend wrote to Otey, for secession seemed imminent. The old bishop was sore distressed; his labors now seemed destined only for sectional, not national, benefit. "To what quarter shall we look," he wrote to Polk in his anguish, "if such men as you and Elliott deliberately favor secession?" A mixture of fear and joy permeated the atmosphere at Sewanee, as Elliott deposited in the cornerstone a number of historical church documents, an 1860 almanac, and several silver coins. The South was to have its university.[90]

Southern nationalism demanded rigid adherence and relentless vigilance. It permitted no deviance from the path of proslavery, agriculture, and sectional chauvinism. Southern nationalism required proper training and right thinking, orthodox behavior and orthodox beliefs. The central purposes of both education and religion, now, were to define, inculcate, and enforce orthodoxy, thus helping to prepare the Southern mind for separate nationhood.

89. James Hervey Otey Diary, December 2, 1859, James Hervey Otey Papers, Southern Historical Collection; Eaton, *Freedom-of-Thought Struggle*, pp. 229–30; *Richmond Enquirer*, December 23, 1859; *Savannah Republican*, January 27, 1860.
90. Eaton, *Mind of the Old South*, p. 215; Chitty, *Reconstruction at Sewanee*, p. 64.

CHAPTER SIX

The Mission and Destiny Allotted to the Anglo-Saxon Race

Between 1819 and 1845 the United States added no new territory to its domain. After the Missouri Compromise, slave and free states continued to be admitted to the Union in pairs, maintaining the sectional balance in the United States Senate. As American settlers continued to press westward, however, and as American nationalistic feelings intensified, a growing number of citizens came to believe that the United States must expand its borders. Though some policymakers feared the consequences of acquiring new territory, by the 1844 election of James K. Polk it seemed clear that a majority of Americans desired territorial expansion.

The desire to extend the nation's boundaries was deeply rooted. Optimistic American nationalism quite naturally led many Americans to believe, as did the delegates to the Memphis commercial convention in 1849:

> . . . the age in which we live is one of great achievements in arts and sciences and in human progress. The nations of the world are engaged in the great race for position and for empire. It becomes our country to aim as high and to realize as soon as may

be that bright and glorious destiny for which God and nature
seem to have reserved her.[1]

These and similar feelings reflected a belief in the "Manifest
Destiny"—a term first used by John L. O'Sullivan, a New
York editor, in 1845—of the American nation. If American institutions were superior, and if a world-wide "race for position
and empire" was on, then it was necessary for Americans to
engage in the contest for new territory. "The North Americans *will* spread out far beyond their present bounds," proclaimed DeBow. "They *will* encroach again and again upon
their neighbors. . . . The isthmus cannot arrest—nor even the
St. Lawrence!! Time has all this in her womb." A Philadelphia
editor saw America bounded on the "East by sunrise, West by
sunset, North by the Arctic Expedition, and South as far as we
darn please." An Alabama editor neatly explained the reason
for expansion: to bring "moral and material well being to the
disintegrating communities and decaying races" of the North
American continent.[2]

American expansionism in the 1840's, however, had other
more immediate origins. The widespread American desire to
expand was akin to the buoyant nationalism that during the
same decade in France, Prussia, Italy, Austria, Hungary, and
elsewhere challenged for a season the royalty of old Europe.
The expansionists of the United States called themselves

1. Quoted in Arthur A. Ekirch, Jr., *The Idea of Progress in America, 1815–1860*,
reprint ed. (Gloucester: Peter Smith Publisher, 1951), p. 228.
2. Frederick Merk, *Manifest Destiny and Mission in American History* (New York:
Alfred A. Knopf, 1963) is a recent and stimulating study of expansionist feeling and rhetoric. See also Julius W. Pratt, "Origin of Manifest Destiny,"
American Historical Review 32 (1927): 795; Albert K. Weinberg, *Manifest Destiny: A Study of Nationalist Expansion in American History* (Chicago: University of
Chicago Press, 1935), p. 62; *DeBow's Review* 6 (1848): 9; Thomas A. Bailey, *A
Diplomatic History of the American People*, 9th ed. (Englewood Cliffs, N.J.: Pren-
tice-Hall, 1974), p. 285; *Tuskegee (Ala.) Republican*, quoted in Robert E. May,
The Southern Dream of a Caribbean Empire, 1854–1861 (Baton Rouge: Louisiana
State University Press, 1973), p. 5, a first-rate study on which the ensuing dis-
cussion heavily relies.

"Young America" and looked with approval at the triumph of their ideals across the waters.[3]

Expansion in the mid-1840's was also the result of the convergence of a number of forces—economic, social, and political—that caused Americans to intensify their search for a national identity. The accelerating pace of change was making Americans insecure. The ruthless development of the frontier and the emergence of an industrial economy in the North produced anxieties alongside prosperity. In the South, too, change was rapid. By the mid-1840's, though the cotton economy was beginning its recovery in the lower South, and in the upper South the transition from tobacco to grain had been successfully accomplished, leadership seemed slowly but surely to be following economic power westward.[4]

The seaboard Southerner's confidence in the future stability of his way of life was undermined; the churches were on the verge of separation; abolition activity was on the rise in the North; and there was no guarantee that the economy would continue to improve. As a result, the seaboard Southerner's optimism was tentative, his anxieties genuine. Even so vocal a nationalist as Simms in the 1840's detected a "lack of permanence, stability, and finish" in American life. Calhoun noted that "modern society seems to me to be rushing to some new and untried condition. . . ."[5] While some Southerners joined reform movements to correct these ills of society, most pre-

---

3. Robert C. Brinkley, *Realism and Nationalism, 1852–1871* (New York: Harper and Brothers, 1935); David M. Potter, *The Impending Crisis, 1848–1861*, New American Nation series, ed. Richard B. Morris and Henry Steele Commager (New York: Harper and Row, 1976), pp. 13–15; Bailey, *Diplomatic History*, pp. 269–70; *Congressional Globe*, 32 Cong., 1 sess., p. 177.

4. Somkin, *Unquiet Eagle, passim*, deals effectively with the theme of American restiveness during the 1840's. Southerners were similarly uncertain. See Chapter Four for a discussion of Southern concerns over "Yankeeness." Chapter Three discusses the economic readjustment.

5. Gray, *History of Agriculture* 2: 1027; William Gilmore Simms to P. C. Pendleton, February 1, 1841, *Simms Letters* 1: 224; John C. Calhoun to James H. Hammond, February 18, 1837, *Calhoun Correspondence*, p. 367.

ferred to forget their worries by too loudly protesting the inevitability of America's Manifest Destiny.

Insecurity was present in the newer portions of the South
as well. The frontier planters in Mississippi and Alabama were
brutally and successfully striving to reap ever more profits
from their fertile lands. The return of prosperity seemed only
to heighten their arrogance and strengthen their confidence in
the superiority of their social and economic systems. As they
won, lost, and recovered large fortunes, the "cotton snobs"
increased their influence and power. The pessimism of such
men as Simms and Calhoun was virtually unknown in Mississippi. As a New Orleans paper described frontier life, "no un-
dertaking was deemed too gigantic, no enterprise beyond the
accomplishment of men who had engraved plates, paper in
abundance, and credulity to operate on. . . ."[6] To these Westerners, American expansion was an inevitability.

I

The tendencies of American life plainly disturbed Calhoun,
who as early as 1837 had accused the North of superiority only
in "the art of gain." But despite the differences between South
Carolina and Mississippi, Calhoun knew that in slavery their
fortunes were inextricably united. Slavery was the tie that
bound the Virginia farmer, the Charleston merchant, the black
belt cotton planter, and the New Orleans businessman
together in a commonality of interest. If slavery was threatened, the South was in danger, and in 1844 slavery seemed
threatened by a vocal and growing Northern majority. Looking ahead, Calhoun foresaw an inevitable upsetting of the senatorial balance between slave and free states. Searching for a
way to avoid such a catastrophe, Calhoun and his followers
decided that Texas was the solution. By securing annexation of

6. *New Orleans Daily True Delta*, quoted in Craven, *Coming of the Civil War*, p.
112. See also Fogel and Engerman, *Time on the Cross* 1: 104, which suggests
that the "sanguinity" of Southwestern planters began a steady rise in the
mid–1840's.

that vast and independent republic, Southerners could anticipate safety in the Union. Rhett best expressed the Carolinians' motivation:

> Every census has added to the power of the nonslaveholding States, and diminished that of the South. We are growing weaker, and they stronger, every day. . . . If this [Texas annexation] measure, therefore, will tend to strengthen the weaker interest in the Union it will be moving in strict accordance with the whole spirit of the constitution.[7]

If Texas would ensure the maintenance of sectional political balance, it would also provide a corrective to the tendencies of nineteenth-century life, or so these Southerners thought. The powerful appeal of virgin land was deeply ingrained in the American mind. If society was going wrong, many thought that more land—where the archetypal Jeffersonian farmer might flourish—could restore the lost virtues. A recurrent theme of these South Carolina annexationists was restoration. One spoke of the "re-establishment of our glorious constitution" in Texas. Calhoun saw in the admission of Texas a return to the "Union, as it came down from the hands of its framers."[8]

Anxieties about politics, society, and the economy, then, combined to lead Calhoun to work for the annexation of Texas. In 1843 he got his chance. When Daniel Webster resigned as secretary of state, President Tyler named Abel P. Upshur of Virginia as his successor. The Virginian—whose ideas about Southern society had been clearly revealed when he eloquently opposed democratic reforms in the state constitution in 1829—shared with Calhoun a deep-seated pessimism about the course of American life and a desire to protect

7. Crallé, ed., *Calhoun Works* 2: 629–33; *Congressional Globe,* 28 Cong., 2 sess., Appendix, p. 146. The definitive and masterful study of annexation remains Justin H. Smith, *The Annexation of Texas,* corrected ed. (New York: Barnes and Noble, 1941).
8. Henry Nash Smith, *Virgin Land: The American West as Symbol and Myth* (Cambridge: Harvard University Press, 1950), esp. pp. 152–53; Calhoun to George W. Houk, October 14, 1844, *Calhoun Correspondence,* p. 625.

Southern interests. Together the secretary and the senator laid plans and began negotiations with the Texans to bring about annexation.[9]

Calhoun strongly encouraged Upshur's efforts, advising the secretary to "prepare the publick mind to realize the danger" of failure. Calhoun was disturbed, too, by British abolitionist activities in Texas and feared that administration delay might prove fatal for his plans. Such failure would threaten "the safety of the Union and the very existence of the South." He urged Upshur to conduct a full-scale newspaper propaganda campaign in the South, emphasizing the danger not only of the British designs on Texas but also of the British presence in Oregon and the Caribbean, especially near slaveholding Cuba. The Calhounites in Congress also gave support. For example, the corpulent Alabama Senator Dixon H. Lewis, upset that "there have been so few meetings in the South on the Texas question," promised to exert his ample influence.[10]

But Texas did not come easily. In late April 1844 Congress overwhelmingly rejected annexation. By this time Calhoun was secretary of state, succeeding Upshur, who had been killed in a freakish ship accident. Dejected but not defeated, the small group of Calhounite annexationists redoubled their efforts through the Democratic party press and vowed to make expansion an issue in the 1844 elections. Repudiating Van Buren—who had agreed with Henry Clay, the Whig presidential nominee—not to discuss Texas, expansionist Democrats nominated Polk, who won election on an unequivocal platform of Manifest Destiny. And in the last week of

---

9. Frederick Merk, *Slavery and the Annexation of Texas* (New York: Alfred A. Knopf, 1972) is a provocative study of the annexation movement in the South.
10. Calhoun to Abel P. Upshur, August 27, 1843, quoted *ibid.*, p. 22. See also Upshur to Calhoun, August 14, 1843, *William and Mary Quarterly*, 2d ser., 16 (1936): 554–57; Dixon H. Lewis to Bolling Hall, April 15, 1844, Bolling Hall Papers, Alabama Department of Archives and History; Lewis to Franklin Harper Elmore, May 9, 1844, Franklin Harper Elmore Papers, Southern Historical Collection.

Tyler's administration, Congress, reading the election returns, annexed Texas by joint resolution.[11]

By injecting expansion into the campaign, the Calhoun-ites achieved their objective, but they lost control of the expansion issue. Eagerly the press took up the call for annexation. Accepting the dictum of a Mississippi Democrat that the purpose of the press was "*manufacturing* public opinion," the editors crusaded for expansion. "The South is up," announced the *Richmond Enquirer.* "The cause of Texas is flying like wildfire over that whole region." An Alabama Democratic editor asked "Why annex Texas?" and then gave a long, occasionally inaccurate, and highly inflammatory answer:

> Because the Father of Democracy, the patriotic Jefferson, bought it of France and *paid the money of the nation for it.* . . . Because it will prevent British invasion by land, save us Oregon, and protect our commerce in the Gulf. . . . Because it would extend our free institutions, the principles of human rights and the glad tidings of salvation. . . . Because our British-Whig abettors aid England and Mexico and oppose 'Union and Liberty.' Because annexation will prevent consolidation and protect State Rights.

This explanation, wrote a student of the annexation issue, "probably represented the Texas opinions of half a million voters."[12]

The Texas annexationists, whose aims had been cautious and conservative, had loosed feelings they were incapable of either regulating or satisfying. As the seaboard statesmen lost

11. Eaton, *History of the Old South,* pp. 325–28. Texas was annexed by a joint resolution, which required a majority congressional vote only. The previous attempt in the spring of 1844 had been by treaty, which required two-thirds approval.

12. *Richmond Enquirer,* May 10, 1844; Smith, *Annexation of Texas,* pp. 305–306; Edwin A. Miles, *Jacksonian Democracy in Mississippi,* James Sprunt Studies in History and Political Science, vol. 42 (Chapel Hill: University of North Carolina Press, 1960), p. 164. See also Richard P. McCormick, *The Second American Party System: Party Formation in the Jacksonian Era* (New York: W. W. Norton and Co., 1966), pp. 246–54, a fine study.

control, the booming southwest became the center of expansionist sentiment. The aggressive spirit of modern America, which Calhoun had hoped to curb, now consumed its keeper. When, after questionable provocation, war with Mexico broke out, Southerners—particularly southwesterners—boldly rushed off to fight in proportionately higher numbers than Northerners. "It is Mexico and war," exulted a Georgia frontiersman. "I never saw the people more excited." Senator Henry S. Foote of Mississippi declared that liberty, "a banner of moral regeneration," would be extended to Mexico. A Texan saw the war as "a part of the mission, of the destiny, allotted to the Anglo–Saxon race." Though northeasterners were most vocal, among the slaveholding states the southwest led in the cry for "all Mexico." Foote and Texan Sam Houston joined their eager northeastern colleagues and gave strong and well-publicized speeches in New York in 1848 demanding that the American army swallow up "all Mexico."[13]

All over the South Manifest Destiny seemed to rule. Some Southerners doubtless supported expansion out of desires for sectional gain. Most, however, were fervent expansionists because of their intense American nationalism and were oblivious to any divisive sectional consequences that the war might later produce. A typical Southern view of the Mexican War was stated by the *Jackson Mississippian*:

> The association of men from all parts of the Union, under such circumstances, will be fruitful of good offices, kindly acts, lasting friendships, fraternal feelings, which will last while life endures. When the war is done, and these principles and feelings, hallowed by victory, are carried to the remotest corners of the confederacy, by the return of the citizen soldiery, what an additional cement will it form to the Union?

13. Thomas R. R. Cobb to Howell Cobb, May 12, 1846, in U. B. Phillips, ed., *The Correspondence of Robert Toombs, Alexander H. Stephens, and Howell Cobb*, Annual Report of the American Historical Association for the Year 1911 (Washington: American Historical Association, 1913), 2: 76; *Congressional Globe*, 30 Cong., 1 sess., Appendix, p. 178; Weinberg, *Manifest Destiny*, p. 180; Merk, *Manifest Destiny*, p. 152.

Another Southerner expressed the expansionists' dedication to "the increase of our territory, and consequently the extension of the area of human liberty and happiness. . . ."[14]

Deeply concerned over the emotions they had stimulated, Calhoun and other seaboard Southerners ineffectually tried to brake the expansionist drive. Calhoun was able to restrain South Carolina enthusiasm, crushing Rhett's Bluffton Movement—which threatened secession if, among other things, southwestern territory was not admitted to the Union—and he tried to warn his fellow Southerners that Mexico was "forbidden fruit." Alexander H. Stephens of Georgia agreed, fearing the divisive sectional debate that would inevitably result over the disposition of the new territories. Expansionist sentiment in Virginia rapidly cooled after the Mexican war began. The caution exhibited by the seaboard statesmen was remarkably like that almost simultaneously manifested in Western Europe, where liberal revolutionary movements were being ruthlessly crushed by the old, aristocratic regimes who believed the reformers had gone too far. Indeed, Calhoun's most conservative utterances after 1845 were quite similar to the conservative European theorists' writings that justified smashing the popular uprisings.[15]

In 1846 Calhoun's and Stephens's worst fears were confirmed when Congressman David Wilmot of Pennsylvania offered his famous proviso prohibiting slavery from all territories won from Mexico. For the next five years North and South wrangled over the chief prize of the Mexican conflict, California, and the struggle went a long way toward developing conflicting definitions about the nature and course of American nationalism.

The growth of Southern nationalism in the United States

14. *Jackson Mississippian*, June 3, 1846; *Congressional Globe*, 30 Cong., 1 sess., Appendix, p. 379.
15. Crallé, ed., *Calhoun Works* 4: 308; *Congressional Globe*, 30 Cong., 1 sess., Appendix, p. 379; *New York Herald*, May 15, 1847; Potter, *Impending Crisis*, p. 15; Charles M. Wiltse, "A Critical Southerner: John C. Calhoun and the Revolutions of 1848," *Journal of Southern History* 15 (1949): 299–310.

after 1850 operated at cross-purposes with Northern definitions of American nationalism. Thereafter, Manifest Destiny
became sectional destiny as southwesterners pushed for expansion into the Caribbean to extend the benefits of plantation
slavery and maintain sectional balance in the Senate. Whether
slavery actually could or should expand to survive economically was less important than a growing Southern conviction
that it must. The acquisition of new territories, far from alle-
viating the tensions of American society as Calhoun had
hoped, instead exacerbated them. In deciding upon the fate of
the territories Americans were forced to define themselves as a
nation. Thus began the national tragedy.

II

The citizens of Natchez, Mississippi, were jubilant. It was
March 7, 1851, and their most famous adopted son, John A.
Quitman, was coming home. A month earlier, under indictment by a New Orleans federal court for his part in a "filibustering" expedition preparing to invade Cuba, Quitman had
resigned his position as governor of Mississippi. Now, because
of insufficient evidence, the court had dropped all charges.
When news reached Natchez, according to a telegraphic dispatch, "the night was made voiceful with the roar of the cannon" in celebration. "Fifteen guns were fired for Quitman, and
fifteen for [the] Southern States. Many persons pulled off their
stockings for cartridges, and fired several for mankind in general."[16]

   By 1851 Cuba gave impetus to the cause of Southern nationalism, and there was no more ardent champion for the immediate annexation of the "Pearl of the Antilles" than Quitman. A restless man of action, Quitman had left his Hudson
River birthplace of Rhinebeck in 1819 at the age of twenty-

16. Claiborne, *Life and Correspondence of Quitman* 2: 79. "The word 'filibuster' is
a French and Spanish corruption of the English word freebooter, an appella-
tion which, in former days, [was] frequently assumed by a certain class of
men, who disliked the name of pirate. . . ." *DeBow's Review* 20 (1856): 670.

one.[17] Drawn to Natchez where, he wrote, "much can be done with little money," Quitman rapidly established himself in a law practice and married the daughter of a distinguished Natchez judge and "social arbiter." Through marriage Quitman acquired a large Natchez plantation complete with slaves and soon succumbed to the intoxicating life of a young gentleman planter. To his Northern friends he wrote of morning juleps, hunting and fishing, sumptuous dinners, and "niggers, . . . the happiest people I have ever seen. . . . It is an indolent, yet charming life, and one quits thinking and takes to dreaming."[18]

Quitman's adaptation to Southern life was rapid and his commitment to it was total. In 1834 he organized a small group of Mississippi Nullifiers into a Southern Rights party and earned the epithet of "secessionist" from the dominant Jacksonians. In 1836, after eight years in state government, Quitman was defeated in a bid for Congress because of his extreme views and retired to his law practice and his plantation, where the 1837 depression forced him to remain for ten years. When war with Mexico broke out, he organized the Natchez Fencibles and led his unit to glory in battle. Upon his triumphant return home the tall, white-haired, full-bearded military hero, now at the peak of his fame, was elected Governor in 1849—just at the moment when sectional antagonisms were reaching new heights. With views unchanged and hardened from his ten-year retirement during which he corresponded with Southern men of like persuasion, Quitman stood ready to defend "Southern rights" against any infringement.[19]

17. There is no published biography of Quitman except for Claiborne's old and adulatory work. James H. McLendon, "John A. Quitman" (Ph.D. diss., University of Texas, 1949) is the only complete biography.

18. *A Brief Sketch of the Life, Civil and Military, of John A. Quitman* (Washington: n.p., 1848), p. 5; D. Clayton James, *Antebellum Natchez* (Baton Rouge: Louisiana State University Press, 1968), p. 132; John A. Quitman to his brother, March 21, 1819, October 4, 1823, to Col. Platt Brush, August 23, 1823, in Claiborne, *Life and Correspondence of Quitman* 1: 32, 83–87.

19. Miles, *Jacksonian Democracy in Mississippi,* pp. 63–69, 134; Robert A. Brent, "Mississippi and the Mexican War," *Journal of Mississippi History* 31 (1969):

At the time of Quitman's inaugural in January 1850, a tightening noose of free territory seemed fastened about the Southern neck. The "fifteen sovereignties of the North cannot exclude the fifteen sovereignties of the South from an equal participation in, and control over, the joint acquisition or property of all," exclaimed Congressman Albert G. Brown of Mississippi. "What the Southern people want," declared a correspondent of Congressman Howell Cobb of Georgia, "is the right to take their slave property into the common territory" south of a Missouri Compromise line extended to the Pacific. And beneath the question of legality and fairness lay a deeper concern over territorial restriction perhaps best expressed by Quitman himself in his inaugural address. "I fear," he cried, that Congress, under Northern control, will "confine the slaveholder and the slave for all time to come to the states where the institution now exists." The calamitous result of such confinement would be "a war of extermination" between the races and either "the destruction of our domestic institutions or the dissolution of the Union."[20]

Quitman had cause for concern. Before Congress were a series of measures virtually excluding slaveholders from most of the territory newly acquired from Mexico. In the White House sat Zachary Taylor with an anti-expansionist Whig cabinet determined to admit California as a nonslaveholding state.

The admission of California as a nonslaveholding state was fraught with grave consequences for the South. Politically, a free California meant that the South would lose its Senate veto and the ability to protect its sectional interests. Equally important were the psychological implications of terri-

202–14; Donald Rawson, "Party Politics in Mississippi, 1850–1860" (Ph.D. diss., Vanderbilt University, 1964), pp. 5, 10–11; Claiborne, *Life and Correspondence of Quitman* 1: 160–63, 185–91, 2: 20–21.

20. M. W. Cluskey, ed., *Speeches, Messages, and Other Writings of the Hon. Albert G. Brown* (Philadelphia: James B. Smith and Co., 1859), p. 165; Hiram Warner to Howell Cobb, March 17, 1850, in Phillips, ed., *Toombs, Stephens, and Cobb Correspondence* 2: 186; Claiborne, *Life and Correspondence of Quitman* 2: 23–24.

torial restriction. Congress, by accepting a free California, would in effect be telling the Southern states they were not the equals of free states. Their citizens, with their property (meaning slaves), could not go into the new national territory but those of Northern and Western states could. As usual, Calhoun most eloquently stated the Southern position in a series of resolutions presented to the Senate shortly before his death in March 1850:

> . . . the States composing the Southern portion of the Union cannot be deprived of their full and equal right in the territory acquired from Mexico, or any other belonging to the Union without violating the constitution, perpetrating an act of gross injustice, destroying their equality as members of the Union, and by retarding their growth and accelerating that of . . . the northern portion of the Union, destroying the equilibrium of Government.[21]

Exclusion from the new territories was the more serious to Southerners because they faced—or thought they faced—similar barriers to expansion elsewhere. In the Caribbean the British seemed to be working to block the further spread of slavery. Early in the 1840's David Turnbull, the British consul and an abolitionist, pressed hard for a treaty that would liberate all slaves imported illegally into Cuba after 1820. Not only would such a treaty emancipate a majority of Cuban blacks, who out-numbered whites on the island by a growing margin, but it would also subvert the Cuban plantation system, cause disorder, and, perhaps, bring about that most horrid of all possibilities, race war. Not incidentally, it would also—by causing Southern support to diminish—lessen the chances of Cuban annexation by the United States. Calhoun, for one, had long realized the danger. In 1844, as Tyler's secretary of state, he wrote to his British counterpart that the United States regretted "the avowal, for the first time made to this government, 'that Great Britain desires, and is constantly exerting

---

21. *Calhoun Correspondence*, p. 785.

herself to procure the general abolition of slavery throughout the world.' "[22]

Southern fears of emancipation were shared by the large slaveholders of Cuba. Engaged primarily in sugar planting and constituting a small portion of the total population, the planters, through their organization the Club de la Habana, expressed a desire for annexation by the United States. Some were bothered by archaic Spanish trade laws; others resented their exclusion from the governmental bureaucracy in favor of native Spaniards; all were frightened by the growing British influence and the possibility of emancipation and racial strife. As a result the influential planters, figuring that annexation would not only stay the British influence but also provide a continuous supply of slaves from the states of the upper South, sought the assistance of Americans to make annexation a reality.[23]

Their unlikely agent was Narciso Lopez, dark complexioned, beady eyed, snowy haired, a native Venezuelan who, during the 1840's, had been a member of the Spanish bureaucracy both in Madrid and in Havana and a sympathizer with Turnbull and abolitionism. After business reversals— aggravated by chronic gambling—and his subsequent removal from public office by the Spanish authorities, Lopez turned to the Cuban annexationists and talked privately with members of the Havana Club about a revolution against Spain. The club, aware of Lopez's earlier flirtation with abolitionism, was skeptical about the Venezuelan's real intent, fearing that he would not hesitate to enroll blacks in his cause. Preferring to work with General William J. Worth, an American hero of the Mexican War, the club offered Worth three million dol-

22. Arthur F. Corwin, *Spain and the Abolition of Slavery in Cuba, 1817–1886* (Austin: University of Texas Press, 1967), pp. 75–77; May, *Southern Dream*, pp. 24–25; Basil Rauch, *American Interest in Cuba, 1848–1855* (New York: Columbia University Press, 1948), pp. 38–45, is a valuable work.

23. Corwin, *Spain and Abolition*, p. 78; Franklin W. Knight, *Slave Society in Cuba During the Nineteenth Century* (Madison: University of Wisconsin Press, 1970), pp. 25, 88–92; May, *Southern Dream*, pp. 24–25.

lars in 1848 to land five thousand American veterans on the island and proclaim Cuban independence, but President Polk, learning of the planned uprising, forbade it. Lopez, who was to have led the native Cubans in the struggle, immediately fled Cuba, barely escaping arrest by Spanish officials who condemned him to death *in absentia* and imprisoned many of his associates.[24]

Arriving in New York, Lopez in 1849 began to organize a filibustering expedition. He stopped in Washington en route to meet with Southern congressional leaders, including Senators Calhoun and Jefferson Davis. Calhoun apparently promised support, for in August 1849 Lopez advised the New York press that the South Carolinian hoped Southerners would "flock down there in 'open boats,' the moment they hear the tocsin." Davis declined to lead the movement but suggested Lopez approach Major Robert E. Lee. Lee, too, refused to accept the command of a "foreign power" army. Other American officers, promised ownership of confiscated sugar plantations (a promise of which Lopez's Cuban allies were doubtless unaware), had fewer scruples and joined the expedition which Lopez himself decided to lead. Meanwhile, Cuban pamphleteers stoked fires of annexation in the South. "The Pearl of the West Indies," wrote one, "with her thirteen or fifteen representatives in Congress, would be a powerful auxiliary to the South. . . ."[25]

But the 1849 expedition failed as well. President Taylor ordered Lopez's ships seized and brought several of the Americans involved to trial for violating neutrality laws. The North-

24. Robert G. Caldwell, *The Lopez Expeditions to Cuba, 1848–1851* (Princeton: Princeton University Press, 1915), pp. 43–49; Rauch, *American Interest*, pp. 76–79.
25. Caldwell, *Lopez Expeditions*, pp. 47–56; Anderson C. Quisenberry, *Lopez's Expeditions to Cuba, 1850 and 1851*, Filson Club Publications, vol. 21 (Louisville: John P. Morton and Co., 1906), pp. 28–30; John L. O'Sullivan to John C. Calhoun, August 24, 1849, *Calhoun Correspondence* 2: 1202–03; Rauch, *American Interest*, pp. 111–13; Douglas Southall Freeman, *R. E. Lee: A Biography*, 4 vols. (New York: Charles Scribner's Sons, 1934–1935), 1: 307.

ern press was divided along partisan lines on Taylor's move, but Southern papers eschewed party differences in a common attack on the president. "If the day of Cuba has arrived," cried the *New Orleans Bee*, "nothing can arrest the accomplishment of this great deed." Other papers declared that Taylor had no authority over expeditions departing from the territory of a sovereign state.[26]

Discouraged but not defeated, Lopez decided to transfer his headquarters from New York to New Orleans. Along the way, early in 1850, he stopped in Jackson, Mississippi, to discuss a new Cuban expedition with Governor Quitman and offer him the command. Quitman, although refusing reluctantly, promised not only encouragement but also money and strategic advice. A number of wealthy planters—including John Henderson, an exceedingly wealthy neighbor of Quitman's—purchased two million dollars in bonds to support the movement, and one, L. J. Sigur, who was also editor of the influential *New Orleans Delta*, managed to procure arms from the Louisiana state arsenal. By May the expedition, consisting of about five hundred Americans, was ready to set out.[27]

It, too, was a failure, more comical than tragic. Ostensibly departing for the California gold fields, Lopez and his band set sail for Cuba to the cheers of a large New Orleans crowd and the "winking encouragement" of port officials. Landing in Cuba, the filibusters took the town of Cardenas and planned to advance on Havana, gathering supporters along the way. The citizens of Cardenas, however, were reluctant to join the motley crew but expressed their friendship in the form of unlimited quantities of food and drink. As Spanish troops neared the town, Lopez hustled his staggering force back on board ship crying "Cuba Libré!" With Spanish bullets whizzing about their heads, the drunken filibusters withdrew from Cuba and,

26. *New Orleans Bee*, quoted in Caldwell, *Lopez Expedition*, p. 55; *New Orleans Crescent*, September 4, 1849, *New Orleans Weekly Delta*, September 3, 10, 1849, both cited in C. Stanley Urban, "New Orleans and the Cuban Question, 1849–1851," *Louisiana Historical Quarterly* 22 (1939): 1118.
27. Rauch, *American Interest*, p. 125.

to outrace pursuing Spanish steamers, cast most of their ammunition overboard to lighten the ship's weight and threw all combustible materials onto the fires to steam them to safety. The liberators arrived in Key West only twenty-five minutes ahead of a Spanish warship and quickly dispersed.[28]

Though their leaders and sympathizers were soon indicted in federal court for violating neutrality laws, the returning Americans were hailed as heroes by the Southern press. A New Orleans newspaper supporting Taylor in 1848 recognized that Cuba "appeals with almost irresistible power to the great heart of the nation. . . ." A reception in Mississippi held in Lopez's honor included speeches, banquets, a parade of "a band of music, one hundred ladies, the pupils of the academy, Gen. Lopez and friends, the masonic brethren, and the Sons of Temperance." In Congress Representative William Inge of Alabama and Senator David Yulee of Florida introduced resolutions calling on the president not to thwart efforts to win Cuba for the United States. In June 1850, however, sixteen filibusters—among them Lopez, Quitman, Henderson, and Sigur—were indicted and ordered to stand trial in New Orleans in December.[29]

Just as the indictments were handed down, the debates over California were reaching a crescendo. The omnibus bill devised by Henry Clay and comprising a series of compromise measures—including the admission of California as a free state and the adoption of a strong law requiring fugitive slaves to be returned to the South—was under consideration in Congress. Quitman was well aware of the importance of the potential loss of California by the South. "For the first time in the history of our country, the North is dominant in the federal government," he wrote. "We are now at their mercy, politically speaking." Accordingly he summoned the Mississippi legisla-

28. *Ibid.*, p. 28; Urban, "New Orleans and Cuba," p. 1124–25; Caldwell, *Lopez Expeditions*, pp. 68–74.
29. *New Orleans Bee*, May 14, 1850; Claiborne, *Life and Correspondence of Quitman* 2: 61; Caldwell, *Lopez Expeditions*, p. 77; *Congressional Globe*, 31 Cong., 1 sess., p. 1021; Rauch, *American Interest*, p. 130; May, *Southern Dream*, p. 27.

ture to convene in November 1850 and expressed doubts about the feasibility of concerted action by all the Southern states. The legislature decided to call a special state convention to assemble one year hence with delegates to be elected in September 1851. Privately Quitman admitted that "there is no effectual remedy for the evils before us but secession." To Governor Whitemarsh Seabrook of South Carolina, who promised that his state would follow the lead of Mississippi, Quitman confided that "my views of state action will look to secession."[30]

Next Quitman turned to his indictment and impending trial. Angrily he argued that a federal court had no jurisdiction over an official of a sovereign state. Considering challenging the government "to 'try its strength' " against him, he decided instead to resign in protest and in February 1851 made a public statement warning that "the whole South, patient as she is under encroachment, might look with some jealousy upon the employment of military force to remove a Southern governor. . . ." He did not deny complicity with Lopez but stated that "I have in all things striven to be faithful and true to the rights, the interests, and the honor of the state. For this I have been abused and calumniated by the enemies of the South." To his friend Rhett in South Carolina he indicated that he resigned to avoid "a collision of arms between this state and the general government prematurely. . . ."[31] Though Quitman looked toward an eventual confrontation, he realized the South was not yet united.

The trials of Henderson and two other filibusters already had begun when Quitman arrived in New Orleans early in 1851. "If you are in trouble and need assistance," wrote a Mis-

---

30. Claiborne, *Life and Correspondence of Quitman* 2: 35–36; McCardell, "Quitman and the Compromise," 245–46; Quitman to J. J. McRae, September 28, 1850, to Whitemarsh Seabrook, September 20, 1850, in Claiborne, *Life and Correspondence of Quitman* 2: 44, 37.

31. Quitman to Jacob Thompson, August 15, 1850, "To the People of Mississippi," February 3, 1851, to R. B. Rhett, January 24, 1851, in Claiborne, *Life and Correspondence of Quitman* 2: 62, 65–67, 72.

sissippi militia commander, "fire a cannon, and my brigade will turn out to a man." Such aid was unnecessary, however, as three hung juries caused all charges to be dropped. Vindicated, Quitman returned in glory to Natchez to resume his doomed battle against the Compromise.[32]

While the New Orleans trials were going on, Lopez was planning yet another expedition. The exclusion of California now made Cuba even more attractive. Up to this point filibustering in Cuba—and elsewhere—had been primarily a movement by natives of the island, a movement in which Southerners were willingly caught up. Now, however, the character and purpose of filibustering changed; it became a tool for creating a Southern nationality and precipitating secession. Henderson, while still under indictment, approached Quitman for financial aid for Lopez, adding that "I am quite sure the time is near at hand when [filibustering] must be so appreciated throughout the South." A "Cuban Patriot" implored Quitman in December 1850 to make "the cause of Cuba . . . the rallying banner of the South. . . ." Flattering the Mississippian as a man "possessing influence," the Cuban pointed out that "probable advantages would result to the South."[33]

Quitman's large ego made him vulnerable to such flattery, but at the moment he had more pressing concerns. The Democratic State Rights party was meeting to nominate its candidate for governor, and Quitman actively sought the nomination. Many members of the party, however, realizing that Quitman's extreme views and his association with earlier filibustering activities might damage the party ticket, hesitated to offer him the position. They preferred the more moderate Jefferson Davis, who also opposed the Compromise but was not a secessionist. Yet Quitman had a good deal of support, most of it based on the belief that he deserved vindication by his party.

32. Claiborne, *Life and Correspondence of Quitman* 2: 74.
33. John Henderson to Quitman, November 6, 1850, "A Cuban Patriot" to Quitman, December 13, 1850, in *ibid.* 2: 71, 381; Ray F. Broussard, "Governor John A. Quitman and the Lopez Expeditions of 1851–52," *Journal of Mississippi History* 28 (1966): 118.

After much debate, Davis withdrew and the party with some reluctance nominated Quitman, as one delegate explained, "it being distinctly understood that he stood upon his own platform." The other party candidates, fearing charges of secessionism from the adroit campaigner Henry S. Foote, who was the gubernatorial candidate of a new Unionist party, kept Quitman at arm's length.[34]

Though secession by this time was clearly impracticable, Quitman was still optimistic. "We have high confidence in the result of the canvass before the people," he wrote to the new South Carolina governor, John Means, Seabrook's successor. While actively campaigning for State Rights convention delegates in 1851, he also aided the new Lopez expedition. A fellow dreamer in Georgia wrote hopefully to Quitman that "when the dissolution of the Union, fast consummating, shall have passed, we can admit Cuba into the Southern Confederation."[35]

First, however, it was necessary to forge a Southern nation. Though only Quitman and a few diehard South Carolinians held any hope of success, they reinforced—and perhaps deluded—one another with a regular correspondence during the first half of 1851. Rhett advised that "if we can carry you in Mississippi and [ex-Governor C. J.] McDonald in Georgia, the game is up, and the South will be redeemed without a blow. God grant you success." To a South Carolinian Quitman promised that if the demands of the coming November convention "are not promptly acceded to," Mississippi "will invite her neighboring sister states to form with her a new confe-

34. McCardell, "Quitman and the Compromise," 256–57; Reuben Davis, *Recollections of Mississippi and Mississippians* (Cambridge: Riverside Press, 1890), pp. 315–17; A. M. Clayton Letters and Notes, no date, J. F. H. Claiborne Papers, Southern Historical Collection. On a technicality, Foote had voted against the admission of California, although he claimed in principle to have supported the Compromise.

35. Quitman to John H. Means, May 25, 1851, in Claiborne, *Life and Correspondence of Quitman* 2: 135–36; Thomas Jones Pope to Quitman, May 5, 1851, John A. Quitman Papers, Mississippi Department of Archives and History.

deracy." After a convention of South Carolina Southern rights associations passed a series of bellicose resolutions, Governor Means wrote Quitman that his state "will therefore lead off . . . but [we] trust that our sister states . . . will unite with us . . . to save our institutions from ruin and the South from degradation." In reply Quitman assured Means that "we are separated by state lines, but a common cause unites us. . . . I and my associates regard the cause of Carolina as the cause of Mississippi."[36]

To effect the happy result of a Southern nation, Quitman acknowledged that although "the people of Mississippi have advanced thus far steadily and firmly" to a secessionist position, the final step "is likely to be long and cautiously deliberated on, because the next places them across the Rubicon." A spark was needed, a cause or an action that would unify the state to take that last step. "The slightest exciting cause would carry them onward, yet without it, public sentiment, alarmed by the imaginary evils of an unknown future, may recoil and pause a long time in doubt and uncertainty."[37]

The irrepressible Lopez offered just such a possibility. His new venture seemed much better organized since he was in close contact with a Cuban underground group, La Sociedad Liberatora, whose leader, Joachim Aguero, planned an uprising for the spring of 1851. A filibustering expedition launched from New Orleans and couched in liberationist rhetoric might—by coordinating its assault with an indigenous revolt—not only secure Cuba for the South but also galvanize Southern opinion when the inevitable debate over the island's

36. R. B. Rhett to Quitman, July 22, 1851, J. F. H. Claiborne Papers, Mississippi Department of Archives and History; Quitman to John S. Preston, March 3, 1851; Means to Quitman, May 12, 1851, Quitman to Means, May 25, 1851, all in Claiborne, *Life and Correspondence of Quitman* 2: 123, 133, 135–36. See also other correspondence in Claiborne 2: 123–43. C. J. McDonald, ex-Governor of Georgia, was Quitman's counterpart in that state; Richard Shryock, *Georgia and the Union in 1850* (Durham: Duke University Press, 1926), pp. 350–54.

37. Quitman to Preston, March 29, 1851, in Claiborne, *Life and Correspondence of Quitman* 2: 124.

admission as a slaveholding state began in Congress. Cuba might provide the basis for Southern secession. The son of former President John Tyler wrote to Quitman in July 1851:

> I look to the acquisition of Cuba as of great importance to the South. Through its acquisition the question as to the abidance of the North, *honestly* & *fairly*, by the provisions of the Constitution as to slavery, would be tested while yet the South [has] the *power of resistance* & the privilege of seceding.[38]

The plans of Lopez and Aguero, however, were discovered by the Spanish Captain-General in Cuba, and Aguero, with a small band of followers, fled to the mountains. On July 4, 1851, Aguero issued a proclamation announcing that

> . . . the island of Cuba is unanimously declared to be independent of the Government and Peninsula of Spain, in order that she may be recognized before the world as an independent nation, which has spontaneously placed itself under the proteçtion and auspices of the Republic of the United States, whose form of government we have adopted.

The revolution was on.[39]

Hurriedly Lopez, unprepared, assembled his forces in New Orleans. On August 3 he and four hundred volunteers, mostly Southerners, left New Orleans aboard the only available ship for Cuba. Quitman was to follow later with reinforcements. The filibusters landed on the western tip of Cuba and were thus at some distance from central Cuba, where Aguero was operating. No sooner had the filibusters disembarked than they were surrounded by waiting Spanish forces and captured. Some fifty Americans were executed by firing squad and their bodies left to the mercy of the crowd. Lopez was marched to the center of Havana and, before a throng of twenty thousand, beheaded. The other prisoners were sentenced to hard labor in Spain but were soon pardoned as part

38. Broussard, "Quitman and Lopez," p. 118; John Tyler, Jr., to Quitman, John A. Quitman Papers, Houghton Library, Harvard University.
39. Rauch, *American Interest*, p. 155.

of a general settlement between the governments of Spain and the United States.[40]

When the news of the mass executions reached New Orleans, riots erupted. "American blood has been shed," trumpeted the *Courier*. "It cries aloud for vengeance—vengeance on the tyrant! . . . blood for blood! Our brethren must be avenged! Cuba must be seized!" Mobile, too, experienced similar violent activities. But there was no vengeance, for within days the news of Lopez's death and the collapse of the revolt arrived, and the effect was sobering. Acting quickly President Millard Fillmore, Secretary of State Daniel Webster, and Daniel Barringer, the United States minister to Spain, secured the pardon of the prisoners and an easing of tension in relations with Spain. The impulse to annexation had at least temporarily abated.[41]

For Quitman, steadily losing ground in his campaign in Mississippi, the defeat of Lopez was an added burden. "I have not one moment's leisure on this terrible canvass," wrote the beleaguered candidate to his wife. The convention vote in September repudiated the State Rights party overwhelmingly, and Quitman, humiliated, withdrew his candidacy for the November gubernatorial election and retired to Natchez to assess his future.[42]

Southern nationalism and Southern expansionism were in full scale retreat. Foote, Quitman's victorious opponent, crowed in triumph that "Quitman and Quitmanism are *dead* forever in Mississippi." Indeed, it certainly seemed so. Barringer's son, a student at the University of Mississippi, informed his father that

40. Caldwell, *Lopez Expeditions*, pp. 91–102; Rauch, *American Interest*, pp. 157–60.
41. *New Orleans Courier*, August 21, 1851, quoted in Urban, "New Orleans and Cuba," p. 1159; Rauch, *American Interest*, pp. 161–80.
42. McCardell, "Quitman and the Compromise," 257–60; Quitman to Eliza Quitman, August 13, 1851, Quitman Family Papers, Southern Historical Collection. The convention vote statewide gave the Unionists all but seventeen of the state's fifty-nine counties and a majority of seven thousand votes.

since the execution of Lopez & [the filibusters'] defeat in the Southern States upon their doctrine of Secession, I think they will remain quiet for a while. Their hopes were very high at one time that they would succeed in Cuba and put the Union once more in danger by their efforts to annex Cuba as a slave State.

Yet it was unclear whether expansionism was defeated or merely detained. A Louisianian, nursing his political wounds, suggested that the expansionists were not ready to give up. "I think," he prophesied, "that Cuba is bound to come at last."[43]

III

Not all Southern nationalists favored expansionism. The South Carolinians wanted to unify the South in preparation for a separate existence, and many of them believed expansion was an issue both distracting and divisive. Refusing to cooperate with any party or administration, the Carolinians opposed expansionist schemes as "pleasing deceits—baits manufactured for party purpose—to quiet the South in the progress of the North to mastery in the Union." Never vigorous advocates of rapid, uncontrolled growth, the Carolinians maintained, in the words of Congressman W. W. Boyce, that "if it be possible for a nation to have territory enough, we certainly have it, and whatever else we may need, we do not need any more space."[44]

Likewise, the upper South was unenthusiastic about expansion. New slave territory would intensify the labor shortage that the whole South was experiencing in the early 1850's. Edmund Ruffin questioned the wisdom of adding territory inhabited by suspicious Catholics and inferior races. Still

43. Henry S. Foote to Howell Cobb, July 9, 1851, in Phillips, ed., *Toombs, Stephens, and Cobb Correspondence* 2:242; P. B. Barringer to Daniel M. Barringer, December 2, 1851, Barringer Papers, Southern Historical Collection; J. T. McMurran to L. P. Conner, September 10, 1851, Conner Papers, Louisiana State University, Baton Rouge.

44. *Charleston Mercury*, February 26, 1858; *Congressional Globe*, 33 Cong., 2 sess., Appendix, p. 91.

others opposed expansion simply because it was time for "the country [to] have some quiet."[45] Economically, socially, or politically, men in the upper South denied the necessity and the desirability of expansion.

Even in the southwest, expansion sentiment was hardly unanimous. A Mississippian opposed expansionists' "laboring to introduce a nation of Catholics and foreigners." Congressman John Reagan of Texas regularly attacked Southern expansionists in his state, many of whom engaged in periodic raids into Mexico during the 1850's, for attempting to "break up the Government and organize a Southern Confederacy."[46]

Yet a large number of Southerners after 1850 continued to believe in Manifest Destiny. Even so, not all Southern expansionists had the same motives. Some desired to acquire territory in Cuba, Mexico, or Central America for their own selfish speculative benefit. Others envisioned a widening of the sphere of American economic influence by developing the vast tropical resources. Many favored expansion for political reasons, hoping to protect Southern interests by the creation of tropical slave states—thus preserving the Union's balance of free and slave states. Still others, men like Quitman and Henderson, dreamed of a separate Southern nation encompassing all of Latin America.

The Southern nationalists who participated in expansion activities in the 1850's were largely responsible for propagating the myth that slavery, in order to survive economically, had to expand. It is not clear whether this argument was correct. Recent studies have suggested not that slavery invariably exhausted soil and constantly demanded new outlets, but rather that slavery was highly profitable and becoming more so and that slaveholders' expectations were highly optimistic.[47] But

45. *Congressional Globe*, 35 Cong., 2 sess., pp. 1061, 1347–48; Scarborough, ed., *Diary of Edmund Ruffin*, p. 290.
46. J. F. H. Claiborne to Quitman, August 16, 1855, Quitman Family Papers, Southern Historical Collection; May, *Southern Dream*, p. 241.
47. Fogel and Engerman, *Time on the Cross* 1 *passim*. The leading advocate of the position that slavery by its very nature had to expand economically is Genovese, *Political Economy of Slavery*, pp. 243–70.

behind the expansionists' economic argument was a political argument that slavery—or, rather, the number of slave states—had to increase to survive. In the colorful, exaggerated tradition of Southern politics, Southern nationalists embellished what was an essentially political purpose with grave warnings of the social and economic threats of containment. If they—like the Mississippi editor who "manufactured public opinion"—could convince the Southern public of the necessity of expansion, then any future congressional action barring Southerners from new territories would increase dissatisfaction with the Union. Hence the Gulf state Southern nationalists during the 1850's stoked the fires of Manifest Destiny as they labored to secure the safety of the South.

Foreign intervention continued to pose a threat to that safety. Soon after the execution of Lopez and the cessation of filibustering expeditions to Cuba, a British fleet began patrolling the Caribbean. At the same time the British minister at Madrid began exerting pressure on Spain to emancipate slaves in all Spanish territorial possessions. That such a move was not only a matter of official British policy but also intended to forestall American annexation became clear in a letter to the Spanish minister to London from Viscount Palmerston, the British foreign secretary; he acknowledged that emancipaiton "would create a most powerful element of resistance to any scheme for annexing Cuba to the United States, where slavery exists."[48]

Meanwhile, territorial expansion was a key issue in the American presidential campaign of 1852. All but the most intractable secessionists returned to the Democratic party in 1852 and supported Franklin Pierce of New Hampshire for the presidency on a platform promising expansion into Cuba. Southern expansionists received additional hope from Pierce's inaugural address, in which he straightforwardly declared:

48. Bailey, *Diplomatic History*, p. 290; Corwin, *Spain and Abolition*, pp. 97–98; May, *Southern Dream*, pp. 31–32; C. Stanley Urban, "The Africanization of Cuba Scare, 1853–1855," *The Hispanic American Historical Review* 37 (1957): 30–36.

. . . the policy of my administration will not be controlled by any timid forebodings of evil from expansion. Indeed, it is not to be disguised that our attitude as a nation and our position on the globe render the acquisition of certain possessions not within our jurisdiction eminently important for our protection. . . .

Further solace came from Pierce's cabinet appointments. Secretary of State William L. Marcy of New York was a longtime advocate of annexing Cuba, as was Secretary of War Jefferson Davis. Southerners confidently expected that the president would succeed in acquiring Cuba. "This will be glory enough for his administration," announced a hopeful Virginian.[49]

Particularly encouraging to Southern expansionists was Pierce's appointment of Pierre Soulé—the eccentric senator from Louisiana, a supporter of Lopez and a Southern nationalist in the 1850–51 crisis—as minister to Spain. "He is a secessionist and a filibuster," inveighed the hostile *New York World* with accuracy. Exiled from his native France in 1825 at the age of twenty-four for publishing Republican attacks against the monarchy, Soulé had found a home in New Orleans. He joined the Democratic party and won election to the Senate in 1848. Favoring Lopez's activities, he was a vocal Caribbean expansionist and gave to the cause considerable talents of energy, passion, and imagination. In addition, Soulé had favored resistance to the 1850 Compromise and on occasion betrayed his own hopes for secession. So public were his convictions that the *New Orleans Commercial Bulletin* remarked, "there is no God save Secession, and Soulé is his prophet." His appointment by

49. Craven, *Southern Nationalism*, p. 130; Roy F. Nichols, *Franklin Pierce, Young Hickory of the Granite Hills* (Philadelphia: University of Pennsylvania Press, 1931), pp. 205–215, 235; James D. Richardson, comp., *Messages and Papers of the Presidents*, 20 vols. (Washington: Government Printing Office, 1897–1917), 6:2731–32; Amos Aschbach Ettinger, *The Mission to Spain of Pierre Soulé, 1853–1855: A Study in the Cuban Diplomacy of the United States* (New Haven: Yale University Press, 1932), p. 117. A small group of Southerners tried to maintain the State Rights party and nominated secessionists George Troup of Georgia for president and Quitman for vice president, but that ticket fared poorly.

Pierce signified the administration's commitment both to expansion and, more generally, to an easing of Southern nationalists' concerns.[50]

Soulé, described by a Philadelphia editor as a man "of swarthy complexion, black flashing eyes, and Frenchified dress and speech . . . artificial—brilliant in repartee, yet subject to fits of melancholy; impetuous, yet reserved; proud, but polite . . . ," departed for Madrid to the cheers of New York annexationists. In a singularly inappropriate response to a serenade, Soulé announced his intention to speak "tremendous truths to the tyrants of the old continent." Combined with his well known views "against purchasing Cuba" as an "obsolete idea," Soulé's farewell speech, which left little doubt as to his position, got his mission off to an unfortunate start.[51]

Soulé's passion for the prompt annexation of Cuba was shared by many Southerners, who viewed with growing alarm events transpiring there. Rumors were rife that England was about to establish a free black colony in Cuba "preparatory to the effectual emancipation of slavery in the South." An organization of exiled Cuban slaveholders in New York, through the columns of their newspaper, La Verdad, maintained a propaganda barrage against British influence which, they claimed, looked toward "Africanization" of the Spanish colony. Southern newspapers in 1853 picked up the theme and its terrifying images. "With Cuba as a free negro colony but a few leagues distant from our most populous Slave States," worried a Tennessee editor, "it would not be difficult to destroy the efficiency of that class of our population and render abolition

50. *New York Herald*, November 15, 1853; Amos A. Ettinger, "Pierre Soulé," *Dictionary of American Biography* 17: 405–406; *New Orleans Commercial Bulletin*, September 27, 1852, quoted in Ettinger, *Soulé Mission*, p. 20; M. J. White, "Louisiana and the Secession Movement of the Early Fifties," *Proceedings of the Mississippi Valley Historical Association for the Year 1914–1915* (Cedar Rapids, Ia: Torch Press, 1916), 8: 281.

51. J. Preston Moore, "Pierre Soulé: Southern Expansionist and Promoter," *Journal of Southern History* 21 (1955): 205; Ettinger, *Soulé Mission*, p. 176. Soulé had spoken these words in a Senate speech January 25, 1853, *Congressional Globe*, 32 Cong., 2 sess., p. 119.

desirable with us." Political leaders joined the cry, Unionists as well as secessionists. Congressman V. E. Howard of Texas spoke guardedly of Cuba's being "converted into a black republic." In the Senate Judah P. Benjamin of Louisiana presented his state legislature's resolution expressing fear over "the abolition of slavery in that colony, to the sacrifice of the white race . . . to a barbarous and inferior race." Benjamin added his own apprehensions of "a body of black troops to assist the Spanish troops against the white population of the island."[52]

Quitman weighed all these matters in the quiet of his Natchez plantation home. His humiliation in the 1852 presidential campaign seemed to have ended his public career. Yet the persistent Mississippian opened communication with the Cuban exiles in New York. In May 1853 Quitman decided to accept their offer to organize and lead a new filibustering expedition to Cuba. He demanded sound financial backing and, by April 1854, was ready to gather his filibusters together.[53]

Quitman undertook the expedition for a number of reasons. He was, first of all, still an energetic and ambitious man. His sizable pride had been considerably wounded during the Compromise crisis and its aftermath, and he wanted the mission to succeed so as "not to compromise my own character and reputation." In addition he feared that emancipation in Cuba would strike "a fatal blow . . . at Southern institutions by introducing into a neighboring island the scheme of mixing the white & black races— . . . thus paving the way for the final establishment of a negro or mongrel empire on our borders.

52. Philip J. Weaver to William P. Browne, November 28, 1853, William Phineas Browne Papers, Alabama Department of Archives and History; C. Stanley Urban, "The Abortive Quitman Filibustering Expedition, 1853–1855," *Journal of Mississippi History* 18 (1956): 175–78; Rauch, *American Interest*, pp. 264–68; *Clarksville (Tenn.) Jeffersonian*, September 28, 1853, quoted in May, *Southern Dream*, p. 35; *Congressional Globe*, 32 Cong., 2 sess., p. 81; 33 Cong., 1 sess., pp. 1298–99.

53. Urban, "Abortive Quitman Expedition," 180–81; Rauch, *American Interest*, pp. 268–72.

. . ." Finally, he wanted Cuba for the Southern nation he still envisioned. "By sternly standing by our principles," he had written in 1852, "a time may come for us to strike with effect."[54]

The fledgling Pierce administration, still mapping out its foreign policy, did not discourage Quitman. Of the several options available for acquiring Cuba—purchase, conquest, filibustering—the administration seemed to prefer an internal uprising followed by the liberation by American forces. In July 1853 Quitman met with Pierce, Soulé, and Marcy, and a plan was apparently devised for Quitman to lead a filibustering movement to install in Cuba "a free and liberal government which shall retain and preserve the domestic institutions of the country." The expedition would ignite a revolution, the signs of which, wrote the American consul in Havana, appeared to be growing more and more decided in character." With the European powers engaged in the Crimean War, British intervention seemed unlikely. The happy result would be first an independent republic and then speedily, by joint resolution, annexation, "after the fashion of Texas," lest "we . . . have California over again."[55]

As in 1850 and 1851, a congressional dispute over slavery in the territories gave an added impetus to the efforts of the filibusters. This time it was the Kansas–Nebraska Act, introduced early in 1854, that aggravated sectional relations. Permitting those two territories, which lay above the Missouri Compromise line, to decide for themselves the legality of slavery within their borders, this bill reopened the territorial issue, apparently resolved in 1850. Southerners in both parties supported the bill, and they were aided by the support of Pres-

---

54. Rauch, *American Interest*, pp. 265–66; Quitman to Junta, April 30, 1853, Quitman to W. D. Chapman, June 9, 1852, in Claiborne, *Life and Correspondence of Quitman* 2: 388, 166; Quitman to B. F. Dill, February 9, 1854, Quitman Papers, Mississippi Department of Archives and History.

55. May, *Southern Dream*, pp. 44–45; Claiborne, *Life and Correspondence of Quitman* 2: 389–90; Rauch, *American Interest*, pp. 267, 270–71; A. M. Clayton to Quitman, November 10, 1853, Quitman Papers, Houghton Library.

ident Pierce. Northern antislavery men, however, vigorously opposed the measure, rightly claiming that the Missouri Compromise had been violated. Many Northerners agreed with Congressman Tappan Wentworth of Massachusetts, who said that "if the South pulls down [the Compromise] of 1820, she cannot expect the North to support that of 1850 [including the Fugitive Slave Bill]. They must stand or fall together."[56]

New developments in Cuba added to Southern anxieties. In December 1853 a new Captain-General, Juan de la Pezuela, assumed control in Cuba and soon thereafter instituted a number of reforms which looked, in his own words, toward a "transition from labor that is entirely compulsory, to the organization of labor under a state of complete freedom." To bring about the transition, Pezuela promised to crack down on the illegal slave trade and introduce free apprentices imported from Africa. By May 1854 Pezuela had begun enlisting free blacks and mulattoes in the army for a two-year term with the same rights as Spanish soldiers. Even more disturbing to Southerners was his decree permitting intermarriage between black women and white men.[57]

Pezuela's reforms coincided with the signing of the Kansas–Nebraska Act and the eruption of a new Northern antislavery attack upon the South. Northern editors and congressmen joined the assault. Southern plantations were "negro harems;" Kansas–Nebraska was "a soulless, eyeless monster;" it was time "to work together for the overthrow of the slaveholding dynasty." As for expansion, "there was a time," wrote a New York editor, "when the North would have consented to annex Cuba, but the Nebraska wrong has forever rendered annexation impossible."[58]

Southerners promptly took up the challenge. An Arkansas

56. Craven, *Southern Nationalism*, pp. 178–200; *Congressional Globe*, 33 Cong., 1 sess., p. 734.
57. Corwin, *Spain and Abolition*, pp. 115–16; Urban, "Africanization of Cuba," 30–34.
58. *New York Tribune*, June 22, 1855; *Congressional Globe*, 33 Cong., 1 sess., p. 282; *Milwaukee Daily Free Democrat*, May 9, 1854, quoted in Craven, *Southern*

Democratic district convention in May 1854 declared that the acquisition of Cuba was preferable to "compromise with fanatics and abolitionists." The *Richmond Enquirer* claimed that "Cuba is the only measure of policy in regard to which the people of the South feel a special and present interest." A flood of inquiries on the progress of the filibustering expedition deluged Quitman. Cuba was "the most important subject that now agitates the Southern mind," wrote one correspondent. A student at the University of Mississippi offered "to contribute [his] little mite . . . to see that beautiful island joined in common fraternity with these Southern States." "The desire that Cuba should be acquired as a Southern conquest, is almost unanimous among Southern men . . . ," wrote another. A committee of Mobile citizens, fearing the conversion of Cuba "into a free negro colony," urged Quitman to strike lest Southern institutions "receive a fatal stab through the same blow that reaches the heart of Cuba." Governor John Winston of Alabama and Senator Alexander H. Stephens of Georgia gave active support.[59]

After the passage of Kansas–Nebraska, acquisition of Cuba was almost exclusively a Southern goal, since the uproar over extending slavery into Kansas made it no longer possible for the administration to encourage filibustering. Pierce, hoping to placate anxious Northern Democrats, further proved his determination by issuing a proclamation prohibiting filibustering activities. As in 1851 the New Orleans court acted swiftly, ordering Quitman and his associates to post a large bond which they would forfeit if they should move against Cuba.[60]

Nationalism, p. 186; *New York Courier and Enquirer*, quoted in Bailey, *Diplomatic History*, p. 294.

59. *Arkansas Gazette*, May 19, 1854; *Richmond Enquirer*, June 20, 1854; Josephus Dotson to Quitman, June 6, 1854, A. J. McNeil to Quitman, June 10, 1854, F. C. Jones to Quitman, June 10, 1854, "Your obt. svts." of Mobile to Quitman, June 10, 1854, Quitman Papers, Mississippi Department of Archives and History; May, *Southern Dream*, p. 50.

60. Urban, "Abortive Quitman Expedition," 183.

About the same time, Marcy directed Soulé to negotiate the purchase of Cuba. A second part of Soulé's orders required him, in the event Spain refused to sell, "to detach that island from the Spanish dominion and from all dependence on any European power." Accordingly, in October 1854, Soulé joined the American ministers to England and France—James Buchanan and John Y. Mason—in issuing the Ostend Manifesto, which declared that if Africanization in Cuba continued and Spain refused to sell the island, "we shall be justified in wresting it from Spain if we possess the power." The sabre-rattling Manifesto alarmed not only European nations, which responded angrily, but also antislavery Northerners, who joined the *New York Tribune* in condemning the "manifesto of brigands." After heavy Democratic losses in the 1854 fall elections to the new, antislavery Republican party, Marcy abandoned all efforts to purchase Cuba.[61]

Quitman and his filibusters, meanwhile, were confused by the variety of signals they were receiving. Late in 1854 they still were trying to raise money for an expedition. The need for intervention to prevent Africanization still loomed, and Quitman still hoped to prevent a nation "of inferior and mixed races." "Our destiny is intertwined with that of Cuba," he wrote. A supporter in *DeBow's Review* urged that Cuba was "a Southern question" and "the safety of the South is to be found only in the extension of its peculiar institutions. . . ."[62]

But suddenly the entire situation changed and the filibustering movement collapsed. Soon after the diplomatic fiascoes of 1854 and Marcy's abandonment of the idea of purchase, Spain removed the liberal Pezuela and installed José Gutiérrez de la Concha. Promising "never to meddle with the system" of slavery, the new Captain-General reversed a number of Pezuela's policies. At the same time he brusquely informed the

61. Bailey, *Diplomatic History*, pp. 294–96; Urban, "Abortive Quitman Expedition," p. 185.
62. Quitman to Thomas Reed, August 24, 1854, in Claiborne, *Life and Correspondence of Quitman* 2: 208, 211; *DeBow's Review* 17 (1854): 523–24.

American consul that if Quitman's force invaded, he would arm the Negroes to resist. Gutiérrez de la Concha also asked four British warships to resume patrols of the Cuban coast, which had been unprotected since the Crimean War began. These developments quickly deflated revolutionary desires in Cuba and hastened the demise of Quitman's plans as well.[63]

By March 1855 the movement was dead. Throughout the South recruiters reported their failure to enlist filibusters for the expedition. In mid-March Quitman came to Washington where Marcy, following Pierce's instructions, ordered him to abandon his scheme. Gutiérrez de la Concha's policy changes, the resulting absence of indigenous Cuban support, and, perhaps most important, the growing power of the antislavery movement exhibited in the 1854 elections, made Cuban annexation—by force or by purchase—ill advised if not politically suicidal. Quitman apparently agreed, for in April he resigned as leader of the filibusters. The opportunity "to strike with effect" had to be found elsewhere.[64]

If neither Mississippi nor Cuba offered the opportunity, perhaps in Congress, where like-minded Southern men were growing daily more conscious of their shared plight, Quitman might realize his dream. In July 1855 he accepted his district's nomination for Congress and stated clearly both his fears and his hopes:

> . . . upon all matters connected with our peculiar domestic institutions the South must look to herself. That no national party organization will fully protect us. That while honestly differing on other subjects, the patriot should seek to keep our people united on this, and that therefore it is highly impolitic and injurious in our party contests about issues less vital, to indulge in violent denunciations of those [Southerners] who differ from us politically.[65]

63. Rauch, *American Interest*, p. 299; Urban, "Africanization of Cuba," 40–42; Corwin, *Spain and Abolition*, pp. 124–25.
64. Urban, "Abortive Quitman Expedition,'" 191–93; Rauch, *American Interest*, p. 300.
65. Quitman to William A. Stone, July 19, 1855, Southern Filibusters Collection, Louisiana State University, Baton Rouge.

Quitman won election and set out for Congress to oppose the "politically corrupt combination, planned by cute Yankee genius." He recognized that there would be no "unanimity in the South, even if slavery in the states should be assailed. There were Tories in '76, there will be Tories in '56. *We* shall have to serve the latter as the patriots of the Revolution treated the former." Quitman took up his new duties in Washington, hoping there to find a chance "to strike with effect."[66]

IV

The events following the Kansas–Nebraska controversy were of scant comfort to Southerners. While they had gained a tactical victory in that all the territories were now theoretically open to slaves, their strategic position was hardly propitious. "Come on, then, gentlemen of the slave States," challenged Senator Seward. "We will engage in competition for the virgin soil of Kansas, and God give the victory to the side which is stronger in numbers as it is in right." Kansas became the battleground both symbolically—between slavery and free labor in the abstract—and literally—between slaveholders and non-slaveholders who, in their often violent struggle to win the territory to their own cause, set up rival governments and made "Bleeding Kansas" an ominous prelude to civil war.[67]

Ironically, it was Northern opposition that made Southerners determined both to pass the Kansas–Nebraska bill and to make Kansas a slave state. If the *Charleston Mercury* as usual represented the view of extreme Southerners, there was great reluctance in 1854 to reopen the healing wounds of 1850–51.

66. Quitman to J. F. H. Claiborne, November 18, 1855, in Claiborne, *Life and Correspondence of Quitman* 2: 216.
67. *Congressional Globe*, 33 Cong., 1 sess., Appendix, p. 771; Roy F. Nichols, *The Disruption of American Democracy* (New York: Free Press, 1948), pp. 24–27, 65–66; Allan Nevins, *The Emergence of Lincoln: Douglas, Buchanan, and Party Chaos, 1857–1859*, 2 vols. (New York: Charles Scribner's Sons, 1950), 1: 133–47; Craven, *Southern Nationalism*, pp. 209–15.

"There is no compact sectional sentiment in the South," said the *Mercury*, after the bill had been enacted,

> . . . in favor of the Nebraska and Kansas bill; while at the North there is the most intense hostility to it. What is to be done? Can the South stand listlessly by and see the bill repealed, when this is made the direct issue against her . . . ? If she prizes the citadel, can she neglect the outposts? There is no alternative for the South. When the North presents a sectional issue, and tenders battle upon it, she must meet it, or abide all the consequences of a victory easily won, by a remorseless and eager foe.[68]

Against this background the deteriorating Pierce presidency spun itself out. It was replaced in 1857 by the administration of James Buchanan, the Pennsylvania Democrat with a distinguished diplomatic career which included service as American minister to England. During his ministerial tenure, Buchanan had won Southern support when he signed the Ostend Manifesto. Upon his old shoulders now rested the hope of sectional peace. His term had an inauspicious start. At a preinaugural banquet, a number of guests contracted food poisoning. Among them was Quitman, who never fully recovered. Two days after Buchanan's inauguration, the Supreme Court issued the Dred Scott decision, which denied the right of a Negro to sue in federal court, the authority of Congress to exclude slavery from any territory, and, thus, the constitutionality of the Missouri and all subsequent compromises. Although Southern reaction to the decision was guardedly hopeful, uproar in the North served to intensify the struggle between rights and right in Kansas. Far from resolving the problem, the court had rather further confounded it.[69]

The more the free states demonstrated their willingness to compete for the territories, the more Southern writers and politicians expressed increasing fears of eventual confinement. Albert G. Brown declared in Congress that "when you have

68. *Charleston Mercury*, June 21, 1854.
69. Nevins, *Emergence of Lincoln* 1: 90–100; Nichols, *Disruption of Democracy*, pp. 73, 78, 84; Craven, *Southern Nationalism*, p. 280.

forced into the cotton-growing States of this Union, eight millions of slaves, and have left them no outlet, you will have that sort of disaster which you would have if you dammed up the mouth of the Mississippi River. There must be an outlet for them." Thomas Clingman of North Carolina feared slavery would be "pent up within a territory which after a time will be insufficient for their subsistence, and where they must perish from want, or from collision that would occur between the races." A contributor to *DeBow's Review* claimed that Southerners, in order to avoid a "war of races," would "in self-defense be compelled to conquer parts of Mexico and Central America, and make slave territory of that. . . ." Another contributor foresaw "in the course of not a very long time, the negro race will become too populous to be advantageously employed as slaves." If "*their limits never be extended*," the Southern states would face "a contest of some sort . . . between that [slave race] and the white race." The denial of any territorial outlet, said the *Mercury*, would inevitably result in emancipation and "the loss of liberty, property, home, country—everything that makes life worth living."[70] Whether or not the fears were realistic, they were certainly genuine.

With Kansas in dispute and with Cuba effectively removed from Southern grasp, at least for the time being, the exploits of William Walker in Nicaragua began to arouse Southern interest. A more unlikely hero would have been hard to find. Shy, unhandsome, standing only five and a half feet tall and weighing only one hundred pounds, Walker, born in Tennessee in 1824, had moved from one failure to another. He received an M.D. degree from the University of Pennsylvania but found medical practice not to his liking. He then studied law and joined the New Orleans bar but had few clients. Next he entered journalism and became editor of the *New Orleans*

---

70. *Congressional Globe*, 32 Cong., 1 sess., p. 194; Clingman quoted in Genovese, *Political Economy of Slavery*, p. 250; *DeBow's Review* 13 (1852): 13; *Charleston Mercury*, quoted in William Barney, *The Road to Secession* (New York: Praeger Publishers, 1972), p. 51.

Crescent in 1848, attacking filibustering movements against Cuba. He fell hopelessly in love with a beautiful deaf mute woman in New Orleans and mastered the sign language to advance his courtship only to see his beloved carried away by the yellow fever. He then moved to California where, in addition to leading a stormy life as a lawyer and editor, he organized a quixotic "colonizing" expedition into Baja California, proclaimed himself president, but was soon forced by angry Mexicans back across the border to face arrest and trial for violating neutrality laws. He was acquitted. Soon after, in 1854, he resumed his editorial duties in California, inveighing against the "hot-headed and narrow-minded . . . ultra-slavery men" as "the most active and efficient agents abolitionists can have in the Southern States."[71]

Walker could not stay in one place for very long. His eyes turned to an offer from Nicaragua, which was immersed in another of those periodic revolutions that had occurred with regularity since the five Central American states declared their independence from Spain and abolished slavery in 1824. By the mid-1850's the conflict in Nicaragua was not between Royalists and Democrats but between two factions that can only be described as "ins" and "outs." Trading violent ascendancy, they regularly proscribed their political enemies, moved the capital from one city to another, and elected a new president. During the six years preceding Walker's involvement, Nicaragua had had fifteen presidents.[72]

Walker was not the only man interested in the Nicaraguan situation. Americans had long been interested in shortening the travel time between the East coast and California, and the

71. William O. Scroggs, *Filibusters and Financiers: The Story of William Walker and his Associates* (New York: Macmillan Co., 1916), pp. 9–69; William O. Scroggs, "William Walker," *Dictionary of American Biography* 19: 363–64; Laurence Greene, *The Filibuster: The Career of William Walker* (Indianapolis: Bobbs–Merrill Co., 1937), pp. 20–27, is written in the "popular" vein, while Albert H. Z. Carr, *The World and William Walker* (New York: Harper and Row, 1963), pp. 3–13 is a psychobiography of a worthy subject.
72. Scroggs, *Filibusters and Financiers*, pp. 82–83.

discovery of gold in California in 1849 made an isthmian route even more desirable. To travel overland across the United States meant facing the hazards of mountains, deserts, and Indians, while the alternative, a steamship journey around the tip of South America, was impractically long. In 1851 the American railroad entrepreneur Cornelius Vanderbilt arranged with the Nicaraguan government a lucrative, monopolistic contract providing transportation across the isthmus. The Accessory Transit Company was soon conveying twenty-four thousand Americans per year.[73]

Meanwhile, in 1854 one of the proprietors of Walker's California newspaper visited Nicaragua, was impressed with its potential for great wealth, and made contacts with the leaders of the "Democratic" faction, which was just then in revolt against the incumbent regime. Eagerly the Democrats responded to a suggested intervention by Americans. Soon Walker began to organize an expedition of Americans, who signed a contract granting them 170 acres of land apiece and designating them as "colonists." In May 1855 "Colonel" Walker and fifty-eight colonists set sail, and by October his forces, with the assistance of the Transit Company, had put the foes of the Democrats to rout. Walker ordered the opposition leader executed, set up a figurehead president, and declared himself commander-in-chief. Pleased with the prospect of stability, the Transit Company began ferrying new recruits from the United States free of charge. The ambitious Walker—doctor, lawyer, and now chief—had thus apparently succeeded at least.[74]

Though enthusiasm for Walker's filibustering exploits was high in the South, his was not at the outset a Southern movement in either composition or purpose. The primary motivation was greed or, more politely, as Walker himself stated,

73. May, *Southern Dream*, pp. 85–87; William O. Scroggs, "William Walker and the Steamship Corporation in Nicaragua," *American Historical Review* 10 (1904): 792–94.
74. Scroggs, "Walker and the Steamship Corporation," 794–95 signing a contract as colonists, the filibusters hoped to avoid neutrality law violations.

"the sweets of adventure or the rewards of fame." The recruits numbered more Northerners than Southerners, and they were, as a whole, "a band of brigands, pirates, and cutthroats." Still, the Southern press probably exceeded the North in supporting Walker's efforts "for the establishment of American institutions in Nicaragua." Slavery was, of course, an American institution. Moreover, Southerners in government tended to support the North Carolina-born minister to Nicaragua, John Hill Wheeler, who—believing "the race of Central Americans . . . incapable of self-government"—urged without success that Pierce recognize the Walker regime.[75]

Walker, however, faced the same political obstacles as his predecessors. Stabilization of the government proved impossible. Immediately after the execution of the opposition leader in November 1855 a new cabal began taking shape to oust the American intruders, receiving support from anti-American elements in other Central American states. Walker, intervening in an internal power struggle for control of the Transit Company, annulled the original company contract and sold exclusive rights to Vanderbilt's opponents, who had helped Walker gain power. The significance of the blunder soon became clear when Vanderbilt, in February 1856, employed his considerable influence to end the free transport of immigrants to Nicaragua, to support the rebels against Walker, and to urge the Pierce administration to intervene. Once again, Walker faced an imminent reverse.[76]

The demands of Vanderbilt and the wishes of the Democratic party did not coincide. In May 1856 Pierce—under great pressure from his party, which was about to adopt a strong

75. William Walker, *The War in Nicaragua* (Mobile: S. H. Goetzel and Co., 1860), p. 32; May, *Southern Dream*, p. 91; *Richmond Whig*, January 7, 1848; *Richmond Daily Dispatch*, March 30, 1856, quoted in May, *Southern Dream*, p. 100; Randall O. Hudson, "The Filibuster Minister: The Career of John Hill Wheeler as United States Minister to Nicaragua, 1854–1856," *North Carolina Historical Review* 49 (1972): 283, 291–92.
76. May, *Southern Dream*, pp. 102–103; Scroggs, *Filibusters and Financiers*, pp. 270–85.

pro-Walker position in its nominating convention—agreed to receive the minister from Nicaragua, thus officially recognizing Walker. Soon thereafter Walker's puppet president defected to the rebels and his minister left Washington. Walker had himself elected president—only a very few voted—and in July sent a new emissary, Appleton Oaksmith, to Pierce who, denied renomination by his party, refused to receive him.[77]

Unrecognized by Pierce, unsupported by the Transit Company, and unloved by a growing number of Nicaraguans, Walker looked around desperately for help. Ready to assist were two Southerners whose position he readily adopted in return for their support. One was Quitman, who had spoken out in Congress recently against the neutrality laws in support of "that patriotic band which has lately transplanted the principles of democracy from United States to Nicaraguan soil." Quitman urged that "the isthmus must be in friendly hands or in our own. To delay in seizing or securing it is to commit an act of moral treason. . . ." The other was Soulé, an old friend from New Orleans days, who had recently written into the Democratic platform an endorsement of "the efforts which are being made by the people of Central America to regenerate that portion of the continent which covers the passage across the Inter-oceanic Isthmus." Soulé engaged to raise funds in New Orleans to support Walker's government.[78]

August 1856 was the critical month. In Washington, Oaksmith won Quitman's support and together, during a long evening meeting on August 4, they appealed to Pierce for recognition. Although Quitman continued almost daily to urge recognition, Pierce stubbornly refused. Meanwhile, on August 20, Soulé arrived in Nicaragua—ostensibly to negotiate, on behalf of the Bank of Louisiana, a $500,000 loan to Walker,

77. May, *Southern Dream*, pp. 102–104; Scroggs, *Filibusters and Financiers*, pp. 196–208.

78. Claiborne, *Life and Correspondence of Quitman* 2: 348, 350; Kirk H. Porter and Donald Bruce Johnson, comps., *National Party Platforms, 1840–1960*, 2d ed. (Urbana: University of Illinois Press, 1961), p. 26; Moore, "Pierre Soulé," pp. 208–10.

which was signed one week later. Yet Soulé and Walker also discussed other matters. The Louisiana investors behind Soulé believed that profits could be harvested from tropical Nicaragua only through forced, colored labor—either impressed natives or imported African slaves. Moreover, the Louisianians had never really lost interest in Cuba. They hoped to use Nicaragua as a base for a movement against the long desired island.[79]

Although Soulé doubtless pressed his case with considerable effect, Walker probably already knew what had to be done. Just before Soulé's arrival Walker had written a confidential note to Don Domingo de Goicuria, a Cuban nationalist who had allied with Walker's filibusters in return for pledges of later aid for Cuban independence. The note promised that "Cuba must and shall be free, but not for the Yankees. Oh no! that fine country is not fit for those barbarous Yankees. . . . The only way to cut the expanding and expansive democracy of the North, is by a powerful and compact Southern federation, based on military principles." Several weeks later, on September 22, Walker issued a decree paving the way for a reinstitution of slavery in Nicaragua. Soulé was well pleased.[80]

If Walker's purpose was, as he later claimed, "to bind the Southern States to Nicaragua as if she were one of themselves" by his decree, he had not failed. The *New Orleans Daily Delta* called Nicaragua a "home for Southern men." A Virginian in Nicaragua wrote to the *Tuskegee* (*Alabama*) *Republican* that Walker had triumphed "in the name of the white race" and

79. May, *Southern Dream*, pp. 104–105; Scroggs, *Filibusters and Financiers*, pp. 209–10; Moore, "Pierre Soulé," pp. 212–13.
80. William O. Scroggs, "William Walker's Designs on Cuba," *Mississippi Valley Historical Review* 1 (1904): 208; Moore, "Pierre Soulé," p. 213; May, *Southern Dream*, pp. 106–107. There is no hard evidence linking Walker's change of position to the new Southern influence, nor, specifically, is there evidence attaching conditions to the Louisiana loan. It seems highly likely, however, that the adaptable Walker readily acceded, whether coerced or not, to the wishes of his New Orleans benefactors, knowing that to do otherwise would jeopardize his already tenuous position.

now held out an opportunity "to you and your slaves, at a time when you have not a friend on the face of the earth." In November 1856, at a New Orleans rally to honor a Nicaraguan army official, the *Courier* reported that "at no time was the cheering more hearty than when he spoke of Southern institutions being planted in Nicaragua." "Walker is not a liberator, he is a slaver," wrote a supportive Texas editor.[81]

At the same time, Northern support evaporated. Goicuria, enraged by the slavery proclamation and the private memorandum on Walker's intentions toward Cuba, published the damaging correspondence in the *New York Herald.* The *New York Times* revealed the fears of many Northerners that Walker's real purpose was a "Southern Slave Empire." Manifest Destiny in Nicaragua was now sectional.[82]

Though Walker's Southern support was considerable, he had made his pitch for it too late. The rebel forces, aided by Vanderbilt, were gaining in strength and by spring the "gray eyed man of destiny," as Walker's supporters called him, was surrounded. On May 1, 1857, Walker surrendered and returned on a U.S. Navy ship, still claiming to be president of Nicaragua, to a hero's welcome in New Orleans.[83]

A triumphal tour followed as Walker began laying plans to make a new foray. From New Orleans to Memphis, Louisville, Cincinnati, Washington, and New York and thence south again to Charleston, across Georgia to Nashville, Mobile, and back to New Orleans, Walker repeated the message to Southerners that his effort was "the only means, short of revolution, whereby [you] can preserve [your] present social organization." In his wake sprang up branches of a Central

81. Walker, *War in Nicaragua*, p. 263; Moore, "Pierre Soulé," p. 215; May, *Southern Dream*, pp. 108–109; *New Orleans Louisiana Courier*, November 25, 1856; *Quitman (Texas) Free Press*, quoted by Earl W. Fornell, "Texans and Filibusters in the 1850's," *Southwestern Historical Quarterly* 59 (1956): 419–20.
82. Scroggs, *Filibusters and Financiers*, p. 224; *New York Times*, November 25, 1856.
83. May, *Southern Dream*, pp. 109–10; Scroggs, *Filibusters and Financiers*, pp. 249–307.

American League, and news of active recruiting emanated from Nashville, Charleston, Savannah, Mobile, and New Orleans, as well as elsewhere.[84]

By November the new Walker expedition sailed out of Mobile only to be overtaken by Commodore Hiram Paulding of the United States Navy. Surrounded by American gunboats, the little filibuster announced quietly, "I surrender to the United States," came to Paulding's cabin, and, in the Commodore's words, "wept like a child."[85]

Paulding's arrest of Walker caused even greater anxiety about the administration's position on the extension of slavery. The Southern press and the Southern politician reached new heights of outrage. The Natchez *Mississippi Free Trader* argued that if the government would not assist Walker's filibustering efforts, "the people will do it and any attempt to suppress them in their action will only lead to bitter sectional strife and dissentions." The *Tuskegee Republican* expressed the "indignation in the breasts of those, who feel an interest in the preservation of Southern institutions." Congressman L. Q. C. Lamar of Mississippi called for "American Liberty with southern institutions planted upon every inch of American soil." Quitman, who was now very ill and would not live the year, angrily called for the repeal of neutrality laws "or we shall soon be surrounded by impassable barriers to our progress." The legislatures of Texas, Tennessee, Alabama, and Virginia considered resolutions censuring Paulding. The Montgomery Commercial Convention endorsed Walker's motives. The *Charleston Mercury* voiced the conviction which Quitman had reached long ago, to which Walker professed allegiance, and to which the press, politicians, and commercial conventions were now moving: ". . . on the subject of slavery the North is utterly antagonistic to the South. The South and the North, on this sub-

---

84. Scroggs, *Filibusters and Financiers*, pp. 317–19; Walker, *War in Nicaragua*, pp. 260–61.
85. May, *Southern Dream*, p. 115; Scroggs, *Filibusters and Financiers*, p. 329.

ject, are not only two Peoples, but they are rival, hostile Peoples."[86]

Still, the South was far from unanimous. The most radical pronouncements came from the southwest, which had always been the center of expansionist activity. Some in the upper South hesitantly supported Paulding. Senators John J. Crittenden of Kentucky, James Mason of Virginia, and James Pearce of Maryland spoke out against Walker. Even in the western South a few, including the editor of the *Memphis Daily Appeal* and Congressman John Reagan of Texas, dared to dissent.[87]

But in general Walker was the darling of the South. The strength of his support became evident as he made another glorious tour in the early spring of 1858. A banquet in Richmond, a tumultuous welcome in Mobile, a private party in the home of Yancey, and a public barbecue in Montgomery and rallies in Mississippi highlighted Walker's journey. In Aberdeen, Mississippi, reported the *Prairie News*, "he closed his speech by appealing to the mothers of Mississippi, to bid their sons buckle on the armor of war, and battle for the institutions, for the honor of the Sunny South." Walker requested aid for "the cause, not for himself but for the cause of Nicaragua's freedom [and] the cause of the South." So enraptured were his listeners that, on the spot, they pledged $10,000. When, in May 1858, the New Orleans court dropped pending charges against Walker for neutrality law violations, his stature was further enhanced.[88]

And his ambition was further whetted. In December a

---

86. Percy Lee Rainwater, "Economic Benefits of Secession: Opinions in Mississippi in the 1850's," *Journal of Southern History* 1 (1935): 460; May, *Southern Dream*, pp. 115–16; *Congressional Globe*, 35 Cong., 1 sess., p. 279; Quitman to J. F. H. Claiborne, February 4, 1858, in Claiborne, *Life and Correspondence of Quitman* 2: 254; *Charleston Mercury*, February 1, 1858.

87. May, *Southern Dream*, pp. 119–20, 192–93.

88. Scroggs, *Filibusters and Financiers*, pp. 337–39; May, *Southern Dream*, p. 126; Rainwater, "Economic Benefits of Secession," p. 462.

new expedition was fitted out and prepared to leave Mobile. Composed, in the words of a close associate of Walker, of men "mostly of the class found about the wharves of Southern cities," the little band made it to within sixty miles of the Central American coast when its ship hit a coral reef and sank. Returning to Mobile on a British ship, the adventurers met a welcome that was by now routine and an equally routine prosecution and acquittal.[89]

After three failures Walker's act was beginning to grow a bit stale. His followers began to drift away, and despite his conversion to Catholicism there was little interest in New Orleans for another try. Perhaps the general decline of interest in divisive undertakings was a reflection of a more general state of calm that encompassed the Union during the first nine months of 1859. Buchanan now had time to negotiate with England a reduction of the British presence in the Caribbean, and it was agreed that the British island of Ruatan would be returned to Honduras. A contributor to *DeBow's Review*, upset by diminishing concern in the South for expansion, stated that "the political policy of *non-expansion* to the South is not compatible with her self-security. . . ."[90]

During the winter of 1859–60, while the country was in turmoil over John Brown's raid upon Harper's Ferry, Walker continued to scheme how to regain the presidency of Nicaragua. Managing to gather a small force, he planned to reenter his former dominion in August 1860 with the help of Englishmen on Ruatan who were upset with the cession of that island to Honduras. The pathetic company attacked Honduras but was quickly routed; Walker was arrested by the British navy and turned over to Honduran authorities. On the morning of September 12, 1860, his slight frame stood in proud

89. C. W. Doubleday, *Reminiscence of the Filibuster War in Nicaragua* (New York: G. P. Putnam's Sons, 1886), p. 201; Scroggs, *Filibusters and Financiers*, p. 376.

90. May, *Southern Dream*, p. 130; Scroggs, *Filibusters and Financiers*, p. 381; Nevins, *Emergence of Lincoln* 1: 298; Craven, *Southern Nationalism*, pp. 289, 305; *DeBow's Review* 26 (1859): 216.

defiance before a firing squad. Moments later, mangled by the bullets of two volleys, William Walker lay dead in the hot tropical sun.[91]

The reactions ran from relief to indifference. Those Southern newspapers that noted his execution—for more exciting events were then taking place—did so without emotion. His staunchest New Orleans supporter, the *Commercial Bulletin*, announced merely that "the mad and unwarrantable enterprise of the great filibuster has ended in disaster and defeat." And, with the Republican Lincoln elected and the Union about to break up before his eyes, James Buchanan proudly announced to Congress in December the demise of filibusterism, claiming the credit for himself. It was probably the greatest achievement of a dismal term.[92]

Hardly anyone noticed.

V

"The first field of our operations is Mexico; but we hold it to be our duty to offer our services to any Southern State to repel a Northern army. . . . The Southern States must foster any scheme having for its object the Americanization and Southernization of Mexico. . . ."[93] Thus began the initiation ritual of that most bizarre offshoot of Southern expansionism, the Knights of the Golden Circle.

Founded in the late 1850's by George Bickley, an Indiana-born reprobate, the Knights represented expansionism in its most exaggerated form, filibustering sentiment carried to its extreme. Racist, belligerent, Protestant, swaggering, "aristocratic," and provincial, the K. G. C. was a caricature of South-

91. Craven, *Southern Nationalism*, esp. pp. 305–11. The full impact of the Brown raid is discussed in Chapter Seven. See also Scroggs, *Filibusters and Financiers*, pp. 368–93; May, *Southern Dream*, pp. 130–32.
92. Scroggs, *Filibusters and Financiers*, pp. 394–95.
93. *An Authentic Exposition of the "K. G. C." "Knights of the Golden Circle;" or, A History of Secession from 1854 to 1861. By a Member of the Order* (Indianapolis: C. O. Perrine, 1861), p. 81.

ernism. Its name described its purpose: a "Golden Circle," radiating from Havana, would extend from Maryland through Missouri, Texas, Mexico, Central America, northern South America, and the West Indies, delineating the limits of a mighty, independent slave empire. Its ritual was a baffling catechism of numerical cryptograms. At one point the qualifications for membership were announced. The candidate

> must have been born in 58 (a Slave State) or if in 59 (a Free State) he must be a citizen; 60 (a Protestant) and 61 (a Slaveholder). A candidate who was born in 58 (a Slave State) need not be 61 (a Slaveholder) provided he can give 62 (Evidences of character as a Southern man).

Among other pledges the initiates vowed that "should my State or any other 76 (Southern State) be 77 (invaded) by 68 (Abolitionists) I will muster the largest force I can, and go to the scene of danger. . . ."[94]

To achieve the primary aim of the K. G. C., which was to make Mexico "Americanized and Southernized," Bickley made the Southern rounds dutifully in 1860, but only in Texas did he receive encouragement. With Southern attention focused on the 1860 campaign and the possible election of a Republican president, recruits were hard to come by. Walker's fate caused further discouragement. No invasion attempt was ever launched, and the K. G. C. shifted emphasis from expansion to secession.[95]

In the end, the greatest effect of the K. G. C. was not its success in the South but the response it received in the North. A Wisconsin Senator vastly exaggerated the K. G. C. as evidence of widespread "Southern fanaticism." *An Authentic Ex-*

94. Ollinger Crenshaw, "The Knights of the Golden Circle: The Career of George Bickley," *American Historical Review* 47 (1941): 23–50; C. A. Bridges, "The Knights of the Golden Circle: A Filibustering Fantasy," *Southwestern Historical Quarterly* 44 (1941): 287–302; *An Authentic Exposition*, pp. 83–84.
95. George Bickley to E. H. Cushing, November 15, 1860, in Jimmie Hicks, ed., "Some Letters Concerning the Knights of the Golden Circle in Texas, 1860–1861," *Southwestern Historical Quarterly* 65 (1961): 85; Crenshaw, "Knights of the Golden Circle," p. 40.

position of the order appeared in Indiana in 1861 while *A Full Exposure of the Southern Traitors* revealed the secret ritual to Bostonians the same year. In reality, the influence of the K. G. C. was practically nonexistent. It extended so far that the order could claim several secession delegates to the Texas convention, but no further.[96] Viewed in isolation, the K. G. C. would seem to be an aberration hardly deserving attention. But viewed in the context of the developments of the 1850's, the organization seems perhaps the logical extension of Southern expansionist rhetoric.

"Kansas, Cuba, South America all loomed up as inviting Southern *expansion* outlet & development. The *dream* has been sadly dissipated. The galling *reality* is too recent . . . ," wrote a frustrated Alabamian in 1858. Though Lopez, Quitman, Soulé, Walker, and their sympathizers may not have succeeded in winning additional territory for the South, they did indeed make the Southern public feel a need for expansion, and they made it aware of the prejudice of the general government against the acquisition of additional slave territory. The recurrent frustrations of the filibusters combined with bungling government policy toward the territories fed the ideology of Southern nationalism, which had long argued, in the words of fire-eating South Carolina Congressman L. M. Keitt, that "the only way the South can save herself is to spread south, get new territory, and spread her institutions, and cut loose from the North."[97]

Though expansionism was dormant during the secession crisis, it was far from dead. Thinking Southerners, convinced that slavery must expand or die, concluded that it would never

96. Crenshaw, "Knights of the Golden Circle," p. 47; May, *Southern Dream*, pp. 150–51; *Congressional Globe*, 36 Cong., 1 sess., 2: 1632.

97. William F. Samford to C. C. Clay, Jr., October 20, 1858, Clay Papers, Duke University; Susan S. Keitt to "Father," February 25, 1860, Lawrence M. Keitt Papers, Duke University. For additional examples of "Americanizing" rhetoric see Samuel R. Walker, *Cuba and the South* (n.p., 1854), p. 4; *Mobile Daily Register*, January 23, 1858; Claiborne, *Life and Correspondence of Quitman* 2: 207, 335–36; *DeBow's Review* 25 (1858): 504; and C. Stanley Urban, "Ideology of Southern Imperialism," *passim*.

be allowed to expand so long as the South remained part of the United States. But once secession took place, the *Vicksburg Weekly Sun* predicted:

> . . . we verily believe that the overthrow of the Union would not only perpetuate slavery where it now exists and establish it more firmly, but would necessarily lead to its widespread extension. The Southern States once constituted as an independent republic, the acquisition of Mexico, Central America, Cuba, Santo Domingo, and other West India Islands would follow as a direct and necessary result. . . .[98]

Manifest Destiny now meant a strong, expansive—and Southern—nation.

98. *Vicksburg Weekly Sun*, October 29, 1860, quoted in Rainwater, "Economic Benefits of Secession," p. 463.

CHAPTER SEVEN

The Man and the Hour Have Met

I

After the Nullification crisis, politics, so far as the Southern nationalists were concerned, was a matter of following the lead of Calhoun. At the height of the tariff imbroglio, the *Charleston Mercury* had boldly announced that "the friends of the State" should adopt "the proud names of WHIGS, and the friends of ANDREW JACKSON and of consolidation . . . the name of TORIES. . . . Every man now in South Carolina is a whig or a tory." The designation of Whig spread rapidly through the South and, with the resolution of the tariff dispute, into the North as well. By 1834 a heterogeneous group of men, united, as one newspaper said, only in their determination to contain "the sea of Jacksonism," had formed a loosely organized party that took the name of Whig.[1]

It was an odd coalition. At the top were Calhoun, the leader of the states' rights, anti-tariff group, among whom were both sectionalists and the small number of Southern nationalists, and Henry Clay, leader of the National Republi-

1. *Charleston Mercury*, December 17, 1832, *U.S. Telegraph*, January 2, 1834, quoted in Arthur C. Cole, *The Whig Party in the South* (Washington: American Historical Association, 1914), pp. 18, 31; Glyndon G. Van Deusen, "The Whig Party," in *History of U.S. Political Parties*, ed. Arthur M. Schlesinger, Jr., 4 vols. (New York: Chelsea House Publishers, 1973), 1: 333–39.

cans, whose "American System" program of a national bank, a protective tariff, and internal improvements fostered a very different kind of anti-Jacksonism. Though it was clearly impossible to get such a disparate group to agree on anything, the Whigs made the election of 1836—in which they nominated three regional candidates to oppose Vice President Martin Van Buren—sufficiently close, particularly in the South, to alarm the Democrats. Early in 1837 Van Buren men began to send out signals to the Calhounites in hopes of reconciliation.[2]

The Democratic overtures fell on receptive ears in the South. The Whig coalition was unstable, and the retirement of Jackson removed the one element of party unity. The Clay–Calhoun alliance could not long endure purely as an opposition party, yet to adopt a positive policy would require taking a stand on the tariff, on banks, and on internal improvements that would automatically alienate some portion of the fledgling party. Nullifiers feared the Northerners would dictate the stand of the Whigs, since the larger portion of the party (providing forty-five of its seventy-three electoral votes in 1836) resided in the nonslaveholding states. Some Northern Whigs in 1836 had gone so far as to couch their anti-Jackson sentiments in antislavery rhetoric. Many of the Nullifiers agreed with Francis W. Pickens, a Calhoun lieutenant, in fearing a Whig coalition. Pickens believed that the Nullifiers must preserve their "independence and separate existence. It is an unnatural alliance for us to sustain the measures of those who are opposed to us in feeling and interest."[3]

2. Joel A. Silbey, "Election of 1836," in *History of American Presidential Elections*, ed. Arthur M. Schlesinger, Jr., 4 vols. (New York: Chelsea House Publishers, 1971), 1: 577–600; Richard C. Bain and Judith H. Parris, *Convention Decisions and Voting Records* (Washington: Brookings Institute, 1973), pp. 20–24. The electoral votes of Maryland and Kentucky went to William Henry Harrison, and those of Georgia and Jackson's home state of Tennessee went to Hugh Lawson White. Van Buren barely managed to carry North Carolina, Mississippi, and Louisiana. The independent South Carolina legislature awarded that state's electoral votes to Willie P. Mangum, a North Carolina congressman who, unlike White, had voted against the Force Bill.
3. Francis W. Pickens to Richard K. Crallé, June 18, 1837, Francis W. Pickens Papers, Duke University.

Calhoun welcomed Van Buren's inaugural statement favoring "a strict adherence to the letter and spirit of the constitution" and promising not "the slightest interference with [slavery] in the states where it exists." The president's declaration that "the less government interferes with private pursuits, the better for the general prosperity" found wide acceptance in the South. Recognizing "a natural conflict in the non slaveholding states, which tends to throw the democratick party on our side . . . , of which we see strong proof on the abolition question," Calhoun instructed his followers to return to "the original Jackson party. . . . Such of our friends who take a different view will be woefully disappointed in the end."[4]

Calhoun strongly believed that the laissez-faire principles of the Democrats generally provided the surest protection of Southern interests. By cooperating with that party Calhoun hoped for "union among ourselves at the South," presumably by the disappearance of the Whigs in favor of a united Southern party. Such a sectional party, though allied with the Democrats, would constitute a small but influential third political force which "would oppose any act of the party that did not accord with our principles and policy." Hoping thereby to "throw our weight, where it will be the most effective to advance our own intersts," Calhoun was certain that "our control will be felt to the last with powerful effect."[5]

Obediently, many Calhounites in other Southern states swore allegiance to the party of Jackson. In Mississippi Quitman, as a "strict disciple of the political school in which Jefferson, and more recently Calhoun, were able expounders and teachers," urged his small band of followers to "co-operate freely and boldly with all genuine Republicans, be they Democrats or Nullifiers. . . ." In Alabama Congressman Lewis effected a similar alliance with the Democracy, while in Virginia

4. Edward M. Shepard, *Martin Van Buren*, American Statesman Series, ed. John T. Morse, Jr. (Boston: Houghton, Mifflin, and Co., 1896), pp. 244–84; John C. Calhoun to Dr. Danall, October 26, 1838, Calhoun to Duff Green, July 27, 1837, *Calhoun Correspondence*, pp. 376–77, 409.
5. Calhoun to Dr. Danall, October 26, 1838, *Calhoun Correspondence*, pp. 409–10.

the young Calhounite Robert M. T. Hunter and his circle followed the Carolinian. Two North Carolina and three Georgia congressmen also made the switch and encouraged their constituents to follow their example.[6]

Among the Nullifiers were the Southern nationalists, whose number was very small and whose aims differed from Calhoun's. Members of this faction within a faction also became Democratic partisans after 1837. Still smarting from their defeat during Nullification and realizing that the paucity of their numbers did not permit them to break with their less radical fellow Nullifiers, the Southern nationalists remained followers of Calhoun. Surrendering tactical positions for strategic goals, they actively sought roles in the Democratic party. By 1840 even such a hardliner as Rhett was extolling the "wonderful leadership" of Van Buren.[7]

The political vicissitudes of William Lowndes Yancey of Alabama exemplify the problem that the Southern nationalist had of working within the Democratic party. Yancey was representative of a new type of politician that began to emerge in the mid-1840's. Though a native of Georgia, Yancey was a man of the west, who had joined the hordes forsaking the old soil to pursue the gleam of a cotton fortune. Like other young western planters, Yancey was loyal not so much to the Union, in whose shaping neither he nor his state had played a part, as to his region, whose solidarity of interest he quickly comprehended and hoped to defend through the Democratic party. Unlike older Southern leaders, Yancey and his kind appeared on the political scene after the campaign techniques of the party system had become well established. Men like Yancey were not repulsed by democracy and its potential for excess; they accepted democracy, believed in it, and reveled in its practice.

6. John A. Quitman to T. Bole and S. Shackelford, December 13, 1838, in Claiborne, *Life and Correspondence of Quitman* 1: 165–67; Cole, *Whig Party*, pp. 48–50. The North Carolina congressmen were Samuel T. Sawyer and Charles B. Shepard, those from Georgia Walter T. Colquitt, Edward J. Black, and Mark A. Cooper.
7. White, *Robert Barnwell Rhett*, p. 45.

The tall, handsome Alabamian with deep set eyes and a prominent nose and chin had overcome numerous frustrations in his rise to political leadership. Yancey was born in Georgia in 1814. His father, an Abbeville, South Carolina, lawyer and friend of Calhoun, died in 1817 and Mrs. Yancey was remarried in 1822 to a teacher at Mt. Zion Academy in Georgia. Yancey's new stepfather, Nathan Beman, sold his three slaves for a tidy profit and took his family to Troy, New York, where he became pastor of the First Presbyterian Church. Troy was in the heart of New York's famed "burned-over district"— repeatedly scorched by the flames of religious revivalism—and Beman joined the campaign. It was from Beman's pulpit that Charles G. Finney launched his revival in 1826, sowing the seeds of righteousness that would later bear abolitionist fruit.

Yancey's childhood in Troy was not placid, for his stepfather and mother quarreled constantly and their marriage rapidly deteriorated. Beman preached abolition and piety while he squandered the Yancey children's inheritance and even prohibited Mrs. Yancey from seeing her children for long periods of time. Young William finally escaped in 1830 to Williams College, which he attended for three years before returning, without a degree, to South Carolina.[8]

The next few years were tempestuous. Yancey spent one year in the law office of Benjamin F. Perry, a leading Unionist in upcountry Greenville and, in 1834, became editor of the *Greenville Mountaineer*. In his first editorial Yancey took the unfashionable position that "we will oppose everything savouring

---

8. Ralph B. Draughon, Jr., "The Young Manhood of William L. Yancey," *Alabama Review* 19 (1966): 28–37; Eaton, *Mind of the Old South*, p. 204. The only available biography of this deserving subject is John Witherspoon DuBose, *The Life and Times of William Lowndes Yancey* (Birmingham: Roberts and Son, 1892), which is massive but uneven, dated, and uncritical. Two valuable dissertations are Ralph B. Draughon, Jr., "William Lowndes Yancey: From Unionist to Secessionist, 1814–1852" (Ph.D. diss., University of North Carolina at Chapel Hill, 1968) and Austin Venable, "The Role of William L. Yancey in the Secession Movement" (Ph.D. diss., Vanderbilt University, 1937), both excellent studies. A recent and outstanding study of antebellum Alabama is J. Mills Thornton, "Politics and Power in a Slave Society: Alabama, 1800–1860" (Ph.D. diss., Yale University, 1974).

of Nullification and Disunion. . . . We do not believe that South Carolina is a sovereign." A year later, in 1835, Yancey entered the plantation gentry by his marriage to Sarah Caroline Earle, daughter of a well-to-do Greenville planter, whose dowry included thirty-five slaves. In 1836 the couple moved to Alabama and rented a plantation, and in 1839 William and his brother Benjamin purchased two newspapers in Wetumpka, near Montgomery.[9]

By 1840 Yancey's political beliefs appeared to be changing. He wrote that "demagogues at the North, to subserve their insidious designs, . . . are endeavoring to undermine the institution with which our political and social existence is identified." Perhaps he had Nathan Beman in mind, for in 1837, while his mother was visiting her children in the South, Beman wrote to her, "You can't return to the North. Should you be rash enough to do it, you will not *find* me." Although Mrs. Beman attempted to return to Troy, the minister ordered her to leave the house and offered her a small amount of money as compensation. He was now free, he wrote, to work for "the cause of the oppressed." Meanwhile the Yanceys, still holding the bill of sale from Beman's earlier slave dealings, wrote a scathing essay against their stepfather and tried unsuccessfully to have it published in the Troy newspaper. Perhaps, too, Yancey was expressing a sense of personal frustration, for a year earlier, after a feud between his and his neighbor's overseer, Yancey's entire black labor force was poisoned.[10]

With redoubled vigor Yancey returned to the law, built up a good practice, and entered politics. Troubled by abolitionist support of the Whig party in 1840, Yancey became an active Democrat and polished his oratorical skills in a speaking

9. *Greenville Mountaineer*, November 22, 1834, quoted in Austin L. Venable, "William L. Yancey's Transition from Unionism to State Rights," *Journal of Southern History* 10 (1944): 334.
10. *Wetumpka Argus*, March 4, 1840; Nathan Beman to Caroline (Yancey) Beman, April 3, 1837, Benjamin Cudworth Yancey Papers, Southern Historical Collection, University of North Carolina, Chapel Hill; Eaton, *Mind of the Old South*, p. 205; DuBose, *Life and Times of Yancey*, pp. 83–84.

tour of Alabama for the reelection of Van Buren. A year later he won election to the state legislature where, against the opposition planter establishment, he championed the apportionment of representation on the basis of white population only. In 1844, running on an expansionist platform, he was elected to Congress. During his first term he was an eloquent Calhounite who, though delivering spellbinding speeches on the glorious future of the Union, was upset at the rebelliousness of some Northern Democrats on economic issues.[11]

By 1846 Yancey was totally disillusioned. Protesting the defection from the party ranks of certain Northern and Western Democrats on crucial votes involving the tariff and river improvements, Yancey resigned his seat. "If principle is dearer than mere party association," he remarked, "we will never again meet in common Democratic convention a large body of men who have vigorously opposed us on principle." Only "one brilliant exception (Mr. David Wilmot)" of Pennylvania was faithful to the tenets of Democracy. And so Yancey withdrew from public affairs and came home to Alabama.[12]

In Yancey's resignation letter he praised the party loyalty of Congressman Wilmot. Within a month, however, Wilmot threw the whole South into a state of alarm with the introduction of his Proviso, which prohibited slavery in the territory won from Mexico. After a decade of suppression the issue of slavery now forced itself upon Congress and almost immediately old party distinctions began to blur. Calhoun, who still led the Southern forces in Congress, warned his Northern Democratic allies that "all the energy of men like you" was

11. Venable, "Yancey's Transition," 340–42; Eaton, *Mind of the Old South*, p. 205. In the Alabama legislature, doubtless with his mother in mind, Yancey sponsored legislation to amend marriage laws to permit married women to keep control of their property.

12. *Mobile Weekly Advertiser*, July 25, 1846, quoted in Malcolm C. McMillan, "William L. Yancey and the Historians: One Hundred Years," *Alabama Review* 20 (1967): 174–75; DuBose, *Life and Times of Yancey*, pp. 153–54; Eaton, *Mind of the Old South*, p. 206; Austin L. Venable, "The Public Career of William Lowndes Yancey," *Alabama Review* 16 (1963): 203.

required "to save the Union from the fanaticks and the demagogues. . . ." He warned that the South "has made up her
mind, both as to her rights, morally and politically, and her capacity to defend them. . . ."[13]

Calhoun himself was torn between his lifelong devotion to
the South and his equally long devotion to the Union—and to
his own ambition to be president. Eighteen forty-eight might
well be his last chance. In 1847 he called for a united Southern
party, ostensibly to prove "by our promptitude, energy, and
unanimity" that "we stand ready to defend our rights and
maintain our perfect equality, as members of the Union."
Many viewed Calhoun's declaration as a move to force a likely
deadlocked three-way presidential election into Congress.
Simms and Hammond in South Carolina thought they recognized Calhoun's real intent, as did a number of Democratic
organs.[14]

An increasing number of Southerners was deciding that
a unified response was necessary. In September 1846 a mass
meeting in Russellville, Alabama, called on the South to
"speak out on this question of usurpation" and on Southerners
to "require pledges from all seeking their votes for high offices,
that our *rights* in the Southern States should be *protected.* . . ."
The following spring the Virginia legislature adopted strong
resolutions, introduced by Lewis E. Harvie, a Southern nationalist, declaring that passage of the Wilmot Proviso would
force the people of Virginia to choose between "abject submis-
sion . . . or determined resistance . . . at all hazards and to the
last extremity."[15]

13. Calhoun to ————, November 7, 1846, *Calhoun Correspondence*, pp.
710–11.

14. Joseph G. Rayback, "The Presidential Ambitions of John C. Calhoun,
1844–1848," *Journal of Southern History* 4 (1938): 342–45; William Gilmore
Simms to James H. Hammond, March 29, 1847, *Simms Letters* 2: 287–92;
Hammond to Simms, April 1, 1847, Hammond Papers; *Jackson Mississippian*,
March 12, 1847.

15. *Calhoun Correspondence*, p. 716; Denman, *Secession Movement in Alabama*, p.
3; Shanks, *Secession Movement in Virginia*, pp. 22–23.

These Virginia resolutions received warm praise from a growing number of Southerners who believed the time for action had arrived. Albert G. Brown, governor of Mississippi, warned that if the North refused "to let us alone on this subject" of slavery extension, "the South must be united" to "defend our rights with those means which God and Nature have placed in our hands. . . ." The Texas legislature passed resolutions similar to those of Virginia, and an Alabama Democratic convention adopted the Virginia resolutions verbatim.[16]

Old party allegiances were beginning to crumble as the nation prepared for the presidential election of 1848. In Alabama Yancey hoped that "the foul spell of party which binds and divides and distracts the South can be broken. . . ." After the New York Democratic state convention resolved that slavery should not be permitted in any of the territories acquired from Mexico, Yancey introduced a series of resolutions at the Alabama Democratic convention in February 1848 that came to be known as the Alabama Platform. Announcing that "the Democratic party is, and should be, co-extensive with the Union," Yancey's resolutions pledged that Alabamians would "neither . . . recognize as Democrats or . . . hold fellowship or communion with those who attempt to denationalize the South and its institutions," or "to array one section in feeling and sentiment against the other." The Platform further pledged "under no political necessity whatever to support for the offices of President and Vice-President . . . any persons who shall not be openly and unequivocally opposed to . . . excluding slavery from the Territories of the United States. . . ."[17] So instructed, the Alabama delegation, with Yancey in the lead, headed for the nominating convention in Baltimore.

16. James B. Ranck, *Albert Gallatin Brown, Radical Southern Nationalist* (New York: D. Appleton-Century Co., 1937), pp. 49–56; Craven, *Coming of the Civil War*, p. 233; Denman, *Secession Movement in Alabama*, p. 11.

17. A. B. Moore, *History of Alabama* (University: University of Alabama Press, 1934), p. 195; Ames, *State Documents on Federal Relations*, p. 245; Denman, *Secession Movement in Alabama*, pp. 9–12; DuBose, *Life and Times of Yancey*, pp. 212–14.

The Alabama Platform stopped short of endorsing secession, although it did take new ground in denying that neither Congress nor the territorial legislature had the power to exclude slavery. Lewis Cass of Michigan, a leading candidate for the nomination, had earlier agreed that Congress had no such authority but suggested that the inhabitants of the territory might. Yancey's Platform was meant to eliminate even that possibility.[18]

In general the Southern Democratic press, after initial approval, backed away from the Alabama Platform as too extreme. In Yancey's own Alabama press sentiment was almost unanimously opposed to the Platform. Whig papers promised to eschew "particular local considerations," which "ought not to interfere with the great national measures which we are attempting to carry out." Democratic editors were hesitant to attack Yancey for fear of alienating his bloc of supporters, since it was uncertain just how large his following was.[19]

The nominating conventions blurred party lines. The Whigs turned to the old war hero Zachary Taylor, a Louisiana slaveholder. The Democrats, meeting in Baltimore, passed a rule requiring all delegates to support the party nominee, a rule that prompted some New York delegates, elected on an antislavery platform, to walk out. They later helped to form a Free Soil party whose antislavery ideology grew in strength through the years. Yancey then presented the Alabama Platform, which was voted down by 216 to 36. He and one colleague made a dramatic withdrawal, and the convention proceeded to nominate Cass.[20]

The old party system seemed on the verge of disintegration. North and South stood poised against one another in

18. Denman, *Secession Movement in Alabama*, pp. 10–11.
19. *Ibid.*, p. 11; Shryock, *Georgia and the Union*, pp. 164–65; Cole, *Whig Party*, p. 136.
20. Denman, *Secession Movement in Alabama*, pp. 12–13; Craven, *Coming of the Civil War*, p. 235. The thirty-six supporters of Yancey were distributed as follows: Maryland 1, South Carolina 9, Georgia 9, Florida 3, Alabama 9, Arkansas 3, Tennessee 1, Kentucky 1. DuBose, *Life and Times of Yancey*, p. 220.

1848 as party lines wobbled before the onslaught of sectional interests. The Democratic party in the South, in which so many Southerners had trusted for so long, was divided between two groups. On one side were the party regulars or national Democrats, mostly Calhounites, who wanted to work out the South's salvation within the Union. On the other side was the small but vocal group of Yanceyites, who spoke a new language of regional grievances and regional resistance. As the campaign of 1848 began, the party system was about to undergo its sternest test.

II

The 1848 campaign saw a growing rift between the two components of the Southern portion of the Democratic party. The margin of Yancey's defeat on the Alabama Platform was a rough gauge of his support in the South, but he was not dismayed. He stopped in Charleston on his way home from Baltimore and gave a blistering speech against the Democratic party. The angry Alabamian attacked Cass for deviating from the party creed on internal improvements and declared that Southern delegates by accepting this unprincipled and equivocal defender of slavery "had sacrificed their principles to an election. . . ." Yancey called for a Southern convention to nominate candidates on the Alabama Platform. The Calhounites—still supporting their man—eagerly circulated the idea, but there were few supporters and the movement proved abortive. Calhoun soon declared his neutrality.[21]

While few chose with Calhoun to sit out the campaign, the Whig nomination of Taylor threatened to pry loose many of the states' rights men from their Democratic allies. Yancey made only two speeches, both attacking Cass. Beverley Tucker praised Taylor as "worthy to be trusted with civil authority. . . ." Many Calhoun Democrats doubtless agreed with

---

21. Rayback, "Presidential Ambitions of Calhoun," p. 351; DuBose, *Life and Times of Yancey*, p. 221.

a South Carolina Calhoun loyalist that Taylor was the best
candidate to "enable the Country to relieve itself of the con-
joint and infamous burdens of Hunkerism [yearning for party
office] and abolitionism." At the same time the Whig strategy
of running a Southerner made possible a strange coalition of
Taylor supporters. Making no attempt to maintain a national
cohesion, the Whig press in the North touted Taylor vaguely
as "an honest man," trustworthy "on this very question of slavery," while the Southern organs of Whiggery proclaimed Old
Rough and Ready as "a Southern man with national principles," as "one of ourselves."

The Southern Democrats—forced to portray the Northerner Cass as more reliable on the Wilmot question than a
Louisiana slaveholder—were placed in an untenable position.
How to answer the Whigs was the problem since, as one Democrat lamented, "their speeches consist of three parts—miscellaneous abuse of Cass and the Democrats, comments on the
danger to slavery, and the impossibility of trusting any Northern man. . . ." Whigs, he complained, "don't care a fig what
you prove on them about their Northern allies. They don't
profess to think alike—and they will give up the Northern
Whigs freely . . . if they can involve the Northern Democrats
in the same odium."

The results of the 1848 election proved how extensive
were the Southern defections to the Whig candidates. The
November voting placed Georgia, Florida, and Louisiana in
the Whig column alongside the staunch Whig states of Maryland, North Carolina, Kentucky, and Tennessee. The Democratic margin in Virginia, Alabama, and Mississippi was sub-
stantially reduced.[22]

Southern Democratic leaders were stunned at the defec-

---

22. DuBose, *Life and Times of Yancey*, pp. 222–29; Beverley Tucker to James H.
Hammond, November 20, 1848, Hammond Papers; J. Hamilton to Calhoun,
April 24, 1847, *Calhoun Correspondence*, p. 1118; *American Presidential Elections* 2:
877; *Savannah Republican*, April 18, 1848; Shryock, *Georgia and the Union*, p.
167; W. H. Hull to Howell Cobb, July 22, 1848, Howell Cobb Papers, University of Georgia; Cole, *Whig Party*, p. 133.

tions. "We know of no Democrat of standing who voted for Taylor," wrote a concerned Georgian to Howell Cobb. "Is it not extraordinary that so large a wing of the democratic party has deserted without a solitary leader at their head? The rank and file have deserted by regiments. . . ." A Florida newspaper characterized the election as "one of the richest specimens of a thorough shuffling of cards which it has ever been the lot of man to witness." In a strong position, the defectors were in no mood to rejoin the Democrats. From Alabama Yancey defiantly refused overtures from state Democratic leaders, stating that a reunion would be possible only "with an acknowledgment of the truth of my position and not before."[23] That acknowledgment would not come for eight more years. The future of the party of Jackson seemed doubtful.

Meanwhile, there was still the pressing matter of the territories won from Mexico pending before Congress. At the same time, a bill abolishing the slave trade in the District of Columbia was under discussion. Troubled by these developments, Calhoun summoned all Southern representatives and senators to his office early in 1849 in a bold attempt to forge a united Southern party. A circular from the Charleston Committee of Correspondence sent to numerous Southern political leaders immediately after the election laid the groundwork. The signers claimed "that they were a people before they were a party,—were Southrons long before they became divided into Whigs and Democrats. They now look but to the South—the South in danger. . . . They respectfully suggest . . . the cooperation of all the leading minds of the Southern Country." In bringing this document before the Southern congressional caucus, Calhoun's purpose, as always, was to assert Southern rights in the Union "by arresting the aggression of the North and causing our rights and the stipulations of the constitution

23. James F. Cooper to Howell Cobb, November 11, 1848, *Toombs, Stephens, and Cobb Correspondence*, p. 137; *Jacksonville News*, quoted in Norman A. Graebner, "1848: Southern Politics at the Crossroads," *The Historian* 25 (1962): 21; DuBose, *Life and Times of Yancey*, p. 228.

in our favour to be respected. . . ." Secession was a dreadful last resort to be avoided as long as possible.[24]

Calhoun and four others drew up an *Address of the Southern Delegates in Congress to their Constituents* which, though firm, was generally not hostile toward the North. "If you become united," they wrote to their constituents, "and prove yourselves in earnest, the North will be brought to a pause, and to a calculation of consequences." After bitter wrangling between Taylor Democrats, Whigs, and Calhounites over the wording of the *Address*, only 48 of the 121 Southerners signed it—46 of 73 Democrats and only 2 of 48 Whigs. The only delegations whose entire membership signed were South Carolina and Mississippi. It seemed that Southerners in Washington wished to give Taylor a chance.[25]

Ill and distressed by his failure, Calhoun conferred with his loyal lieutenant Rhett. Time was running out on the Nullifier, who was now suffering from heart disease and chronic congestion of the lungs. "Mr. Rhett," Calhoun muttered, "my career is nearly done. The great battle must be fought by you younger men." Breaking into tears, the feverish old Carolinian admitted "my only regret at going—the South—the poor South!"[26]

Calhoun's feebleness opened the way for a new, more vigorous generation of Southern leaders, a generation that included many outright advocates of Southern nationalism. Many of these new men were hostile or contemptuous toward the older sectional leaders, who had tried to maintain Southern rights within the Union. "I am no Calhoun man," confided a young Georgia Democrat and Southern nationalist who supported Taylor. "He is in fact off the stage; the coming battle is for other leadership than his, a leadership that is of this generation, not of the past." Indeed the Southern firebrands, who

24. Circular in Benjamin Cudworth Yancey Papers; Calhoun to John H. Means, April 13, 1849, *Calhoun Correspondence*, p. 765.
25. Crallé, *Calhoun Works* 6:312; Potter, *Impending Crisis*, pp. 85–86.
26. J. P. Thomas, ed., *The Carolina Tribute to Calhoun* (Columbia: Richard L. Bryan, 1857), p. 369.

had constituted a minority within a minority during the 1830's, were now entering the prime of their lives and boldly wished to present an alternative to the stale doctrines of a passing generation. In South Carolina during the 1848 elections the impetuous Rhett had demanded that "South Carolina, unaided and alone, meet the contest" and "force every state in the Union to take sides, for or against her. She can compel the alternative—that the rights of the South be respected, or the Union be dissolved." Other Southern nationalists saw opportunity in the election of Taylor, the ascendancy of the Whigs, and the impending demise of the old parties. Governor John B. Floyd of Virginia warned early in 1849 that if Congress prohibited slavery in the territories, "the dissolution of our great and glorious Union will become necessary and inevitable."[27]

The actions of President Taylor helped unite Southerners in opposition to his administration. In April 1849 Taylor sent Thomas Butler King of Georgia to California to arrange that vast territory's immediate application for statehood, bypassing the territorial stage altogether and thus seeming to prevent slavery from coming in. Any remaining trust Southerners had in the president was dispelled in August 1849 when Taylor himself announced, "The people of the North need have no apprehension of the further extension of slavery."[28]

As the Southern states prepared for the 1849 congressional elections, political parties were in a state of flux. Anti-Taylor Whigs, states' rights Democrats, and those states' rights Whigs who had not followed Calhoun into the Democratic party in the 1830's began to join forces with the Democratic regulars. Virginia, which voted in April, set the pattern followed in other states. Its fifteen-man delegation changed from nine Democrats and six Whigs to thirteen Democrats, one Taylor Whig, and one Southern Rights Whig. Southern Whigs soon began taking a decidedly anti-Wilmot—and, there-

27. Coit, *John C. Calhoun*, pp. 487, 491; Henry L. Benning to Howell Cobb, July 1, 1849, *Toombs, Stephens, and Cobb Correspondence*, p. 171; *Charleston Mercury*, September 29, 1848; Shanks, *Secession Movement in Virginia*, p. 24.
28. Potter, *Impending Crisis*, p. 87; Cole, *Whig Party*, p. 138.

fore, anti-Taylor—stance to avoid electoral disaster. The message was clear: party differences were coming to mean less and less, soundness on Southern rights more and more. Banks, tariffs, and internal improvements were now less important than the rights of Southerners to take their property wherever they chose.[29]

Just as there was a shift in issues, so was there a change in Southern leadership. Mississippi took over from South Carolina the leadership of Southern resistance. The sons of the seaboard who had followed the cotton westward now prepared to wrest control of their destiny from their aging fathers. Virtually a one-party state in 1849, Mississippi issued a call for a Southern convention to meet in Nashville the following June, warning that the passage of the Wilmot Proviso or the abolition of slavery in the District of Columbia would force "the slaveholding states, to take care of their own safety, and to treat the nonslaveholding States as enemies. . . ."[30] The call represented new leadership, but not new ideas. Calhoun himself encouraged the Mississippians, writing that

> the call should be addressed to all those who are desirous to save the Union and our institutions, and who, in the alternative (should it be forced on us) of submission or dissolution would prefer the latter. No State could better take the lead in this great conservative movement than yours.[31]

Meanwhile, efforts got under way for one last compromise to save the Union. Early in 1850 Henry Clay introduced his Omnibus Bill, and Daniel Webster soon rallied to his old colleague's side. The third member of the great triumvirate, Calhoun, by then emaciated, weak, and near death, rose feebly in the Senate to call for a constitutional amendment—the only

29. *Richmond Enquirer*, April 13, 1849; Shanks, *Secession Movement in Virginia*, p. 27; *Tribune Almanac, 1849*, p. 3, *1850*, p. 4. Two other exceptions, Arkansas and Florida, had only one congressman apiece.
30. Cleo Hearon, "Mississippi and the Compromise of 1850," *Publications of the Mississippi Historical Society*, XIV (1914): 65.
31. Crallé, *Calhoun Works* 4: 542–73.

protection now possible, he claimed—to restore "the original equilibrium between the two sections" by guaranteeing Southern rights in the territories.[32] Within a month he was dead and, as the clouds of sectional strife thickened, Southerners waited for a new leader to emerge.

Calhoun's fears for the Union were well founded. An incredible rise in secession feeling had taken place in the year between Taylor's election and the convening of Congress in December 1849. Many Southern Whigs followed Senator Robert Toombs of Georgia into the "Southern Movement" after the party caucus rejected his resolution placing the party firmly against the Wilmot Proviso and against abolition of slavery in the District of Columbia. From all parts of the South came alarming reports and dire prophecies. Alexander H. Stephens, a Georgia Unionist and Whig, noted a "general . . . feeling among the Southern members for a dissolution of the Union. . . ." The Georgia legislature in February 1850 called a state convention and warned that Wilmot or any other form of antislavery measure would "induce us to contemplate the possibility of disunion." In Virginia the *Richmond Enquirer* called the Omnibus Bill worse than "all the ravings of Northern Fanatics," and M. R. H. Garnett, an eloquent young disciple of Beverley Tucker, circulated an incendiary pamphlet entitled *The Union Past and Future*, which called for a Southern nation. The Alabama legislature vowed never to submit to a compromise of principle on Southern rights in the territories.[33]

Even in the states where Whig legislatures could prevent the sending of delegates to Nashville or the expression of extreme sentiments—the traditional Unionist strongholds of

32. *Congressional Globe*, 32 Cong., 1 sess., Appendix, p. 282.
33. Cole, *Whig Party*, p. 153; H. D. Foster, "Webster's Seventh of March Speech and the Secession Movement, 1850," *American Historical Review* 27 (1922): 250; *Richmond Enquirer*, February 5, 1850; [M. R. H. Garnett], *The Union Past and Future: How It Works and How To Save It. By a Citizen of Virginia* (Charleston: Walker and James, 1850); Denman, *Secession Movement in Alabama*, pp. 23–25.

Maryland, Kentucky, North Carolina, and Louisiana—there was a sizable increase in secession feeling. Maryland's legislature promised to join "with her Southern sister states in the maintenance of the constitution with all its compromises." From Kentucky came word that the idea "of a Southern Confederacy . . . is a dazzling allurement." In North Carolina a vocal minority was "calculating the advantages of a Southern Confederacy." Governor Joseph Walker of Louisiana endorsed the Mississippi resolutions of October 1849.[34]

In all these states, however, there is little evidence to suggest that the Southern nationalists were coordinating their efforts with one another or, indeed, that they were in control of the situation in their own states. To be sure, the ideas of separate nationhood that they had early and often expressed were now more widely held and generally respectable. But this development came about despite rather than because of the efforts of the Southern nationalists. Men like Garnett and Toombs spoke out only after ascertaining the sentiment in their states. Yancey was silent. It seemed clear that these and other Southern nationalists were riding a wave and not causing or controlling it.

Many of these political leaders viewed the trends of Southern opinion with a heavy heart. Like the American colonists of 1776, these Southerners felt a hesitancy and a genuine sadness about abandoning old ties. What made them Southern nationalists was their feeling that, despite such reluctance, separation must come. Toombs stated plainly his reasons for adopting Southern nationalism. Declaring his "attachment to the Union . . . under the Constitution of our fathers," the Georgian charged the Northern majority with "attempting to fix a national degradation upon half the States of this Confederacy" by driving "us from the territories . . . purchased by the common blood and treasure of the whole people." A dying Calhoun summarized the feelings of many when, after ponder-

34. Foster, "Webster's Seventh of March Speech," 253–54; James K. Greer, "Louisiana Politics, 1845–1861," *Louisiana History* 12 (1929): 570.

ing the changes in Southern attitudes, he sadly acknowledged that perhaps "disunion is the only alternative that is left us."[35]

Though these politicians recognized the rising tide of secession feeling, only in South Carolina and Mississippi—the only states whose delegates unanimously supported Calhoun's Southern Address—was there anything like a coordinated "conspiracy" to separate the South from the Union. These were the only states where the various elements of Southern nationalism had wide appeal. Citizens of these two states were not distracted by intrastate political disputes in 1849. While other Southern states were holding constitutional conventions during the years of the Compromise crisis and debating the territorial issue in lively but fragile old party alliances, South Carolina and Mississippi, both of which had long ago worked out their internal governance, were already in general agreement on basic ideological notions. A racist defense of slavery surely had its strongest appeal in Mississippi and South Carolina, the only two states where the black population exceeded the white in 1850. South Carolina had flirted for a season with economic diversity, but Mississippi, unlike its neighbors, had no cities of any size and was one of the most agricultural states of the South. South Carolina, through Simms, had long led in the movement for literary independence, while in Mississippi calls for educational and religious self-sufficiency were strident. Though separated by geography and 150 years of history, South Carolina, quiescent symbol of past glories, and Mississippi, dynamic token of future wealth, were one in spirit in desiring a Southern nation in 1849.[36]

35. Calhoun to Hammond, February 16, 1850, *Calhoun Correspondence*, p. 781; Foster, "Webster's Seventh of March Speech," p. 251. There are no accounts of this specific period that provide evidence that Yancey was actually involved in fomenting disunion sentiment, though many accounts misleadingly suggest that Yancey was playing an active role. See, for example, DuBose, *Life and Times of Yancey*, p. 249; Craven, *Coming of the Civil War*, p. 265.

36. The congressional delegations of both South Carolina and Mississippi were entirely Democratic. During the period from 1845 to 1852 the following states waged bitter, partisan battles over revisions of their state constitutions: Louisiana, Kentucky, Maryland, Virginia, Missouri, North Carolina, and

In Mississippi Quitman, soon to be elected Governor, expressed his sympathies for secession but confided that until elected he would not be able to give a public avowal, lest the charges of disunion being leveled by his opposition stick. Quitman's smashing election victory seemed to convince the Carolinians that Mississippi was ready to take the lead. By early 1850 the chances of a "Southern movement" were enhanced by the cooperation of these two states.

But if leaders in these two states were in agreement, they had little if any influence beyond their own borders, where old alliances and internal bickering made unanimity on the territorial issue virtually impossible. Earlier in 1849 Governor Seabrook of South Carolina had written to all the Southern governors seeking advice and urging cooperative action. Though their replies are not known, when a Mississippi convention, instigated by Calhoun, met in October 1849 to call for a Nashville convention, Daniel Wallace, an agent of Seabrook, was working actively behind the scenes meeting with convention delegates and receiving valuable information. Several delegates, he reported, told him "that if South Carolina *had attempted to lead*, in the struggle for southern rights, the results would have been disastrous for the cause. . . . [I]t was part of their policy to keep South Carolina as much out of sight as possible."[37]

The most convincing evidence that secession sentiment ran wide but not deep in all the states except Mississippi and South Carolina and that the Southern nationalists were not in control came in the days following Daniel Webster's famous "Seventh of March Speech," in which the great Whig statesman appealed "not as a Massachusetts man, nor as a northern man, but as an American" for "the preservation of the Union." Here was nationalism of an American, not Southern kind, a

---

Alabama. Fletcher M. Green, "Democracy in the Old South," *Journal of Southern History* 12 (1946): 16. See also Table 3, Appendix I and Dodd and Dodd, *Historical Statistics of the Southern States*, pp. 34–37, 46–49.

37. Daniel Wallace to Whitemarsh Seabrook, October 20, 1849, Whitemarsh Seabrook Papers, Southern Historical Collection.

challenge to Americans North and South to define their nation broadly and without bloodshed. Not only Whigs but also many Democrats in the South instantly recognized in Webster's speech a tone of conciliation, a degree of tolerance, that suddenly made the Compromise less threatening. When abolition editors labeled Webster "Benedict Arnold" and called his speech "a terrible mistake," Southerners were the more encouraged. Perhaps the South could yet stay in the Union; perhaps most Northerners still intended to live by the Constitution.[38]

Soon after Webster's speech, the Southern Whig press began to alter the terms of the Compromise debate to make the issue Union or secession. Southern nationalism began rapidly to wane; support of the Compromise seemed to grow. The Southern press began to moderate, led by the Whigs who sought to make a partisan issue of the new terms of the Compromise question. A Virginian observed that a number of politicians in the Old Dominion "have gone over to the compromises." In state after state, the secessionist impulse was subsiding.[39]

Most of the Southerners in Congress were unaware of the rapid change in feeling back home. A few, like Toombs, who only a few months previously had exclaimed, *"I am for disunion,"* began to move back to their Whig allies who were now rallying around the Compromise as true to the Whig philosophy of positive government. Most, though, continued to espouse Calhoun's warnings that passage of the Compromise imperiled the Union.[40]

After the death of Calhoun, leadership of the Southerners in Congress devolved upon Senator Jefferson Davis of Mississippi who, during the hot summer days of 1850, led the Southern Democrats in battle against the Compromise on the Senate

38. *Congressional Globe*, 31 Cong., 1 sess., Appendix, pp. 269–76; Craven, *Southern Nationalism*, p. 77.
39. Foster, "Webster's Seventh of March Speech," p. 255, 267–70; Craven, *Southern Nationalism*, p. 77.
40. *Congressional Globe*, 31 Cong., 1 sess., p. 27.

floor. Born in Kentucky in 1808, Davis was reared on a small plantation in Mississippi. After graduating from West Point in 1828 he acquired fame and fortune through his labors on a large Mississippi plantation, a meteoric rise in state Democratic politics, and gallant service in the Mexican War. Tall and striking in appearance with deep-set eyes and high cheekbones, Davis was an extroverted, charming young politician fiercely loyal to his friends, stubbornly intolerant of his enemies, and supremely confident of his own ability to lead.[41]

Although he was in full agreement with Calhoun on the need for Southern unity, Davis stopped short of endorsing the idea of a constitutional amendment to guarantee Southern rights in the territories. He supported the coming Nashville convention, though he cautioned that its purpose should be not "revolutionary" but "preventive." He preferred "an equal right to go into all territories—all property being alike protected," but would have accepted the extension of the Missouri Compromise line to the Pacific. He hoped that at Nashville the South might unite on such a policy.[42]

That convention was to be the grand attempt to secure Southern unity. But at the June gathering, some like Rhett and Tucker urged immediate secession, others like Hammond and Judge William Sharkey of Mississippi counseled delay, and Maryland, Kentucky, Missouri, North Carolina, and Louisiana were unrepresented. The deep division was not over the maintenance of Southern rights, but over the means of protection. The convention's address was prepared by Rhett but

41. Coit. *John C. Calhoun*, pp. 488–90. The best biographies of Davis are William E. Dodd, *Jefferson Davis* (Philadelphia: George W. Jacobs and Co., 1907) and Clement Eaton, *Jefferson Davis* (New York: Free Press, 1977). Hudson Strode, *Jefferson Davis*, 3 vols. (New York: Harcourt, Brace, and Co., 1955–64) is uneven and uninterpretative. Helpful though partisan and guarded is Varina Howell Davis, *Jefferson Davis, Ex-President of the Confederate States of America: A Memoir*, 2 vols. (New York: Belford Co., 1890). A full, critical biographical study of Davis is still to be written.

42. Hearon, "Mississippi and the Compromise," pp. 110–11; *Congressional Globe*, 31 Cong., 1 sess., pp. 520, 1578.

amended before adoption. Its resolutions called for extension of the Missouri Compromise line and vowed opposition to "any law imposing onerous conditions or restraints upon the rights of masters to remove their property into the Territories of the United States. . . ." Agreeing to reassemble if its demands were not met, the convention adjourned.[43]

On July 31, 1850, the old order passed as the Omnibus Bill was voted down. Henry Clay left Washington for a long vacation. Webster became secretary of state under Fillmore, who had assumed the presidency upon Taylor's death. A rudderless Congress, a land of unanswered questions, a people yearning for peace awaited leadership from a new generation. Taking over the direction of the territorial adjustment from Clay was Stephen A. Douglas of Illinois, who skillfully separated the Compromise measures and reintroduced them one by one. Manipulating the presence of senators on the floor when each bill came to a vote, Douglas achieved the passage of all the Compromise measures. Davis and eight Southern colleagues in the Senate lodged a protest, both as a symbol of their eternal opposition and as an explanation to their Southern constituents.[44]

By the early fall of 1850, the old alignments in the South had faded and three new factions emerged. There were, first, the unconditional supporters of the Compromise, mostly Whigs, who remained loyal to the notion of positive government, but a few old Jacksonians as well. A second faction consisted of those who opposed the Compromise but continued to

43. Potter, *Impending Crisis*, p. 104; Dallas T. Herndon, "The Nashville Convention of 1850," *Transactions of the Alabama Historical Society, 1904*, ed. Thomas McAdory Owen (Montgomery: Alabama Historical Society, 1906), 5: 203–38; St. George L. Sioussat, "Tennessee, the Compromise of 1850, and the Nashville Convention," *Mississippi Valley Historical Review* 2 (1915): 313–47; *Resolutions, Addresses, and Journal of Proceedings of the Southern Convention, Held at Nashville, Tennessee, June 3d to 12th, Inclusive, in the Year 1850* (Nashville: H. M. Watterson, Printer, 1850), pp. 23–24.

44. Holman Hamilton, *Prologue to Conflict: The Crisis and Compromise of 1850* (Lexington: University of Kentucky Press, 1964), pp. 132–51; Davis to F. N. Elmore, April 13, 1850, in Rowland, ed., *Jefferson Davis* 1: 323.

sustain Calhoun's hope for Southern unity and rights within the Union. This group comprised mostly Democrats who adhered to the idea of negative government plus a few of the old Whig Nullifiers who had never followed Calhoun into the Democratic party. Finally there were the Southern nationalists, the Yancey men, who believed that with the passage of the Compromise the "last extremity" had been reached and that secession—preferably cooperatively by the aggrieved states—must follow. All three groups concurred on the right of secession but disagreed as to its expediency at present.

The Nashville debacle had seemingly proved that without further organization the dreams of the Southern nationalists were beyond realization. Yet these veteran opinion manufacturers were not about to surrender without a fight. Soon after Nashville Rhett returned to Charleston where he prophesied "the beginning of a Revolution." He was feted throughout the summer at a number of public gatherings in South Carolina. To offset growing fears that South Carolina did not care about the positions of the other slaveholding states, Rhett for the first time carried his campaign outside the Palmetto State. At a rally in Macon, Georgia, Rhett and Yancey addressed a throng of over eight hundred supporters. "A common cause and a common fate now unites the Southern States," cried Rhett. "Wherever there is a Southern heart to beat with indignation at Southern wrongs,—there a Southern tongue may tell the story of their existence, and counsel their redress." They repeated this maneuver several days later at a similar rally in Walterboro, where the two fire-eaters urged Georgia to take the lead in seceding from the Union and promised that their states would follow close behind.[45]

In the 1850 congressional elections, Georgia, the "Empire State of the South," was a crucial battleground. Already resistance feeling was subsiding in the upper South and the new

45. White, *Robert Barnwell Rhett*, pp. 108, 111; Rhett, Speech at Macon, Georgia, Mass Meeting, August 22, 1850, Rhett Papers, Southern Historical Collection.

Union party was successfully making the issue not the Compromise itself but a simple choice of secession or Union. The Virginia General Assembly declined an invitation by South Carolina to participate in a second Southern convention, viewing such a move as "calculated to destroy the integrity of this Union." The influential *North Carolina Standard* called on the North to "respect and enforce the Fugitive Slave Law as it stands." Kentucky had never desired resistance and Tennessee, under old Whig and now Unionist influence, also acquiesced. When in September Georgia Governor George W. Towns, a Southern nationalist, called an election to be held in November for a special state convention where Georgians might "deliberate and counsel together for mutual protection and safety," the issues of the campaign and the importance to the rest of the South were immediately recognized.[46]

The choice in Georgia was Union or secession, and the election turned on the question of slavery. At their state convention the Southern Rights party, composed of Southern nationalists and some old Calhounites, viewed the election as "a question of life and death to the white race of the South." White supremacy, threatened by the continuation of the Union, could be preserved only in a separate nation. Over and over again the Southern Rights men sounded the theme, appealing especially to the nonslavholding whites whom, they argued, a meddlesome Congress wanted to make "the associates and equals if not the inferiors of the African race." In response, however, the combined Unionist efforts of Toombs, Stephens, and Cobb proved overwhelming. Well known, highly respected, and "safe" on the slavery question, these men gave repeated assurances that the Compromise did not threaten slavery. Governor Towns lamented "that probably 19/20 of the old state rights group are submissionists." His as-

46. Shanks, *Secession Movement in Virginia*, p. 39; *North Carolina Standard*, November 13, 1850, quoted in J. Carlyle Sitterson, *The Secession Movement in North Carolina*, James Sprunt Studies in History and Political Science, vol. 23 (Chapel Hill: University of North Carolina Press, 1939), p. 74; Craven, *Southern Nationalism*, pp. 108, 104.

sessment proved accurate, as Unionists carried all but ten of Georgia's ninety-three counties and won a statewide victory of almost two to one. When the convention assembled moderation prevailed and the resulting Georgia Platform, which accepted the Compromise while promising defiance of any "encroachment on Southern rights," dealt a grave blow to Southern nationalism.[47]

Alabama capitulated next. Yancey, practicing the partisan skills he had mastered during the 1840's, organized twenty-five Southern Rights clubs in fourteen counties, intending to restore the "constitution . . . to the original objects for which it was formed." He received backing from powerful editors in Montgomery and Mobile, but Governor H. W. Collier preferred to await the outcome of the Georgia elections and the reassembling of the Nashville convention in November. When the Georgia results and the sorry efforts of the poorly attended Nashville assembly became known, Collier declared his neutrality. Though Yancey continued to warn that "the whole country will become one vast African population . . . seeking for an outlet" and finding it "by an overthrow of the body politic, drowning all distinctions between the white and black man," Unionists argued with effect that disunion would "hasten beyond any other possible contingency the destruction of that peculiar property. . . ." With the issues so defined, Collier won reelection in August and Unionists won five of seven congressional seats and two-thirds of the seats in the state legislature.[48]

Only Mississippi and South Carolina remained. In Sep-

47. *Georgia Telegraph*, October 8, 1850, quoted in J. C. Gardner, "Winning the Lower South to the Compromise of 1850" (Ph.D. diss., Louisiana State University, 1974), p. 112; *Milledgeville Federal Union*, October 1, 1850, quoted in Horace Montgomery, "The Crisis of 1850 and its Effect on Political Parties in Georgia," *Georgia Historical Quarterly* 24 (1940): 317. For a detailed discussion of the Georgia campaign, see Shryock, *Georgia and the Union*, pp. 308–19. George W. Towns to Seabrook, September 25, 1850, Seabrook Papers.
48. Denman, *Secession Movement in Alabama*, pp. 38–64; *Montgomery Advertiser*, March 26, 1851; Lewy Dorman, *Party Politics in Alabama From 1850 Through 1860* (Wetumpka, Ala.: Wetumpka Printing Co., 1935), pp. 43–64.

tember 1850 Governor Quitman reported to Seabrook that secession sentiment was strong in his state and accurately predicted that the legislature, meeting in November, would summon a state convention to determine the means of resistance. The special election for Mississippi convention delegates was scheduled for the first week in September 1851 and coincided with the campaign for the governor, who would be chosen during the regular elections in November. Meanwhile in South Carolina, as in Mississippi, Southern Rights associations were organizing, as their founders claimed, "for the purpose of procuring unity of action and disseminating light among the people." Even though other states might succumb, these two seemed ready to stand firm.[49]

In Mississippi a Union party came together around Senator Henry S. Foote, who was nominated for governor. Censured by the state legislature for supporting the Compromise (though he voted with Davis against admitting California), the bumptious little senator called on Mississippi Unionists to "censure the censurers" and to accept the Compromise while remaining watchful for any further encroachment. Foote, noted for "excessive garrulity and total want of discretion," took to the stump to attack Quitman and skillfully mobilized the resources of the Democratic press to present the electorate the choice between "secession and acquiescence." As a Democratic leader of an essentially Whig movement, Foote, by quick and determined action, was able to seize the initiative and much of the old party machinery from Quitman, who was then embroiled in the filibuster controversy.[50]

Over the objections of many loyal Democrats, that party changed its name to the State Rights party and nominated

49. Quitman to Seabrook, September 29, 1850, Seabrook Papers; N. W. Stephenson, "Southern Nationalism in South Carolina in 1851," *American Historical Review* 36 (1931): 318–19.
50. Henry S. Foote, *A Casket of Reminiscences*, rev. ed. (New York: Negro Universities Press, 1968), p. 353; Hearon, "Mississippi and the Compromise," p. 179; Davis, *Recollections of Mississippi*, p. 320; *Columbus Democrat*, January 18, 1851; McCardell, "Quitman and the Compromise," 250–54.

Quitman. Many had preferred the moderate and more popular Davis. But Davis declined the nomination, claiming poor health. He was, in fact, suffering from a serious eye infection and lay prostrate for much of the 1851 campaign.[51]

As elsewhere, in Mississippi the State Rights men spoke of the threat posed to slavery by an activist government. They prophesied *"the social and political equality of the negro and the white man."* Davis attacked the Compromise as a governmental "usurpation" of power and as a "violation" of the "plain principles of the Constitution." Urging the nonslaveholder not to support Foote, Davis exclaimed that "no white man, in a slaveholding community, is the menial servant of any one. . . . The distinction between the classes . . . is a distinction of color." In response, the Unionists did not disagree over the future of slavery or its value, but they insisted that the Compromise did not threaten slavery and that Southern resistance was unwarranted. They continued with success to force the issue of Union or secession. After a raucous canvass punctuated by vicious invective and, at one point, the exchange of physical blows, the Unionists elected a large majority of convention delegates. Quitman resigned from the ticket and the State Rights party asked Davis to take his place. Though the new candidate made only a few campaign appearances, he came very close to defeating Foote in November. Still, the elections seemed to be a clear-cut victory for Unionism. Any lingering doubts about Mississippi's readiness to withdraw from the Union were dispelled by the state convention which, approving the Compromise, denied even the right of a state to secede.[52]

In South Carolina events proceeded in a somewhat similar

51. Davis, *Recollections of Mississippi*, pp. 315–17; McLendon, "John A. Quitman," p. 318; McCardell, "Quitman and the Compromise," 256–57; Craven, *Southern Nationalism*, p. 111.

52. *Jackson Mississippian*, January 31, 1851; Rowland, ed., *Jefferson Davis* 2: 70–73. For a detailed study of the campaign see especially Gardner, "Winning the Lower South," pp. 258–75, and Hearon, "Mississippi and the Compromise," pp. 205–12.

fashion, although in the Palmetto State the division was not between Union and State Rights but between those favoring cooperative resistance and those advocating separate state action. "History, honor, and our own consistency force upon us what some may think the terrible alternative of *separate state action*," cried the *Charleston Mercury*. In February 1851 delegates, mostly secessionists, were duly elected to a state convention by a very low turnout of voters, but the convention did not meet until Mississippi acted. The decline of resistance feeling in Mississippi led Rhett to call for separate secession in which, he was still confident, South Carolina would be joined by the other Southern states. The state legislature had earlier issued a call for a Southern convention to meet in Montgomery in 1852 and, though it was by now clear that the convention would never meet, election of delegates to it became the battleground over secession in South Carolina.[53]

For Rhett and his allies, who strenuously canvassed the state prior to the October vote, it was a grand but futile effort. Repeatedly declaring that by secession "South Carolina will never be permitted to become a St. Domingo," the separate action men evoked a vision of "black slaves, turned loose upon the community. . . ." The cooperationists—led by, among others, Rhett's old rival Hammond—agreed on the dreadful nature of such a scene but pointed to other states' acquiescence and the inexpediency of separate action.[54]

In late September 1851 the Northern Lights flashed across the South Carolina sky. One observer considered the spectacle an ill omen for secession and claimed that "it added to the panic among the ignorant classes which resulted in the defeat of the Secession Party. . . ." Only one congressional

53. *Charleston Mercury*, October 1, 1850; White, *Robert Barnwell Rhett*, pp. 118–20.
54. *Speech of the Hon. W. F. Colcock Delivered Before the Meeting of Delegates from the Southern Rights Association of South Carolina at Charleston, May 20, 1851* (Columbia: South Carolinian Office, 1851), p. 22; *Edgefield Advertiser*, July 24, 1851, quoted in Gardner, "Winning the Lower South," p. 353; White, *Robert Barnwell Rhett*, pp. 122–23.

district, Rhett's own, went for secession delegates. All the rest
voted for cooperationists. It was time, said one editor, for
Rhett and his men to "hang up their fiddles," for it was not
likely they would ever hear their "favorite tune played successfully in the United States."[55] Rhett soon resigned his Senate
seat.

III

The political warfare of 1850–51 took its toll. Davis, echoing
the feelings of his following, longed for "the earlier period of
our history," for "the times of those who formed this union.
. . . We have . . . lost something of that purity," he lamented,
"and the voice of honesty is drowned in the clamor of a phara-
saical sect" of extremists. A South Carolinian recognized, a bit
more pragmatically, that "when old party lines are once broken down effectually, my life upon it, the Southern Rights
men will sweep the whole South." Like Davis, he desired to
restore a Democratic party of cooperation with sympathetic
Northern allies.[56]

The approach of the presidential election in 1852 helped
accelerate the healing of the wounds. While the Southern
Whig party, permanently estranged from its Northern wing
over the slavery issue, looked to a continuation of its Union alliance with pro-Compromise Democrats, the Democrats
dropped "Southern Rights" from their name and tried to recall
the Union Democrats to the fold. Davis, who had not deserted
the party during its fling with radicalism, became a central,
unifying figure in this movement. Acknowledging that by
"preaching *under the cloak of Southern Rights*" they had alienated
a portion of their membership, the Democrats called conventions in a number of states to effect a reconciliation. The

55. Maxcy Gregg Sporting Journal, vol. 2, September 29, 1851, South Caroliniana Library; Lillian A. Kibler, *Benjamin F. Perry, South Carolina Unionist*
(Durham: Duke University Press, 1946), p. 277.
56. Rowland, ed., *Jefferson Davis* 2: 37, 39; Speech of James Orr, May 4, 1851,
Orr Papers, South Caroliniana Library.

Whigs, on the other hand, isolated, were stifled in their efforts to maintain the Union party. In Mississippi and Georgia, for example, the Union ranks dwindled rapidly. Mississippi Whigs called for a state Union convention, but when it met it endorsed the Democratic platforms of 1840, 1844, and 1848. In Georgia, Toombs and Stephens persisted without success in calling for the continuation of the Union party.[57]

The result was the swelling of the Democratic ranks. Capitalizing on the antislavery character of the Northern Whigs, the Democratic press asserted that "the only hope of the South in the impending struggle . . . lies in the success of the national Democratic party." The appeal was aimed primarily at younger men who might ordinarily have been expected to join the electorate in roughly equal proportions of Whigs and Democrats. A Georgian reported just such a development to Cobb. Many a young Southerner faced the dilemma of John H. Claiborne of Virginia, whose "ancestry all the way down . . . to the gates of my father's house were Whigs." Observing conditions and reading such pamphlets as *Why Old Line Whigs Should Attach Themselves to the Democratic Party*, Claiborne and many of his contemporaries became "convinced that the true policy of our Government consisted in carrying out the principles promulgated by Democratic formula. . . ." Leading Whigs such as Toombs and Stephens refused to support Winfield Scott, the Whig nominee in 1852. Although voter turnout was lower in 1852 than in 1848, the Democratic presidential vote was higher in every slaveholding state except Alabama, Georgia, and Tennessee. In every Southern state except Virginia and Texas the Whig totals in 1852 were considerably lower than 1848. Scott carried only four states—two of them, Kentucky and Tennessee, in the South, by slim majorities.[58]

57. *National Intelligencer*, April 18, 1851, quoted in Cole, *Whig Party*, p. 212, also pp. 214–15.

58. *Nashville American*, January 16, 1852, quoted *ibid.*, pp. 218–19; Philip Clayton to Howell Cobb, May 5, 1851, Cobb Papers, University of Georgia; Potter, *Impending Crisis*, p. 234; John Herbert Claiborne, *Seventy-Five Years in Old Virginia* (New York and Washington: Neale Publishing Co., 1904), p. 132;

Though most Southern nationalists rejoined the Democratic party, a few extremists fielded a separate ticket of George M. Troup of Georgia for president and Quitman for vice president. It failed miserably. Yancey realized that "voting for that ticket" was "merely an effort to . . . keep together the Southern Rights party, with a view to ulterior usefulness." He advised his followers "to avoid all efforts to irritate the feelings and excite the opposition of two great national parties in the South. *These are the ranks from which we expect to draw recruits. . . .*" In effect, then, he was urging Southern nationalists either to support Pierce or to sit the election out.[59]

From this time until the late 1850's, Southern nationalism had very little expression within the political party system. Instead the idea of a Southern nation began to permeate activities outside the political process. After 1854 the commercial conventions became gatherings primarily of disgruntled Southern nationalist politicians. Proslavery polemics grew more racist and more openly supportive of a Southern nation as the new, young Yanceyites found political advancement often thwarted by the somewhat older and somewhat wealthier regular Democrats, whose defense of slavery was generally in the paternalistic vein.[60] Literary and educational Southern nationalism found new and vocal adherents. Though Southern nationalists had tried politics and failed, their ideas had found new outlets.

Schlesinger, ed., *History of Presidential Elections* 2: 918, 1003. The increase of the Whig vote in Virginia and Texas in 1852 was 13,448 and a mere 486 respectively, while the Democratic increases were, respectively, a whopping 17,272 and 2,884. In the states where the Democratic total dropped in 1852 from its 1848 figure, overall turnout dropped by a higher percentage, and the Whig vote plummeted even further. In Alabama the Whig vote was but half its 1848 total, in Georgia only one third, and in staunchly Whig Tennessee seven-eighths.

59. Yancey to G. W. Gayle, quoted in DuBose, *Life and Times of Yancey*, p. 270.

60. See Chapter Two. For evidence on the relative youth of the Yanceyites and the relative wealth and age of their opponents, see Thornton, "Politics and Power in Alabama," pp. 155–56. Information gleaned by Ralph Wooster, *The Secession Conventions of the South* (Princeton: Princeton University Press, 1962), pp. 34–35 lends further support.

The Southern leaders of the Democratic party, the so-called National Democrats, the regulars, were by and large Southern sectionalists who favored supporting the national party and exercising sectional influence within its councils. The leader of this group was Davis. Among the other significant figures were Cobb of Georgia, John Slidell of Louisiana, Henry A. Wise of Virginia, Benjamin Fitzpatrick of Alabama, and James L. Orr of South Carolina, who was leading a group of younger men determined to bring the party system into the Palmetto State.[61]

These National Democrats did not deny the right of secession, merely its expedience. On many matters they entirely concurred with the Southern nationalists. They agreed, for instance, that the constitutional rights of the South must be protected. Davis viewed the fugitive slave law, which some Northern states were openly flouting, "as a right, not to be estimated, as some seem to suppose, by the value of the property, but for the principle which is involved." Secession would be justified if such constitutional rights continued to be denied, but National Democrats professed hope that right-minded Northerners would see the injustice of their ways.[62]

Davis, as Calhoun's political heir, chose to work within the national party. A close personal friend of Pierce, Davis readily left his unwilling retirement to serve as secretary of war. As a policymaker Davis proved creative and skillful. During his tenure he equipped the army with modern rifles, improved conditions at West Point, raised the salaries of servicemen, developed new tactics, and planned the annex to the Capitol. More important, Davis urged Pierce to send Soulé to Madrid and John Mason of Virginia, also a supporter of Cuban annexation, to France. He arranged with Slidell for that sena-

61. Joel H. Silbey, "The Southern National Democrats, 1845–1861," *Mid-America* 47 (1965): 176–90; Nichols, *Disruption of American Democracy*, pp. 4, 57, 354–55; Dorman, *Party Politics in Alabama*, pp. 80–82.

62. Rowland, ed., *Jefferson Davis* 2: 35. See also Walter N. Crenshaw to Bolling Hall, Jr., January 11, 1851, Hall Papers, Alabama Department of Archives and History, for a clear statement of the National Democrats' position.

tor's important though unsuccessful bid to aid the Cuban filibusters by suspending the neutrality laws in 1854. He sent
James Gadsden of South Carolina to negotiate the purchase of
a tract of land in what is now southern Arizona and New Mexico with the intent of securing a southern route for a projected
transcontinental railway, which he encouraged Pierce to support. Indeed it seemed that the South, through Davis, was certain of both influence and protection in the Pierce administration. National Democracy seemed to be working.[63]

Perhaps Davis's and the South's involvement in Washington explains both the virtual unanimity of Southern support
for Kansas–Nebraska and the virtual absence of Southern ani-
mosity toward the North while the bill was under consideration in the Congress. Davis himself obtained for Douglas a
private conference with Pierce, during which the president
gave his approval to the repeal of the Missouri Compromise.
Northern hysteria in the spring of 1854 was met by Southern
passivity. The *Richmond Enquirer* thought the introduction of
the bill showed the national party was "truer to the South than
her own sons." The Southern Rights press gave grudging support to the bill's repeal of the 1820 Compromise, refusing, like
the South Carolina *Edgefield Advertiser* to go "into ecstasies
over the mere abstract renunciation of gross error." Maryland
newspapers gave hardly any news of the passage of the bill.
The usually combative *Charleston Mercury* called the bill "a
thing of so little practical good, that it is certainly not worth
the labor of an active struggle to maintain it." An Alabamian
stated his inability "to comprehend, or credit, the excitement,
that is said to prevail in the North," for in his own state, there
was "no excitement, no fever, on the subject."[64]

As it seemed that Southern rights were secure under

63. Dodd, *Jefferson Davis*, pp. 133–47.
64. *Ibid.*, p. 149; *Richmond Enquirer*, January 7, 1854; *Edgefield Advertiser*, Feb-
ruary 22, 1854 quoted in Craven, *Southern Nationalism*, p. 196; J. McCardell,
"Maryland and the South, 1854–1861: A Content Analysis" (Seminar paper,
Johns Hopkins University, 1973); *Charleston Mercury*, June 21, 1854; J. L. M.
Curry to C. C. Clay, Jr., July 5, 1854, Clay Paper, Duke University.

Pierce, Southern nationalists began drifting back to the Democratic party. Quitman was elected to Congress as a Democrat, and Albert G. Brown went to the Senate from Mississippi. Alabama Yanceyites reentered the party and won election to Congress. In Georgia, Toombs declared his "Democratization" in 1855. In Virginia Hunter moved away from extreme Southern positions in a growing feud with the popular National Democrat Wise, who portrayed himself and his party as the surest champion of Southern rights in the Union.[65]

While the Democratic party gained new Southern recruits by its presidential policies, its growth was also stimulated by a new movement that threatened briefly to form a powerful opposition party. By 1855 the nativist movement, a fusion of all sorts of disparate political elements, included in the South a large number of erstwhile Whigs and some Union Democrats of the kind who led the Unionist movements in 1851. Such prominent Whigs as John J. Crittenden and Governor Charles Morehead of Kentucky, gubernatorial candidates Pierre Dubigny in Louisiana and Thomas Flournoy in Virginia, and former Congressman Henry Hilliard of Alabama joined with such former Democrats as Sam Houston of Texas, Jeremiah Clemens of Alabama, and James B. Shepard of North Carolina to form a party that advocated different policies in different sections of the country. In the states of the upper and western South that bordered on free territory, the Know-Nothings—as the nativist party members were called—took an anti-immigrant stance, arguing that the ignorant masses settling in the North were prey for abolitionists. In the lower South, the appeals were somewhat different, emphasizing the Northern Democratic "violation of plighted faith" in supporting repeal of the Missouri Compromise. Skillfully fielding ex-Democrats in Democratic districts and old line Whigs in former Whig

65. Claiborne, *Life and Correspondence of Quitman* 2: 210–13; Ranck, *Albert Gallatin Brown*, pp. 135–36, 149; Dorman, *Party Politics in Alabama*, pp. 94–95; Horace Montgomery, *Cracker Parties* (Baton Rouge: Louisiana State University Press, 1950), p. 155; Shanks, *Secession Movement in Virginia*, pp. 46–52.

strongholds, the Know-Nothings—"Whiggery in disguise,"
charged the Democrats—girded for a strong fight.[66]

Southern Democratic fears of nativism were compounded
by the direction the new party was taking in the North.
Though the true antislavery party—the Republicans—had
been founded by anti-Nebraska Northerners in 1854, it was
not at all clear in 1855 either that nativism was but a passing
fancy, that Republicans would subsume the Know-Nothings,
or that Democratic supremacy in the South was assured. It
was hardly encouraging to Southern Democrats in 1855 to
witness the strength of Know-Nothingism in such citadels of
abolitionism as Massachusetts and New York. Nor did astute
Southern politicians fail to note the ideological compatability
of Know-Nothingism and Republicanism. Ninety-two of the
congressmen elected in 1854 were both antislavery and nativist.[67]

In Southern states, the Know-Nothing movement
brought out the old Southern nationalists to battle for the Democracy. Quitman's close 1855 victory was won against a
Know-Nothing opponent. The narrow Democratic victory in
1855 took place after a campaign punctuated, in the words of
one participant, by gatherings at which "it was not unusual to
hear the click of a dozen pistols. . . ." In Alabama, Democrats
faced a strong Know-Nothing opposition. Yancey attacked the
nativists and the Democrats triumphed. In those states less
inclined to resistance in 1850, where Unionism was very
strong, the Democratic campaign isolated the nativists as
threatening extremists. The rout of nativism in the South gave

66. W. Darrell Overdyke, *The Know-Nothing Party in the South* (Baton Rouge:
Louisiana State University Press,1950), esp. pp. 83–126, is the best general
study of the nativist movement in the South. James H. Broussard, "Some De-
terminants of Know-Nothing Electoral Strength in the South, 1856," *Louisiana
History* 7 (1966): 5–20, supplies convincing evidence of the largely Whig origins
of the party, confirming the earlier work of both Cole and Philip Morrison
Rice, "The Know-Nothing Party in Virginia," *Virginia Magazine of History and
Biography* 40 (1947): 61–75, 159–67. See also Craven, *Southern Nationalism*,
pp. 240–45; *Arkansas Gazette*, August 10, 1855.
67. Potter, *Impending Crisis*, pp. 250–51.

a temporary, illusory unity to the now swollen Democratic party in which old Southern nationalists soon discovered they had considerable clout.[68]

Nativism was in retreat as 1856 began. As the Republican menace grew stronger in the North, Know-Nothings deserted their party in the South and many immediately joined the Democrats. A rejuvenated Democratic party prepared to name its presidential candidate. Southerners expected to have a large role in the selection. Though their innermost hopes may still have been of a Southern nation, Yancey and the Southern nationalists declared their allegiance to the Democratic party. Yancey's efforts against the Know-Nothings made him a central figure in the Alabama state Democratic convention in January 1856. As chairman of the Resolutions Committee, Yancey offered and the convention accepted a modified version of the old Alabama Platform. The new declaration, reiterating the right to protection of property in the territories, affirmed that Congress had no power to interfere with slavery there. Only the Supreme Court could rule on decisions made by a territorial legislature. When the national convention later incorporated both provisions into its 1856 platform and nominated James Buchanan, Yancey, satisfied, had every reason to hope that a Democratic victory would "[settle] the Union once more on the fair basis of Justice and equality." It had been eight years since Yancey had withdrawn from politics vowing to wait for his party to come to him. In 1856 it arrived, restored him to the head of the Alabama delegation, and pledged itself to the principles he had long held.[69]

68. Overdyke, *Know-Nothing Party*, pp. 139–43, 206–207; Colin S. Tarpley to Stephen A. Douglas, November 15, 1855, quoted in Percy Lee Rainwater, *Mississippi, Storm Center of Secession, 1856–1861* (Baton Rouge: Otto Claitor, 1938), p. 33; Dorman, *Party Politics in Alabama*, p. 102; Percy Scott Flippin, *Herschel V. Johnson of Georgia: States Rights Unionist* (Richmond: Dietz Printing Co., 1931), p. 69; Clement Eaton, "Henry A. Wise and the Virginia Fire Eaters of 1856," *Mississippi Valley Historical Review* 21 (1935): 499.
69. Craven, *Southern Nationalism*, p. 242; Venable, "Public Career of Yancey," p. 206–209; DuBose, *Life and Times of Yancey*, pp. 318–20.

The Republican nominee was John C. Frémont, and as his candidacy gained support in the North some Southerners during the summer and fall of 1856 contemplated responses to a Republican victory. The Georgia Platform of 1850, to which Southerners generally subscribed, had promised resistance to any further encroachments upon slavery. By 1856 some Southern moderates—so called for their support of the Georgia Platform in 1850—were vowing to follow through on that document's pledge. "The election of Fremont would be the end of the Union, and ought to be," wrote Toombs. A Virginia congressman feared that a successful "[Republican] presidential candidate would probably fill every Federal Office in the *South* with a *Free Soiler!*" A Mississippian wrote that Frémont's success would require "immediate, prompt, and unhesitating secession."[70]

These sentiments were not, however, typical. Expressions of extreme Southernism were still more likely to be heard from outside the political process. Those who, like Yancey, had tried and failed within the party system and came back to try again accepted the Democratic party and worked hard to elect Buchanan over his chief opponent in the South, Millard Fillmore, the Know-Nothing nominee. There was no clearer evidence of Southern complacency than in the response—or nonresponse—to a call by Governor Wise, who summoned all the Southern governors to a meeting in Raleigh, North Carolina, in September 1856 to discuss the Republican threat. Only the governors of North and South Carolina bothered to attend. It hardly mattered that Buchanan carried only five nonslaveholding states; the Democratic party was in control, and Southern institutions seemed safe.[71]

No sooner had nativism been destroyed and Buchanan elected than a series of jolts began to split the Southern Democrats back into two factions. Immediately after Buchanan's in-

70. Potter, *Impending Crisis*, p. 262; W. O. Goode to E. W. Hubard, January 20, 1856, Hubard Family Papers, Southern Historical Collection; Rainwater, *Mississippi, 1856–1861*, p. 38n.
71. DuBose, *Life and Times of Yancey*, pp. 323–34; Eaton, "Wise and the Fire Eaters," p. 501; Nichols, *Disruption of American Democracy*, pp. 60–61.

augural, the Supreme Court handed down the Dred Scott decision, which ruled that the Missouri Compromise—and, in effect, any territorial compromise—was unconstitutional. Buchanan hoped that the Democrats would rally behind this decision, but he was mistaken. While Southerners generally applauded it, Douglas denounced the decision openly.

Appalled that so formidable a leader as Douglas would fail to give the decision his full support, Yancey concluded that he and other Southern rights men must work to capture the Democratic party. To that end, in the spring of 1858, he announced his candidacy for the Senate. For his platform he took only one issue, which represented a complete break with traditional Democratic belief in negative government. Yancey now insisted upon congressional *protection* of slavery in the territories. If the party failed to heed this uncharacteristic demand, Southerners, Yancey argued, would be bound to withdraw their support. And if the Democrats persisted in their folly, and if the Republicans won the presidency in 1860, it would be necessary to dissolve the Union.[72]

Yancey's move effectively divided both the legacy and the constituency of the Democratic party in the South. The Southern nationalists made themselves claimants of Jackson's mantle. The Yancey men retained the Jacksonian organizational methods and the strident, self-confident assurance of a movement that recognized, like the Jacksonians of old, the nature of the enemy and the means to salvation. Free soil became the symbol of inequality and subservience. Proposals for territorial restrictions on slavery, abolitionist attacks, and the emergence of the Republican party confirmed Yancey's direst prophecies and gave credence to his charge that the South now faced a new, ominous threat. Yancey's attacks upon the National Democrats, who preferred compromise, helped undermine the Democratic voter's confidence in his leaders.[73]

---

72. Dorman, "Party Politics in Alabama," p. 143; Venable, "Public Career of Yancey," p. 210; Nichols, *Disruption of American Democracy*, p. 217.
73. I rely unabashedly for the basis of this interpretation on the excellent work of Jonathan Mills Thornton, "Politics and Power in Alabama," pp. 289, 438,

The Davis regulars were in a genuine dilemma. They opposed the disruptive tactics of the Yancey men, but they shared the Yanceyites' concern over the growing Northern threat. With Douglas on one side and Yancey on the other, the Southern regulars were paralyzed. Their situation was hardly enhanced by Douglas's well publicized remark in the summer of 1857 that "it matters not what way the Supreme Court may decide" on slavery in the territories. "The people have the lawful means to introduce it or exclude it as they please."[74]

The battle for the soul of the Democratic party was on, and at the Montgomery commercial convention in 1858 Yancey met with his sympathizers to lay careful plans. It was time for the Southern nationalists to reenter politics, to make their final demands and, if unsatisfied, to withdraw themselves from the party and their states from the Union. With Edmund Ruffin, Yancey left Montgomery to organize a League of United Southerners, an organization whose motto proclaimed, "A Southern Republic is our only safety." Embarking on a speaking tour to promote both his League and his senatorial candidacy, Yancey emphasized his willingness to work within the party, to "elevate and purify" it—a necessary concession for a man seeking its endorsement—but warned that the time might come when Southerners "would throw off the shackles both of parties and of the government, and assert their independence in a Southern Confederacy." Privately the ambitious Alabamian was even less moderate. To a supporter Yancey confided that his real hope was to "fire the Southern heart, instruct the Southern mind, . . . and, at the proper moment, by one organized concerted action, we can precipitate the Cotton States into a revolution."[75]

441–42, 466–67. See also Davis, *Recollections of Mississippi*, p. 324; Nichols, *Disruption of American Democracy*, p. 251.

74. Nichols, *Disruption of American Democracy*, p. 221.

75. Austin Venable, "William L. Yancey and the League of United Southerners," *The Proceedings of the South Carolina Historical Association, 1946* (Columbia: South Carolina Historical Association, 1946), p. 6; *Montgomery Advertiser*, July 21, 1858; Craven, *Coming of the Civil War*, pp. 399–400.

Yancey and his men took up the familiar Democratic tools and rhetoric. One Southern nationalist urged that it "be made to appear" that Southern rights in the territories were threatened. Attacking the regulars for being more concerned with their own advancement than with the future safety of the South, the Yanceyites took on the Buchanan men in state contests. The Alabama National Democrats, charging Yancey with fomenting disunion, moved to thwart him. In a Virginia reversal of previous roles, Wise feuded with Hunter and employed Yanceyite rhetoric to advance his campaign for Hunter's Senate seat. In Georgia Yanceyite Joseph E. Brown battled with the Cobb organization. In Louisiana Slidell, a Buchanan man, contested with Soulé, a Douglas supporter. In Mississippi Davis and Brown forces bitterly attacked one another. In South Carolina, meanwhile, Rhett and the *Mercury* cheered the Yanceyites on, and even Hammond lent support.[76]

Yancey. Wise. Soulé. Joseph Brown. Albert Brown. Rhett. Hammond. All were self-made men. All had emerged from poverty to challenge the political establishment. They were all good Democrats and had mastered the art of opinion manipulation. All were racist defenders of slavery. All of them had suffered repeated frustrations, economic and political. They had no use for an establishment, they said, though they had formed a different kind of establishment themselves. Now they were emerging from obscurity, moving to control the Democratic party. And if they failed, they promised a revolution.

The National Democrats vigorously responded. Davis made an Independence Day speech in Maine defending his party and the Union and attacking "trifling politicians" who, like "mosquitoes around the ox," wished to disrupt the Union. The Alabama National Democrats Clay and Fitzpatrick began to work to defeat Yancey. Even old Whigs pitched in. Daniel

76. John H. Davis to Milledge L. Bonham, January 20, 1858, Milledge Luke Bonham Papers, South Caroliniana Library; Nichols, *Disruption of American Democracy*, pp. 251–52.

M. Barringer of North Carolina, Taylor's minister to Spain, exclaimed, "*Surely—surely it is time for the South—the entire South and all Conservative men everywhere to be fraternal and united in the face of dangers which beset us!*"[77]

Although Yancey made few apparent gains in 1858—few Southerners joined his League, few of his comrades won election, and his own bid for the Senate was frustrated—he had clearly shaken the regulars. A few old Whigs were encouraged by the Democratic schism to reconstruct a Union party, while the National Democrats found themselves moving ever closer to Yancey's position. For example, Davis, under heavy press attack for his Maine speech and his New England tour that followed it, hastily returned home to address the Mississippi legislature and announce that if a Republican should be elected president in 1860, "I should deem it your duty to provide for your safety outside the Union." The regulars, schooled in the art of compromise, now had to compromise with the Yanceyites to preserve a semblance of political unity. They were moving very close to a position of demanding federal protection of slavery in the territories, a position completely contradictory to the traditional Democratic policy of noninterference in the territories and therefore certain to rend the party in two.

If the South seemed becalmed as 1859 began, it was not because the National Democrats had destroyed secession; it was, rather, because fundamental differences between North and South now seemed to have replaced differences between parties or factions. More and more Southern newspapers, pamphleteers, and politicians were declaring "that our interest is radically different from that of the Northern people; . . . that in every aspect in which Union can be viewed, it is a permanent evil to the South." Instead the calm of 1859 bespoke the growing realization of a common ground, the inevitable result of the fact that—for the National Democrats in the

---

77. Rowland, ed., *Jefferson Davis* 3: 271–74; Nichols, *Disruption of American Democracy*, p. 252; Daniel M. Barringer to W. A. Houck, August 6, 1858, Barringer Papers.

South, to both their Republican adversaries and their Yanceyite critics—there was precious little left to concede.[78]

IV

It was a cold, dreary January morning in 1861. His feeble
body wracked with the pain of chronic neuralgia, his dyspeptic
stomach churning in agony, Senator Davis had spent a
wretched night pacing the floor of his Washington home. In a
few hours he was to make his farewell address to the Senate
and the government he had served so long and so well. Mississippi's state convention had voted the state out of the Union
and, along with South Carolina, Mississippi had acted as Davis
had foretold in 1858. Then it was only political rhetoric; now it
was a stark reality. Secession had triumphed; compromise had
failed. It was Davis's last duty to justify, before his colleagues
and the sundered Union he had labored to preserve, his state's
and the South's action.

As he walked back and forth composing his words, his
bony hands clasped behind him, his sharp face pinched in distress, Davis must have mused over the events of the last several
years. Vainly had he tried—ever since returning to the Senate
in 1857, against mounting odds—to keep the South united in
the Democratic party and the Democratic party true to Southern needs. It was more than one man or group of men could ac-
complish. But he had warned them, North and South. In his
tour of New England in 1858 he had become convinced that
the preachments of Yancey were ignorant claptrap. "The difference" between the two sections, he had written to his old
friend Pierce, "is less than I had supposed." Castigated at
home for his wanderings by a state press that was long experienced in the art of opinion manufacturing, Davis had returned
home to warn the North of the consequences of electing a

78. Rowland, ed., *Jefferson Davis* 3: 356; Nichols, *Disruption of American Democracy*, p. 219; Herbert Fielder, *The Disunionist: A Brief Treatise Upon the Evils of
the Union Between the North and the South, and the Propriety of Separation and the
Formation of a Southern United States* (n.p., 1858), p. 72.

Republican president: ". . . such a result would be a species of revolution by which the purposes of Government would be destroyed and the observance of its mere forms entitled to no respect." Still, in 1858 there had been hope. "I have not considered," he told his fellow Mississippians, "the remedies which lie within that extreme [secession] as exhausted, or ever been entirely hopeless of their success."[79]

Had that extreme now been reached? Did Davis really believe, as he had often declared in the preceding years, that Lincoln's election on the Republican platform of free soil meant dissolution of the Union? Whether he himself truly believed them or not, Davis's terms—the election of a Republican president—became throughout the South the accepted definition of that vague, foreboding expression, "the last extremity." All the Democrats in South Carolina, including Orr, accepted such a definition in 1858. After the John Brown raid the Alabama legislature resolved to call a state convention if a Republican should be elected. Georgia Democrats began to talk openly of secession if their party should be defeated. In Virginia, Wise affirmed that "our union with nonslaveholding States cannot continue."[80]

Brown's raid had certainly aroused the South. South Carolina papers like the *Mercury* might regard the raid as a "small affair," but probably no Northern outrage could have moved South Carolina in 1859; the Palmetto State was ready and waiting, aware that the Harpers Ferry episode was, in the *Mercury's* words, but "a sign of the times and of the temper and intentions of the northern majority." Distant, frontier states, to whom Brown's threat seemed far away might believe with the *Arkansas Gazette* that "too much importance has been attached to this matter." But Davis had known better. He had

79. Rowland, ed., *Jefferson Davis* 3: 498, 356, 343.
80. Harold Schultz, *Nationalism and Sectionalism in South Carolina, 1852–1860* (Durham: Duke University Press, 1950), p. 166; Denman, *Secession Movement in Alabama*, pp. 77–79; Haywood J. Pearce, Jr., *Benjamin H. Hill, Secession and Reconstruction* (Chicago: University of Chicago Press, 1928), p. 32; Shanks, *Secession Movement in Virginia*, p. 92.

heard Wise's call on Virginia to "organize and arm"; Alabama Governor A. B. Moore's message advising his legislature to organize volunteer corps in every county, proposing a tax to raise $200,000 to arm the troops; the conservative Tennessee legislature's call for Southerners "to unite in crushing out" Republicans, who were sweeping the 1859 elections in the North, as "traitors to their country and as deadly enemies to the public peace. . . ."[81]

He had heard Christopher G. Memminger of South Carolina announce that "every [Northern] village bell which tolled its solemn note at the execution of Brown proclaims to the South the approbation of that village of insurrection and servile war." Memminger, lately come to a Southern nationalist position, recognized the threat posed by abolitionist support of the Brown raid. In late December 1859 he was beginning a sensitive, vital mission to the Virginia legislature. The South Carolina legislature had decided that a Southern convention must meet, and it had named Memminger, a longtime Unionist who now admitted "that the Union cannot be preserved," to "urge our Carolina view" upon Virginia.[82]

South Carolinians held high aspirations for Memminger's success in "giving direction," as one congressman wrote, "to what may be a vague desire on their part to deal an effective blow at the North." Another Carolinian offered advice on Memminger's address to the Virginia legislature. He should state that Brown's raid was an "outrage. We consider it equally an attack upon S. Carolina. . . . We stand with Virginia in this

81. *Charleston Mercury*, November 14, 1859; *Arkansas Gazette*, November 12, 1859; Shanks, *Secession Movement in Virginia*, p. 92; Denman, *Secession Movement in Alabama*, p. 77; Campbell, *Attitude of Tennesseans*, p. 95.
82. Potter, *Impending Crisis*, p. 383; C. G. Memminger to William Porcher Miles, January 3, 1860, Isaac W. Hayne to William Porcher Miles, January 5, 1860, Miles Papers; Miles to Memminger, January 10, 1860, Christopher Gustavus Memminger Papers, Southern Historical Collection. Two excellent accounts of the Memminger mission are Steven Channing, *Crisis of Fear: Secession in South Carolina* (New York: W. W. Norton Co., 1970), pp. 112–30, and Ollinger Crenshaw, "Christopher G. Memminger's Mission to Virginia, 1860," *Journal of Southern History* 8 (1942): 334–49.

fray & all its consequences." With such language the Virginians might be led while "letting them suppose that they are leading. It is so with political communities."[83]

Memminger was, however, upset with the state of mind in the Old Dominion. Hunter and Wise both craved the presidency, and neither would use his considerable influence to aid the Carolinian's mission. Memminger's reports made Palmetto secessionists "heartsick," said one, "at the prospect of uniting the South. . . ." Rhett concluded that "so long as the Democratic party, is a 'National' organization, . . . and so long as our public men trim their sails with an eye to either its favor or enmity, just so long need we hope for no Southern action." By early February it was clear that Virginia would do nothing, and the Carolinians decided that they "must act and 'drag her along' . . . in the event of the election of a Black Republican President. . . ." Memminger questioned even that possibility, suspecting in his final report that "the Black Republicans will evade an issue by giving us a new candidate in place of Seward, . . . and so I fear we can make up no issue in advance, but must await events."[84]

Despite some disclaimers in the Southern press, then, Brown's raid was certainly not a "small affair." Rising in the Senate to speak in support of Virginia Senator James Mason's Harpers Ferry Invasion Resolutions, Davis charged that there existed in the North "a conspiracy against a portion of the United States, a rebellion against the constitutional government of a State." Those in the North who had financed Brown's foray had violated "every obligation to the social compact, the laws, the Constitution, the requirements of public virtue and personal honor."[85]

83. Miles to Memminger, January 10, 1860, W. W. Boyce to Memminger, January 14, 1860, Memminger Papers.

84. Shanks, *Secession Movement in Virginia*, pp. 63–64; Nichols, *Disruption of American Democracy*, p. 294; Miles to Memminger, January 18, 1860, February 3, 1860, Memminger Papers; R. B. Rhett to Miles, January 29, 1860, Memminger to Miles, February 4, 1860, Miles Papers.

85. Rowland, ed., *Jefferson Davis* 4: 107, 109.

Back home the language had been even less temperate, as Yancey and his followers seized upon the Brown raid to prove once again the truth of their prophecies, the correct identification of the enemy. A pro-Yancey editor claimed that Brown's raid, "like a meteor . . . in its lurid flash," had disclosed "the width and depth of that abyss which rends asunder two nations, apparently one." Alabama Democrats had gathered in January 1860 to name delegates to the national convention at Charleston in April. In attendance were new men—young men, Yancey men—ready to stage their coup. Speaking in support of resolutions that both attacked "the Vandal hordes of Black Republicanism" and promised withdrawal from the national convention if the Democratic party failed to adopt the Alabama Platform, Yancey, his voice ringing with the satisfaction of a triumph long awaited and finally achieved, invoked the trinity of

> Liberty, the Constitution, the Union, three in one and, therefore, inseparable and indissoluable; the first an inalienated and undying principle, the last two valuable only as the machinery planned and operated for the protection of the first; and in that light, and that alone, sacred and worthy of preservation, and in that estimate only to be held inseparable from the first.

The new Alabama Platform of 1860 called for congressional protection of slavery in the territories.[86]

In the Senate Davis's colleague Brown introduced resolutions of an identical kind. Brown prophesied the effect of a Republican victory on the nonslaveholding whites, many of whom, as good Jacksonians, had long supported the National Democrats:

> The Negro will intrude into his presence—insist on being treated as an equal—that he shall go to the white man's table, and the white man to his—that he shall share the white man's bed, and the white man his—that his son shall marry the white man's

86. *Mobile Register*, October 25, 1859, quoted in Craven, *Coming of the Civil War*, p. 411; Dorman, *Party Politics in Alabama*, p. 155; DuBose, *Life and Times of Yancey*, pp. 444–45.

daughter, and the white man's daughter his son. In short, they
shall live on terms of perfect social equality. . . . Then will com-
mence a war of races. . . .[87]

John Brown's raid had personalized the Republican threat
and sent the rank-and-file Southern Democrats rapidly ahead
of their national leaders. Following behind, Davis and his colleagues tried to catch up in order to bring the party back to a
position compatible with its Northern allies. To the Senate
Davis admitted that there existed among Southerners in early
1860 "a thorough conviction that their self-respect, their
safety, their loyalty to the Constitution, their allegiance to the
rights to which they were born, require them to take that last
and regretful step whenever they are reduced to that alternative." Davis was at the time drawing up his own set of resolutions to counter those of his fiery colleague Brown. Davis introduced his resolutions on February 2, placing himself in
effect side by side with both Yancey and Brown even as he
tried to keep the party together. They declared that Congress
was bound to protect slavery in the territories "if experience at
any time should prove that the Judiciary does not possess
power to ensure adequate protection." While Brown scoffed at
the splitting of hairs, border state Democrats hastily referred
the resolutions to a Senate caucus for modification, and Davis
gloated over the similarity between his resolutions and those
offered by Calhoun in 1837. Meanwhile, Democratic conventions in South Carolina, Florida, Mississippi, Louisiana,
Texas, and Arkansas were committing themselves to the new
Alabama Platform. While Davis wrung his hands and racked
his brain, Yancey was firing the Southern heart.[88]

Soon after the Memminger mission ended in February,
the Mississippi legislature tried to take the lead. It called for a
general Southern convention to meet in Atlanta in June, and it
commissioned Peter B. Starke, a Virginia native, to return to

---

87. Rainwater, *Mississippi, 1856–1861*, pp. 147–48.
88. Rowland, ed., *Jefferson Davis* 4:167; Nichols, *Disruption of American Democracy*, pp. 283–84; *Congressional Globe*, 36 Cong., 1 sess., p. 658.

the Old Dominion as an agent of Southern solidarity. The Virginia legislature, however, declined to elect delegates to the Atlanta convention and, when Tennessee likewise rejected the idea of a convention and Alabama declared that separate state action was the only real alternative to staying in the Union, the movement collapsed.[89]

By the time the Democrats convened in Charleston at the end of April two things seemed clear. The prospect of cooperative action seemed less likely than the prospect of separate state action; and South Carolina's hope for secession and support lay not to the north but to the west. Although the Democrats—or at least the convention delegates—in the deep South seemed mostly committed to Yancey's platform, delegates from Maryland, Virginia, North Carolina, Tennessee, Kentucky, and Cobb-controlled Georgia were not. This split was to become more important during the twelve months between the Democratic convention and the outbreak of hostilities, but its magnitude would become apparent as soon as the Charleston gathering began.[90]

Yancey and his disciplined troops came to Charleston determined to have their way or walk out. In their mind the situation was clear, the choices obvious. The Republicans stood a real chance of winning the presidency and controlling the vast executive patronage with a mandate wholly Northern. Once in office, as Southern Democrats feared, Republicans might use the patronage power to undermine the slaveholding civilization. The party would certainly not appoint slaveholders to office; rather, they would turn to nonslaveholding whites, convince them that they had no stake in slavery, and foment a social revolution. Albert Brown, spokesman of piney woods Mississippi, had had just such a vision, as had DeBow, whose 1860 tract on the interest of the nonslaveholder in slavery was well publicized and well timed. No wonder Yanceyites stood

89. Robert W. Dubay, "Mississippi and the Proposed Atlanta Convention of 1860," *Southern Quarterly* 5 (1966–67): 347–62.
90. Dumond, *The Secession Movement*, p. 34.

firm in their demands; no wonder the election of a Republican president had become the fulcrum of Southern nationalism.

Though the Yancey men had no one candidate, they had their principles. As Yancey lectured, the delegates—after a week of wrangling in the Charleston heat—had failed to produce a platform:

> We have come here, then, with the twofold purpose of saving the country and saving the Democracy; and if the Democracy will not lend itself to that high, holy and elevated purpose; if it cannot elevate itself above the mere question of how perfect shall be its personal organization and how widespread shall be its mere voting success, then we say to you, gentlemen, mournfully and regretfully, that in the opinion of the State of Alabama, and, I believe, of the whole South, you have failed in your mission, and it will be our duty to go forth and make an appeal to the loyalty of the country to stand by that Constitution which party organizations have deliberately rejected.[91]

When the convention refused to adopt the Alabama Platform, Yancey marched out of the hall. In 1848 he had marched almost alone. In 1860 his delegation followed him, with those of Mississippi, Louisiana, South Carolina, Florida, and Texas close behind. The breach was irreconcilable, as a reassembled portion of the party in Baltimore nominated Douglas and the Southerners, reconvening in Richmond, selected Vice President John C. Breckinridge of Kentucky as their nominee on a platform calling for congressional protection of slavery. The Democratic party, the last binding cord of the Union, had snapped.[92]

Painfully Davis recalled the depths of his grief when he received the news. He had urged the Mississippians by telegraph from Washington not to follow Yancey. As the party unraveled in Charleston, Southerners and Northerners in Congress exchanged bitter charges and, on one occasion, ac-

91. *Speech of William L. Yancey of Alabama Delivered in the National Democratic Convention, Charleston, April 28, 1860* (Charleston: Walker, Evans, and Co., 1860), p. 3.
92. Nichols, *Disruption of American Democracy*, pp. 303–22.

tual blows. As the fracas between a Virginian and a Wisconsin man broke out, one Southern congressman revealed, "I never said a word to anybody but quietly cocked my Revolver in my pocket. . . ." Senator Hammond observed that "a general fight in one or the other House with great slaughter is always on the tapis. . . . No two nations on earth are or ever were more distinctly separate and hostile than we are here."[93]

But Davis had tried valiantly to keep party and Union together. In May, failing to convince Mississippians that the South could secure its damands only by staying in the convention, he had offered revised resolutions to the Senate declaring that "intermeddling . . . with the domestic institutions" of a state "on any pretext whatever . . . is in violation of the Constitution" and stating that "if the judicial and executive authority do not possess means to insure adequate protection to Constitutional rights in a Territory . . . it will be the duty of Congress to supply such deficiency." Pleading for acceptance Davis had proclaimed, "For thirty years I have walked the deck of the old Democratic ship. . . . If I leave, . . . I mean to stand on a platform . . . about which . . . there is no equivocation, no doubt, no hesitation." Though the resolutions passed the Senate, the Douglas Democrats stood firm in opposition and the Yanceyites declared that the resolutions failed to go far enough.[94]

Despite Davis's exertions, neither party nor national unity seemed possible. The election of 1860 was a four-way contest. Abraham Lincoln, the Republican nominee, seemed assured of a victory over a divided opposition of Douglas, Breckinridge, and John Bell of Tennessee, candidate of the Whiggish Constitutional Union party. In one last effort to re-unite the party, Davis tried to persuade the three anti-Republicans to withdraw in favor of one candidate whom they

93. Martin J. Crawford to Alexander H. Stephens, April 8, 1860, quoted *ibid.*, p. 286; Hammond to Marcellus Hammond, April 22, 1860, Hammond Papers.
94. Rowland, ed., *Jefferson Davis* 4: 250–51, 282; *Congressional Globe*, 36 Cong., 1 sess., p. 2325.

all could support. Though Breckinridge and Bell agreed, Douglas refused.[95]

The course of the campaign seemed only to intensify sectional division. "Every day adds to the probability of Lincoln's election," wrote a South Carolinian as the Republicans swept the early fall local elections in the North. Stumping the country North and South, Yancey repeatedly endorsed Breckinridge. At Memphis he announced, "The country, my friends, has for many years been alarmed for its fate under this government." It was time to "be *men* in the hour that tries men's souls." At Albany, New York, he warned, "Do not destroy our self respect; do us not that injustice, which, when done to a worm, it turns on the heel that crushes it; which, when done to the brute creation, gives evidence of some sort of resistance." The announced secessionist, perhaps hoping to enhance his position when the hour of decision arrived, seemed to be looking to a continuation of the Union and the Democratic party. Davis, meanwhile, forced by circumstances into a common cause with Yancey, conducted a vigorous campaign in Mississippi for Breckinridge. But when questioners forced Davis to address the consequences of a Republican victory specifically, a correspondent detected "a vagueness, an uncertainty, a disconnection and a wandering. . . ." His continual avoidance, even when pressed, revealed that in his heart Davis still hoped for a compromise of some sort.[96]

Even before the presidential election the restless Carolinians were ready to move. In October Governor William H. Gist sent letters to the other Southern governors in yet another

95. Strode, *Jefferson Davis* 1: 358.
96. Isaac W. Hayne to Hammond, September 15, 1860, Hammond Papers; DuBose, *Life and Times of Yancey*, pp. 491–92, 514; *Natchez Courier*, October 10, 1860, quoted in Rainwater, *Mississippi, 1856–1861*, p. 153. The best study of the 1860 campaign in the South is still Ollinger Crenshaw, *The Slave States in the Presidential Election of 1860* (Baltimore: Johns Hopkins Press, 1945). For additional instances of Davis's waffling on the question of responses to a Republican victory, see Rowland, ed., *Jefferson Davis* 4: 540–41, and *Jackson Mississippian*, October 10, 1860.

effort to secure cooperative action, but the responses were not encouraging. The executives of North Carolina and Louisiana replied that their states would not secede merely over Lincoln's election. Governor Brown of Georgia predicted his constituents "would determine to wait for an overt act," while Governor A. B. Moore of Alabama said his state would "not secede alone—but if two or more States will cooperate with her she will secede with them. . . ." M. S. Perry of Florida was unwilling to lead but promised to follow. Only John J. Pettus of Mississippi eschewed talk of following. He planned to summon his legislature, call a Southern convention, and push for secession.[97]

But Gist's mind was already made up. He called the South Carolina legislature to meet on November 5, the day before election day, to name electors and take whatever action "deemed advisable for the safety and protection of the State." On October 25, before Gist could possibly have received any replies from the other governors, he met at Hammond's home with most of the state's congressional delegation, and there the conspirators decided to move for secession immediately if Lincoln was elected. Eleven days later, misrepresenting what the governors had communicated, Gist informed the legislature that "the indications from many of the Southern States justify the conclusion that the secession of South Carolina will be immediately followed, if not adopted simultaneously by them, and ultimately by the entire South."[98]

At the same time old Edmund Ruffin was writing to Yancey that secession must soon come. "You are the man for this

97. William H. Gist to Thomas O. Moore, October 5, 1860; John W. Ellis to Gist, October 18, 1860; Thomas O. Moore to Gist, October 26, 1860; A. B. Moore to Gist, October 25, 1860; Joseph E. Brown to Gist, October 31, 1860; M. S. Perry to Gist, November 9, 1860; John J. Pettus to Gist, October 26, 1860, all William H. Gist Papers, South Caroliniana Library.

98. *Charleston Mercury*, October 16, 1860; J. D. Ashmore to Miles, November 20, 1860, Miles Papers; Nichols, *Disruption of American Democracy*, pp. 366–67; William H. Gist Message No. 1 to the Members of the Senate and House of Representatives, November 5, 1860, Gist Papers.

great work," wrote the Virginian. "Will you be the [Patrick] Henry for this impending contest? Move in at once, and I would stake my life on the venture that your success will not be less complete and glorious than that of your great example."[99]

The news of Lincoln's election set the machinery in motion. The old regular Democrats were stunned and paralyzed and, as their campaign rhetoric had shown, they had no policy to offer. Once again—and for the last time—the Yanceyites claimed to have the answers and exposed the vulnerability of the regulars. "Let us act for ourselves," cried Yancey to a large Montgomery audience the day after Lincoln's election. With momentum now in their favor the secessionists pressed forward. Spurred by a false rumor that Toombs had resigned from the Senate, the South Carolina legislature called a state convention to meet in December, and Senators Chesnut and Hammond thereupon resigned their Senate seats.[100]

Elsewhere the shocking reality of pledges now demanding fulfillment caused Governor Moore of Alabama—following the legislature's instructions passed after the Brown raid—to call a special convention election for December 24. Pettus summoned his legislature to meet in Jackson on November 26. Soon after assembling, it scheduled an election of state convention delegates for December 20. Florida's legislature likewise decided to hold a state convention, scheduling election of its delegates for December 24. The Georgia legislature slated its convention election for January 2, and Louisiana's Governor Moore set his state's vote for January 7. The states that had walked out of the Democratic convention were now seriously preparing to walk out of the Union.[101]

99. Edmund Ruffin to Yancey, October 29, 1860, quoted in Craven, *Edmund Ruffin*, pp. 190–91.

100. DuBose, *Life and Times of Yancey*, p. 539; Channing, *Crisis of Fear*, pp. 241–51; Schultz, *Nationalism and Sectionalism*, pp. 227–33; Charles E. Cauthen, "South Carolina's Decision to Lead the Secession Movement," *North Carolina Historical Review* 18 (1941): 360–72.

101. Denman, *Secession Movement in Alabama*, pp. 92–93; Rainwater, *Mississippi, 1856–1861*, pp. 180–93; Dorothy Dodd, "The Secession Movement in

As at Charleston, however, the upper and border states stood fast. The legislatures of Alabama and Mississippi sent commissioners to these states to persuade them of the need to unite. A propaganda barrage soon followed, as the well oiled Southern nationalist press flooded the South with secession pamphlets. Manipulation of opinion, that old Democratic technique, was now wrecking the Union. "Read and send to your neighbor," boldly demanded the front page of an incendiary pamphlet entitled *The South Alone Should Govern the South*, which called for a *"Southern Confederacy . . .* as one of the independent nations of the earth." Another pamphleteer declared that the South was now united by "a common *danger* and a common *interest.*" Still another reminded that "it is suicidal to defer action until the commission of . . . 'an overt act'. . . . The Republican party['s] . . . success is a declaration of war against our property and the supremacy of the white race. The election of Lincoln is *the* overt act." Chesnut stumped Carolina, Yancey Alabama. Everywhere the cry resounded: the election of Lincoln was a violation of constitutional rights. His administration would be "just such a government as incited the Revolutionary patriots to throw off British allegiance. They [too] denied the right of a foreign people, of the same blood, language, religion and government, to legislate for them." In that statement was the essence of Southern nationalism, intended to unite the slaveholding states.[102]

As the course of the lower South moved inexorably toward secession, the National Democrats, believing that a res-

Florida, 1850–1861," *Florida Historical Quarterly* 12 (1933): 3–24; Thomas Conn Bryan, "The Secession of Georgia," *Georgia Historical Quarterly* 31 (1947): 89–111; Willie M. Caskey, *Secession and Restoration of Louisiana* (Baton Rouge: Louisiana State University Press, 1938), pp. 20–40; Nichols, *Disruption of American Democracy*, pp. 376–77; Potter, *Impending Crisis*, pp. 490–96.

102. Denman, *Secession Movement in Alabama*, pp. 111–12; Rainwater, *Mississippi, 1856–1861*, pp. 166–67; John Townsend, *The South Alone Should Govern the South And African Slavery Should Be Controlled By Those Only Who Are Friendly To It* (n.p., 1860), p. 16; Henry King Bergwyn, *Considerations Relative to a Southern Confederacy* (Raleigh: Standard Office, 1860), p. 15; J. L. M. Curry, *Perils and Duties of the South* (n.p., 1860), p. 10; DuBose, *Life and Times of Yancey*, pp. 540, 550–51.

toration of the Union was more likely to be obtained in Washington than on the stump in their respective states, grappled with possible policies of reconciliation. Later Davis remembered well how he had labored for the Union to the point of exhaustion. He had conferred with Buchanan, urging him not to reinforce federal forts in the South. He had urged the Senate to work out a solution at once, but a compromise committee, which included Davis and Toombs, was not appointed until December 20. The councils of Union were divided and unsure, those of secession aggressive and confident.[103]

Yet the outward confidence belied an inner dread. More than a few secessionists feared that in Washington "some wretched compromise may be patched up" which "would arrest the current of Southern feeling. . . ." Swift action was still needed. On December 6 South Carolina elected its convention. A week later seven senators and twenty-three representatives from nine different states announced that "we are satisfied the honor, safety, and independence of the Southern people are to be found only in a Southern Confederacy—a result to be obtained only by separate State secession." The South Carolina convention assembled on December 17 and, on the day the Senate committee was finally appointed, December 20, voted unanimously to secede from the Union. The convention immediately sent forth commissioners to the other states to discuss the formation of a Southern nation. At the same time the Alabama and Mississippi commissioners were working in other states to effect separate state action under the guise of cooperation.[104]

The Senate committee meanwhile groped for a solution. It considered and rejected—the Republicans on Lincoln's instructions voting against any compromise—proposals ranging from a dual executive to an extension of the Missouri Compro-

103. Nichols, *Disruption of American Democracy*, pp. 402–14.
104. L. Q. Washington to James Chesnut, December 10, 1860, Letters to James Chesnut, South Carolina Historical Society, Charleston; Potter, *Impending Crisis*, pp. 492–93; Dumond, *Secession Movement*, pp. 134–36.

mise line. The Southern press grew more and more pro-secession as the news spread that Alabama, Mississippi, Georgia, and Florida had elected pro-secession delegates—eager, young, and wealthy men. As the senators from those states realized what was happening and tried to grab control of the situation, the work of the committee was doomed. At that moment Jefferson Davis and the rest realized that compromise was impossible. Jointly they sent to their respective conventions a series of resolutions advocating immediate secession and urging the formation of a Southern government.[105]

With Republican intransigence on one side and imminent secession on the other, Davis, with great reluctance, supported secession in alliance with his Southern colleagues. But, his body exhausted, his will thwarted, his heart sick, he could not quite bring himself to affix his name alongside that of his archenemy Brown on a separate telegram prepared by Brown for the Mississippi convention that joined a flood of messages now cascading southward from Washington. "Hope is dead," it announced. "Secede at once."[106]

And so, on this cold January 21, Davis prepared to leave the Senate. Before departing home for the Capitol he unburdened his sorrow in two letters. To a friend from his youthful days at West Point Davis wrote of the "necessity to transfer our domestic institutions from hostile to friendly hands." To Franklin Pierce, with whom he had worked so well and so closely, Davis sadly announced that "the hour is at hand which closes my connection with the United States, the independence and Union for which my Father bled and in the service of which I have sought to emulate the example he set. . . ." Again he wrote of the "necessity" of secession and the "horror"

105. Nichols, *Disruption of American Democracy*, pp. 440–45; Donald E. Reynolds, *Editors Make War: Southern Newspapers in the Secession Crisis* (Nashville: Vanderbilt University Press, 1970), *passim;* Wooster, *Secession Conventions*, pp. 34–35, 61–62, 76, 93–96.
106. *The War of the Rebellion: A Compilation of the Official Records of the Union and Confederate Armies*, ser. 1 (Washington: Government Printing Office, 1880), 1: 443–44; ser. 4, 1: 29.

of civil war. Then, laying aside his pen, he left for the Senate.[107]

Mallory and Yulee of Florida, Clay and Fitzpatrick of Alabama spoke before Davis. Though still weak, the Mississippian arose, his posture erect, his eyes peering dejectedly from the hollows of an exhausted face. Mississippi, by seceding, he stated, knowingly "surrenders all the benefits (and they are known to be many), deprives herself of the advantages (they are known to be great), severs all the ties of affection (and they are close and enduring) which have bound her to the Union." But the act was a necessity, and Davis explicitly stated the reasons for his state's withdrawal:

> Then, Senators, we recur to the compact which binds us together; we recur to the principles upon which our Government was founded; and when you deny them, and when you deny to us the right to withdraw from a Government which thus perverted threatens to be destructive of our rights, we but tread in the path of our fathers when we proclaim our independence and take the hazard.[108]

Bidding farewell, Davis strode from the silent chamber for the last time. Finally he, too, had adopted the idea of a Southern nation as a means of restoring fundamental, constitutional rights. As Davis regretfully left Washington and the Union, that idea was beginning to take shape as a separate Southern government.

Six weeks after his dramatic, emotional departure from the Senate, Jefferson Davis, president-elect of the Confederate States of America, arrived in Montgomery, Alabama, to assume office. He was greeted by Yancey, prophet of the day of deliverance, keeper of the flame of Southern nationalism. At

107. Davis to George W. Jones, January 20, 1861, quoted in Strode, *Jefferson Davis* 1: 386–87; Davis to Franklin Pierce, January 20, 1861, in Strode, ed., *Jefferson Davis: Private Letters, 1823–1889* (New York: Harcourt, Brace, and World, 1966), p. 22.

108. Rowland, ed., *Jefferson Davis* 5: 42, 44.

last the two men who had composed the political counterpoint of the turbulent 1850's stood shoulder to shoulder. For at least a fleeting moment, their dissonance had become harmony. Doubters needed only to hear Yancey introduce Davis to the welcoming Montgomery throng. "The man and the hour," he joyously proclaimed, "have met."[109]

109. Dodd, *Jefferson Davis*, p. 223.

Conclusion

The American nation created in 1787 was based upon a loose consensus on the principles for which the American Revolution had been fought. Giving greater precision to the definition of those principles after 1787—and especially after 1830—was a central problem of American history in the years preceding the Civil War. The quest involved systems of economy, modes of literature, methods of education, practices of religion, and the conduct of politics. It raised basic, inevitable questions that demanded answers. And the tensions it produced caused a civil war.

Proceeding from a general commitment to the Constitution and a set of shared experiences in the Revolution, Americans moved in different directions in attempting to work out their national purpose. Their disputes became subsumed by the slavery issue, out of which sprang sectional ideological configurations that eventually proved incompatible. Each side, North and South, claimed to be remaining true to constitutional values and accused the other of violating constitutional principles. In the South the grievances developed out of a growing sense of minority, inferior sectional status and took an increasingly extreme form. By 1860 a large number of Southerners were convinced that their interests and those of the nation at large—which was controlled by a Northern and seemingly hostile majority—were incompatible. They decided that only in a separate Southern nation could they preserve their constitutional rights. Reluctantly they broke up the Union they had long cherished and served.

Nothing would be more indicative of the Southerners' real purpose than the constitution adopted by the Confederate States of America and the officials chosen to govern the new nation. The constitution would be a virtual duplicate of the United States Constitution. The government would consist of moderate men who had mostly been Unionists until the secession winter. Jefferson Davis would be named president, Alexander H. Stephens—the Georgia Unionist—vice president. Members of the cabinet would include Robert Toombs of Georgia, Stephen Mallory of Florida, Judah P. Benjamin of Louisiana, and that longtime opponent of expansion, John H. Reagan of Texas. Of the Southern nationalists, Rhett, Ruffin, Hammond, and Simms would play no role in the new government. Yancey would receive a diplomatic assignment and be sent out of the country. DeBow would fill a minor post in Louisiana. The Confederacy, created to restore constitutional rights, would have as its purpose conservation and not innovation. In such a government radicals could have no place.

Four years of bloody conflict would follow, and the Union would be restored. During the Civil War both the Union and the Confederate governments would be forced by events to move toward greater organization and increased centralization in the economy, the military, constitutional interpretations, the conduct of foreign policy, and the structure of politics.

By 1865, with the South defeated and slavery destroyed, the United States would be dramatically changed. The exigencies of wartime would lay the foundation for a modern political state. A new set of shared experiences would become the basis for a dynamic, integrated, more truly national America. Ironically, Southern nationalists, taking a strong states' rights position, had heightened the tensions that would produce a new American nationalist ideology. Southerners had forced Americans to think about their nature and purpose as a nation and hastened the emergence of a modern, integrated, and more genuinely United States.

APPENDIX I

SOUTHERN POPULATION DATA, 1790–1860

Source: Jesse T. Carpenter, *The South as a Conscious Minority, 1789–1861: A Study in Political Thought* (New York: New York University Press, 1930), pp. 22–23; Donald B. Dodd and Wynelle S. Dodd, eds., *Historical Statistics of the South, 1790–1970* (University, Ala.: University of Alabama Press, 1973).

Table 1: Total White Population, 1790–1860

Year	North	South	Southern Percentage of Total
1790	1,900,616	1,271,390	40.1
1800	2,602,881	1,693,449	39.4
1810	3,653,308	2,192,686	37.5
1820	5,034,220	2,809,963	35.8
1830	6,871,302	3,633,195	34.6
1840	9,557,063	4,601,893	32.5
1850	13,330,650	6,184,477	31.7
1860	18,825,075	8,036,699	29.9

Southern states are those south of and including Maryland, Kentucky, and Missouri.

Table 2: Distribution of Seats in the House of Representatives, 1790–1860

Year	North	South	Southern Percentage of Total
1789	35	30	46
1790	59	47	44
1800	77	65	46
1810	105	81	43
1820	123	90	42
1830	142	100	41
1840	141	91	39
1850	147	90	38
1860	163	85	35

Table 3: Rate of Population Growth in Selected Southern States

Years	Virginia	South Carolina	Alabama	Mississippi
1790–1800	16.7	38.8	—	—
1800–1810	8.7	20.1	623.7	311.9
1810–1820	6.9	21.1	1313.9	141.0
1820–1830	11.3	15.6	142.0	81.1
1830–1840	−1.8	2.3	90.9	175.0
1840–1850	9.2	12.5	30.6	61.5
1850–1860	9.0	5.3	25.0	30.5

Table 4: Relationship of White to Black Population in Selected Southern States, 1790–1860 (in thousands)

Year	S.C. White/Black	Va. White/Black	Miss. White/Black	Tenn. White/Black
1790	140/108	442/305	—	31/3
1800	196/149	514/365	4/3	91/13
1810	214/200	551/423	16/14	215/45
1820	237/265	603/462	42/33	339/82
1830	257/323	694/517	70/66	535/146
1840	259/335	740/498	179/196	640/188
1850	274/393	894/526	295/310	756/245
1860	291/412	1047/548	353/437	826/283

APPENDIX II
South Carolina During the Nullification Era

Source: William W. Freehling, *Prelude to Civil War: The Nullification Controversy in South Carolina, 1816–1836* (New York: Harper and Row, 1965), p. 8.

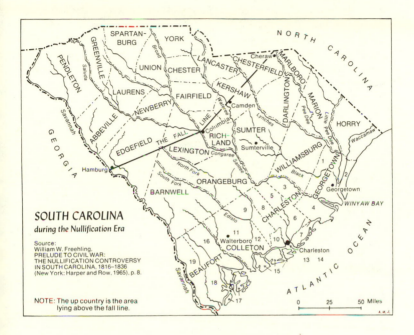

SOUTH CAROLINA
during the Nullification Era

Source:
William W. Freehling,
PRELUDE TO CIVIL WAR:
THE NULLIFICATION CONTROVERSY
IN SOUTH CAROLINA, 1816–1836
(New York: Harper and Row, 1965), p. 8.

NOTE: The up country is the area
lying above the fall line.

1. Prince George Winyaw Parish
2. All Saints Parish
3. St. Stephen's Parish
4. St. James Santee Parish
5. St. John's Berkley Parish
6. St. Thomas-St. Dennis Parish
7. Christ Church Parish
8. St. James Goose Creek Parish
9. St. George Dorchester Parish
10. St. Andrew's Parish

11. St. Bartholemew's Parish
12. St. Paul's Parish
13. St. Philip's Parish
14. St. Michael's Parish
15. St. John's Colleton Parish
16. Prince William's Parish
17. St. Helena Parish
18. St. Luke's Parish
19. St. Peter's Parish

Note: The upcountry is the area lying above the fall line.

APPENDIX III

Leadership Groups in the Nullification Crisis

Sources: Dumas Malone, *Public Life of Thomas Cooper, 1783–1839* (New Haven: Yale University Press, 1926); William W. Freehling, *Prelude to Civil War: The Nullification Controversy in South Carolina, 1816–1836* (New York: Harper and Row, 1965); John B. O'Neall, *Biographical Sketches of the Bench and Bar of South Carolina*, 2 vols. (Charleston: S. G. Courtenay, 1859); *Cyclopedia of Eminent and Representative Men of the Carolinas of the Nineteenth Century*, 2 vols. (Madison, Wis.: Brant and Fuller, 1892); Edwin L. Green, *George McDuffie* (Columbia: The State Co., 1936); Laura A. White, *Robert Barnwell Rhett: Father of Secession* (New York: Appleton–Century–Crofts, 1931).

Table 1: Seven South Carolina Southern Nationalist Leaders during Nullification

Name	Age in 1832	Residence
Thomas Cooper	73	Columbia
Warren Davis	39	Pendleton
James Hamilton	46	Charleston
E. W. Johnston	—	Columbia
George McDuffie	42	Pendleton
Francis Pickens	27	Edgefield
Robert B. Rhett	32	Beaufort

Table 2: Ten South Carolina Unionist Leaders during Nullification

Name	Age in 1832	Residence
Langdon Cheves	56	Charleston
William Drayton	56	Charleston
William Elliott	44	Charleston
Daniel Huger	53	Charleston
Benjamin F. Hunt	40	Charleston
Hugh S. Legaré	35	Charleston

Occupation	Education	Political Experience
Educator	England	Pa. Judiciary, 1804–10
Law–Planter	?	Congress, 1827–35
Law–Planter	?	Congress, 1822–29, Gov. 1830
Editor	?	None
Law–Planter	S.C. Col.	St. Leg., 1818–20, Cong. 1834
Law–Planter	S.C. Col.	St. Leg., 1832–34
Law–Planter	none	St. Leg., 1826–32

Occupation	Education	Political Experience
Law–Planter	Prep.	St. Leg., 1802–10, Cong., 1810–15
Lawyer	England	Cong., 1825–33
Planter	Harvard	St. Leg., 1817–32
Law–Planter	Princeton	St. Leg., 1804–19, 1830–31
Law	Harvard	St. Leg., 1818–32
Law–Writer	S.C. Col.	St. Leg., 1820–30

Table 2 (continued)

Name	Age in 1832	Residence
Henry Middleton	62	Charleston
Benjamin F. Perry	27	Greenville
James L. Petigru	43	Charleston
Joel Poinsett	53	Charleston

Table 3: Ten Calhounite Nullifiers during the Nullification Crisis

Name	Age in 1832	Residence
Robert Barnwell	31	Beaufort
A. P. Butler	36	Edgefield
John C. Calhoun	50	Abbeville
James H. Hammond	25	Columbia
William Harper	42	Charleston
Robert Y. Hayne	41	Charleston
Stephen D. Miller	45	Summerville
Henry L. Pinckney	38	Charleston
William C. Preston	40	Columbia
Robert J. Turnbull	57	Charleston

Occupation	Education	Political Experience
Planter	England	St. Leg., 1802–10, Gov., 1812; Cong., 1815–19; Min. to Russia, 1820–30
Law–Editor	Prep.	None
Lawyer	S.C. Col.	S.C. Atty. Gen., 1822–30
Pol/Diplomat	England	St. Leg., 1816–20, Cong., 1821–25, Min. to Mexico, 1825–29

Occupation	Education	Political Experience
Law–Planter	Harvard	St. Leg., 1826–28, Cong., 1829–33
Law–Planter	S.C. Col.	St. Sen., 1824–33
Politician	Yale	Cong., 1811–17, Cabinet, 1817–25, Vice Pres., 1825–32
Law–Editor	S.C. Col.	None
Law–Planter	S.C. Col.	U.S. Sen., 1826, St. Leg., 1827–28
Law–Planter	Prep.	St. Leg., 1814–18, S.C. Atty. Gen., 1818–22, U.S. Sen., 1823–32, Gov. S.C., 1832–34
Law–Planter	S.C. Col.	Cong., 1817–19, St. Sen., 1822–28, Gov. S.C., 1828–30, U.S. Sen., 1830–33
Law–Publisher	S.C. Col.	St. Leg., 1816–32
Law–Planter	S.C. Col.	St. Leg., 1828–34
Planter	England	None

APPENDIX IV

ATTITUDE AND SUBJECT OF ARTICLES
IN THE *Southern Literary Messenger*, 1848–61

Table 1: Summary of Articles, 1848–61

Total Articles	Year	Southern Sectional	Southern National	Politics	**Subjects Lit.
43	1848	0	0	0	14
50	1849	0	0	0	27
34	1850	0	0	0	14
31	1851	3	0	2	16
37	1852	2	0	0	14
28	1853	1	0	0	16
34	1854	4	0	3	14
35	1855	1	0	1	15
27	1856	5	0	0	15
25	1857	5	0	1	8
25	1858	4	0	0	9
30	1859	2	0	0	13
31	1860	5	0	3	17
23	1861	0	5	4	12

Table 2: Distribution of Southern Sectionalist Articles by Subject**

1851—Politics 2, Travel
1852—Economy, Agriculture
1853—Literature
1854—Politics 2, History 2
1855—Economy
1856—Slavery 2, Education 2, Literature

** Only the most recurrent subjects are listed.

| of Articles | | | **Subjects of Articles | | |
Hist.	Educ.	Travel	Relig.	Slav.	Sci.
9	0	5	0	0	1
6	1	3	0	0	1
8	1	2	0	0	1
4	2	1	3	0	0
3	1	6	3	0	0
2	1	4	1	0	0
2	0	3	1	0	1
2	1	5	0	0	0
2	2	1	0	2	0
4	1	6	4	1	0
5	2	2	0	2	0
9	1	2	0	0	0
6	1	2	0	0	1
1	0	0	1	0	2

1857—History 2, Politics, Slavery, Education
1858—Slavery 2, History, Economy
1859—Literature 2
1860—Politics 3, Literature 2
1861—Politics 4, Literature 1

APPENDIX V

SOUTHERN EDUCATION AND RELIGION DATA TO 1860

Source: Donald G. Tewksbury, *The Founding of American Colleges and Universities Before the Civil War* (New York: Arno Press, 1969), pp. 211–20; *Seventh Census of the United States: 1850* (Washington: Robert Armstrong, Public Printer, 1853), *passim*.

Table 1: Church colleges and State Universities and Year of Founding

State	State University (Year Founded)	Baptist College (Year Founded)
Alabama	(1819)	Howard (1841)
Arkansas	—	—
Florida	—	—
Georgia	(1785)	Mercer (1837)
Kentucky	—	Georgetown (1829)
Louisiana	(1848)	—
Maryland	—	—
Mississippi	(1844)	Miss. College (1830)
North Carolina	(1789)	Wake Forest (1838)
South Carolina	(1801)	Furman (1850)
Tennessee	(1794)	Union (1842)
		Carson–Newman (1851)
Texas		Baylor (1845)
Virginia	(1816)	Richmond (1840)

Methodist College *(Year Founded)*	*Presbyterian College* *(Year Founded)*
Southern (1856)	—
—	—
—	—
Emory (1836)	Oglethorpe (1835)
Wesleyan (1836)	
Lagrange (1847)	
—	Centre (1819)
Centenary (1825)	—
—	—
—	—
Trinity (1852)	Davidson (1838)
Wofford (1851)	Erskine (1850)
—	Tusculum (1794)
	Maryville (1842)
	Cumberland (1843)
	Bethel (1850)
—	Austin (1849)
	Hampden–Sydney (1783)
Randolph–Macon (1830)	
Emory and Henry (1839)	

Table 2: Percentage of Southern Population Belonging to Major Religious Denominations in 1850

State	Baptist	Methodist	Presbyterian	Episcopal	Catholic
Alabama	43.2	38.4	13.3	1.5	1.2
Arkansas	30.8	42.7	17.8	0.6	2.6
Florida	26.6	44.5	13.1	8.4	4.1
Georgia	50.9	37.8	6.5	1.5	0.7
Kentucky	43.5	24.9	14.8	1.1	3.6
Louisiana	15.2	30.3	8.7	4.8	34.5
Maryland	4.2	47.9	5.9	15.8	8.2
Mississippi	38.7	41.1	16.4	1.5	1.1
N. Carolina	35.2	38.7	11.0	2.7	0.2
S. Carolina	36.0	35.9	14.7	6.3	1.3
Tennessee	31.2	39.8	21.6	1.2	0.2
Texas	16.8	51.9	13.1	1.6	10.6
Virginia	28.9	37.8	12.1	9.3	0.9
All South	34.6	37.4	12.9	4.4	2.5

Percentages were computed by dividing the total number of "sittings" (i.e., church accommodations) by the number of members of each denomination in each state. The figures above do not account for those citizens who, when asked by the census taker, responded that they belonged to no church.

APPENDIX VI

Methodology

Part One: Who Were the First Southern Nationalists?

My method of drawing up the list of men who became Southern nationalists during the Nullification crisis was, if anything, too cautious. I began by listing from the three standard authors on Nullification—Boucher, Freehling, and Houston—the names of every South Carolinian to whom either secessionist sympathies or secessionist rhetoric were attributed before 1833. I supplemented this list with names obtained during the course of primary research at a number of Southern libraries. I next attempted to locate and read every available statement that the men on my list made during the years 1828 to 1833. From this research I quickly narrowed down my list. Anyone for whom I could locate no hard evidence of Southern nationalist sympathies I eliminated summarily.

Some of the omissions may seem curious. Hayne, for example, is not included, nor is Turnbull. Yet neither of these men advocated a Southern nation. Though Turnbull did mention secession and even a Southern confederacy, he viewed secession as a means of preserving the Union, a Southern confederacy as a union of the Southern states within the existing Union.

Other omissions, which would have buttressed my argument, I made reluctantly. William C. Preston, A. P. Butler, and James H. Hammond—all upcountry Nullifiers—were parvenu planters. But I have found no evidence that they actually supported secession at this time, much less any proof that by 1833 they were Southern nationalists. There is the additional strange case of James Chesnut of upcountry Camden, a man who also fit the pattern of Southern nationalists and who in 1831 actually remarked in a letter to his local paper that

"a Southern Confederacy, consisting of the cotton growing
states, presents the surest hope & best prospect of success.
. . ."* Yet I excluded him from my final list because in the
1832 election he ran on the Union ticket.

For the information on the Southern nationalists to have
any meaning, however, there must be a "check group" of
Union and Calhounite leaders against which to compare the
data on the Southern nationalists. Accordingly, I drew up lists
of leaders of both groups. This information, presented in Appendix III, Tables 2 and 3, shows the sharp differences between the Southern nationalist leaders on the one hand and the
Calhounites and Unionists on the other.

If anything, then, my list of Southern nationalists is too
conservatively drawn. I do believe, however, that it makes a
number of strong suggestions about the origins of Southern nationalism.

Part Two: Content Analysis

In performing the content analysis of the *Southern Literary
Messenger* for this chapter, I selected at random four issues for
each year from 1848 through 1861. The selection was not ca-
pricious but according to a set pattern of three-year cycles. For
1848 I chose the issues of March, June, September, and December; for 1849 those of January, April, July, and October;
for 1850 those of February, May, August, and November; and
so on through the 1850's. For 1861 I chose January, February,
and March, since by April Virginia had seceded and war had
begun.

After selecting the issues, I read every original prose contribution. The *Messenger* had two, sometimes three, sections:
original prose and poetry, book notices, and, periodically, an
"Editor's Table" of correspondence, gossip, and miscellaneous
news. After reading a selection, I categorized it and eventually

---

* Chesnut–Miller–Manning Papers, South Carolina Historical Society,
Charleston.

arrived at a series of categories, according to subject, in which each article could be placed. Politics I defined as any article dealing in a partisan way with one or more political issues; those articles that dealt exclusively with slavery (some from economic, some from political, some from historical perspectives), I placed in a separate category of slavery. Literature included works of original prose (most of them quite awful), criticism, and occasional essays. The other categories—education, travel, religion, science—are self-explanatory. Those subjects that seemed to come up infrequently I relegated to a "miscellaneous" category, and I have not listed them in Appendix IV.

The tone of an article was of greatest importance. An article classified "Southern sectional" had at least a mention of the South in a nonbelligerent, Unionist way. Works of fiction set in Virginia were not so defined; works of fiction set in Virginia that emphasized the peculiarly Southern aspects of Virginia life were. An article was classified "Southern national" only when it advocated disruption of the Union and the founding of a Southern nation. There were no such instances until 1861.

ESSAY ON SOURCES

It would be impossible and not particularly useful merely to list the sources consulted in the preparation of this study. I have chosen instead to let my footnotes stand as my bibliography. I have stated when necessary in my footnotes the particular value of various sources, and I have tried to indicate both my own assessment of their strength or weakness and their relationship to my own view of a subject. In the following essay I will discuss only my most important sources and only those sources not evaluated in the footnotes.

PRIMARY SOURCES

Manuscripts

The historian of the antebellum South is fortunate that so much manuscript material remains preserved in Southern libraries. The value of manuscripts to this study was generally to reveal what Southerners were thinking privately about sectional events. These views sometimes differed from their public posture. As a result, manuscripts were a vital source.

Probably the most extensive holdings are in the Southern Historical Collection at the University of North Carolina, Chapel Hill. The Daniel M. Barringer Papers are especially useful on both matters of North Carolina politics from 1835 to 1860 and issues of diplomacy with Spain during the Taylor administration. The John Francis Hamtramck Claiborne Papers contain much material on antebellum politics in Mississippi, particularly the involvement of Quitman. The collection of Franklin Harper Elmore Papers, though small, has valuable materials on the machinations of the Calhounites in the 1840's.

The Benjamin F. Perry Papers contain the political observations of an influential upcountry South Carolina Unionist editor. Exceedingly valuable are the Christopher Gustavus Memminger Papers, which give in minute detail the events of that South Carolinian's Virginia mission in 1860. Probably the most important collection, however, is the well scoured William Porcher Miles Papers, which convey in an inimitable, personal way the feelings of a South Carolina congressman and his numerous correspondents of all political persuasions during the late 1850's. A small collection of political letters written by James L. Orr in the 1850's exists in the Orr–Patterson Papers. A large and rich collection of Quitman Family Papers contains much of value on that Mississippian's turbulent career, though it is stronger in the area of family and plantation life than in politics. The Robert Barnwell Rhett Papers are not voluminous but are nevertheless helpful on political issues from 1835 to 1852. The Benjamin Cudworth Yancey Papers, the best manuscript source on the Yanceys, is somewhat disappointing and has nothing for the years after 1852.

On issues of religion and education, three collections, in particular, are helpful. The John S. Martin Papers reveal the attitudes of a Southern Methodist at the time of the 1844 schism. The James Hervey Otey Papers and Diary and the Leonidas Polk Papers are important sources on the founding of Sewanee.

The Manuscript Division of the Library of Congress also contains several very important collections. Among these, the extensive James Henry Hammond Papers, covering almost every detail of his public and private life, are highly valuable. Less rich but still helpful are the Jefferson Davis Papers, many of which have been published in Rowland's volume, cited below, covering politicial events of the 1850's. The diary and papers of Edmund Ruffin are a very important source on agriculture and politics. The William Cabell Rives Papers contain useful material on antebellum Virginia politics. I found the small collection of Whitemarsh Seabrook Papers to be of great use, especially concerning the South Carolina involvement in the reaction to the 1850 Compromise.

The South Caroliniana Library at the University of South Carolina, Columbia, is also strong in manuscripts dealing with antebellum politics. The James Orr Papers, the Milledge Luke Bonham Papers, and a small collection of R. B. Rhett Papers contain information on politics in the 1850's. The William Henry Gist Papers are not extensive, but they include Governor Gist's correspondence with other Southern governors in the fall of 1860. There is some helpful material on South Carolina politics in the Hammond, Bryan, Cumming Family Papers and the James Louis Petigru Papers. A small collection of James Henry Hammond Papers supplements the material at the Library of Congress. The Williams–Chesnut–Manning Papers are valuable on the relationship of state and national politics throughout the antebellum period. In addition to information on the Nullification crisis, the Robert Y. Hayne Papers are useful on railroad development and other attempts at economic diversification in South Carolina during the 1830's.

The South Caroliniana Library also holds manuscripts dealing with antebellum cultural and intellectual developments. A collection of unpublished William Gilmore Simms letters contains insights on the problems of Southern literature, as do the Hugh Swinton Legaré Papers. The Francis Lieber Collection and the William C. Preston Papers reveal much about life at South Carolina College, and the James Henley Thornwell Papers deal both with literature and education and, in great detail, with religion. Useful in sketching in the background of social and cultural life in antebellum South Carolina are Maxcy Gregg's "Sporting Journal" and a small collection of H. Greenleaf letters.

In the Perkins Library at Duke University there exist several essential manuscript collections. On political developments, see the Armistead Burt Papers, the Lawrence M. Keitt Papers, the James Henry Hammond Letters, and the Francis W. Pickens Papers—small collections but valuable. The Clement C. Clay Papers are rich in material on antebellum Alabama politics, and the Campbell Family Papers are equally helpful on Virginia. The James D. B. DeBow Papers, the only manuscript source for this important figure, are especially strong on the fortunes of *DeBow's Review* but are, on the whole, disappointing. The Paul Hamilton Hayne Papers contain insights on the Charleston literary scene in the late 1850's, and the exceedingly useful George Frederick Holmes Papers and Letter Book are vital on matters of literature and education. There are also typed copies of all of Tucker's letters to Hammond taken from the Hammond Papers at the Library of Congress.

The collections in the Louisiana State University Library, Baton Rouge, are strongest on the filibustering incidents of the 1850's, though there is also material on other topics as well. The Quitman Family Papers and the Pierre Soulé Papers are especially helpful on Southern involvement in Cuba and Latin America. The Southern Filibusters Collection, though pretentiously titled, is small and a bit disappointing. Of the other holdings, most rewarding are the (Samuel A.) Cartwright Family Papers, which cover that active and peculiar man; the (Lemuel Parker) Conner Papers, which deal with Louisiana plantation and political life; and the (Joseph B.) Stratton Papers, which reveal the vicissitudes of life as a frontier minister.

In the Mississippi Department of Archives and History, Jackson, are three collections of inestimable value. The J. F. H. Claiborne Collection covers the years 1807–61 and touches upon virtually every aspect of life not only in Mississippi but also in the South. It is especially strong on politics. The Henry Hughes Papers, Diary, and Scrapbook vividly reveal the transformation of Southern proslavery thought from paternalism to racism. In the Quitman Correspondence and Papers, covering the years 1842–55, are numerous useful items on state politics and Cuban filibustering.

There are several important collections in the Alabama Department of Archives and History, Montgomery. Alabama politics receives great attention in the William Phineas Browne Papers, the Bolling Hall Papers, and the John J. Seibels Papers. The Benjamin F. Perry Papers include material on South Carolina politics. The William Lowndes Yancey Papers are not very helpful, containing a number of printed speeches, and little revealing correspondence. For literature, the Alexander B. Meek Papers are valuable.

Other libraries have smaller but still helpful holdings. By far the most useful material at the University of Georgia in Athens is the voluminous collection of Howell Cobb Papers, which may be consulted only with permission of the Cobb family. The Thomas R. R. Cobb Papers and the Joseph E. Brown Papers, also at Georgia, are both helpful for developments during the secession winter. At the South Carolina Historical Society, Charleston, the Chesnut–Miller–Manning Papers and the Letters to James Chesnut are valuable on politics in South Carolina in the 1850's. The newly acquired items in the Robert Barnwell Rhett Collection add to the information on politics a number of letters revealing the touching, private side of that abrasive fire-eater. The Quitman Papers in the Houghton Library at Harvard University are essential to a full understanding of Southern designs on Cuba.

Statistical Sources

These sources are of greatest value in defining the background against which the events I have discussed took place. The most important statistical sources are the *Statistical View of the Population of the United States From 1790 to 1830 Inclusive* (Washington: Duff Green, 1835); United States Bureau of the Census, *Historical Statistics of the United States, Colonial Times to 1957* (Washington: Government Printing Office, 1960); United States Census Office, *Seventh Census, 1850* (Washington: Robert Armstrong, 1853); and Donald B. and Wynelle S. Dodd, *Historical Statistics of the South, 1790–1970* (University, Ala.: University of Alabama Press, 1973). The *Tribune Almanac* contains complete election returns from 1838 through the rest of the antebellum period. Lewis C. Gray, *History of Agriculture in the Southern States to 1860*, 2 vols. (Washington: Carnegie Institute, 1933) has valuable tables on Southern agricultural progress.

Official Documents

The single most important official document is the *Congressional Globe*, where changing ideas on the relationship between the South and the Union are readily observed. For the Nullification period, Herman V. Ames, ed., *State Documents on Federal Relations: The States and the United States* (Philadelphia: University of Pennsylvania Press, 1900–1906) and *State Papers on Nullification: Including the Public Acts of the Convention of the People of South Carolina, Assembled at Columbia, November 19, 1832 and March 11, 1833* (Boston: Dutton and Wentworth, 1834) are indispensable. On the breakup of the churches, especially valuable is *The Debates of the General Conference of the Methodist Episcopal Church, May, 1844* (New York: L. J. McIndoe, Printer, 1845).

Newspapers

A study of Southern nationalism would not be possible without a heavy reliance on newspapers. The extensive collection of newspapers at the Library of Congress is generally satisfactory, but I consulted selected holdings at other libraries as well. A complete run of the most significant organ of Southern nationalism, the *Charleston Mercury*, is not available in any one location, but a visit to the Library of Congress, the Boston Athenaeum, and the South Caroliniana Library permits a thorough study of the *Mercury*. Though no other paper matched the extremism and consistency of the *Mercury*, the Democratic press throughout the South was an accurate barometer of secession feeling. I found the following especially useful and reasonably complete: the *New Orleans Delta*, the *Jackson Mississippian*, the *Arkansas Gazette and Democrat* (Little Rock), the *Augusta (Georgia) Constitutionalist*, and the *Richmond Enquirer*.

Periodicals

Periodical literature from the antebellum South, despite a usually short life span, is a vital source. *DeBow's Review* is exceedingly important for all manner of economic information as well as essays on a wide variety of subjects. Edmund Ruffin's *Farmer's Register* and the Agricultural Society's *American Cotton Planter* are important for agricultural developments. Of the many literary journals, the most valuable are the *Southern Literary Messenger*, the *Southern Quarterly Review*, and the short-lived *Magnolia* and *Russell's Magazine*. All these journals are available in Widener Library, Harvard University.

Pamphlets

The pamphlet was an important vehicle of political expression in the antebellum South. An emotional stump speech often reached a wider audience when it was later published in pamphlet form. Fortunately for the historian of the antebellum South, a large number of these pamphlets have been preserved. Most of the pamphlets cited in this study may be found in one of four sizable collections. The Rare Book Room in the library of the University of North Carolina, Chapel Hill, has a Southern Pamphlet Collection of great size and value. The Toner Collection in the Rare Book Room of the Library of Congress, supplemented by items available through the Main Reading Room, is equally useful. Widener Library at Harvard has a surprisingly good collection of pamphlets, and at the Boston Athenaeum may be found several pamphlets not available elsewhere. In addition, the South Caroliniana Library has a collection of rare broadsides. Especially interesting is the *Address, 1851, of the Southern Rights Association of the University of Virginia to the Young Men of the South*, which reveals a strong tendency toward Southern nationalism.

Published Correspondence

The published correspondence, speeches, and other writings of many leading Southerners are indispensable. Among the most helpful collections for political affairs are: Richard K. Crallé, ed., *The Works of John C. Calhoun*, 6 vols. (New York: D. Appleton and Co., 1855); J. Franklin Jameson, ed., *Correspondence of John C. Calhoun*, Annual Report of the American Historical Association for the Year 1899, 2 (Washington: Government Printing Office, 1900); and *Selections From the Letters and Speeches of the Hon. James H. Hammond of South Carolina* (New York: J. F. Trow and Co., 1866). These three collections show the unique concerns of South Carolinians for Southern welfare. For the view of three leading Georgians, see U. B. Phillips, ed., *The Correspondence of Robert Toombs, Alexander H. Stephens, and Howell Cobb*, Annual Report of the American Historical Association, 2 (Washington: Government Printing Office, 1913). Useful for political events in Mississippi and the South is J. F. H. Claiborne, *Life and Correspondence of John A. Quitman*, 2 vols. (New York: Harper and Brothers, 1860) and Dunbar Rowland, ed., *Jefferson Davis, Constitutionalist: His Letters, Papers, and Speeches*, 10 vols. (New York: J. J. Little and Ives Co., 1923). On developments both literary and political, Mary C. Simms Oliphant et al., eds., *The Letters of William Gilmore Simms*, 5 vols. (Columbia: University of South Carolina Press, 1952–56) is first-rate.

Memoirs

Personal reminiscences are very helpful in understanding men and events more clearly. John Herbert Claiborne, *Seventy-Five Years in Old Virginia* (New York and Washington: Neale Publishing Co., 1904) is valuable for the Old Dominion. For South Carolina, two very interesting sources are Judge John B. O'Neall, *Biographical Sketches of the Bench and Bar of South Carolina*, 2 vols. (Charleston: S. G. Courtenay, 1859) and Benjamin F. Perry, *Reminiscences of Public Men* (Philadelphia: J. D. Avil and Co., 1883). Valuable for a vivid account of life in frontier

Mississippi are Reuben Davis, *Recollections of Mississippi and Mississippians* (Cambridge: Riverside Press, 1890) and Henry S. Foote, *Casket of Reminiscences* (reprint ed., New York: Negro Universities Press, 1968). William Walker, *The War in Nicaragua* (Mobile: S. H. Goetzel and Co., 1859) is a necessary though biased source on Southern involvement in Central America.

Other Published Primary Materials

A number of proslavery publications proved useful. *The Pro-Slavery Argument* . . . (Charleston: Walker, Richards, and Co., 1852) contains essays by Dew, Harper, Hammond, and Simms. E. N. Elliott, ed., *Cotton is King and Proslavery Arguments* (Augusta, Ga.: Pritchard, Abbott, and Loomis, 1860) is an enormous anthology of proslavery writing. Also valuable are George Fitzhugh's two books, *Sociology for the South, or the Failure of Free Society* (Richmond: A. Morris, 1854) and *Cannibals All! or Slaves Without Masters*, ed. C. Vann Woodward, John Harvard Library (Cambridge: Harvard University Press, 1960), which introduce and refine comparisons between Northern and Southern labor systems. Daniel R. Hundley, *Social Relations in Our Southern States* (New York: Henry B. Price, 1860) is an excellent defense of social mobility (for whites) in the antebellum South. William A. Smith, *Lectures on the Philosophy and Practice of Slavery* (Nashville: Stevenson and Evans, 1856) reveals the thinking of an ardently Southern Methodist minister. An abolitionist's account of the denominational schisms is William Goodell, *Slavery and Anti-Slavery: A History of the Great Struggle in Both Hemispheres* (New York: W. Harned, 1852). William K. Scarborough, ed., *The Diary of Edmund Ruffin: Volume 1, Toward Independence, October, 1856–April, 1861* (Baton Rouge: Louisiana State University Press, 1972) is exceedingly valuable on the politics of secession.

SECONDARY SOURCES

This portion of the bibliography is necessarily very selective. I have annotated secondary sources in my footnotes whenever it seemed necessary either to show a work's relationship to my own study or to delineate this study's position on matters of current historiographical debate. In the following paragraphs I will discuss only those secondary works that have been of greatest value to me in preparing this volume.

General Studies in Southern History

Of the large number of works that fall into this category, several were instrumental in helping me to shape my thinking. Still useful though dated is Samuel Chiles Mitchell, ed., *The South in the Building of the Nation*, 10 vols. (Richmond: Southern Historical Publishing Co., 1909). More recent and considerably more helpful are two volumes in the History of the South series edited by Wendell H. Stephenson and E. Merton Coulter. Charles S. Sydnor, *The Development of Southern Sectionalism, 1819–1848* (Baton Rouge: Louisiana State University Press, 1948) is especially strong on politics, though Sydnor's discussion of social and cultural developments is also excellent. Avery O. Craven, *The Growth of Southern Nationalism, 1848–1861* (Baton Rouge: Louisiana State University Press, 1953) gives a thorough treatment of political events but neglects expressions of Southern nationalism in other areas, concluding that there really was no such thing as Southern nationalism. Craven's *The Coming of the Civil War* (revised ed., Chicago: University of Chicago Press, 1966) goes considerably further in analyzing comprehensively the many elements of Southern nationalistic thinking.

Three books by Clement Eaton are also of great merit and utility. *A History of the Old South*, 2nd ed. (New York: Macmillan Co., 1966) is a solid, textbook account of the antebellum years. *The Freedom-of-Thought Struggle in the Old South* (revised ed., New York: Harper and Row, 1964) emphasizes the

Southern abandonment of Enlightenment rationalism in favor of religious and sectional orthodoxy. *The Mind of the Old South* (revised ed., Baton Rouge: Louisiana State University Press, 1967) is a brilliant series of biographical essays on which I have relied heavily.

Of the numerous studies of Southern particularism, Lester B. Baltimore, "Southern Nationalists and Southern Nationalism, 1850–1870" (Ph.D. diss., University of Missouri, 1968) studies eight leading Southern nationalists in various fields but does not link them to a common ideology. Jesse T. Carpenter, *The South as a Conscious Minority, 1789–1861: A Study in Political Thought* (New York: New York University Press, 1930) is a fine study of the growing Southern feeling of shared minority status. David M. Potter, *The South and the Sectional Conflict* (Baton Rouge: Louisiana State University Press, 1968) is a penetrating collection of essays by one of the greatest Southern historians. "The Historian's Use of Nationalism and Vice Versa" is the most pertinent essay contained therein.

The Roots of Southern Nationalism

Southerners' perception of their distinctiveness existed from the earliest days of the American nation, a topic well discussed in John Richard Alden, *The First South* (Baton Rouge: Louisiana State University Press, 1961). The best and fullest discussion of the Virginia and Kentucky resolutions is Adrienne Koch and Harry Ammon, "The Virginia and Kentucky Resolutions: An Episode in Jefferson's and Madison's Defense of Civil Liberties," *William and Mary Quarterly*, 3rd series, 5 (1948): 145–76. Glover Moore, *The Missouri Controversy, 1819–1821* (Lexington: University of Kentucky Press, 1953) is a complete and authoritative account, especially strong on Southern reactions to the Compromise.

Southern nationalism was born during the Nullification crisis. By far the best account of that dispute is William W. Freehling, *Prelude to Civil War: The Nullification Controversy in South Carolina, 1816–1836* (New York: Harper and Row,

1965), which overstates Southern guilt over slavery but which correctly and skillfully demonstrates the volatile relationship between abolition attack and economic decline. James M. Banner, Jr., "The Problem of South Carolina," in *The Hofstadter Aegis,* ed. Stanley M. Elkins and Eric McKitrick (New York: Alfred A. Knopf, 1974), pp. 60–93 is a concise and elegant survey of the distinctive features of the Palmetto State.

Several biographies of leading Nullifiers are also of great value, especially Dumas Malone, *The Public Life of Thomas Cooper, 1783–1839* (New Haven: Yale University Press, 1926) and Laura A. White, *Robert Barnwell Rhett: Father of Secession* (New York: Appleton–Century–Crofts, 1931). The two best biographies of Calhoun are Margaret Coit, *John C. Calhoun: American Portrait* (Boston: Houghton, Mifflin, and Co., 1951) and the magisterial Charles M. Wiltse, *John C. Calhoun* (New York: Russell and Russell, 1944–51).

The Proslavery Argument

The most recent and stimulating studies of slavery have come from the eloquent pen of Eugene D. Genovese. His first book, *The Political Economy of Slavery: Studies in the Economy and Society of the Slave South* (New York: Vintage Books, paperback ed., 1967), promulgates the thesis that the antebellum South was a seigneurial society in which a dominant planter class maintained political and social hegemony. *The World the Slaveholders Made* (New York: Pantheon Books, 1969) modifies the earlier argument and includes an incisive essay on George Fitzhugh as one of the first critics of capitalism. *Roll, Jordan, Roll: The World the Slaves Made* (New York: Pantheon Books, 1974) examines slave culture. Taken together, these books provide the most comprehensive—though Marxist—view of slavery that now exists. They are invaluable. An equally provocative interpretation that challenges the Genovese position is Robert W. Fogel and Stanley Engerman, *Time on the Cross: The Economics of American Negro Slavery,* 2 vols. (Boston: Little, Brown, and Co., 1974).

On the development of the proslavery argument there have been numerous works. William S. Jenkins, *Pro-Slavery Thought in the Old South* (Chapel Hill: University of North Carolina Press, 1935) remains the best survey. Two provocative articles offer opposing explanations of the emergence of the argument. Ralph Morrow, "The Proslavery Argument Revisited," *Mississippi Valley Historical Review* 48 (1961): 79–94 emphasizes planter guilt. David Donald, "The Proslavery Argument Reconsidered," *Journal of Southern History* 37 (1971): 3–18 argues that the slavery defense was a means of reestablishing order in the midst of rapid social and economic change. The history and durability of racial attitudes is the central theme of both George Fredrickson, *The Black Image in the White Mind: The Debate on Afro-American Character and Destiny, 1817–1914* (New York: Harper and Row, 1971) and William Stanton, *The Leopard's Spots: Scientific Attitudes Toward Race in America, 1815–1859* (Chicago: University of Chicago Press, 1960), both of which have been of great assistance. Alison H. G. Freehling, "Drift Toward Dissolution: The Virginia Slavery Debate of 1831–1832" (Ph.D. diss., University of Michigan, 1974) is a fresh and controversial interpretation of the context of the Dew essay, which argues that Dew was an advocate of tariffs and internal improvements and his essay a forward-looking, optimistic disquisition.

The most useful biographies of proslavery theorists are Stephen S. Mansfield, "Thomas Roderick Dew: Defender of the Southern Faith" (Ph.D. diss., University of Virginia, 1968); Elizabeth Merritt, *James Henry Hammond, 1807–1864* (Baltimore: Johns Hopkins University Press, 1923); Robert C. Tucker, "James H. Hammond, South Carolinian" (Ph.D. diss., University of North Carolina, 1958); Harvey Wish, *George Fitzhugh: Propagandist of the Old South* (Baton Rouge: Louisiana State University Press, 1943); and C. Vann Woodward's excellent introduction to the previously cited John Harvard Library edition of Fitzhugh's *Cannibals All!*

Commercial Conventions

Many Southerners viewed commerce as the way to economic self-sufficiency. Robert R. Russel, *Economic Aspects of Southern Sectionalism, 1840–1861* (Urbana: University of Illinois Press, 1932) is still an essential work on this subject. Of the several general surveys of the commercial conventions—a subject that deserves a fresh look—the best is Herbert Wender, *Southern Commercial Conventions, 1837–1859*, Johns Hopkins Studies in Historical and Political Science, series 48, no. 4 (Baltimore: Johns Hopkins University Press, 1930). Otis C. Skipper, *J. D. B. DeBow, Magazinist of the Old South* (Athens: University of Georgia Press, 1958) is a full biography of DeBow, although Robert F. Durden, "J. D. B. DeBow: Convolutions of a Slavery Expansionist," *Journal of Southern History* 17 (1951): 441–61 is more analytical. Diffee William Standard, *"DeBow's Review, 1846–1880: A Magazine of Southern Opinion"* (Ph.D. diss., University of North Carolina, 1970) is a solid study of that journal.

But agriculture remained the foundation of Southern distinctiveness. The Southern agricultural revolution receives extensive treatment in two studies by Avery O. Craven. *Soil Exhaustion as a Factor in the Agricultural History of Virginia and Maryland, 1606–1860*, University of Illinois Studies in the Social Sciences, vol. 13 (1925) emphasizes the exhaustive nature of the tobacco economy, while *Edmund Ruffin, Southerner: A Study in Secession* (New York: D. Appleton Co., 1932) is a fine study not only of that cranky Southern nationalist but also of agriculture as a basis of Southern nationalism. On the cotton planters' conventions see two extremely helpful works by Weymouth Jordan, "Cotton Planters' Conventions in the Old South," *Journal of Southern History* 19 (1953): 318–35 and *Rebels in the Making: Planters' Conventions and Southern Propaganda*, Confederate Centennial Studies, no. 7, ed. William Stanley Hoole (Tuscaloosa, Ala.: Confederate Publishing Co., 1958). The best general study of the campaign to reopen the African slave trade is Ronald T. Takaki, *A Pro-Slavery Crusade: The Ag-*

itation to Reopen the African Slave Trade (New York: Free Press, 1971), which includes a composite study of the supporters of reopening.

Literature

Several general studies of Southern literature are very helpful. Jay B. Hubbell, *The South in American Literature, 1607–1900* (Durham: Duke University Press, 1954) is an authoritative study of both major and minor literary figures. Hubbell's "Literary Nationalism in the Old South," in *American Studies in Honor of William K. Boyd*, ed. David Kelly Jackson (Durham: Duke University Press, 1940), pp. 175–220 is the only account of an important and neglected topic. Benjamin T. Spencer, *The Quest for Nationality: An American Literary Campaign* (Syracuse: Syracuse University Press, 1957) places Southern writers in the mainstream of the quest for a distinctive national literature. William R. Taylor, *Cavalier and Yankee: The Old South and the American National Character* (New York: Harper and Row, paperback ed., 1961) traces the evolution of the Cavalier–Yankee antithesis in literature. Drew Gilpin Faust, *A Sacred Circle* (Baltimore: Johns Hopkins University Press, 1978) offers a close and penetrating analysis of the dilemma of Southern intellectuals during the antebellum period.

Agriculture—and, more particularly, the plantation—became after 1832 a central theme in Southern literature. Francis Pendleton Gaines, *The Southern Plantation: A Study in the Development and Accuracy of a Tradition* (New York: Columbia University Press, 1924) examines the plantation myth. Dorse H. Hagler, "The Agrarian Theme in Southern History to 1860" (Ph.D. diss., University of Missouri, 1968) is also of some aid.

Among the biographies of literary figures, several are of outstanding merit. The most useful studies of Simms are Jon L. Wakelyn, *The Politics of a Literary Man: William Gilmore Simms*, Contributions in American Studies, no. 5 (Westport, Conn.: Greenwood Press, 1973), which emphasizes Simm's

political activities, and the controversial article by John W.
Higham, "The Changing Loyalties of William Gilmore
Simms," *Journal of Southern History* 9 (1943): 210–23. A good
analysis of Simm's conflicting loyalties is John C. Guilds, Jr.,
"Simms's Views on National and Sectional Literature,
1825–1845," *North Carolina Historical Review* 34 (1957):
393–410. John Donald Wade, *Augustus Baldwin Longstreet: A
Study in the Development of Culture in the South* (New York: Mac-
millan Co., 1924) is a thorough study of Longstreet's move-
ment from conservative critic of frontier excesses to Southern
nationalist. Two valuable studies of Tucker are Robert J.
Brugger, "A Secessionist Persuasion: The Mind and Heart of
Beverley Tucker of Virginia" (Ph.D. diss., Johns Hopkins
University, 1974), a psychobiography, and Gerald Lee Wil-
son, "Nathaniel Beverley Tucker, 'Aristocratic Paternalist':
The Search for Order and Stability in the Ante-Bellum South"
(Ph.D. diss., University of North Carolina, 1973).

Education and Religion

The simultaneous growth of religious and sectional orthodoxy
has never been comprehensively examined. Several important
works in religious history now make such a study possible.
Among the many important general surveys, three stand out in
excellence. Sydney Ahlstrom, *A Religious History of the American People* (New Haven: Yale University Press, 1972) is a recent, rich study. Walter P. Posey, *Frontier Mission: A History of
Religion West of the Southern Appalachians to 1861* (Lexington:
University of Kentucky Press, 1966) is a lively account of the
vicissitudes of the denominations on the frontier. Though old,
William Warren Sweet, *The Story of Religions in America* (New
York: Harper and Brothers, 1930) is still useful on the schisms
over slavery.

Every denomination now has a very good general history.
Ernest T. Thompson, *The Presbyterians in the South*, 3 vols.
(Richmond: John Knox Press, 1963) and C. Bruce Staiger,
"Abolitionism and the Presbyterian Schism of 1837–1838,"

Mississippi Valley Historical Review 26 (1949): 395–413 are fine studies of the problems of the antebellum Presbyterian church. William Wright Barnes, *The Southern Baptist Convention, 1845–1953* (Nashville: Boardman Press, 1954) and Mary B. Putnam, *The Baptists and Slavery* (Ann Arbor: University of Michigan Press, 1913) are adequate studies of the Baptist schism. The best studies of the Methodist breakup are Donald G. Mathews, *Slavery and Methodism: A Chapter in American Morality, 1780–1845* (Princeton: Princeton University Press, 1965); John Nelson Norwood, *The Schism in the Methodist Episcopal Church, 1844: A Study of Slavery and Ecclesiastical Politics* (Alfred, N.Y.: Alfred Press, 1923); and Lewis M. Purifoy, "The Methodist Episcopal Church, South, and Slavery" (Ph.D. diss., University of North Carolina, 1965).

Southern education has also received considerable study. Edgar W. Knight, *Public Education in the South* (Boston: Ginn and Co., 1922) is helpful, but Donald G. Tewksbury, *The Founding of American Colleges and Universities Before the Civil War* (New York: Arno Press, 1969) is more recent and comprehensive. Albea Godbold, *The Church College of the Old South* (Durham: Duke University Press, 1944) surveys the denominational institutions and presents impressive research; it is an invaluable study. A competent survey of Southern educational nationalism is John S. Ezell, "A Southern Education for Southrons," *Journal of Southern History* 17 (1951): 304–27, which includes some interesting statistics on where Southerners sent their sons to college. Among the most valuable institutional studies are Alma Foerster, "The State University in the Old South" (Ph.D. diss., Duke University, 1939); Allen Cabaniss, *The University of Mississippi: Its First Hundred Years* (Hattiesburg, Miss.: University and College Press of Mississippi, 1971); and Arthur B. Chitty, Jr., *Reconstruction at Sewanee* (Sewanee, Tenn.: University Press, 1954).

Several biographies are also quite helpful. Neal C. Gillespie, *The Collapse of Orthodoxy: The Intellectual Ordeal of George Frederick Holmes* (Charlottesville: University of Virginia Press, 1972) is an excellent and incisive examination of Holmes's life and thought. Frank Freidel, *Francis Lieber, Nineteenth Century Liberal* (Baton Rouge: Louisiana State University Press, 1947) is an outstanding study of a lonely, brilliant educator in intellectually moribund South Carolina. William M. Polk, *Leonidas Polk, Bishop and General*, 2 vols. (New York: Longmans, Green, and Co., 1915), though adulatory and uncritical, contains some important correspondence.

Manifest Destiny

The general concept of Manifest Destiny has received extensive and stimulating treatment. Albert K. Weinberg, *Manifest Destiny* (Baltimore: Johns Hopkins Press, 1935) is an attack on American expansionism both historical and contemporary. Frederick Merk, *Manifest Destiny and Mission in American History* (New York, Alfred A. Knopf, 1963) stresses the popularity of expansionism while Merk's *Slavery and the Annexation of Texas* (New York: Alfred A. Knopf, 1971) is suspicious of Southern expansionist desires. Robert E. May, *The Southern Dream of a Caribbean Empire, 1854–1861* (Baton Rouge: Louisiana State University Press, 1973) is a valuable and exhaustive study of Southern designs in Latin America on which I have relied heavily. An interesting article on the motivations behind Southern expansionism is C. Stanley Urban, "The Ideology of Southern Imperialism: New Orleans and the Caribbean, 1845–1860," *Louisiana Historical Quarterly* 39 (1956): 48–73, which argues that intentions changed from benevolence to outright racist imperialism between 1850 and 1860.

A number of studies on specific Southern moves in the Caribbean are of great merit. On Cuba, Basil Rauch, *American Interest in Cuba, 1848–1855* (New York: Columbia University Press, 1948) is thorough and generally reliable as a survey. Robert G. Caldwell, *The Lopez Expeditions to Cuba, 1848–1851* (Princeton: Princeton University Press, 1915) is old but still useful. Arthur F. Corwin, *Spain and the Abolition of Slavery in Cuba, 1817–1886* (Austin: University of Texas Press, 1967) deals competently with a central concern of Southern expansionists. Ray F. Broussard, "Governor John A. Quitman and the Lopez Expeditions of 1851–1852," *Journal of Mississippi History* 28 (1966): 103–20 and C. Stanley Urban, "The Abortive Quitman Filibustering Expedition, 1853–1855," *Journal of Mississippi History* 18 (1956): 175–96 are both vital studies.

Biographies are also useful. There is no recent full-length biography of Quitman, but Claiborne's study may be supplemented by James McLendon, "John A. Quitman" (Ph.D. diss., University of Texas, 1949). Amos Aschbach Ettinger, *The Mission to Spain of Pierre Soulé, 1853–1855: A Study in the Cuban Diplomacy of the United States* (New Haven: Yale University Press, 1932) colorfully tells of Soulé's escapades in Spain, but in many ways a more penetrating sketch of Soulé is J. Preston Moore, "Pierre Soulé: Southern Expansionist and Promoter," *Journal of Southern History* 21 (1955): 203–23. Walker has been the subject of extensive study. William O. Scroggs, *Filibusters and Financiers: The Story of William Walker and His Associates* (New York: Macmillan Co., 1916) is a full and valuable study which argues Walker's Southern nationalism with great effect. Albert H. Z. Carr, *The World and William Walker* (New York: Harper and Row, 1963) is a psychobiography.

Politics and Parties

This topic has been extensively treated. Among the most valuable general studies are Arthur C. Cole, *The Whig Party in the South* (Washington: American Historical Association, 1914); Richard P. McCormick, *The Second American Party System: Party Formation in the Jacksonian Era* (New York: W. W. Norton and Co., 1966), which emphasizes the beginnings of party organizations; David M. Potter, *The Impending Crisis, 1848–1861*, New American Nation series, ed. Richard B. Morris and Henry Steele Commager (New York: Harper and Row, 1976), which elegantly places the political events of the 1850's in a broad ideological context; and Roy F. Nichols, *The Disruption of American Democracy* (New York: Macmillan Co., 1948), a superb analysis of the breakdown of the Democratic party. All these works are helpful in understanding the role of Southerners in the party system and the effect on Southern politicians of the various sectional political clashes in the antebellum years.

On specific political issues several works are of especial importance for the emphasis they place on the South. For the Wilmot Proviso, see Chaplain Morrison, *Democratic Politics and Sectionalism* (Chapel Hill: University of North Carolina Press, 1967). The impact of the Compromise of 1850 on the South is well treated in J. C. Gardner, "Winning the Lower South to the Compromise of 1850" (Ph.D. diss., Louisiana State University, 1974). On the Know-Nothing party see W. Darrell Overdyke's comprehensive study, *The Know-Nothing Party in the South* (Baton Rouge: Louisiana State University Press, 1950). The impact of the John Brown Raid is treated in Ollinger Crenshaw, "Christopher G. Memminger's Mission to Virginia, 1860," *Journal of Southern History* 8 (1942): 334–49. Crenshaw's thorough *The Slave States in the Presidential Election of 1860* (Baltimore: Johns Hopkins Press, 1945) remains unequalled.

Of the many studies of state politics of varying quality, several stand out as exemplary for their depth and insight. Among these are Henry T. Shanks, *The Secession Movement in Virginia, 1847–1861* (Richmond: Garrett and Massie, 1934); J. Carlyle Sitterson, *The Secession Movement in North Carolina*, James Sprunt Studies in History and Political Science, vol. 23 (Chapel Hill: University of North Carolina Press, 1939); Harold Schultz, *Nationalism and Sectionalism in South Carolina, 1852–1860* (Durham: Duke University Press, 1950); Horace Montgomery, *Cracker Parties* (Baton Rouge: Louisiana State University Press, 1950); Clarence P. Denman, *The Secession Movement in Alabama* (Montgomery: Alabama State Department of Archives and History, 1933); Percy L. Rainwater, *Mississippi: Storm Center of Secession, 1856–1861* (Baton Rouge: Otto Claitor, 1938); and Willie M. Caskey, *Secession and Restoration of Louisiana* (Baton Rouge: Louisiana State University Press, 1938). Of special value and extraordinary merit is Jonathan Mills Thornton, "Politics and Power in a Slave Society: Alabama, 1800–1860" (Ph.D. diss., Yale University, 1974).

Southerners' activities during the secession winter have also been exhaustively studied. Of particular usefulness are the following: Steven A. Channing, *Crisis of Fear: Secession in South Carolina* (New York: W. W. Norton and Co., 1970), which emphasizes Southern racial fears; Charles E. Cauthen, "South Carolina's Decision to Lead the Secession Movement," *North Carolina Historical Review* 17 (1941): 360–72, which explains the Palmetto State's impatience to act after so many previous failures by other states; Donald E. Reynolds, *Editors Make War: Southern Newspapers in the Secession Crisis* (Nashville: Vanderbilt University Press, 1970), which traces how press attitudes changed from the fall of 1860 to the early spring of 1861; and Ralph Wooster, *The Secession Conventions of the South* (Princeton: Princeton University Press, 1962), which contains valuable statistical data on the background of secession convention delegates.

Almost every important figure in the secession crisis has received biographical treatment. For this study the most valuable biographies were the dated but still essential William E. Dodd, *Jefferson Davis* (Philadelphia: George W. Jacobs and Company, 1907), which is yet to be superseded; Ralph B. Draughon, Jr., "William Lowndes Yancey: From Unionist to Secessionist, 1814–1852" (Ph.D. diss., University of North Carolina at Chapel Hill, 1968), which is especially strong on Yancey's early years; John Witherspoon DeBose, *The Life and Times of William Lowndes Yancey* (Birmingham: Roberts and Son, 1892), which is adulatory, delightfully biased, and occasionally insightful; and Austin Venable, "The Role of William L. Yancey in the Secession Movement" (Ph.D. diss., Vanderbilt University, 1937), which concentrates on Yancey's activities during the 1850's.

Index

Abernethy, Thomas P., 13*n*
abolitionism (*see also* proslavery argument; slavery), 24, 37, 44–45, 51–54, 56, 59, 63–64, 66–67, 69, 96, 111, 125, 129, 137, 149–51, 155–57, 160, 164, 183–200, 217–18, 232–33, 239–40, 254–61, 263, 274, 279, 281, 286, 292, 297–98, 307, 311–15, 321
Accessory Transit Company, 265–67
Adams, John, 14, 16, 18
Adams, John Quincy, 31, 33, 45
Adams, Samuel, 62–63
Adger, John B., 203*n*
African Labor Supply Association, 140
african slave trade, 75, 88, 92, 133–40, 259, 268
Agassiz, Louis, 77
agriculture, 174, 211
  science of, 40, 107–9, 131
  in seaboard south, 21, 29, 51–53

and slave labor, 46, 51
and southern economic development, 91–134, 143, 151, 170, 204, 212–13
Agricultural Association of the Planting States, 130, 132, 134
Aguero, Joachim, 247–48
Ahlstrom, Sydney, 217*n*
Alabama, 72–73, 177
  agricultural economy of, 100, 230
  and secession, 331–32
  and slavery issues, 81–82, 192, 285, 323
  on succession, 331–32
  on territorial rights, 293
Alabama Baptist Association, 184
Alabama Platform:
  1848, 285–87, 313
  1860, 323, 326
Alden, John Richard, 13*n*–14*n*
Alderman, Edwin A., 215*n*
Alexander, G. R., 84*n*
Alien and Sedition Acts, 16, 38

Allen, William, 115n
Ambler, Charles Henry, 26n–27n, 51n
American Anti-Slavery Movement, 185
American Colonization Society, 24–25
American Cotton Planter, 131, 134n
American Dictionary of the English Language, 19
American Grammar, 19
Americanism, 150, 154, 166
American literature, 141–76
American Reader, 19
American Revolution, 6, 13–15, 18, 175, 261, 331, 336
American Spelling Book, 19
Ames, Herman V., 31n, 285n
Ammon, Harry, 17n
Anderson, J. R., 128
Andrew, James O., 197–98
Aquinas, Thomas, 211
Arator, 107
Arieli, Yehoshua, 7n
Aristotle, 211
Arkansas Gazette, 126–27, 320
Atlantic Monthly, 169

Bacon, Francis, 208
Bailey, Thomas A., 228n, 252n, 259n
Bain, Richard C., 278n
Baldwin, M. A., 130, 162
Baltimore American, 11
Bank of the United States, 22
Banner, James M., 18n, 28n
Baptist denomination
    on education, 179–82, 201–202, 217
    on slavery, 178, 183–84, 188–93
Baptist, The, 190
Baptist Magazine, 189
Barnard, Frederick A. P., 207
Barnes, Gilbert H., 186n
Barnes, William W., 189n

Barney, William, 263n
Barnwell, Robert W., 182
Barringer, Daniel M., 5n–6n, 12n, 249, 250n, 318
Bascom, H. B., 200n
Batterson, Herman G., 218n
Beauchampe, 148
Bell, John, 327
Beman, Nathan, 281–82
Benjamin, Judah P., 255, 338
Benning, Henry L., 291n
Benson, Lee, 201n
Bergwyn, Henry K., 331n
Bernstein, Barton J., 135n, 139n
Berry, Henry, 52
Betts, Leonidas, 208n, 211n
Beverly, John, 107
Bible, and proslavery argument, 50, 54, 78–79, 183–84
Bickley, George, 273, 274n
Black, Edward J., 280n
Bledsoe, Albert, 87, 90, 208, 215
Blue Ridge Railroad, 222
Bluffton Movement, 64–65, 110, 113, 201, 235
Bohner, Charles H., 153n–54n
Bole, T., 280n
Bone, W. P., 207n
Border Beagles, 148
Boucher, Chauncey S., 32n
Boyce, Ker, 96, 129
Boyce, W. W., 250
Branch, J., 105n
Brashear, R. B., 74, 84
Breckinridge, John C., 326–28
Brent, Robert A., 237n
Bridges, Hal, 206n
Brinkley, Robert C., 229n
Britain:
    on abolition, 189–90, 194, 232–33, 239–40, 254–55, 259–60, 272
    in Caribbean, 239, 272
    and Cuba, 232–33, 239–40, 256
Broussard, James H., 312n

Broussard, Ray F., 245*n*, 248*n*
Brown, Albert G., 203, 205, 238, 262, 285, 311, 317, 327, 329, 333
Brown, J. Thompson, 53
Brown, John, 225–26, 272, 313, 320–24, 330
Brown, Joseph, 317, 329*n*
Browne, William P., 255*n*
Bruce, Kathleen, 128*n*
Bruce, Philip A., 215*n*
Brugger, Robert J., 161*n*
Bryan, Thomas C., 331*n*
Bryant, William Cullen, 148
Buchanan, James, 259, 262, 273, 313–14, 317, 332
Burnet, Elizabeth W., 61–62
Burt, Armistead, 68*n*

Cabaniss, Allen, 207*n*
Caldwell, Robert G., 241*n*, 243*n*, 249*n*
Calhoun, James E., 34*n*, 96*n*
Calhoun, John C., 18–19, 23, 31–37, 40–41, 44, 46, 58, 62–65, 68, 69*n*, 72, 96, 113–21, 200, 201*n*, 229–35, 239, 277–81, 283–84, 287–98, 300, 309, 324
California, 164, 242, 264
    admission in Union, 74, 235, 238–39, 243, 245, 291, 303
    and gold discovery, 265
Cannibals All!, 87–89
Capers, William, 194–96
capitalism, 166–67, 173, 214
Cappon, Lester L., 18*n*
Caribbean, and expansionism, 236, 239, 252–53, 272
Carlyle, Thomas, 86
Carpenter, Jesse T., 15*n*, 24*n*, 75*n*
Carroll, Charles, 11–12
Carruthers, William Alexander, 152
Cartwright, Samuel, 76–77, 82–83, 90, 143*n*
Caskey, Willie M., 331*n*

Cass, Lewis, 286–88
Cassels, Samuel J., 178*n*
Catholicism, 211, 250–51, 272
Cauthen, Charles E., 330*n*
Central America, and expansionism, 251, 263, 266–67, 272, 274
Central American League, 269–70
Channing, Edward T., 19, 144, 330*n*
Channing, Steven, 320–22
Charles, Joseph, 15*n*
Charleston Courier, 202
Charleston Mercury, 68, 70, 111, 118, 135, 157, 170, 201, 223, 261–63, 270, 277, 305, 310, 317, 320
Chesnut, Senator James, 3–4, 9, 36*n*, 330–31, 332*n*
Cheves, Langdon, 36
Chitty, Arthur B., Jr., 216*n*, 218*n*, 222*n*–23*n*, 225*n*
Christian Index, 180–81
church, 229
    affiliated colleges, 178–88, 202–4, 206–9
    and state, 193–98, 216–17, 220–21
Cincinnati Convention, on abolition, 194
Civil War, 5, 122, 261, 334, 336, 338
Claiborne, J. F. H., 59*n*, 169*n*, 236*n*–38*n*, 244*n*, 246*n*–47*n*, 251*n*, 259*n*, 261*n*, 267*n*, 271*n*, 280*n*, 307, 311*n*
Clapp, J. M., 170
Clarkson, Thomas, 66
    letters, 68
Clay, C. C., Jr., 84*n*, 114–15, 275*n*, 310*n*
Clay, Henry, 18–19, 114, 154, 200, 243, 277–78, 292, 299, 334
Clemens, Jeremiah, 311
Clingman, Thomas, 263
Cloud, Dr. Noah B., 131
Club de la Habana, 240
Cluskey, M. W., 238*n*
Cobb, Howell, 234*n*, 238*n*, 250*n*,

Cobb, Howell (*continued*)
    288*n*, 289, 291*n*, 301, 307,
    309, 325
Cobb, Thomas, R. R., 234*n*
Cobbs, Bishop Nicolas, 218, 223
Coit, Margaret, 32*n*–33*n*, 115*n*, 291*n*,
    298*n*
Cole, Arthur, C., 277*n*, 280*n*, 286*n*,
    288*n*, 291*n*, 293*n*, 307*n*, 312*n*
colleges, in antebellum south,
    179–83, 185, 202, 210
Collier, Gov. H. W., 130, 302
Colquitt, George W. T., 280*n*
Columbia Telescope, 40
Commerce in South (*see also* indus-
    trialization, manufacturing),
    121, 123, 91–140
Commercial Bulletin, 273
commercial conventions movement,
    91–92, 96–106, 114–19,
    126–33, 270, 308
    Augusta Convention (1837),
        96–100, 104
    Charleston convention (1854),
        131–33
    Macon convention (1839), 105–6
    Memphis convention (1845),
        114–19, 131
    Montgomery Commercial Conven-
        tion, 270, 316
    Southern Commercial Convention,
        138
    Virginia trade convention (1838),
        99–100
Compromise of 1850, 74, 81, 129,
    172, 245, 253, 255–57, 261,
    295, 297–306
Concha, José Gutiérrez de la, 259–60
Confederate States of America, 334,
    338
Congregationalists, 185, 187
Congress:
    and Alien and Sedition Acts, 16
    on California admission, 238–39,
        291
    on Cuba annexation, 240—43, 248
    on Kansas-Nebraska act, 310
    on Mexican War, 239, 289
    on Mississippi River improvement,
        116–18, 283
    on Nullification, 163
    on secession, 174
    on slavery, 63–64, 69, 74, 136–37,
        262, 324
    on Southern territorial rights, 273,
        284, 292–93, 297–301, 313,
        326–27
    on taxation, 21, 40, 42, 62, 69, 283
    on Texas annexation, 230–33
conservatives, 70
Constitution, U.S. 14–16, 18, 31, 35,
    43, 51, 62, 66, 156, 172, 199,
    231, 239, 248, 294, 297–98,
    304, 309, 323–24, 326–27
Constitutional convention:
    finance program of, 15
    sectional strife and, 15–16
Continental Army, 14
Continental Congress, 14
Cooke, Philip Pendleton, 152
Cooper, James Fenimore, 141, 150,
    182, 289*n*
Cooper, Mark A., 280*n*
Cooper, Thomas, 38–40, 45–46, 145
copyright law, 159
Corwin, Arthur F., 240, 252*n*, 257*n*
cotton gin, 28
Cotton is King, 90
cotton trade:
    and slavery, 28–31, 263
    and Southern economy, 72–73,
        93–95, 99, 103–5, 113, 123,
        230
Coulter, E. Merton, 8*n*, 179*n*
Crallé, Richard K., 35*n*, 231*n*, 235*n*,
    278*n*, 292*n*
craniology, 77
Craven, Avery O., 8*n*, 25*n*, 30*n*, 58*n*,
    107*n*–8*n*, 110*n*–11*n*, 140*n*,
    229*n*, 253*n*, 257*n*, 261*n*,

272*n*–73*n*, 286*n*, 295*n*, 297*n*,
301*n*, 310*n*, 312*n*–13*n*, 323*n*
Crenshaw, Ollinger, 274*n*–75*n*, 309*n*,
321*n*, 328*n*
Crimean War, 256, 260
Crittenden, John J., 311
crop rotation, 107
Cuba, 232, 263
and annexation in U.S., 239–40,
248–49, 254, 309–10
and slave importation, 239–40,
257, 269
Southern invasion of, 232–60
Spanish domination of, 240–41,
248–49, 257, 264
Current, Richard N., 33*n*
Curry, J. L. M., 310*n*, 331*n*
Cushing, E. H., 274*n*

Daniel, Robert N., 202*n*
Davidson, Chalmers, 115*n*
Davidson, Philip G., 17*n*
Davis, A. B., 105*n*
Davis Jefferson, 72, 84, 89, 241,
245–46, 253, 297–99, 303–4,
306, 309–10, 316–20, 323–24,
326–28, 332–35, 338
Davis, Thomas, 218
Davis, Warren, 40, 45–46, 97*n*,
100*n*, 126*n*, 145*n*
Dearing, William, 92–93, 103
DeBow, James D. B., 58, 72, 74,
79–81, 83–84, 87–89, 119–27,
131, 134, 136, 138–40,
155–57, 203, 205, 228, 327,
338
DeBow's Agricultural Journal, 124
DeBow's Review, 68, 72, 74, 88, 102*n*,
119–25, 134, 140, 143*n*,
155–56, 205, 224, 263, 272
Declaration of Independence, 11
Democratic politics, 38, 75*n*, 139,
149, 152, 161–62, 164, 175–76
and secession, 278–80, 282, 282,

284–91, 297–98, 300, 303,
306–9, 312–28, 330
and territorial balance, 231–33,
253, 258, 262, 264–68
Denman, Clarence P., 81*n*, 131*n*,
286*n*, 302*n*, 321*n*, 330*n*–31*n*
Depression:
1820's, 93–94, 103–4, 237
1830's, 22–29, 93, 106
Deschamps, Margaret B., 186*n*
Dew, Mary, 181
Dew, Thomas, 53–60, 66–67, 70–71,
74, 76, 86, 121, 209
Dew, William, 181
Dill, B. F., 256*n*
District of Columbia, 289, 292–93
Dodd, Donald B., 27*n*
Dodd, Dorothy, 330*n*–31*n*
Dodd, W. E., 56*n*, 310*n*, 334*n*
Dodd, W. F., 298*n*
Dodd, Wynelle S., 27*n*
Dodge, A. C., 114
Dodson, E. Griffith, 51*n*
Donald, David, 141*n*–42*n*
Dorman, Lewy, 302*n*, 309*n*, 311*n*,
313*n*–14*n*, 323*n*
Doubleday, C. W., 272*n*
Douglas, Stephen A., 117–18, 299*n*,
315–16, 326–27
"drapetomania," 82
Draughon, Ralph B., 281*n*
Drayton, William, 36
Dred Scott controversy, 172, 262,
315
Dubigny, Pierre, 311
DuBose, John W., 281*n*–82*n*, 285*n*,
288*n*–89*n*, 308*n*, 313*n*–14*n*,
323*n*, 328*n*, 330*n*
Duboy, Robert W., 325*n*
Duffy, John, 83*n*
Dumond, Dwight, 24*n*, 186*n*, 325*n*,
332*n*
Duvall, S. P. C., 168*n*
Duyckinck, E. A., 160*n*, 174*n*
"dysaethesia," 82

Eaton, Clement, 56*n*–57*n*, 61*n*–62*n*,
    65*n*, 161*n*, 180–81*n*, 183*n*,
    201*n*, 207*n*, 219*n*–20*n*, 223*n*,
    226*n*, 233*n*, 281*n*–83*n*, 298*n*,
    313*n*–14*n*
economic development:
    early American system of, 15,
        18–20
    in North, 91, 94–95, 110–11, 212
    in South, 91–140, 208
        and banking systems, 98, 101
        and commercial conventions,
            96–106
        seaboard states, 21, 29, 51–53,
            72, 93, 103, 229
        and slave holding, 22–30, 34, 37,
            39–40, 44–46, 52–53, 72–75,
            96, 111–13, 122–125, 132–40
        and territorial expansion, 251–52
    in Southwest, 103, 107
Edgefield Advertiser, 310
educational movement
        and religion in South, 177–83,
            202–26, 350–51
        and Southern nationalism, 7–8,
            19–20, 132, 203, 295, 308
Ekirch, Arthur A., 228
Elements of Algebra, 206
Elliott, E. N., 58*n*, 90
Elliott, Stephen, 42*n*, 216*n*–17*n*,
    218–21, 226
Elliott, William, 36
Elmore, Franklin Harper, 232*n*
Emancipation, 24–26, 28–29, 52–53,
    56, 66, 80, 111, 162, 193–94,
    240
Emerson, Ralph Waldo, 141, 145
empiricism, 208
Engerman, Stanley, 94*n*, 104*n*, 229*n*,
    251*n*
English Baptist Union, 190
Enlightenment, 76, 208
environmentalism, 76
Episcopal churches in South, 182,
    216–24

Essai sur l'inegalite des races humaines,
    83
Essay on Calcareous Manures, 108
Essay on Liberty and Slavery, 208
Essays on Domestic Industry, 114
Ettinger, Amos A., 253*n*–54*n*
Europe, revolutionary movements of,
    235, 256, 259
Ezell, John S., 178*n*, 206*n*

Farmer's Register, 108–9
Faulkner, Charles J., 52
Faunt, Joan R., 115*n*
federalism, 16–17, 18*n*
Fielder, Herbert, 319*n*
filibuster movements
    in Cuba, 248
    in Nicaragua, 264–73, 303, 309–10
Filler, Louis, 24*n*
Fillmore, Millard, 249, 299, 314
Finlay, J. B., 204*n*
Finney, Charles G., 185
Fitzhugh, George, 50, 85–90, 134,
    143, 214
Fitzpatrick, Benjamin, 309, 317, 334
Flournoy, Thomas, 311
Floyd, John B., 51, 208, 291
Foerster, Alma, 183*n*, 203*n*
Fogel, Robert W., 94*n*, 104*n*, 229*n*,
    251*n*
Foote, Henry S., 234, 246, 249, 250*n*,
    303–4
Foreign Mission Board, 188, 190–92
Fornell, Earl W., 269*n*
Foster, H. D., 293*n*–95*n*, 297*n*
Fox, Early Lee, 24*n*
Frederickson, George, 50*n*–51*n*, 83*n*
Freehling, Alison H. G., 31*n*–33*n*
Freehling, William W., 12*n*, 29*n*,
    31*n*–33*n*, 39*n*–41*n*, 44*n*–48*n*,
    57*n*, 337*n*
Freeman, Douglas, 16*n*, 241*n*
Free Missionary Society, 191–92

Free Soil party, 286
Freidel, Frank, 207*n*
Frémont, John C., 314
French Revolution, 66
frontier development, 229–30
Fugitive Slave Bill, 172, 257, 301, 309
Fuller, Richard, 191
fundamentalism, 76, 78, 181
Furman, James C., 202

Gadsden, James, 96, 99, 310
Gaines, Francis P., 153*n*
Galusha, Elon, 191
Gamble, John G., 105
Gardner, J. C., 302*n*, 305*n*
Garnett, M. R. H., 82*n*, 293–94
Garrison, William Lloyd, 4, 24, 44, 51, 59
Geertz, Clifford, 4, 14
Genius of Universal Emancipation, The, 24
Genovese, Eugene D., 50*n*, 104*n*, 129*n*, 263
George Balcombe, 76, 162
Georgia, 73, 177, 192, 195, 198
  agriculture of, 94
  on secession, 301–2, 307, 329, 333
Georgia Methodist Conference (1837), 184, 195
Georgia Platform, 302, 314
Georgia Scenes, 156
Gertrude, 163
Gholson, J. H., 52
Giddings, Joshua, 89
Gillespie, Neal C., 208*n*–11*n*
Gist, William H., 328–29
Gliddon, George R., 76, 83
Gobineau, Arthur de, 83
Godbold, Albea, 179*n*–80*n*, 183*n*, 202*n*
Goicuria, Don Domingo de, 268
Goldthwaite, George, 130
Goodell, William, 185*n*, 190*n*–92*n*, 194*n*

Goshen Baptist Association, 190
Govan, Thomas P., 105*n*
Gracchus, Caius, 25
Graebner, Norman A., 289*n*
grain production, 95, 109, 113, 123, 128, 229
Gray, Lewis C., 22*n*, 44*n*, 75*n*, 105*n*, 113*n*, 128*n*, 229*n*
Grayson, William J., 73, 87
Green, Edwin L., 39*n*–40*n*, 46*n*
Green, Fletcher, 296*n*
Green, Nathan, 207
Green, William M., 218*n*
Greene, A. L. P., 200*n*
Greenville Mountaineer, 281
Greer, James K., 294*n*
Gregg, William, 114, 132
Guilds, John C., 147*n*
Guthrie, James, 114
Guy Rivers, 148
Gwathney, Edward M., 153*n*
Gwynn, Colonel Water, 222

Hale, Will T., 115*n*
Hall, Bolling, 309*n*
Hall, James, 141–42
Hamilton, Alexander, 15
Hamilton, Holman, 299*n*
Hamilton, James, Jr., 41–42, 45–46, 105
Hammond, Benjamin, 60
Hammond, James J., 58, 60–71, 74, 77, 79, 84, 90, 109–10, 121, 122*n*, 150, 155, 163, 164*n*, 174*n*, 200–201, 229*n*, 288*n*, 295*n*, 305, 317, 327, 328*n*, 338
Harper, Chancellor William, 36, 58, 68, 71, 86, 90, 102, 121, 209
Harper's Ferry, 272, 320–24, 330
Harper's Magazine, 157
Harris, Joel C., 215*n*
Harris, Seymour E., 222*n*
Harris, Congressman S. W., 130

Harrison, William Henry, 278n
Hartford Convention, 17–18, 34–35
Harvie, Lewis E., 284
Haskins, David G., 217n–18n
Hawthorne, Nathaniel, 141, 143, 145
Hayes, Carlton J. H., 6n
Hayne, Robert Y., 12, 97, 98n, 101,
    103–4, 145n
Hearon, Cleo, 47n, 59n, 292n, 298n,
    304n
Helper, Hinton R., 84, 156–57
Hemphill, W. Edwin, 18n
Henderson, John, 242–43, 244n, 251
Henry, Patrick, 29, 63
Hill, D. H., 206
Hillard, George, 207n
Hillhouse, D. P., 105n
Hilliard, Henry W., 105n, 311
Holcombe, James P., 166
Hollis, Daniel W., 207n
Holman, C. Hugh, 147n, 165n,
Holmes, George Frederick, 64n, 66n,
    87, 149, 208–15
Home Mission Society, 188–189,
    192
Honduras, 272
Hoole, W. Stanley, 161n
Hooper, Johnson Jones, 160, 162
Hopkins, James F., 19n
Houk, George W., 231n
House of Representatives
    South's membership in (1789–
        1820), 23
    and tariff bill, 31
Houston, David F., 32n
Houston, Sam, 139, 234, 311
Howard, V. E., 255
Hubard, R. T., 73n
Hubbell, Jay B., 142n, 144n–45n,
    156n–57n, 161–64, 166n
Hudson, Randall O., 266n
Huger, Daniel, 36
Hughes, Henry, 72
Hughes, J. J., 105n
Hull, W. H., 288n

Hume, D., 208
Hunter, J. L., 105n
Hunter, R. M. T., 43, 209n, 280,
    311, 317, 322

Illinois Central Railroad, 117
Impending Crisis, The, 84, 156–57
Indigenous Races of the Earth, 83
industrialization
    in North, 91, 95, 110–11, 212, 229
    in South, 92, 95, 104, 114, 128
Industrial Resources, 123
Inge, William, 243
Ingraham, Joseph H., 74n

Jackson, Andrew, 11, 33, 43–44, 47,
    315
Jackson Mississippian, 122, 234
James, D. Clayton, 237n
Jameson, J. Franklin, 23n
Jefferson, Thomas, 13, 15–18, 34, 63,
    233
Jenkins, William S., 26n, 49n,
    52n–53n, 56n, 77n, 185n
Johannsen, Robert W., 117n
Johnson, Allen, 53n, 56n, 97n
Johnson, Donald B., 267n
Johnston, A. S., 69n
Johnston, E. W., 40, 45–46
Jones, George W., 334n
Jones, J. C., 114, 128
Jones, Joseph Seawell, 5n, 12n
Jordan, Weymouth T., 103n, 105n,
    130n–31n

Kansas-Nebraska Act, 172–73,
    256–58, 261–62, 310
Kansas warfare (1856–1857), 172, 220
Katherine Walton, 165, 167
Keitt, L. M., 275
Kennedy, John Pendleton, 141,
    152–54, 158, 165
Kentucky, 18
    and agriculture, 25
    and state rights doctrine, 16

Kentucky Resolutions, 16
Kibler, Lillian, A., 306*n*
King, Thomas Butler, 97, 291
Knight, Edward W., 179*n*, 202*n*–3*n*,
    218*n*, 221*n*
Knight, Franklin W., 240*n*
Knights of the Golden Circle (K. G.
    C.), 273–75
Know-Nothings, 311–14
Koch, Adrienne, 17*n*
Kohn, Hans, 5*n*

La Sociedad Liberatora, 247
Latin America, 7, 75, 251
Laurens, Henry, 14
La Verdad, 254
Lawson, James, 146*n*, 165*n*
League of United Southerners, 316,
    318
*Lectures on the Philosophy and Practice of
    Slavery*, 58
Lee, Richard Henry, 14
Lee, Robert E., 241
Legaré, Hugh Swinton, 36, 42*n*, 145
Leigh, Benjamin W., 26, 27*n*, 70
Lewis, Dixon, 43, 232*n*
Lewis, Letitia P., 209*n*
liberalism, 182
Liberator, 24, 44
Lieber, Francis, 7*n*, 206*n*–7*n*
Lincoln, Abraham, 273, 327, 330–32
literary nationalism, 8, 19–20, 126,
    160, 166, 169–70, 295, 308
literature (*see also* publications; *specific
    journals*)
    American, 141–76
    British, 147
    European, 144, 147
    Northeastern American, 142,
        156–60, 166–69
    Southern American, 141–76
        on Cavalier-Yankee antithesis,
            147, 152, 154, 166–67
        on frontier life, 160–62
        and mystery romance, 162–63

on plantation life, 153–54,
    166–68
and Revolutionary romance,
    165–68, 174–75
Locke, John, 208
Longfellow, Henry Wadsworth, 141,
    169
Longstreet, A. B., 156, 160, 162, 210
Lopez, Narciso, 240–43, 246–49,
    252–53, 275
Louisiana, 72, 75, 177, 203, 255
Louisiana Purchase, 23
Lowell, James Russell, 142, 145
Lumsden, F. A., 127

Madison, James, 15–17, 34
Magnolia, 149–50, 157
Malcom, Howard, 207
Mallory, Francis, 99, 334, 338
Malone, Dumas, 17*n*, 33*n*, 39*n*,
    45*n*–46*n*, 53*n*, 97*n*
"Mammonism," 86, 213
Mangum, Willie P., 278*n*
Manierre, William R., 213*n*
"Manifest Destiny," 7, 228, 230, 232,
    234, 236, 251–52, 269, 276
manufacturing in South, 104, 114,
    121, 123, 128
Marcy, William L., 253, 256
Marks, Henry S., 115*n*
Marshall, C. K., 143*n*, 204
Marshall, Chief Justice John, 52
Marshall, Thomas, 52
Martin, John S., 184*n*
Martineau, Harriet, 95*n*, 150–51, 167
Martin Faber, 148
Mason, James, 271, 322
Mason, John Y., 259, 309
Mason, W. M., 130
Mathews, Donald G., 190*n*,
    194*n*–95*n*, 197*n*, 199*n*
May, Robert E., 115*n*, 228, 240*n*,
    256*n*, 266*n*–72*n*, 275*n*
McCaine, Alexander, 199*n*

McCardell, John, 43n, 246n, 249n, 303n–04n, 310n
McColley, Robert, 49n
McCormick, Richard P., 233n
McDonald, Gov. C. J., 246
McDuffie, Goerge, 39–40, 45–47, 96, 98
McGehee, Nathan, 105n
McLaughlin, Andrew C., 14n
McLendon, James H., 237n
McLure, James S., 204n
McLure, William, 204n
McMillian, Malcolm C., 283n
McRae, J. J., 244n
Meade, Robert D., 219n
Means, John, 246–47
Meek, Alexander B., 158, 159n
Mellichampe, 148–49
Memminger, Christopher G., 98, 320–22, 324
Memphis Daily Appeal, 271
Meriwether, Robert L., 18n
Merk, Frederick, 232n
Merritt, Dixon L., 115n
Merritt, Richard L., 13n, 16n, 65n
Methodism
  on education, 179–82, 201–2, 210, 217
  on slavery, 178, 189, 193–200
Mexican War, 234–35, 237, 240, 251, 298
Mexico, 164, 263–64, 274, 283
Middleton, Henry, 36
Miles, Edwin A., 233n
Miles, William Porcher, 174n, 321n–22n, 329n
military defense, 21, 116
Miller, Stephen D., 36
Minor, Benjamin B., 171n
minority rights, 47, 155, 161
Mississippi, 75, 177, 203–4, 207
  agriculture economy of, 73, 99–100, 230
  on Nullification, 43, 59
  on secession, 246–47, 292–98
  on slavery, 72, 84, 90, 285, 324
Mississippi Convention
  on Baptist church hierarchy, 188
  on territorial rights, 296
Mississippi Free Trader, 270
Mississippi Friends of Southern Rights, 82
Missouri, 162
Missouri compromise (1819–1820), 4, 23–24, 50, 161, 227, 238, 257, 298–300, 310–11, 315, 332–33
Mitchell, Broadus, 53n, 120n
Mitchell, Samuel C., 179n, 208n
Mobile Medical Society, 77
Monroe, James, 24–25, 32
Montgomery Commercial Convention, 270, 316
Montgomery, Horace, 302n, 311n, 316, 330
Montgomery Mail, 161
Moore, A. B., 320, 329n
Moore, Glover, 23n
Moore, J. Preston, 254n, 267n–68n, 330
Moore, William O., 329n
Morehead, Charles, 311
Morton, Samuel G., 77, 80
Mott, Frank Luther, 145n, 170n–71n

Nagel, Paul C., 6n
Nashville convention, on territorial rights, 163, 296, 298, 300, 302
Natchez Fencibles, 237
national banking, formation of, 15, 19
National Baptist Anti-Slavery convention, 191
national defense, development of, 21, 32
National Democrats, 309–11, 317–19, 323

nationalism, 5–6, 18, 149–50, 152, 154, 174, 227–28, 234, 295–97
National Republicans, 277–78
Nat Turner, 51
Negroes and Negro "Slavery," 89
neutrality laws, 267, 270–71, 310
Nevins, Allan, 56*n*, 261*n*–62*n*
New England
 on abolition, 184, 196–97
 mercantile economy of, 17, 178–79
 on tariff bill, 33
New England Anti-Slavery Society, 184
Newman, A. H., 189*n*, 192*n*–93*n*
New Orleans Bee, 242
New Orleans Commercial Bulletin, 253
New Orleans Crescent, 263–64
New Orleans Delta, 135, 169, 242, 268
New Orleans Medical and Surgical Journal, 82
New Orleans Weekly Picayune, 127
New York Evangelist, 186
New York Herald, 157, 269
New York Times, 269
New York Tribune, 259
Nicaragua, and expansionism, 263–69, 271–72
Nichols, Roy F., 253*n*, 309*n*, 315*n*–19*n*, 322*n*, 324*n*, 326*n*, 329*n*, 331*n*–33*n*
Nile's Weekly Register, 19–20, 92–93
North (*see* Union)
 on abolition, 184–200, 279, 281, 292, 297–98, 307, 311–15
 on education, 205–06, 213
 industry of, 91, 95, 110–11, 212, 229
 party politics of, 156, 158, 277–335
 and religious reform, 184–87, 191–201
 and transportation revolution, 94–96, 206
North American Review, 19, 141, 158
North Carolina, 75

and education, 19
 on Nullification, 43
 on religious reform, 187
Northen, William, 115*n*
Northern Christian Examiner, 157
Northern Literary Messenger, 172–74
Norwood, John N., 194*n*, 198*n*
Nott, Josiah, 72, 77–85
nullification, 6–7, 34–48, 57, 59–62, 64, 69, 91, 94, 101, 106, 144, 148–49, 151–52, 154, 162, 182–83, 201, 237, 276, 278, 281–82, 290, 344–47
Nullification Proclamation, 43

Oaksmith, Appleton, 267
Old Dominion, 51, 56–57, 89, 93, 99, 106–7, 118–19, 161–62, 297, 322, 325
Omnibus Bill, 292–93, 299
O'Neall, John B., 39*n*
Ordinance of Nullification, 42, 44
Oregon, 232–33
Orion, 145
Orr, James L., 309, 320
Ostend Manifesto, 259, 262
O'Sullivan, John, 228
Otey, Bishop James, 216, 218, 225–26
Overdyke, W. Darrell, 312*n*–13*n*
Owen, Thomas McAdory, 115*n*, 299*n*

Palmer, Frederick A., 141*n*–42*n*
Palmerston, Viscount, 252
Parks, Edd Winfield, 159*n*
Parks, Joseph, H., 203*n*
Parrington, Vernon L., 7*n*–8*n*
Parris, Judith, 278*n*
Parsons, C. B., 200*n*
Partisan, The, 149
Partisan Leader: A Tale of the Future, The, 162

Paulding, Commodore Hiram, 270–71

Pearce, James, 271

Pendleton, P. C., 159n, 229n

Perry, B. F., 62n, 132, 281

Perry, M. S., 329

Perry, W. S., 219n

Peterson, Merrill D., 15n

Petigru, James, 36

Pettus, John J., 329–30

Pezuela, Juan de la, 257, 259

Phillips, U. B., 98n

Pickens, Francis W., 40, 45, 278

Pickens Republic, 172

Pierce, Franklin, 123, 252–54, 256–57, 262, 266–67, 309–11, 333, 334n

Pierce, G. F., 198

Pinckney, Charles, 15

Pinckney, Henry Laurens, 36–37

plantation:
  economy, 4, 22–30, 39, 51, 95
    and commercial conventions, 96–106, 126–133
    and slavery issue, 72–73
    and tariff bill, 30–48
  life, 153–54, 166–68, 219–20, 237, 239

planter's conventions, 129–31

Plan of Union (1801), 187

Poe, Edgar Allen, 158

political party systems (*see specific political parties*)
  in North, 156, 168, 277–335
  in South, 8
    and economic development, 92, 95
    and expansionism, 229–31, 251–52, 272
    and secession, 277–335

Polk, James K., 227

Polk, Leonidas, 216–22

Polk, William M., 216n–17n

Pope, Joseph D., 66n

population, and Southern influence in the Union, 25–27, 75, 178, 189, 295, 341–42

Porter, Kirk H., 267n

Portico, 20

Posey, Walter B., 181n, 184n–85n, 188n, 190n, 192n, 194n

Potter, David M., 5n, 229n, 291n, 299n, 307n, 312n, 314n, 332n

Prairie News, 271

Pratt, Daniel, 129

Pratt, Julius W., 228n

Pratt, W. H., 105n

Presbyterian denomination:
  on abolition, 184–89, 200
  on education, 179–82, 201–2
  New School of, 185–88
  Old School of, 185–88

Presidential elections:
  1844, 227, 232
  1848, 291
  1852, 255, 306
  1860, 172, 274, 315, 318, 320, 325, 327–31

Preston, John S., 247n

Preston, William C., 34–35, 152

Priest, Josiah, 78n

proslavery argument (*see also* abolition; emancipation; racism; slavery), 8, 49–50, 70–91, 95, 143, 150–51, 157, 162, 166
  Biblical view of, 50, 54, 78–79, 183–84
  ethnological view of, 78–83, 86, 89
  paternalistic view of, 50–51, 67, 69, 71–72, 75, 78, 85, 87, 95, 111, 121–22, 189, 219
  and politics, 72–90
  and racism, 50, 66–67, 69, 71–73, 75–77, 83, 87, 90, 111, 295, 308, 317
  social order view of, 54–55, 66, 71–72

Southern religious emphasis on, 183–200, 207–8, 219–20
and trade bands, 136–40
Pro-Slavery Argument, The, 71, 151
Pryor, Roger A., 139
publication(s) (*see also* literature; *specific publications*)
and circulation in Southern market, 158–59
of literary periodicals, 141–42, 144–45, 157
and publishing houses, 142, 156, 158–59
public land policies, 69
public school education, 179
Purifoy, Lewis M., 193*n*
Putnam, Mary B., 190*n*, 201*n*
Putnam's Monthly, 169

Quitman, F. Henry, 59*n*
Quitman, John A., 43, 59, 70, 114*n*, 137, 139, 236–38, 242–49, 251, 255–56, 258–62, 267, 270, 275, 279, 296, 303–4, 308, 311–12

racism, and proslavery argument, 50, 66–67, 69, 71–73, 75–77, 83–85, 87–90, 111, 295, 308, 317
railroad development (*see specific railroads*), 113–18, 121–24, 126–27, 265, 310
Rainwater, Percy L., 271*n*, 276*n*, 313*n*, 324*n*, 328*n*, 330*n*–31*n*
Ramsey, George H., 77*n*
Ranck, James B., 285*n*, 311*n*
Randolph, John, 161
Randolph-Macon Alumni Association (1884), 180–81, 207
rationalism, 76, 181, 185, 211
Rauch, Basil, 242*n*, 255*n*, 260*n*
Rawson, Donald, 238*n*

Rayback, Joseph G., 284*n*, 287*n*
Regan, John, 251, 271, 338
Reeves, James E., 192
religion (*see also* church; *specific religions*), 7, 20
and education, 177–226, 202–26, 350–51
and politics, 181–200, 208–9, 295
and government, 193–98, 216–17, 220–21
and slavery issue, 183–200
and social order in South, 210–14
Remini, Robert V., 33*n*
Republican party, and anti-slavery, 125, 133, 259, 273–74, 279, 314–15, 318–33
Reynolds, Donald E., 333*n*
Reynolds, Emily B., 115*n*
Rhett, Robert Barnwell, 39–40, 45*n*–46*n*, 60–71, 76, 132, 135, 137, 231, 235, 244, 246, 280, 290–91, 298, 300, 305–06, 317, 322, 338
Rice, Philip M., 312*n*
Richard Hurdis, 148
Richardson, James D., 253*n*
Richmond convention, on Baptist organization, 190
Richmond Enquirer, 25–26, 52*n*, 53, 74, 111, 214, 233, 258, 293, 310
Ridgely, J. V., 153*n*, 168*n*
Rives, William, C., 114*n*
Roach, Chevillette, 148
Roane, Spencer, 24
Robert, Charles Clarke, 51*n*–52*n*
Rowe, Henry K., 97*n*
Rowland, Dunbar, 309*n*, 318*n*, 322*n*, 324*n*, 327*n*–28*n*, 334*n*
Royalists, 264
Ruff, John, 184*n*
Ruffin, Edmund, 58, 87, 100, 107–13, 124, 134, 139–40, 316, 329, 330*n*, 338
Russel, Robert R., 99*n*, 138*n*

Russell's Magazine, 169
Ryan, Frank W., 170*n*

Samford, William F., 275*n*
Savannah River Baptist Association, 191
Sawyer, Samuel T., 280*n*
Schaff, Rev. Philip, 189*n*
Schlesinger, Arthur M., 278*n*, 308*n*
Schoolcraft, Henry, 141–42
Schultz, Harold, 330*n*
Science, and agriculture, 40, 107–9, 131
Scott, Orange, 194, 197
Scott, Winfield, 196, 307
Scroggs, William O., 265*n*, 268*n*–73*n*
seaboard states, Southern:
  and economic development, 21, 29, 51–53, 72, 93, 103, 229, 233–34
  and expansionism, 233–35
Seabrook, Whitemarsh, 28–29, 244, 246, 296, 303
secession, 3, 9, 157, 162–63, 174, 197, 202, 215, 218, 226
  economic issues of, 92, 110, 128–29, 135, 138–40
  and political party diversity, 277–35
  and slavery issue, 41, 46, 62, 68–69, 72, 80, 83–84, 89
  and territorial balance in Union, 235, 237, 244–48, 250, 253, 274–76
Secession Party, 305
sectionalism, 7, 9, 13–17, 20, 24, 26, 28, 48, 50, 56, 59, 64–65, 70–71, 86, 90–92, 94, 98, 103, 113, 115, 122–23, 129, 165, 172, 174–75, 277, 279, 291–92
  and educational movements, 203–6, 210, 216–18, 223, 226
  and nationalism, 143, 145, 147, 149–50, 154, 309

and religious orthodoxy in South, 182–83, 187, 197, 216–18
  in Southern literature, 143–45, 147, 149–52, 160, 168, 175
  and territorial expansion, 226–76, 262, 269–70
Senate, 134, 152, 292
  on Missouri Compromise, 22–23
  sectional balance in, 227, 230–31, 238–39, 253
  on slavery issues, 74–75, 84, 139, 327
  and tariff bill, 31, 33
"Seventh of March Speech," 296–97
Seward, William H., 89, 172–73, 261
Shafer, Boyd C., 6*n*
Shanks, Henry, 171*n*, 284*n*, 291*n*–92*n*, 301*n*, 311*n*, 321*n*–22*n*
Sharkey, Judge William, 298
Shepard, Charles B., 280*n*
Shepard, Edward M., 279*n*
Shepard, James B., 311
Shepherd, Henry E., 215*n*
Sigur, L. J., 242
Silbey, Joel A., 278*n*, 309*n*
Simms, William Gilmore, 68, 71, 141–52, 154–60, 164–68, 170–71, 174–75, 209, 229–30, 284*n*, 338
Sims, W. D., 53
Singleton, R. W., 64*n*
Sioussat, George L., 299*n*
Skipper, Otis C., 72*n*, 122*n*, 124*n*, 126*n*
slavery (*see also* abolitionism; African slave trade; emancipation; pro-slavery argument; racism), 3, 7, 24–26, 204, 206, 211, 219, 223, 279
  and cotton trade, 28–30, 39
  and tariff issue, 37, 39, 45, 56–57, 59, 62–65, 69, 275
  and territorial expansion, 237–40, 251, 266, 304, 314–17, 323

Slavery Justified, 86

Slidell, John, 72, 309, 317

Smith, George C., 198*n*

Smith, Henry N., 231*n*

Smith, Justin H., 231*n*

Smith, William A., 58, 195–96, 207, 208*n*

Snyder, Louis L., *6n*

social order in South, 29–30, 44–45, 52, 66–67, 167–69, 177, 181, 205, 210–14, 224, 229–31, 237, 269

Society in America, 150

Sociology for the South, 86–87

Somkin, Fred, *6n,* 229*n*

Sons of Temperance, 243

Soulé, Pierre, 253–54, 256, 259, 275, 267–68, 275, 309, 317

South, antebellum (*see* Southern nationalism)

    agriculture of, 5, 21–30, 51–53, 91–134, 170, 174

    early literature of, 141–176, 213

    economic development of, 21–30, 34, 37, 39–40, 44–46, 52–53, 72, 91–140

    educational movement of, 177–83, 202–26

    and industry, 92, 95, 104, 114, 128

    and manufacturing, 104, 121, 123, 128

    North incompatibility, 46, 56–67, 94, 101, 110–11, 121, 124–26, 136, 147, 152–54, 166–74, 277–335

    party politics of, 277–335

    and plantation life, 153–54, 166–68, 219–20

    political climate of, 23, 34, 92, 95, 99, 109, 161–71, 175–77, 181–83

    religious institutions of, 177–226

    social fabric of, 29–30, 44–45, 52, 66–67, 167–69, 177, 181, 205, 210–14, 224, 229–31, 237, 269

and Southwest, 115, 118

and territorial expansion, 227–76

South Carolina, 18, 20, 72, 90, 163, 203

    agricultural economy of, 22–30, 50, 94, 105, 109–10, 121, 230

    history of, 150

    on religious issues, 191, 202

    on secession, 292, 295, 300–305, 319, 328–29, 332

    on slavery, 28–29, 57–60, 100–102, 292

    on tariff issue, 11–12, 32–38, 42–44

South Carolina Exposition and Protest, 34–35, 41

Southern Advocate, 59

Southern Baptist Convention, 193

Southern Christian Advocate, 197

Southern Christian Herald, 184

Southern Commercial Convention, 138

Southern Confederacy, 81, 111, 140, 164, 246, 251, 294, 316, 331–32, 334, 338

Southern General Conference, on abolition, 195–99, 201

Southern Literary Gazette, 147–48

Southern Literary Journal, 145

Southern Literary Messenger, 19–20, 57, 71–72, 106, 118, 144–45, 150, 155, 157, 163, 166, 169, 171–72, 209, 212, 348–49

Southern nationalism, 6, 40, 92, 161, 164, 168–70, 176–215, 220

    and economic issues, 92, 94, 123–25, 133, 136–40

    and educational issues, 7–8, 19–20, 132, 178, 203, 295, 308

    ideology of, 4, 6, 8, 90, 150, 154, 175, 212, 214

    on politics, 280, 294, 308, 311, 315–17, 321, 326

    and proslavery argument, 28–30, 39, 46, 49–50, 69–91

Southern nationalism (*continued*)
on religious issues, 177–83,
202–26, 350–51
on secession, 295–97, 300–302,
331
on sectionalism, 143, 145, 226,
277, 290–91
on territorial expansion, 235–36,
245, 249–54, 275
Southern Quarterly Review, 20, 57, 102,
113, 118, 120, 129, 132, 145,
156, 164, 170–71, 209
Southern Rights party, 81, 173, 203,
207, 226, 247, 301–3, 306,
308, 310
Southern Times, 61
Southern Watchman, 190
Southwest, and expansionism, 115,
118, 227–36, 251, 271
Spain, and Cuban independence,
240–41, 248–49, 257, 259, 264
Spencer, Benjamin T., 20*n*, 142*n*
Spratt, Leonidas, 135–36
Sprunt, James, 233*n*, 301*n*
Staiger, C. Bruce, 184*n*–85*n*
Stanton, Robert L., 204
Stanton, William, 77*n*
Starke, Peter B., 324–25
state legislature
on banking, 22, 150, 278
on churches, 193–98, 216–17,
220–21
on education, 182, 202
and national government, 21,
26–29, 31, 33, 37, 41–42,
47–48
State militia, 21
State Rights party, 59, 165, 233,
245–46, 249, 303–5
states' rights, doctrine of, 16, 148,
161, 287
state universities in antebellum
South, 179, 202–3, 206–7, 217
Staudenraus, P. J., 24*n*

Stephens, Alexander, 89, 234*n*, 235,
258, 307, 338
Stephenson, Wendell H., 8*n*
Stiles, Edward H., 115*n*
Stone, William A., 260
Stover, John F., 117*n*
Stowe, Harriet Beecher, 166–67, 213
Stringfellow, Thornton, 58, 59*n*, 87,
90, 204*n*
Strode, Hudson, 298*n*, 329*n*, 334*n*
sugar plantation, 219–20, 239–41
Sumner, Charles, 142
Supreme Court, 315–16
Swallow Barn, 153–54
Swaney, Charles B., 196*n*
Sweet, William W., 184*n*, 186*n*–87*n*,
190*n*–94*n*, 196*n*–97*n*
Sydnor, Charles S., 19*n*, 177*n*, 190*n*

Tait, Charles, 50*n*
Takaki, Ronald T., 74*n*, 89*n*, 135*n*,
138*n*
Tandy, Jeanette R., 167*n*
Tappan, Arthur, 185, 257
Tappan, Lewis, 185
tariff imbroglio (1830s), 4, 7, 19,
30–48, 53, 56–57, 59, 62–65,
69, 94–96, 98, 104, 110, 162,
188, 201, 277–78, 283
Tarpley, Colin S., 313*n*
Taylor, George Rogers, 21*n*
Taylor, John, 40, 85, 107
Taylor, William R., 74*n*, 95*n*, 127*n*,
143*n*, 152*n*
Taylor, Zachary, 164, 238, 241–43,
286–92, 299, 318
Tennessee, 177, 321
territorial expansion, 8, 75, 227–76,
283–84, 286–93, 297–99
Texas, 251, 274–75
agriculture of, 73
annexation of, 201, 230–33, 256
gubernatorial campaign of 1859,
256

Thomas, David Yancy, 115*n*
Thompson, Ernest T., 186*n*
Thompson, Jacob, 244*n*
Thompson, John R., 171, 212, 213*n*
Thoreau, Henry David, 141
Thornton, Jonathan, 315*n*
Thornwell, James H., 171*n*, 185, 203*n*, 204, 206, 211*n*
Tillett, Wilbur F., 198*n*
Timrod, Henry, 156
tobacco farming, 107, 113, 229
Toombs, Robert, 130, 234*n*, 293–94, 297, 301, 307, 314, 330, 332
Towns, George W., 301
Townsend, John, 331*n*
transportation revolution, 94–102, 113–18, 265
Trent, William P., 145*n*, 165*n*, 171*n*
Triennial Convention, 188–92, 202
Troup, George, 308
Tucker, Nathaniel Beverley, 58, 59*n*, 76, 161, 287, 293, 321*n*
Turnbull, David, 239
Turnbull, Robert, 36–37
Turtt, Thomas E., 105*n*
Tuskegee (Alabama) Republican, 268, 270
Tyler, Alice F., 19*n*
Tyler, John, 209, 231, 233, 239, 248
Tyler, Samuel, 171*n*
Types of Mankind, 83

Uncle Tom's Cabin, 166, 212–13
Union (*see* North)
　and Nullification, 41–44, 62, 163
　on secession, 277–335
　on slavery issue, 37, 56, 63, 65, 81, 161, 166, 300–301
　vs. South, 46, 56–57, 94, 101, 110–11, 121, 124–26, 136, 172–74
　and Southern economy, 46, 56–57
　on tariff issues, 12, 37, 40, 56–57
　on territorial expansion, 227–76

Unionists, 36, 38–39, 42, 50, 221, 246, 255, 281, 293–94, 301–4, 311–12, 321, 338
Union Pacific Railroad, 117
Union Past and Future, The, 293
Union Theological Seminary, 186
United States Bank, 98
University of the South, 215–26
Upshur, Abel P., 26, 27*n*, 57, 70, 231–32
Urban, C. Stanley, 242*n*–43*n*, 252*n*, 255*n*, 257*n*–60, 275*n*
urbanization in South, 104

Van Buren, Martin, 33*n*, 162, 278–80, 283
Vanderbuilt, Cornelius, 265–66, 269*n*
Van Deusen, John G., 98*n*, 114*n*, 118*n*–19*n*, 126*n*, 133*n*, 137*n*, 277*n*
Van Evrie, John H., 89
Venable, Austin L., 283*n*, 313*n*–14*n*, 316*n*
Vesey, Denmark, 28
Vicksburg Weekly Sun, 276
Views and Reviews, 150
Virginia, 152–53, 161–63
　agriculture of, 21–22, 25–27, 31, 72–73, 93–94, 99–100, 106–13, 121, 230
　anti-Hamilton factions and, 15
　on Missouri Compromise, 23
　on secession, 47, 325
　on slavery issues, 50–59, 72, 85, 88–90, 284–95
　on states rights, 16
Virginia Resolutions, 16, 284–85
Virginia State Convention (1829–1830), 26–27

Waddel, John N., 210*n*
Wade, John D., 160*n*
Wadel, Moses, 179

Wakelyn, Jon L., 145*n*, 147*n*, 149*n*, 174*n*

Walker, David, 24

Walker, John W., 50*n*

Walker, Joseph, 294

Walker, Samuel, 275*n*

Walker, William, 263–73

Wallace, Daniel, 296

War of 1812, 5, 17, 32

Ware, N. A., 105*n*

Warfield, Ethelbert D., 17*n*

Warner, Hiram, 238*n*

Washington, George, 15–16

Washington, L. Q., 332*n*

Weaver, Oliver C., 203*n*

Weaver, Philip J., 255*n*

Webster-Ashburton Treaty, 138

Webster, Daniel, 118, 231, 249, 292, 296–97, 299

Webster, Noah, 17, 19

Weinberg, Albert K., 228*n*, 234*n*

Weld, Theodore D., 185

Wender, Herbert, 93*n*, 98*n*, 100*n*, 102*n*, 126*n*, 132*n*

Wesson, J. M., 169*n*

Western Monthly Magazine, 141

West Indies, and slave trade, 189, 241, 274

What Shall Be Done with the Free Negro?, 86

Wheeler, John Hill, 266

Whetstone, J. A., 130

Whig party, 232, 277–79, 282, 286–91, 293, 296–97, 299–300, 303, 307, 311–12, 318

Whiggish Constitutional Union party, 327

Whitaker, Daniel R., 170, 174–75

White, Laura A., 40*n*, 45*n*–46*n*, 62*n*–64*n*, 69*n*–70*n*, 139*n*, 280*n*, 305*n*

Whitfield, Theodore M., 51*n*

Whittier, John G., 142

Wightman, William, 197, 202

Wilde, Richard Henry, 168*n*

Williams, Jack K., 135*n*

Williams, Mary Wilhelmina, 153*n*

Wilmot, David, 235, 283

Wilmot Proviso, 111, 136, 235, 283–84, 288, 292–93

Wiltse, Charles M., 33*n*, 235*n*

Winans, William, 195, 198

Winston, John, 258

Wise, Henry A., 226, 309, 311, 313*n*, 314–15, 322

Wish, Harvey, 85*n*, 87*n*–88*n*, 135*n*, 209*n*, 212*n*

Wood, Gordon, 14*n*

Woodcraft, 167–68

Woodfin, Maude H., 161*n*

Woolens Bill, 33

Wooster, Ralph, 308*n*, 333*n*

Worth, William J., 240

Yancey, William Lowndes, 70, 84, 136–37, 139, 280–84, 286–87, 295*n*, 300, 302, 308, 313–19, 323–26, 328, 330*n*, 331, 335

yankeeism, 147, 152, 154, 160–63, 167–69, 173–74, 176, 197, 213

yellow fever, 77, 264

Young America movement, 149, 164, 228–29

Young, James S., 21*n*

Yulee, David, 243, 334